Immigrant Industry

IMMIGRANT INDUSTRY
Building Postwar Australia

Anoma Pieris, Mirjana Lozanovska,
Alexandra Dellios, Andrew Saniga
and David Beynon

berghahn
NEW YORK · OXFORD
www.berghahnbooks.com

First published in 2024 by
Berghahn Books
www.berghahnbooks.com

© 2024 Anoma Pieris, Mirjana Lozanovska, Alexandra Dellios,
Andrew Saniga and David Beynon

All rights reserved. Except for the quotation of short passages
for the purposes of criticism and review, no part of this book
may be reproduced in any form or by any means, electronic or
mechanical, including photocopying, recording, or any information
storage and retrieval system now known or to be invented,
without written permission of the publisher.

Library of Congress Cataloging-in-Publication Data

A C.I.P. cataloging record is available from the Library of Congress
Library of Congress Cataloging in Publication Control Number: 2024013513

British Library Cataloguing in Publication Data

A catalogue record for this book is available from the British Library

ISBN 978-1-80539-456-3 hardback
ISBN 978-1-80539-457-0 paperback
ISBN 978-1-80539-458-7 epub
ISBN 978-1-80539-459-4 web pdf

https://doi.org/10.3167/9781805394563

Contents

List of Figures   vii

Preface   xi

Acknowledgements   xiii

Introduction   1
Anoma Pieris and Mirjana Lozanovska

Chapter 1
Postwar Immigrant Recruitment Policies, Labour and Accommodation   17
Mirjana Lozanovska, Alexandra Dellios and David Beynon

Chapter 2
Machines for Making Australians: The Military Prehistory of
Migrant Camps   39
Anoma Pieris

Chapter 3
Unfinished Histories of Nation Building: Racialization, Space of Labour
and Industry at Port Kembla Steelworks   67
Mirjana Lozanovska

Chapter 4
Company Town: Housing Labour Migrants on the Snowy Hydro Scheme   99
Anoma Pieris

Chapter 5
Woomera: A Landscape of Displacement and Renewal   132
Andrew Saniga

Chapter 6
Noncompliance and Agency in Migrant Family Life: Greta and
Benalla Migrant Camps 166
   Alexandra Dellios

Chapter 7
Design Experiments in Collective Housing: The Renewal of Commonwealth
Migrant Hostels 190
   Renee Miller-Yeaman

Chapter 8
From Enterprise to Enterprise: Refugees, Industry and Settlement in
an Australian City 221
   David Beynon

Conclusion
Migration Heritage Landscapes in Australia Today 248
   Alexandra Dellios, Anoma Pieris, Mirjana Lozanovska,
   Andrew Saniga and David Beynon

Index 279

Figures

0.1 Sites and localities connected to camps, hostels, infrastructure, industries and company towns and suburbs mentioned in the book. Drawn for author by Renee Miller-Yeaman, 2022 — 9

2.1 Cowra, New South Wales: specifications for the erection and completion of twenty timber-framed buildings and the resiting of three timber-framed buildings in a POW camp, December 1944 — 45

2.2 Bonegilla Military Training Camp, Vic, 1954 — 46

2.3 Rushworth Camp 3, Tatura Group, Vic, 1949 — 47

2.4 Giuseppe Roncari's overseas journeys — 52

2.5 Joe Roncari's journeys within Australia — 53

2.6 Giuseppe Roncari's family home in Cerro Veronese, 1971 — 54

2.7 Giuseppe Roncari's photograph of the monument to *Our Lady of the Prisoner*, Bangalore Camp, Group 1, India, 1940 — 55

2.8 Giuseppe Roncari unpicked the threads from the seams of his uniform to embroider this image of the monument to *Our Lady of the Prisoner* while at the Bangalore Camp, circa 1940 — 55

2.9 A poster appealing for the safe return of the two Roncari brothers taken prisoner during the Second World War, undated circa 1940 — 56

2.10 Joe Roncari greets Angelina on her arrival in Sydney, 31 August 1950 (left), and Joe and Angelina at Warrah, circa 1950 (right) — 57

2.11 The Roncari home at 22 Bent Street Cooma Plan drawn by builder Rodney Parkes, 1954 (above) and photograph, 1950s (below) — 58

2.12 The Roncari home at 5 Belmont Avenue, Dandenong Plan drawn by builder C.L Moon, 1963 (above) and photograph, 2022 (below) — 60

2.13 Decorative detail at 5 Belmont Avenue, Dandenong, 2022 — 61

2.14	The Roncari family	61
3.1	Workers coming out of the Port Kembla Steelworks at the end of their shift, 1955	69
3.2	Map showing the five land grants in Illawarra in 1817	70
3.3	BHP Steelworks, Port Kembla, 1960	73
3.4	A diagram showing the steel production process but omitting the role and labour of the workers	79
3.5	BHP Steel Mill, Port Kembla, Mark Strizic, 1959	81
3.6	Jovanče Kantaroski with his mother in the village Brusnik, SR Macedonia, Yugoslavia prior to his departure, January 1970	83
3.7	Dragan Grozdanovski with friends in Port Kembla, soon after he started working at the BHP Steelworks, Port Kembla, 1963	83
3.8	Watercolour and pencil drawing of 'The Five Islands' by Edward Close, circa 1820	88
3.9	Public Works Department (PWD) plan showing the proposed development of Port Kembla Harbour, including the Inner Basin	89
4.1	Jindabyne Reservoir, 2015	100
4.2	A diagram of the Snowy Mountains Development, 1953	101
4.3	Scenic Jindabyne and the valley of the Snowy River, with the camp in the foreground, 1950	108
4.4	Construction work on pressure tunnel Tumut 1 Power Station, 1958	110
4.5	Snowy towns and work camps, 2022	111
4.6	Cooma North housing, 1951	112
4.7	Cooma North housing layout, 1952	120
4.8	House plans for prefabricated dwellings in Cooma North, 2022	121
4.9	SMA Head Office, Cooma North (snow scene), 1954	122
4.10	Festival of the Snows – Cooma International Club float moves along a Cooma Street during the grand procession, 1958	124
5.1	Two QSL cards linking Woomera with the Soviet Union via amateur short-wave radio, 2002	133
5.2	Details of European immigrant personnel recorded at Woomera from mid-1948 to mid-1949	137

Figures

5.3 CDWH workers meet stockmen from a pastoral station neighbouring Woomera on the lands of the Kokatha People, mid-1948 (above) Canvas tents at Lake Koolymilka construction workers' camp at night, date unknown (below) ... 138

5.4 Immigrant 'bush carpenters' at Lake Koolymilka with Bronislaw Blazejowski (left) and Jerzy Borejko (with saw strapped to waist), circa 1948 (above). Clothes hung out to dry in front of the Workmens' Framed Tent which was a type of prefabricated hut designed by Department of Works and Housing Chief Engineer J.J.W Gray, circa 1949 (below) ... 141

5.5 Woomera nearly fifteen years in the making, date unknown ... 143

5.6 Workers constructing the Pimba to Woomera rail line, 1949 ... 148

5.7 The Phillip Ponds construction workers' camp, circa 1949–50 (above) A survey team in Woomera with Guido Laikve believed to be on the far right, circa 1950 (below) ... 152

5.8 Jonas Meškauskas, Algimantas Žilinskas, Jerzy Szymming and Kostas Tymukas outside canvas tent accommodation at Phillip Ponds construction workers' camp, circa 1949–50 (left); Kostas Tymukas (middle) and Algimantas Žilinskas (to the right) at work in the Drawing Office of the Commonwealth Department of Works and Housing, Woomera, circa 1949 (right) ... 155

5.9 Česlovas Dubinskas and Jonas Meškauskas (in the doorway) in the garden they created adjacent to their rooms in the Commonwealth Department of Works and Housing's Staff Quarters at Woomera West, date unknown (above); two unidentified colleagues of Dubinskas and Meškauskas in the garden showing a degree of cultivation of garden beds, specimen planting and lawn, date unknown (below) ... 157

5.10 The remains of the Pimba to Woomera rail line bridge ... 159

6.1 Greta Camp layout, 1949 ... 171

6.2 Benalla Camp layout, circa 1950 ... 173

6.3 Inside Burlington/Bradmill Industries Mill at Rutherford, circa 1950 ... 176

6.4 Women workers outside the Latoof and Callil factory in Benalla, circa 1950 ... 178

7.1 The Endeavour Migrant Hostel, Randwick (now South Coogee), Sydney, 1977 ... 191

7.2	Residents lining up for meals at the Endeavor Hostel, 1971	193
7.3	The Enterprise Migrant Hostel under construction, Springvale, Melbourne, 1970	194
7.4	New industrial-style kitchens at the Endeavour Hostel, circa 1970–78	200
7.5	Laundry facilities at the Endeavour Migrant Hostel, 1971	204
7.6	Example of a room at the Enterprise Migrant Hostel, 1984	205
7.7	Accommodation blocks elevation, Endeavour Migrant Hostel, 1967	207
7.8	Accommodation block plan, Endeavour Migrant Hostel, 1964	208
7.9	Example of Commonwealth Migrant Flats in Adelaide, South Australia, 1973	212
8.1	Nan Yang Asian Supermarket, Springvale, Victoria, 2022	229
8.2	Lim's Pharmacy, Springvale, Victoria, 2022	230
8.3	Sewing/machining workshop, Keilor Downs, Victoria, 2022	232
8.4	Quang Minh Vietnamese Buddhist Temple, Braybrook, Victoria, 2022	235
8.5	The Guan Di Daoist Temple and Teochew Association, next door to a cabinet-making workshop, Springvale, Victoria, 2022	236
8.6	Angkor Tyres repair workshop, Springvale, Victoria, 2022	238
9.1	Block 19, Bonegilla Migrant Experience, 2012	253
9.2	What remains at the site of the former Greta Migrant Camp, 2019	256
9.3	Past immigrant workers climb the stair tower to the mill at the BHP Steelworks in Port Kembla, 2021	259
9.4	Past immigrant workers point to the coke ovens at the BHP Steelworks in Port Kembla and speak about their experiences and the skill required for their work, 2021	260
9.5	Injured worker and companion at Snowy Mountains Hydro Electric Scheme work camp, 1957–60	264
9.6	Memorial to the Snowy workers who lost their lives during construction of the Snowy Mountains Scheme 1949–74	265
9.7	Wirrawirralu Waterhole (Phillip Ponds), 2021	267
9.8	Vietnamese-Chinese hairdresser (in a shop that once was a clothing factory outlet), next to an East African *injera* bakery and grocery in Footscray, 2020	269

Preface

We respectfully acknowledge the Traditional Owners/Custodians of the lands across Australia discussed in this book and pay our respects to their Elders, past and present. They include for each of our case studies: the Wonnarua, Taungurung and Yorta Yorta peoples, Traditional Custodians of the Maitland region and the Benalla region respectively (Migrant Camps); the Naguraiilam-wurrung people (Rushworth Camp); the Ngunawal, Walgalu, Djilamatang and Ngarigo (Ngarigu) people, the Traditional Owners of the Snowy-Monaro region (Snowy Hydro); the Dharawal (also written as Tharawal) people, the Traditional Owners of the Port Kembla, Illawarra region (Port Kembla Steelworks); the Kokatha people, the Traditional Owners of the land on which Woomera is located (Woomera); and the Wurundjeri Woi-wurrung and Bunurong/Boon Wurrung peoples of the Kulin Nation (Melbourne Suburbs). We use the term 'Indigenous Australians' to describe these Traditional Owner/Custodian groups in our text but remain mindful of the recent changes to these descriptors both in academia and in politics. These include concurrent practices of identification as First Nations' peoples/Aboriginal and Torres Strait Islander peoples/First Peoples.

As members of Australia's diasporic communities, we are all intimately connected to the continent's migration histories, sharing the sense of dislocation and cultural distance described in this book, either learned first-hand or via the experiences of our parents and grandparents. Repositioning this knowledge in relation to Indigenous Australian dispossession through settler colonialism and by disciplinary inquiry from architectural/urban/landscape and heritage studies is among this book's key innovations. The affective experiences of continental European and later Asian labour migrants offer a more heterogeneous record of Australia's industrial development to date, alerting us to forms of racialization unacknowledged in normative histories. We hope to capture its many nuances in the chapters that follow.

This book emerged out of a four-year collaboration for an Australian Research Council Discovery Project DP190101531 on architecture, migrant labour and industry. The research team led by Anoma Pieris (University of Melbourne) comprised Mirjana Lozanovska (Deakin University); Alexandra Dellios (Australian National University); Andrew Saniga (University of Melbourne); and David Beynon (University of Tasmania). The project's intellectual framing by Anoma and Mirjana provided the scaffolding for several activities and outcomes. Anoma's work on wartime camp construction, settler colonialism, diasporic labour, borders and refugees, and Indigenous Australians fused together to offer an unusual approach to a familiar topic. She led the book project, directing and editing the work of the authorial team. Mirjana's decades-long theoretical interrogation of diasporic architecture and migrant housing drove many of the questions raised in the project influencing the book's focus. She curated and convened the project exhibition *Immigrant Networks* (Museo Italiano, November 2022–March 2023) and through collaborative workshops we each designed and created contributions featuring our individual case studies. A day-long workshop, also organised by Mirjana, used the exhibits as a catalyst for a range of scholars from across Australia to discuss *Immigrant Networks* and the nature of exhibiting academic research (outcomes expected to be published in *Landscape Research* in 2025). David Beynon, and his research assistants Freya Su and Van Krisadawat, designed and collated the exhibition catalogue, introducing the experiences of migrants of colour into a body of scholarship weighted towards European perspectives. Alexandra Dellios gave discursive currency to our case studies by asking us to engage with Critical Heritage Studies. Andrew Saniga reminded us of the positionality of Eastern European migrants working in remote Australian arid landscapes during the Cold War. He donated his exhibit for *Immigrant Networks* to the Woomera History Museum, thus 'taking-back' the stories he uncovered in a bid to enhance the Museum's collection.

We included a contribution from Renee Miller-Yeaman, research assistant for a major part of the grant, who developed her chapter in parallel with her doctoral thesis on the Villawood Migrant Hostel in Sydney. Through our collaboration, we explored how, historically, after the Second World War, alongside industrial skills and opportunities associated with labour allocations, forms of inequity (including exploitation and harsh living and working conditions) mediated immigrant experiences of the host environment. We ask what the spatial and material conditions of these experiences convey about their contribution to building postwar Australia.

Acknowledgements

Research for this anthology was funded by an Australia Research Council Discovery Project DP190101531 (2019–2022), *Architecture and Industry: The Migrant Contribution to Nation-Building 1945–1979*, with an interdisciplinary team from The University of Melbourne, Deakin University, the University of Tasmania and the Australian National University. The research was first presented at a public exhibition entitled *Immigrant Networks* held at the Museo Italiano, Co.As.It (Italian Assistance Association) in Melbourne from November 2022 to March 2023 with a catalogue by the same name and a related workshop on 'Migration+Place+Architecture Research: What Next?'. Our thanks to Paolo Baracchi and Ferdinando Colarossi for hosting the exhibition. Our thanks also to Helen Boer and the Estate of Mark Strizic for permission to use his photograph for the cover image and in Chapter 3.

An editors' issue of the journal *Fabrications* 29(2), themed 'Industry + Architecture', was published in 2019 on this topic with a special forum involving a number of authors on 'Industrial Sites and Immigrant Architectures: A Case Study Approach' (pp. 257–72). The following publications are related to this project: Mirjana Lozanovska, 'The Space of Labour: Racialisation and Ethnicisation of Port Kembla, Australia', in Nikolina Bobic and Farzaneh Haghighi (eds), *The Routledge Handbook of Architecture, Urban Space and Politics, Vol I: Violence, Spectacle and Data* (New York: Routledge 2023), pp. 233–49; Anoma Pieris, 'Subaltern-Diasporic Histories of Modernism', in Vikramaditya Prakash, Maristella Casciato and Daniel Cosett (eds), *Rethinking Global Modernism* (New York: Routledge 2021), pp. 251–71; Alexandra Dellios, *Heritage Making and Migrant Subjects in the Deindustrialising Region of the Latrobe Valley* (Cambridge: Cambridge University Press, 2022); Andrew Saniga, 'Layered Landscapes: Links between Brazil and Australia after the Second World War', *Fabrications: The Journal of the Society of Architectural Historians, Australia and New Zealand*, 31(1) (2021): pp. 85–108; Andrew Saniga (with Andrew Wilson), 'A League of His Own: Karl Langer's Landscape Australia', in Deborah van der Plaat and John MacArthur (eds), *Karl Langer: Modern Architect and Migrant in the Australian Tropics* (London: Bloomsbury, 2021), pp. 232–57; Mirjana Lozanovska, 'Port Kembla Steelworks, Australia: Post War Immigrant Histories of Architecture, Urbanism and Heritage', Proceedings of Ngā Pūtahitanga/Crossings: A Joint Conference of the 39th Annual Conference of the *Society of Architectural*

Historians, Australia and New Zealand, and the 19th *Australian Urban History Planning History*, Auckland, New Zealand, 25–27 November 2022; and Renee Miller-Yeaman, 'From Emergency Reception Centres to Housing Experiments: Migrant Accommodation and the Commonwealth Department of Public Works', Proceedings of Historiographies of Technology and Architecture: The 35th Annual Conference of the *Society of Architectural Historians, Australia and New Zealand*, Wellington, New Zealand, 4–7 July, Wellington: SAHANZ, 2018. The story of Giuseppe Roncari was first introduced in a forthcoming Routledge book chapter: Anoma Pieris, 'Exilic Spaces: Assimilation and Cultural Resilience in Post-war White Australia', in Itohan Osayimwese and Felipe Hernandez (eds), *The Routledge Critical Companion to Race and Architecture*. Further discussion of Springvale's diverse settlement was published in David Beynon, Freya Su and Van Krisadawat, 'In from the Periphery: Becoming (G)locally Cosmopolitan in Springvale', *Architectural Theory Review*, 27(2) (2023): pp. 258–276.

Workshops, presentations and plenaries related to this project include: Mirjana Lozanovska (Deakin University, Australia), Roundtable: 'Diasporic Architecture and Australia's Unfinished Histories', *Society of Architectural Historians Australia and New Zealand*, Annual Conference (virtual), Perth, Australia 18–25 November 2020; Mirjana Lozanovska (Deakin University, Australia) and Anoma Pieris (The University of Melbourne, Australia), Session, 'Diasporic Architectural Histories' *Society of Architectural Historians* (SAH) Annual International Conference (virtual), Montréal, Québec, 14–18 April 2021; and Mirjana Lozanovska, 'The Space of Labour: Initial Findings on Port Kembla', 17th Annual Conference, *Australasian Urban History Planning History*, 5–7 February 2020.

Our individual thanks for each project section is given below.

Migrant Camps: My warmest thanks to former residents and dedicated chroniclers of Australia's migrant camps, who were so generous with their time and resources. A special thank you to Sabine Smyth, of Benalla Migrant Camp Inc., for providing access to its extensive photographic archive. Thanks to Alek Schulha, and his epic tome *Beneath the Shadows of Mount Molly Morgan: History & Stories of Greta Camp* (1939–1960), which contained hundreds of invaluable personal stories of residents of Greta Migrant Camp. Jim Klopsteins offered his stories and permission to reproduce his careful map of Benalla Migrant Camp, and Judith Fleming assisted with archival insights into Department of Immigration welfare workers and the treatment of single migrant mothers at Benalla. Thanks are also due to Helen Topor, writer and Benalla heritage advocate, and Professor Bruce Pennay, for their work on migrant camps and their willingness to share research insights. A final thank you to valuable archival institutions like Benalla Migrant Camp Inc., Newcastle Libraries, the University of Newcastle Special Collections and the National Archives of Australia for assisting with this research and making collection material accessible for the exhibition. Thanks also to research assistant Anne Claoue-Long.

Snowy Hydro: I am grateful to the Roncari family members Alexander Roncari, Tosca Roncari, Frank Roncari and Ronald Roncari for sharing their family history and the family photographs included in Chapter 2. Thanks to Patrick Swain at Cooma for information on the housing and workshops and for sharing the notes of workshop manager Bert Knowles. Nick Skobelkin, Laura Greco, Miles Lewis and Gioia Greco provided me with specific insights. Thanks to Shannon O'Boyle for permission to quote her father Ulick O'Boyle's song 'Dozer Driver Man'. Staff at various institutions and archives kindly assisted in sourcing materials and responded to many inquiries, including at the National Archives of Australia (NAA) at Melbourne, Sydney, Canberra and Perth, the National Library of Australia (NLA), the ACT Heritage Library, Tatura War Time Camps and Irrigation Museum, the State Library of New South Wales, Snowy Hydro Discovery Centre and Snowy Monaro Regional Library – Cooma. Thanks especially to Harry Ree at the Powerhouse Collection-Museum of Applied Arts and Sciences for providing me with photographs and liaising with Sandra Byron and Ashley Russell at the Jeff Carter Archive. Thanks to Janet McGaw and Alex Selenitsch for reading drafts of my essays. Thanks to several research assistants, especially Renee Miller-Yeaman, long-time RA on the project, Yoke Lin Wong, Yvette Putra and Michael Pearson, as well as Brian Duong, Catherine Woo and Dhanika Kumaheri, who assisted in drawing and formatting the graphics.

Port Kembla Steelworks: My warmest thanks to the past Port Kembla steelworks immigrant workers who were so generous with their time and keen to tell their stories, and the children who reported on their fathers. Our deepest gratitude to the Macedonian Welfare Association (MWA), Port Kembla, especially Verica Sajdovska and Mendo Trajcevski, and to the Multicultural Communities Council of Illawarra (MCCI), especially Chris Lacey and Pia Solberg. Thanks to the following people who assisted with research on Port Kembla and Wollongong – John Petersen (Heritage, Wollongong), Meredith Walker (Wollongong's Migration Heritage Places Study, 2007), Glenn Mitchell, Henry Lee and Gregor Cullen (Wollongong University), Sandra Pires (Why Documentaries), Craig Nealon (BlueScope), Brent Hilbrink-Watson (Inside Industry), and Franca Facci and Fidelia Pontarolo (Migration Heritage Project). Thanks to staff at the following libraries: Grant White, Stephani Drummond (University of Wollongong Library), Josephine Le Clerc, Luke Watsford and Kate Herford (Deakin University), Hilary Powell and Jenny McConchie (Wollongong City Library), National Library Australia (NLA), National Archives of Australia (NAA), and the State Library of New South Wales (with special thanks to Michael Herlihy and Amanda Hardie). Sincere appreciation to artist Riste Andrievski and photographer Sue Bessell for the use of their works. Thank you to Alexandra Florea for her invaluable long-term research assistance and contribution to this project; to Qiaochu Tang, who assisted with creative research; to Chayakan Siamphukdee for ongoing research; and to Julie Pham for supporting their work.

Woomera: This project would not have been possible without the support of the families of Woomera's European immigrants. The following people have provided photographs, documents, material objects, translations and interviews: Louise Blazejowska; Andrew Domaševičius-Žilinskas; Guido and Õnne Laikve and daughters Elle, Linda, Heidi and Ivi; Peter Lazič; Jonas Mockunas; Lilian Salupalu; Kathleen Tymukas and family; Valda Veigurs; and Margaret Žurauskas. I am indebted to Guido Laikve, who served in Woomera from 1949 to 1951 and was the only remaining immigrant I could locate. Our interviews, together with his own written memoirs, were invaluable. The published memoir of Česlovas Dubinskas was crucial in illustrating the lives and lifestyles of many of Woomera's immigrants along with their trials and tribulations within the Drawing Office of the Commonwealth Department of Works and Housing.

Sincere thanks to the National Archives of Australia; the Australian Lithuanian Archive; and the Woomera History Museum. Special thanks to the wonderful research assistance of Michael Pearson, Jack Wilde, Yvette Putra, Yasmin Rousset and Simeon Chua.

The following people gave much time and effort in assisting with information and other support: Ieva Aras; Lucyna Artymiuk; Heather Cleland; Yana Di Pietro; Robert Freestone; Sue Gibbs; Christine Garnaut; Egle Garrick; Caz Harding; David Hemming; Roger Henwood; Marcus Jones; Vic Jurskis; Avriel Kain; Peter Kanas; Martin Kurvits; Edita Meškauskaitė; Danute Morison; Daina Počius; Lyn Pool; Nicola Pullan; Aldis Putniņš; John Quinn; Adrian Rudzinski; Rudi, Stanys and Clyde Saniga, Algimantas Taškunas; Colin Telfer; Suzy Teska; Peter Tymukas; Frank Vana; Gill Vallak; Eve Wicks; Dennis Willshire; and Mike Wohltmann.

Melbourne Suburbs: Many thanks to the following: Andrew Dao, who as external affairs deputy for the Vietnamese community in Victoria put us in contact with many of our contributors; members of Vietnamese Museum Australia for their time in interviews, discussions and lending key items for our exhibition, in particular Hanh Do (Operations Manager), Kim Bùi-Quang (Deputy Operations Manager), Khuê Nguyên (who lent one of his lovely sketches to the exhibition), Phước Bùi-Quang, Thủy Trần, Diệp Nguyên, Trung Nguyên, Thúy Phan, Hùng Lê, Thanh Trấn, Tiền Trấn, Đinh Nguyên, Kim Liên Trâm and Đức Liêm Trâm; Bon Nguyên for his insights as President of the Vietnamese Community in Victoria; Sophanara Sok for sharing the experiences of Cambodian refugees; two business owners in Springvale who wished to remain anonymous; Councillor Cúc Lam from City of Maribyrnong, who as part of her interview accompanied us to the former Midway Hostel site; Councillor Richard Lim from the City of Greater Dandenong, who shared his visions for the future of Springvale; the Venerable Phước Tấn Thich, Abbott of the Quang Minh Temple, who showed us around the temple and recounted its history and context; Annie Wong of the Teo Chew Association/Guan Di Temple, who provided insights into that temple's history; Rhonda Diffey of the City of Greater Dandenong's Archive for diligently following up permissions for our many requests; Sue Jarvis for allowing use of her fine photographs; Youhorn Chea and Dr Thel Thong for their historical interviews; Chris Keys of the Springvale Historical Society for facilitating access to their archival collection; Jan Trezise of the Enterprise Hostel Committee for assistance with contacts; Wai Kee Yeo for her assistance with interviewing and translating Cantonese-speaking participants, along with Wajie Chan; Trang Nguyễn, who provided initial contacts; Darren Watten of Southern Archaeology, who sourced aerial photographs; the State Library of Victoria for historical photographs of Footscray; and Jane McDougall, who assisted with interviews, videos and provided ongoing moral support. Many thanks to Freya Su and Van Krisadawat, who were instrumental in providing design input, fieldwork/documentary assistance and intellectual engagement with this project.

We would like to thank the publishers at Berghahn Books and the reviewers of the manuscript. Special thanks are also due to our research assistant Melathi Saldin for her invaluable help in preparing the manuscript for review and submission, Belinda Nemec for preparing the index and Gracie O'Malley-Welby for assistance in finalising the proofs.

Introduction

Anoma Pieris and Mirjana Lozanovska

During and after the Second World War, Australia transitioned from a clientist relationship with Great Britain to one with greater awareness of (and anxiety regarding) the surrounding Asia Pacific region while reorienting towards US economic leadership. Industrial dependency gave way to industrial self-determination; a key feature of the mid-twentieth-century nation-building decades.[1] War-displaced refugee and immigrant workers arriving in Australia proved pivotal for this change. This book offers new unexplored insights into the historical conditions, legislative changes and economic context that underscore postwar immigration, industrialization and settlement in Australia through an architectural and spatial analysis of the lasting physical transformations of this era. Whereas heightened transience and material dispossession have deferred recognition of their efforts to a point later in the life journeys of many migrants, when they become economically stable and spatially and socially positioned as individuals, this book highlights their contributions to Australia as occurring earlier: in the backbreaking collective labour and dedicated efforts of communities employed in specific industries on sites often remote from metropolitan centres, at the social and spatial periphery of what are commonly understood to be constitutive sites of national history. Consequently, for the first time, this book expands the limits of migration studies to include contributions as yet underexamined in Australian architectural and social history, but favourable to the goals of plurality and non-elite representation.

Using an interdisciplinary approach that connects the built environment disciplines to critical heritage studies, this book focuses on the historical intersections of migration, industry, architecture and landscape in the period from 1945 to 1979. It examines the inhabitation, inscription, intervention and shaping of the built environment as a legacy of the refugee and migrant populations who were directed to work and labour in Australia's major industries, including construction related to infrastructure, heavy industry and manufacturing, as well as migrant-led entrepreneurial initiatives and networks. The broad influence of migration represents an extraordinary confluence of transnational cultures within Australia's history of modernization. Informed by migration histories of selected case studies that align with key postwar industries, this book highlights the corresponding impact on Australian cities and the wider built landscape, providing valuable architectural insights into economic and social histories of industry, population growth and modernization that have continuing relevance, but have not been viewed through the lens of architectural studies in Australia, to date.

Architectural histories have tended to focus on the contributions of British or anglophone migrants as primary agents of the most progressive features in the nation's development, casting nonanglophone migrants as secondary. In this study, the labour of these peripheral migrant streams takes centre stage. Their contribution is historicized as catalytic for modernization in Australia after the Second World War, a period of postwar reconstruction, shaped by immigration, industry and the settlement of diverse cultural communities following four decades of the *Immigration Restriction Act* of 1901. Federal and corporate funding for major industries together with government policies for population growth enabled nation-building programmes that shaped remote, rural and urban environments into modern industrial landscapes. Populations were drawn from war-destroyed nations, underdeveloped economies and environments divided by political ideologies or wracked by civil war. Focusing on the architecture and landscapes of major but underdocumented industrial sites and their complex social histories, we examine the intersection of the built environment and industrial growth, shifting attention to acknowledging the spatial and material dimensions of the migrant legacy and broadening the social scope of design and planning historiography, including architecture, landscape and domestic living environments. In a contemporary sense, this project speaks directly to both anxieties and aspirations of new refugee and immigrant arrivals by uncovering the extent of the contribution made by war-displaced and immigrant populations to national development in the past.

THEORY AND HISTORIOGRAPHY

In the last two decades, migration theory has become a way of conceptually framing contemporary society.[2] The formation of migration research centres was motivated by national agenda research of the 'migrant problem', but in the 1980s the focus was on immigrant identity and multiculturalism.[3] By connecting this to postmodern and postcolonial theoretical discourse, migration scholarship in Australia has gained international prominence.[4] Lingering colonial structural prejudices have and continue to influence the Australian nation and society, based historically on the racialization of nonanglophone populations in an implicit hierarchy, according to the lineage of immigrant arrivals, and alongside the perceived inferiority of non-white races and the exclusion of Indigenous Australians (Aboriginal and Torres Strait Islander First Nations/Peoples) that shaped mid-twentieth-century politics. The persistence of these racial and cultural biases and associated bigotry into the late twentieth century 'multicultural' decades has been theorized by key scholars, most notably Sneja Gunew, Ghassan Hage and Ien Ang, among others, who alert us through examples to the struggles of Southern European, Middle Eastern and Asian diasporic communities in Australia navigating and unwilling or unable to assimilate into a normative and frequently superficially accommodating forms of anglophone cultural hegemony.[5] More significantly, the issue of how the pervasive late twentieth-century ideologies of 'multiculturalism' have repressed the problematic of 'race' and its historical entanglement with ethnicity and culture in Australia remain underexamined.[6]

Publications written within the postwar period of immigration, especially those that draw on ethnographic research, have become documents of a contemporaneous historiography. Jean Martin's *Refugee Settlers* (1965) details the working lives of migrants and refugees in one industrial town; James Jupp's *Arrivals and Departures* (1966) examines major themes of work, life and community based on surveys of four ethnic groups; and Jerzy Zubrzycki's *Settlers of the Latrobe Valley* (1964) focuses on the assimilation problems of over 500 immigrant male employees of the State Electricity Commission in Victoria, and is probably the first such study.[7] Importantly, these are anthropological and sociological studies rather than initiatives within Australian history, which according to Balint and Simic has only begun to catch up after 2010.[8]

This body of research is also linked to studies on the globalization of place and transnational exchange, and illustrates both the continuing significance and the need for a re-evaluation of migration theory beyond the framework of the nation state.[9] Key among these are explorations of the physical impact of the diversity of cultures inhabiting Australian cities.[10] Architectural histories focusing on émigré architects, their pedagogical and design contribution, include those, for example, by Harriet Edquist and, most recently, Philip Goad et al.[11] As Esra Ackan and Iftikar Dadi explore in their recent anthology the disciplinary lens can also be extended to forced emigration after partition, and migration related discrimination, among deeper ethical and political concerns.[12] The extension of migration theory to immigrant architecture can be understood in three ways: the first on the urban and suburban environments by scholars like Michel Laguerre, Leonie Sandercock, Arijit Sen and Jennifer Johung, and Ian Woodcock;[13] and cultural presence and mobilities, including ephemeral materialities, in a recent architectural project on Australia's Muslim pioneers led by Peter Scriver;[14] the second on immigrant institutions including David Beynon's work on worship places, and the current work by Katherine Bartsch et al. on the Australian mosque;[15] and the third on immigrant housing by scholars Iris Levin and Mirjana Lozanovska.[16] Noteworthy contributions include the anthologies *Drifting: Architecture and Migrancy*, *Ethno-Architecture and the Politics of Migration* and *Migrant Housing: Architecture, Dwelling, Migration* by Australia-based scholars, including Mirjana Lozanovska in this collection.[17] Drawing from critical and postcolonial theories, these works pioneered historiography at the intersection of migration and architecture, and combined ethnographic methods with architectural documentation. The collective labour and industrial contributions of immigrants, and the industrial environments they inhabited and transformed, have not been a focus of scholarly attention, which has created a significant gap in knowledge, leading to the erasure of many key sites of immigrant heritage, following the closure of industrial facilities, the depopulation of related towns and the dispersal of labouring populations. Architectural studies of industrial transformation, including Australia's mining industry, can be expanded through new knowledge on the postwar immigrant contribution to key industries.[18]

Studies on the impact of immigration on Australia's landscape have focused on immigrant gardens and domestic environments, the shaping of a gardening culture, the usage of national parks and the works of émigré professional designers.[19] A comprehensive examination of the immigrant impact on landscapes related to industry and industrial sites in remote and peripheral locations awaits discovery. The analysis of the economic benefits of major industries needs to be studied alongside their positive and adversarial environmental and social impacts.

The approach from critical heritage studies, focusing on post-industrial landscapes is particularly pertinent to case studies such as ours, where the industries have been discontinued and many sites have been abandoned. Viewed from this perspective, our study of immigrant industry intersects with memory studies and critical re-evaluations of intangible heritage addressed most recently by Alexandra Dellios, also an author in this collection.[20] *Remembering Migration: Oral Histories and Heritage in Australia* and books in the Palgrave Macmillan series on Memory Studies are noteworthy.[21] Books focused on the heritage of specific places related to camps and industries are too many to mention here, as are the many immigrant memoirs related to specific camps or industrial sites encountered in the following chapters. Nonja Peters' *Milk and Honey – But No Gold: Postwar Migration to Western Australia, 1945–64* combines these approaches in an academic study.[22] Elaborating on 'heritage corridors', Denis Byrne's work expands this field conceptually towards a geographical stretch of heritage caused by migration and the longer geocultural histories of ongoing migratory travel of Chinese-Australian immigrants, and brings the intangible at an interface with spatial heritage with work on architectures of enterprising immigrants.[23] Our collection fills a much-needed gap in the literature, linking architecture, immigrant labour and industrial development; and is particularly important for the insights it brings from the Australian postcolonial and settler contexts. Pastoral lands from which Indigenous Australian custodians had been brutally evicted during a previous century were requisitioned for wartime military training facilities – displaced persons (DP) camps – industrial work camps and factories, implicating immigrant and refugee-settlers in longer histories of dispossession that pre-dated their arrival in Australia. Major industries that drew immigrant labour from the migrant reception and holding centres accelerated the environmental destruction already initiated through industrial agriculture; their massive infrastructural works or heavy industries, causing lasting ecological trauma. An important innovation in this book is its greater sensitization to issues that have surfaced through ethical awareness of Indigenous Australian and First Nations' peoples' rights and the geopolitical exigencies of global warming, both, at times, directly connected to industrial development. Viewed from this perspective, nation building can be seen as regressive.

By arguing that refugee and immigrant presence, labour and productivity are integral to an understanding of postwar Australian modernization, this book challenges the assumption that refugees 'burden' the Australian economy and society. The period 1945–79 marks a time when the introduction of culturally and racially different refugees and immigrants to Australia irrevocably impacted its social and spatial landscape. Spanning the last four decades and the final demise of the White Australia Policy, this period saw a tremendous impetus for decolonization globally that implicated Australia in significant ways, most markedly in its changing attitudes to cultural diversity and race. There was unprecedented regional transformation, when Asia Pacific nations around Australia achieved political independence, decolonized institutions and reinstated their belief systems. Australia at first relaxed its immigration policies only so far as to encourage the entry of Continental Europeans (preferably Northern Europeans as Southern Europeans were at this stage undesirable); defensively strengthening its racial boundaries and ethnic hierarchy internally and with the expectation that Northern Europeans would willingly assimilate with the anglophone majority. This was not always the case, especially due to recruitment policies that brought in disproportionate numbers of young single men or separated men from their families remaining in the homelands, many of whom fell into alcoholism and depression. Each wave of immigrants was subjected to new modes of discrimination. The influx of large numbers of Vietnamese and Cambodian refugees during the late 1960s and early 1970s forced Australia's borders open by the sheer demographic pressure of a regional humanitarian crisis. Their racialization and distinction from nineteenth-century Chinese immigrants added greater complexity to Australian society.[24] These immigrants were racially and culturally unassimilable, and their cultural and religious practices were often illegible to the white majority.[25]

A focus on nation-building industrial practices contributes original insights and new empirical findings to the studies of culturally diverse urban environments, and migration and postcolonial studies of Australia, with comparative lessons for settler societies. Industry instigated the postwar coexistence of culturally diverse immigrants, which in turn produced temporary environments for cosmopolitanism in its initial stages.[26] The project's findings contribute substantially towards a more inclusive, interdisciplinary, architectural, landscape, urban and social history of immigrants' contribution to nation building, invigorated by new discourses on borders, refugee flows, labour and globalization. The methodologies combine ethnographic and historical research with architectural documentation and other forms of visual records of place. The situated analyses of refugee/immigrant contributions to specific industries central to post-Second World War national development up to the Vietnam War open up this social field to historical questions that are contingent on physical and material evidence. As the physical context for immigrants' everyday struggles, the built landscape provides evidence of their capacity to contribute to the industrial transformation of

Australia. The architecture, urban places and landscapes that hosted these industries and accommodated immigrants in diverse facilities mediated their integration and their continued engagement and investment in Australia. Their own place-making practices, in concert with other immigrants or professionals, became the basis of their social networks.

Our focus on the spatial, physical and material attributes of industrial environments offers a unique lens that complements previous socially focused historical approaches to industrial environments. There are several important historical studies of the Australian Gold Rush-era environments, mining and steel industries, and also convict-era heritage that illustrate this broader field of study, including studies related to irrigation and water politics that politicize industrial development in important ways.[27] These above approaches are comparable to Michael Roller and Paul Shackel's respective foci on specific industrial towns in the United States.[28] Here too, the lens from heritage offers an opening for examining post-industrial sites. Stefan Berger's *Constructing Industrial Pasts* is a recent 2019 publication that aligns with our interest in industrial heritage, as does Christian Wicke et al.'s *Industrial Heritage and Regional Identities*, which includes several international case studies.[29]

Books with a similar scope are rarer in our disciplines, divided between approaches that look more for design innovation or professional engagement than for the social critiques embedded in historical studies.[30] Publications aligned with our interests would include Andrew Johnston's *Mercury and the Making of California* and the much earlier *Building the Workingman's Paradise* on the Tennessee Valley Authority housing schemes.[31] More recently, *The Garden in the Machine* by Avigail Sachs offers an interesting spatial and political counterpoint to Clayton Strange's Soviet, industrial *Monotowns*.[32] Sarah Lopez's *The Remittance Landscape*, connecting the United States and Mexico, resonates with our exploration of how labour, manufacturing and small industries create capacity for immigrant emplacement at the outer suburban periphery or inner city.[33] The cross-disciplinary project *VacantGeelong*, led by Lozanovska with team including Beynon, likewise explores past immigrant worker memories of post-industrial sites.[34]

International interest in migration and refugee studies has expanded exponentially during the past decade, as part of the global interest in its geopolitical significance, not least because of the overlap with border studies, making it a highly interdisciplinary area of research. *Camps Revisited* traces the refugee camps contemporary lineage, and many similar studies recognizing the scale and proliferation of camp spaces have addressed their architecture as contemporary urban and spatial phenomena.[35] Anoma Pieris' *Architecture on the Borderline* and her publication with Lynne Horiuchi, *The Architecture of Confinement*, on wartime incarceration camps, including in Australia, historicizes the practices of diasporic identification and racial segregation in these spaces as connected to DP treatment in migrant camp environments as well as contemporary practices of immigrant processing and detention in carceral facilities.[36] These publications reinforce our study's salience for broader international awareness of human displacement and migrant labour globally. The work of South Asian and African diasporic scholars focused on diasporic home-making have augmented this aspect of immigrant studies more recently, further exploring methods discursively aligned with critical race theory and decolonization.[37] Their scholarship is significant for discursively integrating contemporary refugee and migrant experiences as co-constitutive and for exploring their positionality within the ongoing transformation of Australian identity and border politics, beyond the timeframe covered in this book.

THE SHAPE OF THE BOOK

Immigration centres and industries that employed refugee and immigrant labour in the postwar period can be thought of as nodes in a spatial and labour network, the running of each being dependent on the other. The case study chapters convey this network, its nodal points and intercultural social interactions through a study of the camps, key industrial sites for hydroelectric power generation, defence and raw material production. Examples are drawn from the populous southeastern states: the recipients of the largest numbers of postwar refugees and immigrants, due to their significance in the history of immigration and Australian modernization, and their capacity to convey their co-dependence, and the later dispersal of new immigrants into manufacturing and service industries at the metropolitan periphery. In doing so, the examples reveal how labour and domicile environments of refugees and immigrants shaped Australia internally, highlighting their interaction and competition with other groups.

The first three chapters, including this one, frame the topic of nonanglophone postwar labour migration as pivotal for Australian industrialization and distinctive from other immigrant pathways. Chapter 1, Postwar Immigrant Recruitment Policies, Labour and Accommodation, unpacks histories of migrant settlement and industry in postwar Australia. In exploring these mutually inclusive histories, Mirjana Lozanovska, Alexandra Dellios and David Beynon set the historical scene for the subsequent chapters. The spatial will be a key framework throughout. The spaces under analysis, those that define the immigrant experience of settlement, are the migrant camp, the accommodation centre, the boarding housing and the industrialized workplace. They are deeply implicated in the processes of nation building and industrialization that underpinned the impetus behind Australia's mass immigration scheme. The scheme was not immune to prevailing Anglo-Australian prejudices and preconceptions about the non-British immigrant, but rather was a key mechanism through which these notions were enacted, both socially and economically. Therefore, one cannot unravel these complex postwar histories without considering the role of ethnicity and its function in Australian immigration policy, in the political economy and in the workplaces of a largely Anglo-Australian society.

Chapter 2, 'Machines for Making Australians: The Military Prehistory of Migrant Camps' by Anoma Pieris, aims to build a continuum between immigration and wartime histories rarely connected in migration studies. DP families who came through refugee camps in Europe found living alongside military units in military administered, regimented environments to be challenging. The purportedly benign repurposing of a wartime facility and the placement of immigrant families in military huts raise questions regarding the presumed neutrality of military architecture, the lack of adaptation for civilian accommodation and, where camps were formerly used for prisoner-of-war or internee accommodation, their prior histories of violence. Pieris explores these themes through the architectural facilities and the labour mobilities that knit together the shared military and migration histories of camps. The chapter offers an intimate insight into a sponsored immigrant pathway, relating the story of Italian immigrant Giuseppe (Joe) Roncari's negotiation of Australia's postwar labour landscape through serial dislocations to eventual emplacement.

Having explored the intellectual framing for the book in its broader sense, the remaining seven chapters focus on specific case studies, selecting those most indicative of important intersections of built environment and social histories, beginning with key sites in New South Wales (see Figure 0.1). Architecture and industry are core to nation-building agendas and their histories tend to align with progressive narrative framings. In the postwar period (1945–79), the BHP Steelworks (Broken Hill Proprietary) in Port Kembla, Australia, expanded into a 'scene of Australia's great industrial growth'.[38] Urban and economic growth, expansion, technological innovation and power – BHP directors, their agency, networks and genealogy – dominate the histories of the steelworks and Port Kembla as a place. In Chapter 3, 'Unfinished Histories of Nation-Building: Racialization, Space of Labour and Industry at Port Kembla', Mirjana Lozanovska offers an alternative way to tell the story of Port Kembla, reorienting a dominant progressive historiography of industrialists towards labour migrants, and from this perspective developing a theory of industrial architecture as a space of labour. The chapter develops a thesis that nation building, industrialization and modernization are contingent on labour, and illustrates how the making of modern societies involves labour, increasingly as its invisible infrastructure. Focusing on postwar immigrants working at the Port Kembla steelworks and drawing upon labour histories, statistical data, findings and ethnographic participant work, the chapter argues that racialization and ethnicization structure the space of labour and the architectural landscape of industry, as well as its modernizing subtext.

In Chapter 4, 'Company Town: Housing Labour Migrants on the Snowy Hydro Scheme', Anoma Pieris examines the towns and associated work camps created for the federally funded postwar industrial project with the largest immigrant workforce in postwar Australia. Using Indigenous Australian dispossession and environmental impacts as new lenses for critiquing the pioneering rhetoric, Pieris peals back layers of the Scheme's 'development ecology', in which human expertise and labour are enmeshed. The chapter focuses on the human dimension of the Scheme rather than

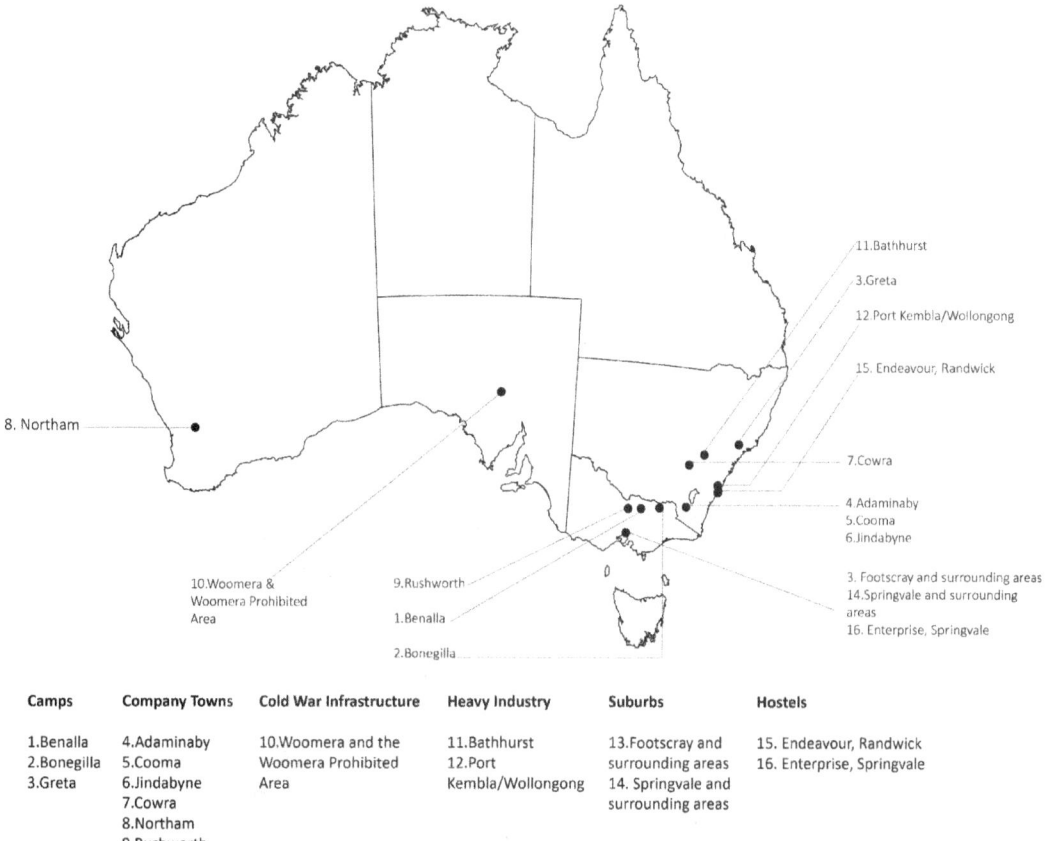

Figure 0.1 Sites and localities connected to camps, hostels, infrastructure, industries and company towns and suburbs mentioned in the book. Drawn for author by Renee Miller-Yeaman, 2022.

its engineering achievements, exploring its construction phases and material culture: the ephemeral camp sites and prefabricated accommodation that housed the largely immigrant workforce. It argues that Cooma North, the company town was an international settlement, its diversity sustained by the ongoing presence of multinational contracting companies, their staff and immigrant workers, rather than 'the birthplace of multiculturalism', as it is often described.

The Department of Defence's Anglo UK–Australian joint project to test and develop long-range weapons in Australia's arid region commenced in 1947 and reached a peak in the 1970s and 1980s. In Chapter 5, 'Woomera: A Landscape of Displacement and Renewal', Andrew Saniga examines how the rocket and missile-testing range at the Woomera Prohibited Area in South Australia necessitated complex infrastructure as well as a service town, Woomera Village, servicing workers and scientists involved in the Cold War military project. Some 400 Eastern and Central European DPs, sent to Woomera to work for the Commonwealth Department of Works and Housing, were significant in enabling the project in a time of labour shortage, engaging in everything from mixing concrete to drafting plans. Their environmental and living conditions, their socialization and their manoeuvring into semi-professional roles launched some individuals on lifelong career trajectories. But set against the backdrop of what was undoubtedly Australia's first and most overt participation in the Cold War international politics and relations, the DPs' immigrant workers' origins in war-torn Europe sat uneasily with public, political and unionist perceptions, particularly those linked with communism and communist states.

In Chapter 6, 'Noncompliance and Agency in Migrant Family Life: Greta and Benalla Migrant Camps', Alexandra Dellios draws on published and unpublished testimony, digital storytelling and oral histories from former immigrant residents of Australia's postwar Immigration Centres (or 'camps') to explore the limits of agency and noncompliance within the spaces of Greta and Benalla migrant camps in the period from 1949 to 1961. Dellios accounts for an immigrant's individual ability to influence their social environments, for themselves and for their families, and thus operates as a corrective to accounts that may limit their position within the historiography to that of victim, on the one hand, or (free agent) success story, on the other. Much of this detail can only be captured through the storytelling of immigrants. As members of diverse families, they could demonstrate noncompliance, outright defiance, and creative acceptance or adaptation – depending on their familial circumstances and desires while living within Australia's camp system. Through themes of family separation under the two-year work contract with the Commonwealth, the creative building of informal economies of exchange and work, and the pressures (as well as the benefits) of childrearing in a semi-regulated but communal setting, the struggle and compromise between agency and structure is made clear.

During the post-Second World War nation-building era in Australia, the domestic, as produced through public housing, was a site for innovation in construction technologies and programmatic arrangements. Arguably, government-sponsored domestic design experimentations can merge with broader social agendas and nation-state policy directives. In Chapter 7, 'Design Experiments in Collective Housing: The Renewal of Commonwealth Migrant Hostels', Renee Miller-Yeaman investigates the overlap between design and social experimentation in housing through strategies used to accommodate immigrants and refugees entering the country. Miller-Yeaman argues that constant adjustments in accommodation type, from provisional practices to testing out new models for collective living, mark the trajectories of Commonwealth migrant hostel sites. Focusing on two hostels, The Endeavour in Sydney and The Enterprise in Melbourne, the chapter examines designs that originated within the Commonwealth Department of Public Works in conjunction with Commonwealth Hostels Ltd (CHL). Their templates for temporary, collective living were aligned with dwelling arrangements seen in medium-density housing rather than the ex-military facilities. Architectural approaches to government-sponsored design reveal how housing provision in Australia is inextricably linked to migration discourse as it emerges in understandings of the nation in the second half of the twentieth century.

Concurrent economic and demographic developments impacted immigrant accommodation and employment in the 1970s. A noteworthy decline in government-supported industrial projects as major employers of new immigrants and refugees occurred alongside the first major influx of immigrants from Asia since the mid-nineteenth-century Gold Rush. Without federal support to catalyse their economic integration, this new wave of settlers, largely refugees from the Vietnam War, had to find employment in smaller pre-existing industries and, more pointedly, develop new industries and enterprises to establish themselves. It was this aspect of their industrial activity that transformed suburban built environments in a manner that has been critical to the broader development of Australia's cities. In Chapter 8, 'From Peripheries to Centres: Refugees, Industry and Settlement in an Australian City', David Beynon explores the impact of refugees who resided at Melbourne's migrant hostels from mid-1970s onwards, in particular The Enterprise Migrant Hostel in Springvale and Midway Migrant Hostel in Maribyrnong. Beynon explores the relation of this broader reluctance to the relative neglect of refugee-instigated urban settlement in Australian architecture and urban planning discussions, despite its profound cultural and economic impact. Many of these hostels' residents were of Asian backgrounds – Vietnamese, diasporic Chinese, Lao, Cambodian, Sri Lankan, Timorese and others – and represented a distinct change to Australia's demography at the time. The chapter explores individual or family stories that link refugee arrival, settlement and developments in commerce, industry and community in the cities of Greater Dandenong and Maribyrnong, the municipalities in outer-suburban Melbourne, Victoria where the Enterprise and Midway migrant hostels were respectively located.

Studies of immigrant communities in Australia often adopt ethnic perspectives, echoing the policies of multicultural differentiation, whereas architecture is able to explore spatial and material conditions as settings for multiple ethnic practices that converge or overlap. Migration, the mobility of peoples into and within the continent, has been a constant across Australia's settler history. However, the public recognition of settler-colonial Australia as a 'migrant nation' is limited in scope. The origins of a 'multi-ethnic' Australia are placed in the mass post-Second World War immigration scheme. In the heritage management landscape, the privileged position of white settler narratives serves to conceal histories of Indigenous Australian dispossession, of interethnic and sectarian conflict, unequal labour relations and working conditions for non-English-speaking immigrants, and the race-based inequality that has shaped the settlement experiences of many.

Our concluding chapter is entitled 'Migration Heritage Landscapes in Australia Today'. It is an exploration of the status and direction of 'immigrant heritage' – especially as it pertains to authorized, national and industrial heritage – in Australia and it offers multiple, and sometimes conflicting, questions about the heritage and public history of post-Second World War immigration, industrialization and architecture. These are not prescriptive conclusions about immigrant heritage, but rather nodal points of discussion, which draw from each of our site-based research with immigrant and implicated community groups.

Anoma Pieris is Professor of Architecture at the Melbourne School of Design. Her most recent publications include the anthology *Architecture on the Borderline: Boundary Politics and Built Space* (2019) and *The Architecture of Confinement: Incarceration Camps of the Pacific War* (2022), co-authored with Lynne Horuchi. She was guest curator with Martino Stierli, Sean Anderson and Evangelos Kotsioris of the 2022 MoMA exhibition *The Project of Independence: Architectures of Decolonization in South Asia, 1947–1985*.

Mirjana Lozanovska is Professor in Architecture and Director of the Architecture Vacancy Lab at Deakin University. Her work investigates the creative ways that architecture mediates human dignity through multidisciplinary theories of space. Her books include *Migrant Housing: Architecture, Dwelling, Migration* (2019) and *Ethno-Architecture and the Politics of Migration* (2016). Her creative works include *Venetian Blinds* (European Cultural Centre, Venice 2021), and, with David Beynon, Cameron Bishop, Diego Fullaondo and Anne Scott-Wilson, the exhibition *Iconic Industry* (2017, National Wool Museum, Geelong). She was co-editor of Fabrications: *Journal of the Society of Architectural Historians Australia and New Zealand* from 2018 to 2021.

NOTES

1. Cochrane, *Industrialization and Dependence*.
2. Appadurai, *Modernity at Large*.
3. Martin, *Refugee Settlers*; Jupp, *Arrivals and Departures*; Junankar, *Recent Immigrants*; Castles, Booth and Wallace, *Here for Good*; Castles and Kosack, *Immigrant Workers*.
4. Hage, *White Nation*; Hage, *The Diasporic Condition*; Gunew, *Haunted Nations*; Jordens, *Alien to Citizen*; Papastergiadis, *The Turbulence of Migration*; Perera, *Australia and the Insular Imagination*.
5. Gunew, *Haunted Nations*; Hage, *White Nation*; Ang, *On Not Speaking Chinese*.
6. Ang, *On Not Speaking Chinese*, 100.
7. Zubrzycki, *Settlers of the Latrobe Valley*.
8. Balint and Simic, 'Histories of Migrants and Refugees in Australia', 380
9. Hannerz, *Transnational Connections*; Hou, *Transcultural Cities*.
10. Sandercock, *Cosmopolis II*; Fincher and Jacobs, *Cities of Difference*.
11. Edquist, *Frederick Romberg*; Goad et al., *Bauhaus Diaspora*; Lozanovska and McKnight, 'Émigré Architects and the Australian Architecture Establishment'.
12. Ackan and Dadi, *Art and Architecture of Migration and Discrimination*.
13. Woodcock, *Multicultural Sense of Place*; Laguerre, *Minoritized Space*; Sen and Johung, *Landscapes of Mobility*; Sandercock, *Cosmopolis II*.
14. Scriver, 'Mosques, Ghantowns and Cameleers'.
15. Beynon, 'Hybrid Representations'; Bartsch et al., The Australian Mosque.
16. Lozanovska, 'Abjection and Architecture'; Levin, *Migration, Settlement, and the Concepts of House and Home*; Lozanovska, *Migrant Housing*.

17. Cairns, *Drifting*; Lozanovska, *Ethno-Architecture*.
18. Crawford, *Building the Workingman's Paradise*; and see also the chapters in Aitchison, *The Architecture of Industry*.
19. Armstrong, 'Making the Unfamiliar Familiar'; Aitken, *Cultivating Modernism*; Thomas, *Moving Landscapes*; Saniga, *Making Landscape Architecture*.
20. Dellios, *Histories of Controversy*; Dellios and Henrich, *Migrant, Multicultural and Diasporic Heritage*.
21. Darian-Smith and Hamilton, *Remembering Migration*.
22. Peters, *Milk and Honey– But No Gold*.
23. Byrne, *Counterheritage*; Byrne, 'Heritage Corridors'; Byrne, 'Dream Houses in China'.
24. Ang, *On Not Speaking Chinese*.
25. Viviani, *The Indochinese in Australia*.
26. Jacobs and Malpas, 'Immigration, Indigeneity and Identity'; Hall, *The Migrant's Paradox*.
27. Reeves and Nicholls, *Deeper Leads*; Eklund and Fenley, *Earth and Industry*; Eklund, *Steel Town*.
28. Roller, *An Archaeology of Structural Violence*; Shackel, *Remembering Lattimer*.
29. Berger, *Constructing Industrial Pasts*; Wicke, Berger and Golombek, *Industrial Heritage and Regional Identities*.
30. Examples of these include Aitchison, *The Architecture of Industry*; and Thomas, Amhoff and Beech, *Industries of Architecture*.
31. Johnston, *Mercury and the Making of California*; Crawford, *Building the Workingman's Paradise*.
32. Sachs, *The Garden in the Machine*; Strange, *Monotowns*.
33. Lopez, *The Remittance Landscape*.
34. Lozanovska et al., *Iconic Industry*.
35. Katz, Martin and Minca, *Camps Revisited*.
36. Pieris, *Architecture on the Borderline*; Pieris and Horiuchi, *The Architecture of Confinement*.
37. Kandasamy, Perera and Ratnam, *A Sense of Viidu*; Carrasco et al., 'A Home for Diaspora'.
38. BHP, *Seventy-Five Years of BHP*, 33.

BIBLIOGRAPHY

Ackan, Esra, and Iftikar Dadi (eds). *Art and Architecture of Migration and Discrimination: Turkey, Pakistan and the European Diasporas*. Abingdon: Routledge, 2023.

Aitchison, Mathew. *The Architecture of Industry: Changing Paradigm in Industrial Building and Planning*. Farnham: Ashgate, 2014.

Aitken, Richard. *Cultivating Modernism: Reading the Modern Garden 1917–71*. Carlton, Vic: Miegunyah Press, 2013.

Ang, Ien. *On Not Speaking Chinese: Living Between Asia and the West*. New York: Routledge, 2001.

Appadurai, Arjun. *Modernity at Large: Cultural Dimensions of Globalization*. Minneapolis: University of Minnesota Press, 1996.

Armstrong, Helen. 'Making the Unfamiliar Familiar: Research Journeys towards Understanding Migration and Place', *Landscape Research*, 29(3) (2004), 237–60.

Balint, Ruth, and Zora Simic. 'Histories of Migrants and Refugees in Australia', *Journal of Australian Historical Studies*, 49(3) (2018), 378–409.

Bartsch, Katherine, Mizanur Rashid, Dijana Alic and Maryam Gusheh. The Australian Mosque Today: Architectural Collaborations, 2020–2023. Australian Research Council Special Research Initiatives, Grant ID: SR200200989.

Berger, Stefan. *Constructing Industrial Pasts: Heritage, Historical Culture and Identity in Regions Undergoing Structural Economic Transformation*. Oxford: Berghahn Books, 2019.

Beynon, David. 'Hybrid Representations: The Public Architecture of Migrant Communities in Melbourne'. Ph.D. dissertation. Melbourne: University of Melbourne, 2002.

Broken Hill Proprietary Company (BHP). *B.H.P. 75 years of B.H.P. Development in Industry*. Broken Hill, N.S.W.: BHP, 1960.

Byrne, David. *Counterheritage: Critical Perspectives on Heritage Conservation in Asia*. Abingdon: Routledge, 2014.

——. 'Heritage Corridors: Transnational Flows and the Built Environment of Migration', *Journal of Ethnic and Migration Studies*, 42(14) (2016), 2351–69.

——. 'Dream Houses in China: Migrant-Built Houses in Zhongshan County (1890s–1940s) as Transnationally "Distributed" Entities', *Fabrications*, 30(2) (2020), 176–201.

Cairns, Stephen (ed.) *Drifting: Architecture and Migrancy*. Abingdon: Routledge, 2004.

Carrasco, Sandra Neeraj Dangol and Majdi Faleh. 'A Home for Diaspora: From the Horn of Africa to Melbourne's Public Housing'. Melbourne School of Design, The University of Melbourne, 2021. Retrieved 7 December 2023 from https://research.unimelb.edu.au/__data/assets/pdf_file/0006/4091325/A-home-for-the-diaspora-small.pdf.

Castles, Stephen, and Godula Kosack. *Immigrant Workers and Class Structure in Western Europe*. New York: Oxford University Press, 1985.

Castles, Stephen, Heather Booth and Tina Wallace. *Here for Good: Western Europe's New Ethnic Minorities*. London: Pluto Press, 1984.

Cochrane, Peter. *Industrialization and Dependence: Australia's Road to Economic Development, 1870–1939*. Brisbane: University of Queensland Press, 1980.

Crawford, Margaret. *Building the Workingman's Paradise: American Company Towns*. New York: Verso, 1995.

Darian-Smith, Kate, and Paula Hamilton (eds). *Remembering Migration: Oral Histories and Heritage in Australia*. London: Palgrave Macmillan, 2019.

Dellios, Alexandra. *Histories of Controversy: Bonegilla Migrant Centre*. Melbourne: Melbourne University Publishing, 2017.

Dellios, Alexandra, and Eureka Henrich (eds). *Migrant, Multicultural and Diasporic Heritage*. Abingdon: Routledge, 2020.

Edquist, Hariette (ed.). *Frederick Romberg: The Architecture of Migration 1938–1975*. Melbourne: RMIT University Press, 2000.

Eklund, Erik. *Steel Town: The Making and Breaking of Port Kembla*. Carlton, Vic: Melbourne University Press, 2002.

Eklund, Erik, and Julie Fenley (eds). *Earth and Industry: Stories from Gippsland*. Clayton, Vic: Monash University Press, 2015.

Fincher, Ruth, and Jane M. Jacobs (eds). *Cities of Difference*. New York: Guilford Press, 1998.

Goad, Philip, Ann Stephen, Andrew McNamara, Harriet Edquist and Isabel Wunsche. *Bauhaus Diaspora and Beyond: Transforming Education through Art, Design and Architecture*. Carlton, Vic: Miegunyah Press, 2019.

Gunew, Sneja. *Haunted Nations: The Colonial Dimensions of Multiculturalisms*. New York: Routledge, 2003.

Hage, Ghassan. *White Nation: Fantasies of White Supremacy in a Multicultural Society*. Sydney: Pluto Press, 1998.

——. *The Diasporic Condition: Ethnographic Explorations of the Lebanese in the World*. Chicago: University of Chicago Press, 2021.

Hall, Suzanne. *The Migrant's Paradox: Street Livelihoods and Marginal Citizenship in Britain*. Minneapolis: University of Minnesota Press, 2021.

Hannerz, Ulf. *Transnational Connections: Culture, People, Places*. New York: Routledge, 1996.

Hou, Jeff (ed.). *Transcultural Cities: Border-Crossing and Place-Making*. Hoboken, NJ: Taylor & Francis, 2013.

Jacobs, Keith, and Jeff Malpas. 'Immigration, Indigeneity and Identity: Cosmopolitanism in Australia and New Zealand', in Gerard Delanty (ed.), *Routledge Handbook of Cosmopolitan Studies* (New York: Routledge, 2012), pp. 516–30.

Johnston, Andrew. *Mercury and the Making of California: Mining, Landscape, and Race, 1840–1890*. Boulder: University Press of Colorado, 2013.

Jordens, Ann-Mari. *Alien to Citizen: Settling Migrants in Australia*. Sydney: Allen & Unwin, 1997.

Junankar, P.N. *Recent Immigrants and Housing*. Canberra: Australian Government Publishing Service, 1993.

Jupp, James. *Arrivals and Departures*. Melbourne: Cheshire-Lansdowne, 1966.

Kandasamy, Niro, Nirukshi Perera and Charishma Ratnam. *A Sense of Viidu: The (Re)Creation of Home by the Sri Lankan Tamil Diaspora in Australia*. Singapore: Palgrave Macmillan, 2020.

Katz, Irit, Diana Martin and Claudio Minca. *Camps Revisited: Multifaceted Spatialities of a Modern Political Technology*. New York: Rowman & Littlefield, 2018.

Laguerre, Michel. *Minoritized Space: An Inquiry into the Spatial Order of Things*. Berkeley: Public Policy Press, 1999.

Levin, Iris. *Migration, Settlement, and the Concepts of House and Home*. New York: Routledge, 2016

Lopez, Sarah. *The Remittance Landscape: Spaces of Rural Mexico and Urban USA*. Chicago: University of Chicago Press, 2016.

Lozanovska, Mirjana. 'Abjection and Architecture: The Migrant House in Multicultural Australia', in G. Baydar Nalbontoglu and Wong Chong Thai (eds), *Postcolonial Space(s)* (New York: Princeton Architectural Press, 1997), pp. 101–29.

——. (ed.). *Ethno-Architecture and the Politics of Migration*. New York: Routledge, 2016.

——. *Migrant Housing: Architecture, Dwelling, Migration*. Abingdon: Routledge, 2019.

Lozanovska, Mirjana, and Julia McKnight. 'Émigré Architects and the Australian Architecture Establishment'. Deakin University. Conference contribution, 2015. Retrieved 4 December 20223 from https://hdl.handle.net/10536/DRO/DU:30081167.

Lozanovska, Mirjana, David Beynon, Cameron Bishop, Diego Fullaondo and Anne Scott-Wilson. *Iconic Industry: Exploring the Industrial Built Fabric of Geelong*. Geelong: Deakin University, 2017.

Martin, Jean. *Refugee Settlers: A Study of Displaced Persons in Australia*. Canberra: Australian National University, 1965.

Papastergiadis, Nikos. *The Turbulence of Migration: Globalization, Deterritorialization, and Hybridity*. Cambridge: Polity Press, 2000.

Perera, Suvendrini. *Australia and the Insular Imagination: Beaches, Borders, Boats, and Bodies*. New York: Palgrave Macmillan, 2009.

Peters, Nonja. *Milk and Honey – But No Gold: Postwar Migration to Western Australia, 1945–64*. Crawley: University of Western Australia Press, 2001.

Pieris, Anoma (ed.). *Architecture on the Borderline: Boundary Politics and Built Space*. New York: Routledge, 2019.

Pieris, Anoma, and Lynne Horiuchi. *The Architecture of Confinement: Incarceration Camps of the Pacific War*. Cambridge: Cambridge University Press, 2022.

Reeves, Keir, and David Nicholls (eds). *Deeper Leads: New Approaches in Victorian Goldfields History*. Ballarat: BHS Publishing, 2007.

Roller, Michael. *An Archaeology of Structural Violence: Life in a Twentieth Century Coal Town*. Gainesville: University Press of Florida, 2018.

Sachs, Avigail. *The Garden in the Machine: Planning and Democracy in the Tennessee Valley Authority*. Charlottesville, VA: University of Virginia Press, 2023.

Sandercock, Leonie. *Cosmopolis II: Mongrel Cities in the 21st Century*. London: Continuum, 2003.
Saniga, Andrew. *Making Landscape Architecture in Australia*. Sydney: UNSW Press, 2012.
Scriver, Peter 'Mosques, Ghantowns and Cameleers in the Settlement History of Colonial Australia', *Fabrications*, 13(2) (2004), 19–41.
Sen, Arijit, and Jennifer Johung (eds). *Landscapes of Mobility: Culture, Politics, and Placemaking*. Burlington, VT: Ashgate, 2013.
Shackel, Paul. *Remembering Lattimer: Labor, Migration and Race in Pennsylvania Anthracite Country*. Champaign: University of Illinois Press, 2018.
Strange, Clayton. *Monotowns: Urban Dreams, Brutal Imperatives*. San Francisco: Applied Research & Design, 2019.
Thomas, Katie Lloyd, Tilo Amhoff and Nick Beech (eds). *Industries of Architecture*. New York: Routledge, 2015.
Thomas, Mandy. *Moving Landscapes, National Parts and the Vietnamese Experience*. Sydney: Pluto Press Australia, 2002.
Viviani, Nancy. *The Indochinese in Australia, 1975–1995: From Burnt Boats to Barbecues*. Melbourne: Oxford University Press, 1996.
Wicke, Christian, Stefan Berger and Jana Golombek (eds). *Industrial Heritage and Regional Identities*. New York: Routledge, 2018.
Woodcock, Ian. *Multicultural Sense of Place: The Case of Sydney Road, Melbourne*. Parkville, Vic: University of Melbourne, 2016.
Zubrzycki, Jerzy. *Settlers of the Latrobe Valley: A Sociological Study of Immigrants in the Brown Coal Industry in Australia*. Canberra: Australian National University Press, 1964.

Chapter 1

Postwar Immigrant Recruitment Policies, Labour and Accommodation

Mirjana Lozanovska, Alexandra Dellios and David Beynon

INTRODUCTION: NATION BUILDING AND IMMIGRATION

Since British colonization, the Australian continent has been quintessentially pictured via its distance from its colonial motherland, Great Britain, and its vastness, with a populace concentrated and dotted along its perimeter and an empty desert centre.[1] Considering Indigenous Australian (Aboriginal and Torres Strait Islander First Nations/Peoples') custodianship and land management, and the many Indigenous nations and languages distributed within the continent, this myth, while consistently revised and revived, is manifestly false and damaging. It is also not true when considering major industries that have shaped the lives of countless peoples living on unceded lands. Dispersed across regional and urban locales, they constitute the economic foundation of colonial and federal nation building and modernization. These industries included manufacturing and production (mining, logging and steel), pastoral and agricultural (wool, sugar cane, wheat, dairy, corn and canola), and energy (gas, coal and hydraulic), and they demanded workers. Following the era of convict labour, a large number of these workers were (assisted) immigrants. This chapter offers a historical and theoretical framework for this anthology, tracing the material and social contexts that migrant workers encountered in Australia.

Following the abolition of convict transportation between 1840 and 1868 (which provided a ready stream of labour since the colony's founding in the more populous southeastern states), Australia turned to other sources to address its labour needs. Since colonization, Australian nation building and immigration went hand in hand.[2] In the four decades from 1860, Afghan and Indian cameleers, often working with Indigenous Australian people, played a crucial role in all expeditions and scientific surveys of the Australian interior establishing the iconic Birdsville track, as well as several other major routes, including the one to Alice Springs.³ Large land grants offered by various governors to white British colonial settlers transformed these landscapes into rural holdings and precipitated the increasing appropriation of Indigenous Australian labour, especially in the interior and on sites that interfaced with immigrant labourers. In the two decades after 1863, over 62,000 Pacific Islanders arrived in Queensland, largely to work on the sugar plantations along the tropical coast, many of them coerced to work in Australia by the blackbirding trade.⁴ German Lutherans began to arrive in South Australia in 1838, escaping the religious politics of the church, establishing the 'German villages' in the Adelaide Hills. The Gold Rush evinced a multiracial and itinerant influx of migrants, which resulted in a Chinese population of 40,000 by 1891, many later establishing market gardens and grocery stores in cities and country towns.⁵ With the United States imposing quota restrictions in 1924, Southern and Eastern European immigrants were redirected to migrate to Australia, many settling into rural communities in Queensland, Victoria and Western Australia, and many others entering transient contract work in logging in the late 1800s and early 1900s. In contrast to histories of immigrant concentration in the major cities of Melbourne and Sydney, a spatial history of immigrant labour reveals the presence and distribution of immigrant communities across regional and rural centres.

Expanding settlement and the economic successes of early 'pioneers' were premised on the violent displacement of Indigenous Australian populations. The genocide of Australia's Indigenous peoples was the ultimate outcome of racial and colonialist ideologies. British colonialism in Australia seeks to deny Indigenous Australian sovereignty and to fundamentally deny Indigenous Australian personhood through the fiction of *terra nullius*. A 'White Australia' and the biological racism that underpinned it continued to justify the colonial project upon Federation in 1901 and beyond. The first act of Parliament was to pass the Immigration Restriction Act 1901, colloquially known as the 'White Australia Policy', which excluded non-Europeans and effectively placed restrictions on any non-Anglo-Celtic peoples from entering the country. The progressive labour policies of strong unions did not extend to non-British labourers. Chinese, Pacific Islanders, Afghan, Indian and other Asian immigrants – along with other non-British settlers in the nineteenth century – faced racism in the 'working man's paradise' of the Australian colonies. History in Australia continues to have a problem with who counts as 'European' due to this anglophone emphasis and its specific conflation of race with culture.⁶ Attempts to define 'Australian identity' up until the 1960s were premised on the White Australia Policy and British race patriotism.⁷ As Gunew has noted, 'Australianness' is assumed to be synonymous with 'Anglo-Celticism'.⁸ Even earlier immigrant identities are absorbed without differentiation in the historiography into a continuum of Anglo-Celtic settler identities or marginalized as minority Others living on the fringes of colonial society.

This book recognizes and wishes to emphasize that non-British migrant labour and its infrastructure are not limited to one short period of Australia's economic history, but are integral and constitutional to Australian nation building since British invasion. Rather than seeking to add non-Anglo-Celtic 'migration history' to 'Australian history', this chapter conceptualizes Australia as fundamentally and always multiracial and intercultural. This recognition exposes the essentialized and systemic racism of Australia's historical narratives. Undeniably, for much of its history, Australia privileged the migration of people from the British Isles.[9] Only in recent decades have non-Anglo-Celtic and non-European immigrants, particularly from Asia, come close to dominating the immigration intake. When restrictions were relaxed on the entry of peoples from the Middle East and Asia, this first came only in the form of temporary visas. From 1957, non-Europeans were eligible for citizenship after fifteen years of residency in Australia; Europeans were encouraged to take up residency after five years. By 1981, with 1,086,716 immigrants from Europe (excluding the United Kingdom and Ireland) and an additional 360,900 from Asia, nonanglophone immigrants made up more than 50% of the immigrant population.[10] There were increasing numbers of refugees and other immigrants from Southeast Asia (particularly Vietnam and Cambodia) from the late 1970s. Before 1975, there were fewer than seven hundred Vietnamese-born people in Australia, largely adopted orphans, Colombo Plan students or the wives of Australian soldiers.[11] By 2001, however, after waves of refugees, associated migration under family reunion programmes and the appearance of second and third generations, the Vietnamese-Australian population had grown to around 300,000.[12] Today, the majority of people seeking to emigrate to Australia are more likely to come from India and China, although many still arrive and stay for decades on temporary visas and under precarious working conditions.[13] The results of the 2021 Census show that over 50% of the Australian population is now born overseas, a percentage that had continued to rise since Australia's mass immigration policy after 1947, with a substantial and accumulative proportion of the population connected to a diversity of nonanglophone nations, cultures and languages.

RECEIVING NEW ARRIVALS: POSTWAR IMMIGRATION SCHEMES

Government-subsidized heavy industry and its demand for production and growth underpin Australia's labour policies in the postwar era. Immigration was the only way to achieve those demands. Australia's immigration policy changed from the Immigration Restriction Act 1901 to a radical mass immigration scheme (or schemes, as it were). The post-Second World War period constitutes the second of Australia's largest migration 'waves' – the first being the period from 1850s to the 1890s of assisted emigration, mainly from the British Isles. Government documents evidence the difficulty and the efforts to reassure the Australian electorate that this mass postwar migration would not alter their society or the anglophone status quo. In hindsight, we can see that the postwar recruitment policy for mass immigration more or less reversed the strategy of the 1901 Immigration Restriction Act, which by 1947 had produced a relatively homogeneous and, due to its racial and ethnically discriminatory agenda, a hegemonic society. The population comprised over 90% Australian born Anglo-Celtic heritage, 8% born in other anglophone countries, with under 2% born in nonanglophone countries, and 0.12% Indigenous Australian peoples.[14]

The Commonwealth Department of Immigration was established in 1945 by Chifley's Labor Government, with Arthur Calwell as its first Minister. In the historiography and in popular accounts, Calwell is lauded as the visionary behind Australia's mass postwar immigration scheme. His Department of Immigration established an extensive bureaucratic arm of government, which continued to develop after the electoral defeat of Labor by Menzies' Liberal government in late 1949. The Department of Immigration administered the recruitment, entry and dispersal of new arrivals to Australia. They saw their job as 'managing' migrant arrivals, their work allocation, and therefore the social and economic impacts of immigration, specifically its impacts on mainstream Anglo-Australia.[15] This view of the function of the Department persisted well into the 1970s, when some functions devolved or came to rest with the Department of Social Services.

Calwell's most cited quotation, 'populate or perish', has generated a skewed understanding of this pivotal moment in Australia's history. In 1945, at the close of the Second World War, Calwell raised the nationalist agenda for security: 'Our first requirement is additional population. We need it for reasons of defence.'[16] However, debates about migration, in which industrial forces played a large part, demonstrate that the pendulum swing in migration policy was propelled by economic growth. The security agenda was partly presented to placate a foretold racist reaction from mainstream Anglo-Australia. Through a radical mass migration policy, the Australian government invested and provided the necessary support to industry and industrialists. It was not migrant subjects that were desired by the Australian government so much as unskilled and semi-skilled labourers to fuel the postwar industrial agenda intended to generate economic growth.

DISPLACED PERSONS

Although politicians and journalists often date the beginnings of multicultural Australia in the postwar era, the immigrant intake remained predominately British and Irish well into the 1960s. The Australian government sought to maintain the racist exclusions contained in the White Australia Policy up until the mid-1960s. However, and as stated, while the immigration campaign targeted firstly immigrants from the British Isles, the numbers were not forthcoming. In order to meet immigrant quotas, the Australian government, influenced by the demands from industry, cast the net wider and embraced immigration from outside the British Isles, beginning with the acceptance of Eastern European refugees (or 'displaced persons') still residing in International Refugee Organization (IRO) camps in war-torn Europe. The acceptance of migrant labour from countries outside of the British Isles was an economic (rather than humanitarian) necessity. After the IRO scheme ended in the early 1950s, the Australian government signed intergovernmental migration agreements with European nations, including the Netherlands, Germany, Italy, Poland, Malta and Greece. Many of these migrants would arrive under assisted passage and were expected to fill labour shortages in industry – consequently, able-bodied young single men were preferred in the immediate postwar era (1947–52) and during the continued industrial growth of the 1960s.

In the wake of the Second World War, millions of stateless people remained in refugee camps in Europe – the aforementioned displaced persons or DPs. Australia's earliest non-British postwar intake were primarily refugees from communism – that is, Eastern European DPs who had fled the falling of the Iron Curtain and had found themselves in refugee camps in Germany, Austria or Italy after the end of the Second World War. These refugees were unable or unwilling to return home; others from Poland or the Ukraine had been displaced during the war and became forced labourers interned in Nazi labour camps. They too feared returning to their home countries, which were now under Soviet control. From 1947 to 1952, approximately 170,000 of these DPs arrived in Australia. The DPs comprised of anti-communist refugees from Latvia, Lithuania, Estonia, Poland, Germany, Austria, Ukraine, Hungary and Czechoslovakia. Historian James Jupp, looking back in 1966 on the agreement signed between Australia and the IRO in 1947, argued that:

> The decision to select *economically assimilable* Displaced Persons in 1947 is often hailed as 'the greatest humanitarian act that Australia has ever undertaken'. In fact it was a coolly calculated drive, in competition with the United States, to draft workers into Australia without upsetting the domestic labour or housing situation. It was humanitarian in that families were allowed to accompany male workers, provided they were healthy. It was less than human in splitting those families on arrival in Australia, sometimes for as much as two years ... Yet Australia, which had fought against indentured labour, was quite happy to impose two years of bonded employment in manual work as its price for humanitarianism.[17]

Calwell remained a dedicated defender of the White Australia Policy well into the 1960s, when the policies behind it began to be dismantled by the McMahon Liberal government. As labour-hungry industries demanded it, the acceptable criteria for migration expanded and racial categories became less tenable. Admittedly, racial prejudices prevailed in the selection of DPs and assisted migrants – this did not disappear with the need to 'populate or perish'. This is seen most clearly in the caps imposed on Jewish migration and on Polish DPs before 1949. The Department of Information (the Department of Immigration's promotional wing) drew on prevailing ideas in scientific racism, promoting to the Australian public, the blue-eyed, blonde-haired 'Beautiful Balt' as the typical DP and thus homogenizing this diverse cohort.[18] Once the IRO numbers dwindled, Australia, which was still in need of workers to fuel its long industrial boom, chose to accept 'less-desirable' or 'economically assimilable' applicants, including single-parent families and family units containing members beyond working age, something Canada and America declined to do during the years of the IRO scheme. All individual refugees arriving in the immediate postwar era were handed, upon arrival, a certificate of registration, which described their occupation as either 'labourer' or 'domestic', regardless of their skills or qualifications; they were 'made equal in status with all their fellow nationals'.[19]

As this book examines, many new arrivals were directed to employment in mining, steelworks and major infrastructure projects, some of them in regional areas of the country. In the early postwar era, decentralization was a government priority.[20] Industry was encouraged by government – through the Decentralization Board – to expand into rural areas, which was in turn aided by the extension of modern electrified train services to major rural centres. Major industries directed the settlement of migrant workers to regional towns, rural agricultural lands and remote sites. As will be relayed in Chapter 3, this included immense steelworks and associated industries in regional New South Wales (NSW), particularly in the Illawarra, as well as state-supported car manufacturing, cement production and open-cut coal mining and electricity production in regional Victoria. These industrial projects drastically transformed the landscapes and rapidly expanded the populations of these regions.[21] However, by the 1960s, the push to decentralize had mostly been abandoned.[22]

THE WORK EXPERIENCES OF POSTWAR ARRIVALS

Nearly two million migrants arrived in waves from the 1950s to the 1970s, some having all or part of their passage covered by the Commonwealth government, and others having to repay lending agencies in their home countries or church organizations in Australia. Many were therefore privy to work contracts with the Commonwealth, which in turn had arrangements with industry. Alongside assisted immigration, an increasingly diverse cohort were arriving via chain migration, sponsored and assisted by family already settled, which also altered Australia's ethnic and cultural demography.

The economic status and standing of most postwar non-British migrants were transformed upon migration. A majority of postwar migrants were rural peasantry (particularly those from Greece, Yugoslavia and Italy); some had already worked in state industries rebuilding the infrastructure of their homelands or as temporary guest workers in Germany, France or Belgium. Upon migration to Australia, they were quickly transformed into Australia's new industrial working classes. By the 1970s, non-English-speaking-background migrants were concentrated in the 'heaviest, dirtiest, most monotonous, most dangerous and least paid jobs', while constituting nearly 30% of the Australian workforce.[23] As labour historians Lever-Tracy and Quinlan argued, Australia's labour market has always been ethnically segmented.[24] In the postwar era in particular, 'skilled' migrants tended to be those from Northern Europe (Scandinavia, the Netherlands and Germany) and the United Kingdom, while migrants from

Southern and Eastern Europe, and, from the 1970s, the Middle East (Lebanon and Turkey) and Southeast Asia were funnelled into 'unskilled' work.[25] In the 1980s, Marxist labour historian Jock Collins reflected on these prevailing patterns in the labour market: 'Migrants from the UK and other English-speaking countries – Anglophones – seem by and large to occupy labour market positions similar to the Australian born.' He identified 'Northern European non-Anglo migrants' as the exception; they tended to manifest labour market relations similar to English speakers, but 'migrants from other non-English-speaking countries – the Italians, Greeks, and Yugoslavs being numerically the largest of these – are concentrated in different jobs'.[26] Cutting across the country of origin axis is gender – regional industrial growth towns did not have many jobs for women, and jobs in certain service industries (healthcare, social work and domestic labour, as well as textile factories) remained 'women's jobs'. The gendered dimension to the exploitation of non-English-speaking migrant labour is explored below. Non-English-speaking migrant groups, particularly those from Southern Europe and Asia, also had higher rates of small business ownership and self-employment – this was the case with early Greek settlers in the colonial period too, as it was with Southeast Asian refugees arriving from the 1970s. It largely relates to discrimination in the labour market and the nonrecognition of overseas qualifications (see Chapter 8).[27]

INDUSTRY, TRADE UNIONS AND GOVERNING MIGRANT LABOUR

Entangled with government's ethnicized and racialized categories that sought to uphold the hegemony of an anglophone mainstream were the powerful influences of major industries – including the State Electricity Commission of Victoria, Australian Paper Mills, Electric Power Transmission (EPT) and, of course, the Broken Hill Proprietary company (BHP). The directors of the monolithic BHP company gained membership to the Commonwealth Immigration Planning Council (CIPC). In contrast to an understanding that immigrants from the United Kingdom continued to be a priority and preferred, Lever-Tracey and Quinlan demonstrate industry's desire for workers who were more readily 'exploitable', as evident in their specific targeting of Southern European and Middle Eastern immigrants. Refugees from Vietnam also started to settle in substantial numbers after 1975 and while the impetus for the arrival of the Vietnamese was more due to their need to escape the conflict in their homeland, they were also a ready source of exploitable labour. Some contemporaneous accounts indicate that immigrant workers from the United Kingdom, both skilled and unskilled, were perceived to be troublesome by large employers because of the standard of unionized labour they expected.[28]

Aside from the leaders of industry, mass labour immigration necessarily involved trade unions, which in 1945 complicated the aligned strategies between government and industrialists. In the postwar period, a number of major unions continued to favour the enforcement of the White Australia Policy, with only a minority of radical left-wing unions (like the Building Workers' Industrial Union, the Waterside Workers' Federation and the Seamen's Union) siding with the policy of the Communist Party of Australia from the 1950s, which opposed the White Australia Policy. While generally supporting 'planned immigration', larger mainstream unions were initially against mass immigration from underdeveloped countries, as this, they argued, would undermine local living standards. Negotiations between unions and government in the immediate postwar period were difficult, not least because representatives from major corporations and industrialists, notably BHP, had the ear of then Minister for Immigration Arthur Calwell and were represented on the Immigration Advisory Council (IAC). Calwell was at pains to stress that migrant labour would present 'no competition' to Australian labour, an argument that made mass immigration more palatable to unions.[29] Nonetheless, Calwell 'extracted a number of additional concessions from BHP', including employing 'immigrants in the least attractive jobs', and 'to dismiss those refusing to join the union'.[30] Many of these expectations persisted into the 1960s, and only some unions in the 1960s came to campaign for the rights of their non-English-speaking workers. Notably, the ACTU (Australian Council of Trade Unions) in the late 1950s continued to view migrant labour as a means to prop up the 'bottom of the ladder'.[31]

LANGUAGE, PREJUDICE AND STRUCTURAL RACISM

Prejudices remained and had implications beyond initial acceptance and migration – they affected the migrant's working and intimate lives, the jobs they were afforded, their rights at work and the support services they were denied (or simply not made aware of), the standard of accommodation they were able to access and the government restrictions placed on their personal and familial living circumstances. This was the case for those who arrived as DPs or assisted migrants and worked under a strictly enforced two-year work contract with the Australian government; it was also the case for immigrants arriving in the 1960s and 1970s, who were at the mercy of new industrial management and production methods with very little intervention from government agencies.

The persistence of a racist and institutionally supported Anglocentrism can also be seen in the labels ascribed to migrant groups: the term 'New Australian', initially popularized by Calwell, went out of favour by the 1960s, by which time it was identified as patronizing, but the label was not nearly as bad as the slang term 'reffo' (attached to Jewish refugees arriving from 1938) and the term 'Balts', indiscriminately used both by the government and the media to describe DPs (even those who came from outside the Baltic States of Latvia, Lithuania and Estonia); the offensive terms 'wog' and 'dago' have a much longer lineage in Australia, linked to the migration of Italians, Yugoslavs, Macedonians and Greeks in the nineteenth and early twentieth centuries, and their unofficial use persisted throughout the postwar era as a racial slur.

The arrival of Vietnamese, Cambodian and diasporic Chinese refugees and immigrants in the 1970s and 1980s led to new racist slurs, with 'Asian' serving as a general term with discriminatory overtones, as Ang puts it, deriving from the 'hegemonic assumption that "Australian" culture/identity and "Asian" culture/identity are mutually exclusive, antagonistic categories'.[32]

Despite the prevalence of structural racism and the exclusion of non-Anglo-Celtic Australians from positions of power in unions, workplaces and politics, workplaces inevitably became multi-ethnic spaces as a result of the mass postwar immigration, as did many of the industrial hubs and suburbs in which migrants lived. The postwar mass immigration policy that brought millions of non-Anglo-Celtic immigrant workers into Australia altered the social and cultural fabric, and redirected the futures and modes of modernization of Australian society. Directed to industrial employment, many thousands settled in urban as well as regional, rural and remote sites, transforming the spatial environments, built fabric, composition, order and street atmosphere of these places.

REGIONAL CAMP ACCOMMODATION AS 'PROCESSING' AND 'DISPERSAL' SITES

In returning to the immediate postwar era, the following section offers a historical account of the accommodation and housing options afforded to different migrant cohorts, particularly in regional areas. Importantly, these sites of accommodation had direct relationships to industry and Australia's labour policies. From 1949, the newly established Department of Immigration administered a network of 'reception and training centres' and 'holding centres' that received, processed and assigned work to new migrant arrivals (those who had no family or sponsors in Australia to accommodate them). Officers within the Department worked closely with the Department of Labour and National Service (DLNS) and the newly created Commonwealth Employment Service (CES). Officers of the CES arranged for arrivals to find work where they were most needed. This system of allocation and movement required that migrants accept the jobs allocated to them and report to their local employment office whenever they moved or changed jobs.[33] The majority of these centres – referred to by former residents as 'camps' – were former military training sites in remote and regional areas of Australia, places like Bonegilla in Victoria, Greta in NSW and Northam/Holden in Western Australia (WA). They operated at their peak from 1947 to 1952. But when rural settlement and decentralization waned by the late 1950s and the larger remote centres began to close, incoming migrants were more readily directed to manufacturing and hostels in inner-city suburbs.

As former military establishments, the conditions within these centres were spartan. They proved ill-equipped to accommodate families and children (see Chapter 6), although Departmental historian Ann-Marie Jordens concedes that the mass immigration programme was a large, impressive and mostly efficient administrative achievement.[34] Crucially, the centres were located at a distance from major urban centres like Sydney or Melbourne, out of sight and mind from the mainstream Anglo-Australian population. Calwell issued a statement regarding the 'revolutionary' provisions made for the reception, accommodation and job allocation of new arrivals. He stressed the necessity of the scheme, recognizing its radical departure from previous immigration policy but stressing its utilitarian and 'well-managed' nature. He assured the public, industry and unions that 'since they will have been selected with a view to meeting our known labour requirements, there will be no difficulty in securing suitable employment with a minimum of delay for all the displaced persons who are brought here'.[35] In the immediate postwar era, with the renewed emphasis on regional and rural industrial expansion, military training sites seemed ideal places for migrant reception centres and not just because the housing shortage compelled the Department to utilize this option.

Regional military training camps were able to act as points of dispersal for labour, both agricultural and industrial. In theory, arrivals who were able to work were processed and allocated employment within two weeks of their arrival at the centre, following an interview with a CES officer. In practice, the time spent at the camp depended on the willingness of migrants to accept allocated work, on housing available (generally another, smaller camp or hostel), on individual family circumstances and on the demand for labour at the time. Over 320,000 displaced people and assisted migrants passed through Bonegilla during its twenty-four years in operation (1947–71) and over 100,000 through Greta from 1949 to 1960.

Alongside the larger Department of Immigration centres like Bonegilla and Greta (both of which operated as reception points and when needed, as 'holding centres' for workers' dependants), the Department set up similar centres at former military training camps from the early 1950s. They established five holding centres in Victoria alone, located at Rushworth, Benalla, Mildura, Somers and West Sale; in NSW, there was Uranquinty and Cowra. Some smaller and marginally better-equipped hostels were marked for British use only (like Elder Park and Gepps Cross in South Australia); all the rest accommodated DPs or assisted migrants from across Europe. With the exception of Bonegilla, the Department closed all centres by the late 1960s, when Commonwealth-assisted migration numbers decreased (chain migration and family reunion streams increased) – and as the government came to realize that the regional and spartan nature of these former military camps were no longer tenable as accommodation solutions for new migrants. This choice was also compelled by the high rates of return emigration for Italian and Dutch migrants.

State governments also managed smaller hostels that accommodated workers (almost exclusively men) employed on state-run projects. For example, NSW Railways and the State Electricity Commission of Victoria had purpose-built wooden barracks or Nissen huts to accommodate the influx of migrant workers. At moments in the 1950s, when numbers exceeded available accommodation, 'tent cities' emerged around sites of industry. Australia's continued housing crisis, matched with huge numbers of incoming migrants, also saw the need for city hostels (like Maribyrnong in Melbourne and Villawood in Sydney, which operated throughout the 1960s and 1970s). These hostels were initially administered by the DLNS; from 1952, they were administered by the newly formed government-funded company Commonwealth Hostels Ltd, which was answerable to the DLNS.[36] These city hostels came to be the main focus of departmental funding from the 1960s, as fewer migrant workers were accommodated in remote centres like Bonegilla and more were placed in work in major cities. City hostels also offered a higher and more modern standard of accommodation and amenities compared to remote camps.

PRIVATE ACCOMMODATION FOR NONASSISTED CHAIN MIGRATION

Not all immigrants had access to the Commonwealth accommodation system. In addition to large numbers of assisted immigrants, immigrants who were sponsored by relatives or self-funded initially lived in accommodation organized by friends or family. The options were not specific to migrants, but they consisted of company hostels (company employees, men only); boarding houses both registered and unregistered; house flats and shared houses; flats and units in purpose-built buildings; garages and sheds; tents and caravans; and houses. The immigrant experience of restricted housing options, and a lack of affordable and adequate housing was compounded by restrictions on non-British access to the Victorian Housing Commission. Until the mid-1970s, only British immigrants had access to social housing in Geelong and this inequity was repeated in the Latrobe Valley. British immigrants were accommodated in prefabricated housing imported from England and reassembled in the Latrobe Valley by the State Electricity Commission. In Wollongong too, nonanglophone immigrants did not have access to social housing, creating British-only districts such as the Dapto estate of prefabricated housing. Once they passed through the hostels, these immigrants had limited choices of housing. Some rented old houses, while families had to share rudimentary accommodation and lived in sheds, old barns and corrugated iron shacks for periods of five to seven years.[37]

Regional industrial sites suffered from planning neglect. In the areas where immigrant labourers settled – Geelong (Corio) in Victoria and Wollongong (Cringila) in NSW – sewerage systems, electricity and running water were lacking and roads were unsealed. The industrial decentralization strategy was a drawcard for immigrants. Immigrants arrived in thousands to work at major industries in Geelong – Geelong Gas Company, Portland Cement, Geelong Small Goods and the giant Ford Motor Complex – which transformed Geelong into Victoria's second-largest city. Immigrant labour doubled the population in the Latrobe Valley in the period from 1947 to 1961.

Despite the hardships experienced in immigrant labour communities, increases in the population reinvigorated the cultures of regional industrial hubs. By the 1950s, almost half of the population of Corio – adjacent to the industrial zone of Geelong – was born overseas; immigrant families arriving in the 1960s shared small run-down weatherboard housing in West Geelong.[38] Polish delicatessens, Ukrainian bakeries, Dutch florists, florists and boot repairs as well as mixed business of Southern Europeans altered Geelong's Pakington Street.[39] By the end of the 1970s, there were nearly 40,000 Vietnamese refugees in Australia, with a majority arriving by boat and by plane. Their concentration in places like Cabramatta in Sydney and Dandenong in Melbourne generated ethnic-specific services and organizations providing support for individuals and families. Here the gender imbalance was more in the nature of work being sought than overall numbers of settlers, with Vietnamese single men becoming the next wave of immigrant labour in major industries, including BHP in Port Kembla.

In the 1940s, due to housing shortages, houses were divided up into single private rooms and became boarding houses. In Wollongong, as in other industrial regional towns, these boarding houses were located near the centre of the town and could not be distinguished from the neighbouring houses.[40] A large majority of immigrants recruited in the postwar period were single men. Boarding houses were a significant component of the housing available to them. The more traditional type of boarding houses were 'adaptions of old hotels, large houses or bungalows'.[41] But the boarding or (perhaps better named) rooming houses that accommodated single male immigrants were within the houses of other immigrants who had established their modest housing and these could be in separate rooms, in the basement level or in a bungalow at the back of the house. In the major cities, these rooming houses and more autonomous flatlettes were located in the inner-city suburbs. In the regional industrial towns, they were often close to major industry, as in Cringila, Port Kembla, an area for which there was little infrastructure, not only in terms of schools and cultural institutions but sewerage as well. Cringila is a stone's throw from Steelworks, an island suburb amidst industrial operations.[42]

SINGLE MEN

Australia's postwar mass migration policies dismissed immigrants' subjectivity – the history of their homelands, the trauma of war and the displacement of economic migration. Berger and Mohr's study documents this passage from emigration to immigration and the scale of ongoing loss caused by the disregard for immigrants' personhood in labour recruitment strategies. A most cruel and inhumane dimension of the Australian postwar mass immigration recruitment strategy was the preference for single, able-bodied men. For many, who were not actually unmarried, this caused a disruption to family, as their wife and children remaining in the homeland were separated for years. Numerous oral accounts have been told about the long periods of family separation – anxiety, remittance finances and work injuries – but their long-term effect is less well understood. Concentrated male immigrant labour in remote sites and industrial growth towns tended to evolve into a masculine culture, sometimes outwardly in a brutality of street environments. For others who were single men, especially those (like the Eastern Europeans) who were not embedded in already settled immigrant communities, the pathway of transition from refugee/immigrant to resident was often precarious. Their trauma was inwardly directed and men fell into mental illness and neglect. In contrast to a happy reunion, the arrival of families, in addition to the single female migrants outlined below, was of estranged members whose troubles continued into subsequent generations. This gendered division of immigrant labour recruitment continues globally well into the twenty-first century.

Due to the notorious shift-work patterns of work in major heavy industries, many single male immigrants shared a room, sometimes with three to six beds. For some, a boarding house was an improvement from the hostel, as it provided the option of a home-cooked meal.[43] For others, the spatial tightness of a room shared with others was a necessity. Many male migrants had left their families in their home countries on the premise that they would save enough funds to pay for their voyage and provide their accommodation on arrival. This separation, which sometimes continued for years, resulted in children who became estranged from their fathers and a breakdown of family life.[44] Work that was risky and arduous, the exhaustion and a male-dominated home and urban environment caused many to drift into alcoholism.[45] Sometimes, boarding houses, as one built by Italian migrants at Cringila, was a place for social gatherings for the Italian community. Immigrant communities and networks also evolved from these shared spaces on arrival into Australia.

UNDERSTANDING THE PIPELINE

From Camp to Industrial Labour

The larger camps that temporarily housed most of the DPs arriving from 1947 to 1952 and the bulk of the assisted arrivals throughout the 1950s operated along transport lines (mainly trains) to disperse people (labour) to where they were needed. People were treated as a 'pool of labour' and they were instrumental in alleviating postwar shortages in essential industries and boosting production.[46] For example, Greta was a one-hour drive from the industrial hub of Newcastle (a former coal mining hub and, from the early twentieth century, the home of BHP Steelworks); Greta was also three hours from Wollongong, another booming postwar regional hub whose heavy industry continued to expand in the postwar era. Many who passed through Greta also found work at the Snowy Mountains Hydro Electricity Scheme. Bonegilla in Victoria was a good recruiting spot for large landowners and farmers seeking fruit pickers or the State Electricity Commission seeking workers for the expanding coal-fired power industry in the Latrobe Valley. People could be sent further afield (as far as North Queensland) from Bonegilla if the demand was there and if individuals accepted such a job allocation. In times of recession, such as the 1952 downturn, this type of temporary work was all that was available and many accepted sixteen-week contracts cutting sugarcane or picking fruit. However, many individuals who passed through Bonegilla, if they did not accept regional job allocations, 'absconded' from their contracts (that is, they failed to report to the CES) and sought employment independently, generally in the nearest city, Melbourne (a four-hour train ride away).

Theoretically, according to the terms of their work contracts and the availability of subsidized housing, assisted migrants could find themselves sent anywhere across the country. Crucially, 'escaping' from Bonegilla did not mean leaving the camp system altogether – migrants could be moved from Bonegilla to, for example, the Gippsland region of Victoria, where migrant workers might be accommodated in the West Sale migrant camp, or further afield to Townsville in northern Queensland, where they might be accommodated in the Stuart migrant camp. The Department of Immigration, in conjunction with the CES, controlled and monitored the movements, employment and accommodation of migrants (under the Aliens Act). As emphasized, this system of monitoring was strictly adhered to in the earliest years of the postwar immigration scheme, but faltered (or became untenable) after 1952 and the end of the DP scheme. Each camp can therefore be seen as nodes in a network, all of which were geared towards the labour market and underpinned by racial anxieties.

From Port to Industrial Labour

In the context of postwar labour histories, Europe is a divided continent between the north and the south. An insatiable demand for labour was sourced from the depleted economies of Spain, Italy, Yugoslavia and Greece, to be directed to the edges of large industrial cities or to vast massive industrial plants in remote rural areas in advanced Northern European economies. Leading migration scholar Stephen Castles (with Heather Booth and Tina Wallace) details the migrant labour campaigns of Belgium, France, the Netherlands, Sweden and Switzerland, stating they 'started about 1945, gained momentum in the fifties, expanded dramatically in the late sixties and early seventies, and then stopped fairly suddenly in 1973/1974'.[47] With 400 recruitment offices in Southern Europe, busloads of immigrant workers were transported to German industries in Munich, Cologne and Hanover, often living in wooden huts or dormitories. Immigrant workers from Southern Europe were key to transnational capital and postwar labour history. It is well known that Southern European labour migrants arriving in the period from 1951 to 1973 tended to settle within pre-existing migrant communities in Melbourne and Sydney (with higher concentrations in Melbourne), as they relied on the ethnic community's financial and social support, public transport and proximity to work sites.

A decentralized industrial scheme resulted in the dispersal of immigrants outside the major cities and concentrations of labour immigrants in the major manufacturing centres. Immigrants were also subjected to itinerant work and often relocated – from steel manufacturing in Port Kembla, to extractive mining industries located in remote sites such as Kalgoorlie, Western Australia, to building the towers for the nation's electric network (Electric Power Transmission [EPT]) in Kwinana, Western Australia. Such spatial histories and dispersed geographies of labour migration provoke questions about earlier spatial histories of nonanglophone immigrants in the 1920s in rural, remote and regional areas of Australia.

Immigrants arriving in the 1950s and 1960s were processed at the pier of the major port in Melbourne (Station Pier) or Sydney, invariably to be loaded up on trains or buses. Many such double-decker buses travelled from the port in Sydney directly to the BHP Steelworks in Port Kembla, where large immigrant groups were allocated and directed to their sites of work. In the 1960s and 1970s, immigrants were also processed at Sydney or Melbourne Airport, often with the first port of arrival in Perth or Darwin. In the period from 1945 to 1979, the largest nonanglophone immigrant cultural presence in Australia was that of the Southern Europeans.[48] By the end of the 1970s, over half a million immigrants from Italy, Yugoslavia and Greece had settled in Australia – they demonstrated concentrated settlement patterns in the inner-city suburbs in Sydney and Melbourne in close proximity to manufacturing industries.[49] Likewise, in industrial growth towns such as Port Kembla and Wollongong, concentrations of Italian-born immigrants had settled in close proximity to the site of the Port Kembla Steelworks, with another group settling in the northern area of Fairy Meadow (where the immigrant hostel had been located), and Yugoslavian-born immigrants had the highest concentration in Port Kembla itself, including in the notorious area of Cringila.

In his comprehensive study *The Impact of Immigration on Australia*, Burnley extends this understanding with a discussion on regional manufacturing and mining towns, including discussions on Wollongong, Newcastle, Geelong and the Latrobe Valley (Victoria) and Whyalla (South Australia).[50] Burnley's maps illustrate settlement patterns and also show that immigrants from the United Kingdom and Ireland settled much further away from the Port Kembla steelworks, some prompted by the social housing in Berkeley (that was not available to nonanglophone immigrants). Immigrants from the Netherlands and Germany also settled at a great distance from the Port Kembla Steelworks site. The hierarchical structure of this distribution tended to be repeated in other regional manufacturing sites, as well as in the peripheral and inner suburban industries of major cities. As Burnley notes: 'Turkish and Macedonian immigrants who arrived in strength in 1968–74 later moved into housing vacated by eastern Europeans, Greeks and Italians. Increasingly, Cringila-Port Kembla became an area of considerable cultural mixture.'[51] Spatial patterns and suburban hierarchies align with the discriminatory structural divisions of labour: ethnicized work allocations were divided between skilled and unskilled migrant subjectivity.

GENDER, POSTWAR MIGRATION AND WOMEN'S WORK

Women and children were not the primary focus of the original immigration scheme or of the camp system set up to accommodate and allocate work to new arrivals. Women with children in particular presented an issue for immigration officials in the early years of the mass immigration scheme, notwithstanding the bureaucratic recognition of their value to nation building as reproductive labour. Classified as a male breadwinner's 'dependants', mothers and children were not bound by the two-year work contract. They were often accommodated in a holding centre, while their husbands and fathers worked off their contracts at industrial or agricultural sites across the country, living in 'men's only' workers' hostels or tent cities. In her account of postwar accommodation, Panich argues that 'women were never accepted as immigrants likely to make a contribution to the workforce' and there was little vision of them being more than 'dependants' in the first instance.[52]

The issue of appropriate childcare for working migrant parents was a longstanding one, both within the network of camps, and in the regional and urban centres in which migrants settled and worked. The director of Cunderdin (WA) Holding Centre pointed to the need for structural and systemic change, to provide housing, schooling and childcare, but only insofar as it would enable women 'to become assimilated into industry'.[53] Those who arrived outside assisted migration made their own informal and community-based arrangements for childcare – the need to work, for both men and women, was too great.

A large oversight in the recruitment policy of industrial decentralization is that regional towns, many dependent on a large male-centred industry, did not have enough employment for women. Rosa Cappiello's novel *Oh Lucky Country* catalogues the desperate struggles of migrant women in Wollongong. She reflects on the exploitation of Macedonian, Turkish, Greek and Maltese women who were 'bussed' daily to Sydney (a 160 km round trip) to work in sweatshops; while Julianne Schultz's, nonfiction study *Steel City Blues* links these women's experiences with data about (un)employment and family life.[54]

Migrant women came to dominate the work floors of small textile factories in regional Australia. In Wollongong and across the Illawarra, migrant women fuelled the textile industry's expansion from the 1940s to the 1970s.[55] The textile, clothing and footwear industry depended on the availability of girls and women, many of them non-English-speaking migrants who did not know their rights in the workplace, often because it had never been communicated to them in their own languages.[56] The poor conditions under which they laboured and their poor representation in trade unions was the subject of some sociological and community reports from the 1970s and 1980s, but by that point, the manufacturing industry was in decline.[57]

Non-Anglo migrant women were also valued as potential domestic labour in private homes or institutions. Separate schemes targeting women from countries like

Spain, Greece and Italy were established in the 1950s and 1960s to bring out women for this explicit purpose. The government also came to realize by the 1960s that immigration recruitment strategies targeting young able-bodied single men caused a large gender imbalance, which in turn created social problems within many immigrant communities. The government tied this to concerns about the high rates of return emigration for migrant men.[58] As Burnley notes, 'the strong male surplus among the immigrants from Czechoslovakia, Hungary, Lithuania, Poland and Ukraine' fostered a sense of social isolation among these men working off their two-year contracts in regional or remote parts of the country.[59]

Many of the single women who came out under migration agreements in the 1960s, such as the Spanish 'Marta Plan', did end up marrying their compatriots and settling in Australia, and in popular parlance their trips have been labelled 'bride flights'.[60] Other single young women came as 'promised' brides from Greece, or were married by 'proxy' in Italy, before migrating to meet their husbands in Australia.[61] Suffice to say, non-English-speaking migrant women in the postwar era fared worse than their male counterparts in the workplace – whether they worked as domestics or in factories.[62] They felt ignored by their unions, vulnerable to ill-treatment by their employers and unsupported by social services, especially in the areas of healthcare and childcare. When the clothing industry declined in the 1980s, many of the migrant women previously employed in this industry moved to outwork and therefore faced (and continue to face) sweatshop conditions and labour exploitation.[63] Despite these issues, clothing industry outwork was (and in a few cases still is) an important source of employment for immigrants from Southeast Asia who arrived around this time.[64] The gendered, arduous but sometimes communal nature of this labour is a subject that will be discussed in relation to correspondents' stories in Chapter 8.

CONCLUSION: INTERTWINING MIGRATION, LABOUR AND NATION BUILDING

Migrant labour is deeply implicated in the processes of nation building and industrialization. As outlined in the introduction to this framing chapter, the need for workers underpinned the impetus behind Australia's mass immigration scheme, in the same way that policies under colonial governments and post-Federation governments were calibrated to recruit the 'right' type of migrant worker. The mass immigration scheme was not immune to prevailing Anglo-Australian prejudices and preconceptions about the non-British migrant; rather, it was designed according to those prejudices. Importantly, and despite racist restrictions to non-British immigration, the story of Australia's colonization and industrial expansion since invasion has always featured diverse peoples, and any comprehensive history of the nation state would recognize the ethnically segmented nature of Australia's labour markets. Pivotally, this book also recognizes the spatial, environmental and aesthetic implications of that labour segmentation.

This chapter has provided a historical canvas from which to understand subsequent chapters. In particular, it accounts for the historically networked nature of migrant camps, centres, and housing with ports and regional/peripheral industrial hubs, and how these give rise to commercial districts. A spatial lens through which the chapters evolve explores the geographic dispersal from sites of arrival and processing to regional/peripheral industrial hubs, and the spatial confinement and constraint within camps or between housing and industry. This networked nature is spatially traced by migrant subjectivities who are both directed and who must navigate systemic exploitation and harsh environments. It is worth reiterating Jock Collins' argument, which features across all chapters in this anthology, that 'perhaps *the* central point in understanding the migrant presence in Australia is that anglophone and non-anglophone migrants have different work experiences'.[65]

Mirjana Lozanovska is Professor in Architecture and Director of the Architecture Vacancy Lab at Deakin University. Her work investigates the creative ways that architecture mediates human dignity through multidisciplinary theories of space. Her books include *Migrant Housing: Architecture, Dwelling, Migration* (2019) and *Ethno-Architecture and the Politics of Migration* (2016). Her creative works include *Venetian Blinds* (European Cultural Centre, Venice 2021) and, with David Beynon, Cameron Bishop, Diego Fullaondo and Anne Scott-Wilson, the exhibition *Iconic Industry* (2017, National Wool Museum, Geelong). She was co-editor of Fabrications: *Journal of the Society of Architectural Historians Australia and New Zealand* from 2018 to 2021.

Alexandra Dellios is Senior Lecturer in the Centre for Heritage and Museum Studies at the Australian National University. She is the author of *Heritage Making and Migrant Subjects in the Deindustrialising Region of the Latrobe Valley* (2022) and *Histories of Controversy: Bonegilla Migrant Centre* (2017), and co-editor (with Eureka Henrich) of *Migrant, Multicultural and Diasporic Heritage: Beyond and Between Borders* (2020). She is Chair of the Editorial Board for *Studies in Oral History*, a founding member of the Australian Migration History Network, and Executive Committee member of the Association of Critical Heritage Studies.

David Beynon is Associate Professor in Architecture at the University of Tasmania. His research involves investigating the social, cultural and compositional dimensions of architecture, and adaptations of architectural content and meaning in relation to migration and cultural change. His current work includes investigations into the multicultural and postcolonial manifestations of contemporary urban environments and the creative possibilities for post-industrial architecture in Australia and Asia.

NOTES

1. Society of Architectural Historians Australia and New Zealand (SAHANZ) Conference, *Distance Looks Back*.
2. Castles, 'Demographic Change', 2.
3. Scriver, 'Mosques, Ghantowns and Cameleers', 19–41.
4. Burnley, *The Impact of Immigration on Australia*, 82.
5. Burnley, *The Impact of Immigration on Australia*, 80.
6. Gunew, *Haunted Nations*, 46–47.
7. Castles, 'Demographic Change', 4.
8. Historians have noted the very term 'Anglo-Celtic' is also problematic: conflating the discriminatory experiences faced by Irish-Catholics under the category 'British' in Australia is a case in point. See Malcolm and Hall, *A New History of the Irish in Australia*, 12; For a critique see Gunew, *Haunted Nations*, 19–20.
9. Beynon, 'Beyond Big Gold Mountain', 187.
10. Lever-Tracey and Quinlan, *A Divided Working Class*, 3
11. Department of Home Affairs, 'Vietnam-Born Community Information Summary'.
12. Thomas, 'Vietnamese in Australia', 1143.
13. Australian Bureau of Statistics, '2021 Census Data'; Thomson, 'Migrant Employment Patterns in Australia', 4.
14. Lever-Tracey and Quinlan, *A Divided Working Class*, 1–5; Australian Bureau of Statistics, 'Census of Population, 1947'.
15. On the role of the Department of Immigration, see Jordens, *Alien to Citizen*. See also Tavan, *The Long Slow Death of White Australia* for policy and entry restrictions extending beyond the postwar era and based on race.
16. NAA: Department of External Affairs, A1066, 1944–1948, G45/1/1, Calwell, Statement to the House of Representatives, 2 August 1945.
17. Jupp, *Arrivals and Departures*, 8 (emphasis added).
18. Persian, *Beautiful Balts*.
19. Kunz, *Displaced Persons*, 163.
20. MacIntyre, *Australia's Boldest Experiment*.
21. Burnley, *The Impact of Immigration on Australia*, 105.
22. Jupp, *Arrivals and Departures*.
23. Moraitis, Constantinou and the Australian Greek Welfare Society, *Ethnics in Industry*, np.
24. Lever-Tracy and Quinlan, *A Divided Working Class*.
25. Jupp, *Arrivals and Departures*, 56–57.
26. Collins, 'Immigration and Class', 11–12.
27. Collins, 'Cosmopolitan Capitalism', 27–35.
28. Lever-Tracy and Quinlan, *A Divided Working Class*, 49.
29. Kunz, *Displaced Persons*, 41.
30. Lever-Tracy and Quinlan, *A Divided Working Class*, 172.
31. As Arthur Monk, the President of the ACTU, told an Australian Citizenship Convention in 1958, cited in Pennay, *Greek Journeys through Bonegilla*, 12.
32. Ang, 'Asians in Australia', 126.
33. Dellios, *Histories of Controversy*.
34. Jordens, *Alien to Citizen*, 1–20.
35. Calwell, cited in Kunz, *Displaced Persons*, 38.
36. Panich, *Sanctuary?*, 39.

37. Zubrzycki, *Settlers of the Latrobe Valley* 1964; Burnley, *The Impact of Immigration on Australia*, 97–121.
38. Australia established Assisted Migration Agreements with Yugoslavia and Turkey in 1967.
39. The Pako Festival continues to celebrate Geelong's multicultural history of immigrants.
40. Walker, *First Accommodation for Migrants*, 16.
41. Ibid.
42. Burnley, *The Impact of Immigration on Australia*, 105–14.
43. As reported by Cathy Edwards (née Baart) when describing her family's experience in Walker, *First Accommodation for Migrants*, 17.
44. Davis, 'Building a Culture', 217–30.
45. Morrisey, Michael and Jakubowicz, *Migrants and Occupational Health: A Report*; Burnley, *The Impact of Immigration on Australia*, 133.
46. Kunz, *Displaced Persons*, 176.
47. Castles, Booth and Wallace, *Here for Good*, 11.
48. Ibid., 140–81.
49. Lever-Tracey and Quinlan, *A Divided Working Class*, 3.
50. Burnley, *The Impact of Immigration on Australia*, 97.
51. Ibid., 109.
52. Panich, *Sanctuary?*, 118.
53. Jordens, *Alien to Citizen*, 68.
54. Cappiello, *Oh Lucky Country*; Julianne Schultz, *Steel City Blues*.
55. Thom, *The Places Migrant Women Found Work in Wollongong 1943–1990*, np.
56. Ibid.
57. Storer, 'But I Wouldn't Want My Wife to Work Here'; National Women's Advisory Council, *Migrant Women Speak*.
58. Simic, 'Bachelors of Misery', 151.
59. Burnley, *The Impact of Immigration on Australia*, 130.
60. The Marta Plan was the informal name for the agreement signed between Australia and Spain in 1957 designed to bring out single Spanish women. Most of them were from poorer rural areas, partly assisted by the Catholic Church and entered the Australian workforce as domestics.
61. Nazou, *Promised Brides*.
62. Alcorso, *Non-English Speaking Background Immigrant Women in the Workforce*, 8–10.
63. Collins, 'Cosmopolitan Capitalism', 34.
64. Thomas, 'Stitching at the Boundaries'.
65. Collins, 'Immigration and Class', 13.

BIBLIOGRAPHY

Archival Records

National Archives of Australia (NAA)

Publications

Alcorso, Caroline. *Non-English Speaking Background Immigrant Women in the Workforce*. Wollongong, NSW: Published for the Office of Multicultural Affairs, Department of the Prime Minister and Cabinet by the Centre for Multicultural Studies University of Wollongong, 1991.

Ang, Ien. 'Asians in Australia: A Contradiction in Terms?', in J. Docker and G. Fischer (eds), *Race, Colour and Identity in Australia and New Zealand* (Sydney: University of New South Wales Press, 2000), 115–130.
Australian Bureau of Statistics. 'Census 2021 Data'. Retrieved 25 February 2022 from https://www.abs.gov.au/statistics/people/people-and-communities/snapshot-australia/2021.
——. 'Census of Population, 1947'. Retrieved 25 February 2022 from https://www.abs.gov.au/AUSSTATS/abs@.nsf/DetailsPage/2109.01947?OpenDocument.
Beynon, David. 'Beyond Big Gold Mountain: Chinese-Australian Settlement and Industry as Integral to Colonial Australia', *Fabrications* 29(2) (2019), 184–206.
Bosworth, Richard. 'Conspiracy of the Consuls: Official Italy and the Bonegilla Riot of 1952', *Historical Studies* 22(89) (1987), 547–68.
Burnley, Ian. *The Impact of Immigration on Australia: A Demographic Approach*. Melbourne: Oxford University Press, 2001.
Cappiello, Rosa R. *Oh Lucky Country*. Brisbane: University of Queensland Press, 1984.
Castles, Stephen. 'Demographic Change and the Development of a Multicultural Society in Australia', *Centre for Multicultural Studies, University of Wollongong, Occasional Paper* 15 (1988), 1–41. Retrieved 6 December 2023 from http://ro.uow.edu.au/cmsocpapers/13.
Castles, Stephen, Heather Booth and Tina Wallace. *Here for Good: Western Europe's New Ethnic Minorities*. London: Pluto Press, 1984.
Collins, Jock. 'Cosmopolitan Capitalism: Ethnicity, Gender and Australian Entrepreneurs'. Ph.D. dissertation. Wollongong: Migration and Multicultural Studies, University of Wollongong, 1998. Retrieved 6 December 2023 from https://ro.uow.edu.au/theses/1898.
——. 'Immigration and Class: The Australian Experience', in Gillian Bottomley and Marie de Lepervanche (eds), *Ethnicity, Class and Gender in Australia* (Sydney: Allen & Unwin, 1984), pp. 1–27.
Davis, Joseph. 'Building a Culture: Architecture and Art in the Illawarra', in Jim Hagan and Andrew Wells (eds), *A History of Wollongong* (Wollongong: University of Wollongong Press, 1997), pp. 217–30.
Dellios, Alexandra. *Histories of Controversy: Bonegilla Migrant Centre*. Melbourne: Melbourne University Publishing, 2019.
Department of Home Affairs. 'Vietnam-Born Community Information Summary', 2016. Department of Home Affairs website. Retrieved 29 January 2024 from, https://www.homeaffairs.gov.au/mca/files/2016-cis-vietnam.PDF.
Gunew, Sneja. *Haunted Nations: The Colonial Dimensions of Multiculturalism*. London: Routledge, 2004.
Jordens, Ann-Marie. *Aliens to Citizens: Settling Migrants in Australia: 1945–75*. St Leonards, NSW: Allen & Unwin, in association with the Australian Archives, 1997.
Jupp, James. *Arrivals and Departures*. Melbourne: Cheshire-Lansdowne, 1966.
Kunz, Egon. *Displaced Persons: Calwell's New Australians*. Canberra: Australian National University Press, 1988.
Lever-Tracy, Constance, and Michael Quinlan. *A Divided Working Class: Ethnic Segmentation and Industrial Conflict in Australia*. London: Kegan Paul, 1988.
Macintyre, Stuart. *Australia's Boldest Experiment: War and Reconstruction in the 1940s*. Sydney: NewSouth Publishing, 2015.
Malcolm, Elizabeth, and Dianne Hall. *A New History of the Irish in Australia*. Cork: Cork University Press, 2019.
Moraitis, Spiro, Con Constantinou and the Australian Greek Welfare Society. *Ethnics in Industry: A Submission by the Australian Greek Welfare Society*. Melbourne: Australian Greek Welfare Society Melbourne, 1976.
Morrisey, Michael, and Andrew Jakubowicz. *Migrants and Occupational Health: A Report*. Sydney: UNSW Social Welfare Research Centre, 1980.

National Women's Advisory Council. *Migrant Women Speak: A Report to the Commonwealth Government*. Canberra: Australian Government Publishing Service, 1979.

Nazou, Panayota. *Promised Brides: Experiences and Testimonies of Greek Women in Australia*. Sydney: Modern Greek Studies Association Australia and New Zealand, 2019.

Panich, Catherine. *Sanctuary? Remembering Postwar Immigration*. London: Routledge, 1988.

Pennay, Bruce. *Greek Journeys through Bonegilla*. Wodonga, Vic: Parklands Albury-Wodonga, 2011.

Persian, Jayne. *Beautiful Balts: From Displaced Persons to New Australians*. Sydney: University of New South Wales Press, 2017.

Scriver, Peter. 'Mosques, Ghantowns and Cameleers in the Settlement History of Colonial Australia', *Fabrications* 13(2) (2004), 19–41.

Schultz, Julianne. *Steel City Blues: The Human Cost of Industrial Crisis*. Ringwood: Penguin, 1985.

Simic, Zora. 'Bachelors of Misery and Proxy Brides: Marriage, Migration and Assimilation, 1947–1973', *History Australia* 11(1) (2014), 149–74.

Society of Architectural Historians Australia and New Zealand (SAHANZ) Conference, *Distance Looks Back*, Sydney, Australia, July 2019.

Storer, Des (ed.). *But I Wouldn't Want My Wife to Work Here: A Study of Migrant Women in Melbourne Industry* (Research Report for International Women's Year). Fitzroy, Vic: Centre for Urban Research and Action, 1976.

Tavan, Gwenda. *The Long Slow Death of White Australia*. Melbourne: Scribe, 2006.

Thom, Louise. *The Places Migrant Women Found Work in Wollongong 1943–1990*. Wollongong: Heritage Office NSW, 2007.

Thomas, Mandy. 'Stitching at the Boundaries: Vietnamese Garment Industry Workers in Transnational Spaces', *Intersections: Gender, History and Culture in the Asian Context* 5 (2001), np.

Thomas, Mandy. 'Vietnamese in Australia', in Melvin Ember, Carol Ember and Ian Skoggard (eds), *Encyclopedia of Diasporas: Immigrant and Refugee Cultures Around the World* (New York: Springer, 2005), pp. 1141–49.

Thomson, Lisa. *Migrant Employment Patterns in Australia: Post Second World War to the Present*. Melbourne: AMES Research and Policy Unit, 2014. Retrieved 6 December 2023 from https://www.ames.net.au/-/media/files/research/history-of-migrant-employment-final.pdf?la=en.

Walker, Meredith. *First Accommodation for Migrants Arriving in Wollongong Post-World War II*. Wollongong: Heritage Office NSW, 2007.

Zubrzycki, Jerzy. *Settlers of the Latrobe Valley: A Sociological Study of Immigrants in the Brown Coal Industry in Australia*. Canberra: Australian National University Press, 1964.

Chapter 2

Machines for Making Australians
The Military Prehistory of Migrant Camps

Anoma Pieris

During the early twentieth century and across two world wars, numbers of overseas-born Australians decreased to less than 10% of the population, which was 96% British and 99% white by 1947.[1] Unsurprisingly, around one million service personnel willingly entered the war to defend British interests in Europe and in the Asia Pacific region. After the war, displaced persons (DPs) and many other sponsored and assisted passage immigrants arriving in Australia had, likewise, experienced first-hand the violence and dislocation of catastrophic humanitarian crises: family separation and break-up, the erection of the Iron Curtain around Soviet Bloc countries, followed by the civil wars of the post-World War decades. These conditions saw the redistribution of people on a global scale. As potential sources of labour, their dispersal aided population-starved settler colonies, like Australia, to grow exponentially, from 7.4 million at the end of the war to 10 million by 1960.[2] The collective camp and hostel environments that received the majority of these immigrant labour conscripts (labour-migrants) mediated their first encounters with the hegemonic Anglo-Celtic culture that greeted them outside the camps. Short-term labour conscription introduced a more palatable variation on the unfree legacies of convictism, Indigenous Australian (Aboriginal and Torres Strait Islander First Nations/Peoples) (nonwaged) labour exploitation, and Asian and Pacific Islander indenture by which settler colonies, like Australia, have historically founded liberal democratic governments and achieved economic prosperity.

For many labour-migrants, barrack and hostel accommodation was the physical threshold to industrial worksites, factories, labour camps and the suburban homes of an idealized Australian life. Detached homes in garden plots had featured in propaganda posters inviting emigration to Australia.[3] The rectilinear military barrack prefigured immigrant entry into the inner city urban or outer suburban property grid, the latter expanding rapidly with population growth after the Second World

War. The abstraction of labour in nation-building industries, in large infrastructure projects, agriculture and heavy industries – often coupled with government strategies for decentralization – for example, individuated new arrivals as potential citizens in preparation for their absorption into and augmentation of Australian society. But equally, and because of these culturally graduated systems, postwar immigrants relied on temporary social networks when navigating environments that were ill-prepared for their arrival. Multilingual and culturally diverse or plural nonanglophone immigrants came together due to the necessity to domesticate military facilities and navigate industrial work regimes. Camp experiences forged intercultural sensibilities that sometimes persisted across labour-migrant networks at least for a generation, before anglophone linguistic assimilation strengthened horizontal relationships. For reasons elaborated in the arguments that follow, these two seemingly contradictory forces of individuation and collectivism became interlinked.

Following a brief introduction of the broader historical context for the repurposing of military camp facilities for refugee and immigrant accommodation, this chapter links aspects of wartime labour deployment to transient labour conscription for federally funded industries. The availability of temporary barracks and tented facilities hastily erected for worker accommodation were foundational to industrial growth both during and after the war. Types of accommodation varied, including in situ construction by local tradespeople following military-type plans, prefabricated housing transported to and assembled on site, and the accumulation of these provisional typologies at industrial work sites (see Chapters 4 and 5). The examples reviewed here are directly linked to military troop accommodation and cover the early phase of migration to Australia, during the 1940s and early 1950s, before purpose-built on-arrival accommodation was introduced. The government's repurposing of camp facilities in a continuous timeline with limited modification suggests troubling synergies between its various military and immigrant programmes. Their architectural assemblages assumed different social functions as though their military genesis was unimportant, or their temporariness obviated the need to consider them as impactful environments. Camp facilities were integral to the lineage of serial displacements that both temporally and spatially punctuated the trajectories of refugee lives. The second part of this chapter introduces Giuseppe (Joe) Roncari, an Italian immigrant who, arriving via pathways of this former military history, was drawn into the postwar industrial landscape. His story, although commencing in serial displacements through prison camps and work camps, diverts into sponsored migration, igniting autonomous efforts at place making at the industrial periphery.

In his 2012 exhibition *flotsamandjetsam*[4] on Bonegilla, the largest of Victoria's migrant camps, artist/architect Alex Selenitsch used the phrase 'Machines for making Australians' to describe this immigrant threshold into Australia. Fleeing postwar Europe, Alex's family passed through migrant camps at Cowra, Rushworth and Bonegilla, before eventually settling in industrial Geelong. The phrase, borrowed for this chapter's title, invokes Swiss architect Le Corbusier's declaration that houses were 'machines for living in', suggesting the links between camp environments, industrialization and citizenship.⁵ His functionalist vision was tested in prototypes for mass-produced housing achieved through the fabrication of standardized elements to generate a series. 'A well-mapped-out scheme, constructed on a mass production basis, can give a feeling of calm, order and neatness, and inevitably imposes discipline on the inhabitants', he wrote.⁶ This desired instrumentality of architecture in disciplining the citizenry, introduced most effectively through industrial workplaces and housing, commenced for many postwar immigrants in austere migrant camp and hostel facilities.

Comparison with the early to mid-twentieth-century United States is instructive. Innovations in worker camp and settlement designs sought to reconcile what Margaret Crawford describes as a fundamental contradiction within American capitalism of the profit-making motive with liberal principles of social rationality.⁷ The Farm Security Administration's migrant camp network created for internally displaced farm workers during the 1930s Depression era introduced settlements with civic amenities.⁸ Worker housing for the Tennessee Valley Authority assumed the character of rural townships.⁹ These tendencies were evident, albeit in more limited ways, when worker populations were wartime internees, passing from industries initiated in internment/concentration camps to agrobusinesses like Seabrook Farms, New Jersey, which accommodated Japanese-American internee and war-displaced European immigrant worker employees in a purpose-designed village.¹⁰ More importantly, in the United States, with the exception of the camp at Fort Ontario, DPs entered through individual sponsorship agreements unmediated by recipient migrant camps. This distinction differentiated the United States from Australia, placing the onus on individual sponsorship, while in Australia the chain of immigration linked camps to camps. In fact, during the early postwar period, DP/migrant camps in Australia were socially segregated sites hastily repurposed from military facilities like those in postwar Europe – for example, in Germany, Italy, Austria, France, the Netherlands and Belgium. Purpose-designed hostels (see Chapter 7) were not introduced until the 1960s.

THE MILITARY CAMPS

Austere military camp environments were used during the Second World War for training patriotic expeditionary forces, incarcerating prisoners of war (POWs) and internees identified as enemy nationals or aliens and housing POW working parties. War-displaced persons and assisted passage immigrants were accommodated in former military camps, often in repurposed and adjacent facilities from the late 1940s to the 1970s. During the mid-twentieth-century postwar decades, the camps transitioned from housing a predominantly male fighting or labour force to also acting as reception and holding centres for women and children, some of whose husbands or fathers were away on industrial work camps and sites as a precondition governing their emigration to Australia. The pragmatic reasoning behind the camps' minimal adaptation ensured that the facilities would remain temporary and encouraged immigrants to seek alternative accommodation following their term of indenture. These preferences were best summarized by G.W. Brown, chairman of the Commonwealth Immigration Advisory Council in 1953. Brown declared that migrant hostels must not be made comfortable enough to satisfy the needs of the less energetic immigrants – enervated by war – observing that 'it's going to be pretty difficult to plan something between a hostel which migrants don't want to live in permanently and a hut In [sic] which they can develop a sense of home ownership.'[11] Protests on camp conditions faced by British immigrants published in the London *People* newspaper threatened reverse migrations if facilities did not improve.[12] While agreeing that conditions were no less 'primitive' than those they had encountered in postwar Europe, either as concentration or DP camps, and disturbed at the continuing military oversight of these civilian facilities, the stated difference was their physical distance from wartime devastation and the hopefulness associated with new beginnings.[13]

The mutation of the camp environment across several functions for different categories of citizens or citizens-in-waiting suggests entanglements of militarization, immigrant labour and temporary accommodation that are yet to be fully explored in migration studies. Our understanding of the camp is also inflected by perceptions of 'New Australians' – immigrants new to anglophone cultural values – a descriptor that disregarded lives lived before arrival in Australia. Among the arguments raised to support this cultural *tabula rasa* was the necessity to suppress strains of wartime political enmity still simmering amongst many former enemy nationalities. The effacement of these political complexities was amplified by Australians' poor knowledge of European politics, due in part to their distance and cultural insulation, but also to the difficulties of communicating cultural knowledge in a foreign tongue. Expectations of the immigrant's deferential newness privileged British immigrant and Anglo-Australian authority as based on continuous uninterrupted and augmented cultural patrimony extending Britain's imperial provenance and the associated racialized colonial social hierarchies.[14]

The novelty and temporariness of camp environments, the rough domesticity of the partitioned military hut interiors and shared amenities echoed the crude subjectivity Australians attributed to Britain's European neighbours, aggravated by wartime impoverishment and prejudice. The right to property, privacy, family cohesion and recovery of peasant or urban cultures lost in their uprooting was conditional on and deferred by this period of labour investment in Australia. The expectation called for immersion in camp or industrial 'total environments' as provisional embodiments of Anglo-Australian values, before absorption into Australian cities and towns.[15] The prominent display of photographs of the British royal family at Bonegilla Immigrant Reception and Holding Centre's Tudor Hall, through which some 300,000 immigrants passed between 1947 and 1971, highlighted Britain's patronage of the host society.[16]

There were several ways in which military systems persisted in the lives of the European DPs, including in labour allocations. The Port Kembla Steelworks (see Chapter 3) was pivotal for Broken Hill Proprietary company (BHP)'s wartime steel manufacture used in the production of armoured vehicles, fighter aircraft and weapons. Baltic immigrants were employed on a Cold War Department of Defence Project, where they lived in active military camps that were established afresh rather than being repurposed facilities: the construction of the Woomera Prohibited Area and Village (see Chapter 5). Elsewhere, the use of repurposed military training camps or administration by the army meant that the military presence mediated many immigrant experiences in their first two years in Australia. Military camps in Victoria repurposed for migrant hostels or reception and training centres included Bonegilla (military training camp and hospital),[17] Benalla and Somers (RAF training camps) and Rushworth, a former wartime internment camp, as well as several other facilities.[18] Immigrants frequently moved between these militarized spaces as jobs became available in adjacent industries. Wasli and Leokadija Denisenko (from Russia/Ukraine and Poland respectively) who arrived in 1950, passed through Bonegilla, Uranquity, Rushworth and then Benalla.[19] Typically, several weeks were spent at Bonegilla awaiting work appointments, alongside language classes, health checks and registration for social services. The camp rituals and routines were likewise modelled after military practices such as the roll call, the linear barrack accommodation, the rudimentary, common messing and bathing facilities, and an overall lack of privacy.

With larger numbers of families arriving, as well as single women with children, military encampments became worker-family dormitories. Work allocation on a designated project, moving the family to a nearby camp or scheduling family leave, and finding independent employment and accommodation was the envisioned pathway to citizenship. This gave the camp network continuous utility through connection to industries. The distance from the camp to the industrial site – i.e., the distance of the family from the worker or the migrant camp from the work camp – became an affective measure of family security. Whereas a preference for young male workers obviated this dependency in some industries, work life was a conduit to immigrant-settler futures rather than an end in and of itself. Protests at Bonegilla in 1949, 1952 and 1961 suggest that delays in work allocation upset the immigrants and in the last incident even provoked their attack on and resultant damage to the employment office.[20] Local trade unions became involved and tensions rose between skilled German workers who were sought after when compared to unskilled Southern Europeans from Italy and Yugoslavia. The internal differentiation of nonanglophone immigrants according to perceptions of their relative merits affected their future prospects.

Migrants at Rushworth Camp 3 in Victoria (December 1948–June 1953), who are the first focus of this chapter, found employment in woodcutting in Greytown, fruit picking in Shepparton orchards or camp-related services at the nearby Puckapunyal, Balcombe, Seymour and Bandiana military camps.[21] The first arrivals were European DP families, followed later by unmarried Italian men.[22] Lt. Col. E.J. Parks, who was appointed director of the Rushworth camp, was formerly at the Uranquity migrant camp, part of the network of military personnel that formed the migrant camp administration. Robert Bain, also a director at Rushworth and later at the nearby Benalla migrant camp, had served in both world wars in addition to having been commander of the nearby Murchison POW Camp 13.[23] Military origins and networks likewise underwrote the organization of several camps elsewhere in Australia, including, in New South Wales, Bathurst (infantry training centre), Greta (military training camp and hospital) and Kapooka (army engineer training camp); in Western Australia, Northam (army camp), Holden Holding Centre (118th Field Hospital) and Cunderdin (Royal Australian Airforce base); and in Queensland, at Wacol (military camp), to name just a few of the repurposed facilities. Using these spaces as temporary accommodation fulfilled an urgent and pragmatic need because they had roads, fences and reticulated services with many additional amenities such as hospitals and recreational buildings previously provided for the military. Many war-displaced adult immigrants placed in regimented barrack environments closely resembling concentration camps found this association disturbing.[24] Providing bare essentials deflected any criticism of preferential treatment of immigrants that might be directed at them by a public suffering from postwar housing shortages, and by returned servicemen seeking land grants and housing placements in the community.

The standardized modular P- and C-series army huts, entered through their gable ends, were raised on stumps like Australian houses, joined by longitudinal bearers and floor joists, their walls raised on platforms built on boarded floors (see Figure 2.1).[25] Each hut had five windows and a ventilation gap covered with bird mesh above the walls. Walls and roof were clad in unpainted corrugated galvanized iron sheets or in timber, as was the case at Greta. These modular structures were highly adaptable as messes, guard huts, canteens, medical aid posts, dental surgeries, recreation huts, classrooms and offices, as well as showers, latrines, laundries, offices and stores. They were designed to be constructed in situ and adapted to varying site conditions, their reliance on local materials and familiar building techniques extending their reusability after the camps were disbanded. Bonegilla, for example, comprised 600 huts arranged in twenty-four blocks scattered across an undulating site, serviced by a railway siding, a water supply, a 600-bed hospital, theatre and a civic centre with gardens and lawns.[26] While the accommodation huts followed military lines, the blocks themselves were scattered throughout the camp plan (see Figure 2.2). The undifferentiated uniformity of corrugated iron and fibre-board surroundings was dispiriting to immigrants who were eager to rebuild lives in Australia, although interior modifications were introduced to individuate units. The 1949 newspapers describe the conversion of army huts to austere five-roomed houses at Greta with electricity and water laid on. A photograph of the conversion of one of these huts in 1951 reveals the ingenuity with which immigrants adapted these facilities.[27]

These first homes for DP and immigrant arrivals in Australia were crude, sparsely furnished containers: cogs in the above-mentioned machines for making Australians.

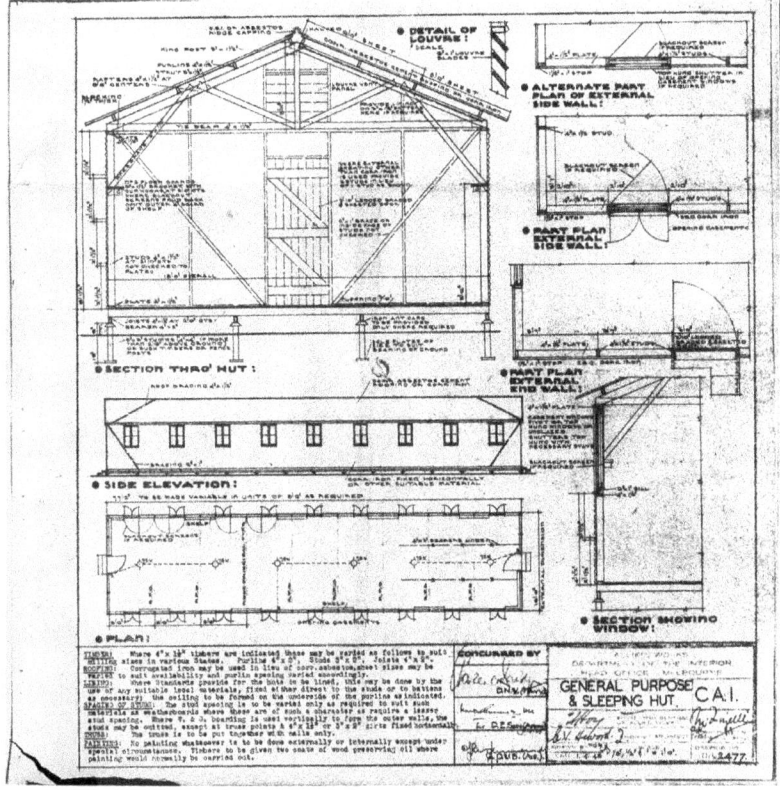

Figure 2.1 Cowra, New South Wales: specifications for the erection and completion of twenty timber-framed buildings and the resiting of three timber-framed buildings in a POW camp, December 1944. Courtesy of the National Archives of Australia, SP155/1, DEF397047, [Box 19], 44/45.

They were modified to simulate urban institutions at a smaller and more impoverished scale – the schools, workshops, gardens and kitchens all simulating spaces to be encountered outside the camp in Australian neighbourhoods. In these provisional waiting rooms in rural borderlands, prospective wage earners and future homeowners were prepared for citizenship. Aligned with military surveillance and industrial labour creation, widely dispersed migrant camps pursued and facilitated key economic imperatives that drove settlement. At Greta, barrack architecture of either corrugated iron Nissen huts or weatherboard and Masonite-clad timber structures formed two distinctive cities named Silver City and Chocolate City. Each barrack could house up to twenty-five people, and the whole facility catered to 6,000 men.[28] Although military lines and military names like 'mess hall' or 'recreation hall' persisted, both 'cities' had their own schools, cinemas, canteens and chapels. Silver City had the camp hospital. At one stage, there were seventeen different nationalities at the camp. Despite recurring tensions over kitchens or work allocations, former wartime enemies cohabited as neighbours uniting in their need to know and enter Australian society, to understand and resist incompatible dimensions of anglophone culture, and to benefit from the

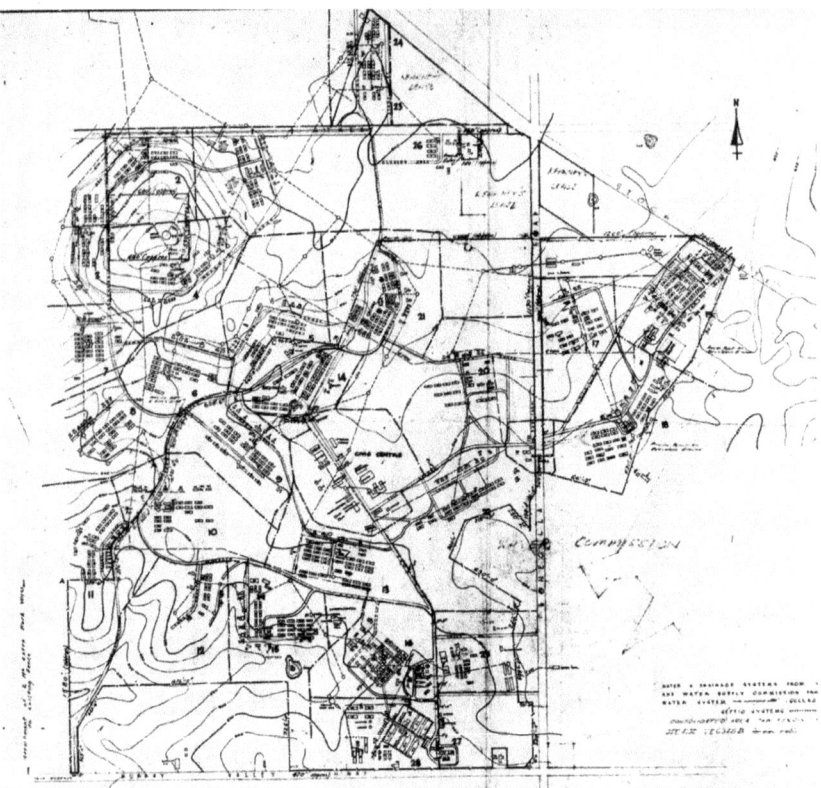

Figure 2.2 Bonegilla Military Training Camp, Victoria, 1954. Courtesy of the National Archives of Australia, B3712-Dr150-Folder4-part1, 1 April 1954.

cultural and linguistic plurality natural to many Europeans. Collapsed in the space of an Australian camp, proximate cultures mingled and national borders were sometimes sharpened, but just as frequently crossed.

Some of the camps had more troubling military associations due to their past incarceration of enemy aliens or overseas refugees of enemy nationality or captured enemy military personnel. The Australian military constructed and ran eighteen POW and internment camps and several other smaller facilities during the war.[29] At Rushworth, a former internment camp site was repurposed for immigrant reception.

RUSHWORTH MIGRANT CAMP

Originally the property of John McEwen, a former Country Party MP for the Goulburn Valley in Federal Parliament, the Rushworth site had been requisitioned during the war for two groups of internees: Camp 3 for overseas German (including Jewish refugees from Nazism) and Italian internees, and Camp 4 for German and later Japanese internees. Both camps were used as a migrant holding centre, but the available records are limited to the former site (see Figure 2.3).³⁰ Between 1941 and 1943, overseas internees from Singapore and Malaya, including 215 Germans and Austrians, 44 Italians and seven other nationalities, many German Templer families from settlements in Palestine but also Italians who were living there, and German Lutheran missionary families from Papua New Guinea, were sent to these camps.³¹ Some 120 huts, divided internally into eight to ten rooms, were organized across four compounds in a diamond-shaped enclosure with a kitchen, mess and washrooms. Because these were family camps, the linear barracks were partitioned and some of them were designated as school buildings.

When they were vacated in 1947, the army gutted several of these facilities, handing over skeleton dormitories to the Commonwealth Department of Works and Housing. Others were itemized for disposal due to the high cost and therefore desirability of building materials after the war.³² The postwar repatriation of prisoners and internees saw a parallel demobilization and internal circulation of former military buildings and building materials producing nonhuman networks and mobilities, but also domesticating buildings in ways that masked their earlier violence. Site auctions dispersed camp huts and vehicles not only to military and government facilities further

Figure 2.3 Rushworth Camp 3, Tatura Group, Vic, 1949. Drawn by Zachariah Dahdoule, 2021. Based on State Library of Victoria: Photo-map of Victoria, Murchison 799 A1. Aerial Survey of Victoria, 1949.

afield but also to nearby townships and farmsteads. Some huts at Rushworth were sent on to 'The Rocket Range', presumably at Woomera; garage buildings from Benalla were requested for vehicle storage and huts at Tocumwal for hospital buildings.[33] The last task was the removal of the dense layers of coiled Dannert razor-wire surrounding the camp, which continued even after the immigrants had arrived. A flurry of official correspondence regarding the scarcity of labour accompanied their slow progress.

The corrugated iron huts lacked lining, heating and power points – which were considered too luxurious for their former overseas internee occupants – inviting necessary improvements alongside new civic facilities, such as a midwifery, kindergarten and church. Unlike in the case of internees, who could appeal only to the International Red Cross, assisted passage labour-migrants voiced their dissatisfaction to their home governments or the media. Cultural expectations were often at odds with government opinion. A letter from the centre director E.J. Parks suggested that while an argument could be raised that making dependants too comfortable was a disincentive to their husbands' seeking outside employment, lack of opportunity was forcing many to seek work at the army camps.[34] Bruce Pennay notes that: 'By 1950, 4,106 of the 4,637 newcomers were employed at the various migrant centres.'[35] T.H.E. Heyes, secretary to the Department of Immigration, responded that placing fire stoves in living rooms was a hazardous Continental habit; fireplaces were confined to open communal buildings, and lining, electrifying or heating their units was out of the question.[36]

Ferdinand Schmertz, who arrived at Bonegilla in 1945 with his parents and sister, described how family members were split – his father sent to the Seymour army camp while he went to Rushworth in May 1949.[37] The 130 huts in the camp were divided into two sections for Germans and Italians. The immigrants helped local workers clear up debris, removing fencing and discovering overgrown gardens and numerous articles left by departing internees. The family was able to reunite by finding jobs in the camp – in the kitchen and the depot. Ferdinand was first a toilet cleaner and member of the mop brigade, later working in the vegetable store. The family left Rushworth in 1950.

Polish immigrant Stanley Spodar, who, likewise, came via Bonegilla in 1949, gives a detailed description of camp life.[38] Skilled in motor mechanics, he was employed as a driver, which gave him greater mobility, including travel to Melbourne for supplies or transporting immigrants' luggage. He observed that the camp had 1,200 persons from twelve nationalities, the men being distributed for work as far as the sugar cane plantations of Queensland, the International Harvester and Ford Factory at Geelong, and nearby hospitals and services. Food was plentiful; a bus service ran to and from Shepparton three times a week and recreation included dances, films once a week, picnics at the nearby Waranga Basin as well as swimming and fishing.[39]

Camp kindergartens and preschools – key institutions for immigrant assimilation – had well-equipped facilities with large playgrounds.[40] Preschool teachers and attendants played surrogate roles in helping children to adjust. Camps at Cairns, Wacol, Greta, Scheyville, Bonegilla, Benalla and Woodside each had one or more play centres for children between the ages of three and five. An Australian-trained preschool teacher was put in charge with 'New Australian' assistants at a ratio of one adult to fifteen students. Crèche services at Greta, Scheyville, Bonegilla, Benalla and Woodside provided for children up to the age of seven whose mothers were in hospital. At Rushworth Migrant Centre School No. 4654 (1949–53), a group of ceilingless uninsulated huts was divided into eight classrooms for primary school education, after which students attended the local high school. Teachers lived at the camp. The school rooms had linoleum floors, blackboards, desks, boot scrapers and a pot-bellied stove for heating, but there were no teaching aids. Outside the camp, the local schoolteachers described continual problems of communicating with the often bewildered, bright children (and parents), who were made conspicuous by their colourful clothing.[41]

Nostalgia for the camp's military heritage or the town's colonial past is often at odds with immigrants' recollections of this first precarious threshold into Australia. Alexandra Dellios has discussed Bonegilla's commemorative transformation – through restoration of one portion of the camp, Block 19 – as the Bonegilla Migrant Experience, a place feted as the birthplace of Australian multiculturalism and a gathering point for nonanglophone memories.[42] The later physical transformation of migrant hostels as experimental housing sites (see Chapter 7), but also their shameful present-day legacy as detention centres, highlights the extraordinary violence that underscores the camps' purported hospitality.

Many British immigrants were co-located in migrant camps, albeit separated from their continental relatives. Around a hundred immigrant boys from Britain were housed at Dhurringile near Tatura, a colonial mansion used as a wartime prison camp for German POWs.[43] At Bonegilla, three of the blocks were reconditioned, partitioned and furnished for British immigrants, but after eight months, following many complaints, they were no longer required to share facilities.[44] Pennay notes they were also eligible for Housing Commission accommodation, unlike the Europeans.[45]

When researching Australia's immigrant camps, it becomes increasingly obvious that fixing the numbers in a given camp or a camp by its population is futile. Numbers waxed and waned across the camp's lifetime. Nor is it possible to trace linear connections between specific camps and industries, because immigrant workers were drawn from many camps. Complicating this demographic further was the employment of sponsored immigrants from outside the migrant camp networks who had a greater degree of autonomy to choose their vocations, as well as immigrants who had served their indenture and stayed on or moved on to another industry. There were also examples of single mothers sent out to work, leaving their children with surrogate mothers in orphanages – a different kind of collective experience that replaced familial interdependency, and, with the increasing purpose design of hostels, the institutionalization of immigrant accommodation in industrial areas as extensions of industrial spaces. This fluid movement of immigrant workers across the camp and industrial site network also has its corollary in wartime labour procurement, continuing a practice by which unguarded Italian POWs captured in North Africa and sent via Indian POW camps to Australia were deployed on wartime industries.

This unexplored connection between Australia's wartime prisoner workforce and diasporic labour is this chapter's next focus, explored through an Italian immigrant's wartime entry and postwar absorption into Australian society. In pursuing his story, the chapter ventures beyond the camp's limits to broader agricultural and industrial projects as part of 'the machinery for making Australians,' in a networked continuum of physical spaces and buildings.

LABOUR NETWORKS AND MOBILITIES

Migrant labour deployment had roots in wartime labour conscription for essential industries.[46] The Department of War Organization of Industry recruited 728,000 men and women war workers by July 1942 under the Allied Works Council (AWC).[47] A Civil Constructional Corps of around 50,000 noncombatant civilian volunteers worked on maritime and civil infrastructural works.[48] By February 1945, when the new Commonwealth Department of Works absorbed it, the AWC had completed over 2,000 major projects, including for the US military.[49] More importantly, the wartime industrial workforce was supplemented by the above-mentioned 13,207 Italian ordinary recruits (ORs) captured in North Africa and transported after a period of incarceration in India, as well as 4,396 others arriving directly from North Africa.[50] C-class unguarded, rural work designed for Italian POWs sustained agricultural production throughout the war.[51]

The 200-or more prisoners typically allotted to each area were distributed from rural control centres throughout the country (except in the Northern Territory), in a fifty-mile radius from each worksite. An Italian to English phrasebook was issued to each prisoner to help him communicate. By March 1945, of the 17,032 Italian POWs in Australia, 10,295 were working in rural industries: in dairy, vegetables, fruit and meat production, poultry, meat fodder and cereals, wool, other rural industries and on mixed farms.[52] Italy's capitulation in 1943 undoubtedly made their circulation less threatening. They set out daily in groups of fifty from thirty-four hostels, either in military camps like Greta or Bonegilla, or in outer metropolitan suburbs like Melbourne's Rowville camp.[53] Bonegilla drew prisoners incarcerated at the nearby Myrtleford POW camp who worked principally at Bandiana on maintaining the services and the storage facilities.[54] They were also stationed at the nearby Hume Camp. At Greta, POWs were housed in the Army Supply Corps Depot and worked at the camp incinerator, the Whitburn Colliery and the Hunter Valley vineyards.[55] These patterns of employment preceded similar arrangements for employing European DPs and assisted immigrants from the same or similar physical camp facilities. Army camps were also used for housing POWs awaiting repatriation, as with Northam Army Camp in Western Australia, which, dating from the closure of the POW camps from 1946 onwards, held up to 3,500 prisoners in its four compounds.[56] They would remain there until November 1946.

The labour deployment of Italian POWs outlasted the war's end and overlapped with the arrival first of overseas internees and later of immigrants and DPs. Eager to trace this connection in its entirety, I pursued the story of Giuseppe (Joe) Roncari (1918–2002), based on a description on a small brass plate on the Cooma-Monaro Commemorative Wall erected to celebrate the town's 150th anniversary in 1999. It read (in block capitals):

> Giuseppe's (Joe) love for this country as a POW brought him back from Verona Italy with his wife, Angelina (Angela) [arriving August 1950 on the ship *Ugolino Vivaldi*]. They came to Cooma in 1953 with his brother Guglielmo and nephew, Angelo [both arriving in September 1952 on the ship *Australia*]. Like many others with hope and enthusiasm and an ethic, they helped build the Snowy. Joe worked as a blacksmith at Guthega, Polo Flat, Island Bend and N.Z. [Aotearoa New Zealand]. Angelina not only raised Ronald, Alex, Tosca and Frank, but also helped other immigrants adjust to their new life in Aust. In 1963 the family moved to Victoria.

Trawling through the White Pages, I found Joe's son Alexander. The family, he said, had paid AU$300 to have the plaque installed. Over several conversations and many photographs, we pieced together a story that could anchor labour-migrant experiences to the period before the war. However, reliance on the memories of his children, who were very young when the family lived in Cooma, and the absence of Giuseppe who had passed away in 2002, prompted greater reliance on photographs. Because Alexander's former training in architecture enabled greater synergy with my built environment lens, house plans and buildings, exterior and interior backdrops gained prominence in conversations about physical layouts and material textures as self-fashioned elements of successive Roncari family homes.

Veronese immigrant Giuseppe (Joe) Roncari had first arrived in Australia as an Italian POW conscripted to work in wartime industries. Serial displacements through numerous provisional camps and dwellings incrementally formalized his integration into Australian society. Giuseppe's navigation of postwar society, as related by three of his four children (Alexander, Tosca and Ronald), follows three phases: as a prisoner-cum-farm labourer following his capture, incarceration and repatriation; his return to Australia – and employment as a smithy on the Snowy River Hydro Electric Scheme; and, finally, interstate migration along with several other Italian immigrant families to work in Melbourne's farm equipment manufactories (see Figures 2.4 and 2.5). To what extent did these work experiences mediate his response to and reception in Australia?

The first phase of Giuseppe's incarceration is similar to several thousands of prisoners captured by the Allies during the Second World War, except that as a peasant youth from Cerro Veronese recruited by the Italian army in 1941, he had only a vague idea of the altered political context (see Figure 2.6).[57] Alexander observes that his father thought he was fighting for King Victor Emmanuel III, not Benito Mussolini. British and Australian forces defeated his anti-aircraft battalion at Elbeida in Libya: his first encounter with foreigners he had been told were barbaric. But when carrying

52 *Immigrant Industry*

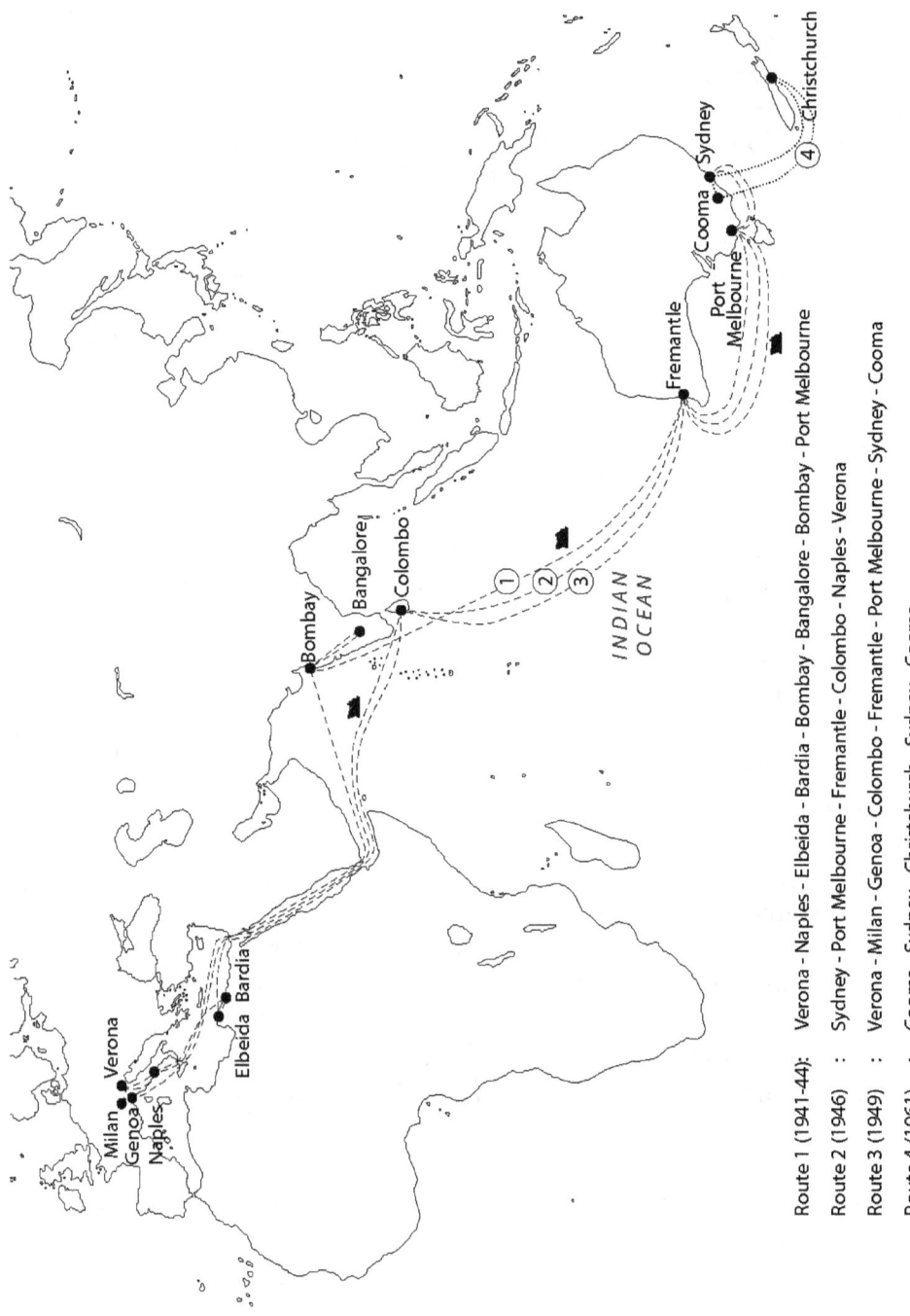

Route 1 (1941-44):	Verona - Naples - Elbeida - Bardia - Bombay - Bangalore - Bombay - Port Melbourne
Route 2 (1946)	:	Sydney - Port Melbourne - Fremantle - Colombo - Naples - Verona
Route 3 (1949)	:	Verona - Milan - Genoa - Colombo - Fremantle - Port Melbourne - Sydney - Cooma
Route 4 (1961)	:	Cooma - Sydney - Christchurch - Sydney - Cooma

Figure 2.4 Giuseppe Roncari's overseas journeys. Drawn for author by Yoke Lin Wong, 2022.

Route 1 (1944-1946) : Port Melbourne - Cowra - Dunedoo - Liverpool - Cowra - St. Ives - Liverpool - Sydney

Route 2 (1949-1954) : Sydney - Warrah - Sydney
       (1954-1963) : Sydney - Guthega - Tumut - Cooma - Jindabyne - Cooma

Route 3 (1963 onwards): Cooma - Dandenong

Figure 2.5 Joe Roncari's journeys within Australia. Drawn for author by Yoke Lin Wong, 2022.

a wounded Australian soldier, clutching a Bible and a cross, he reconsidered his prejudice. Giuseppe recounted this encounter as an invitation to 'come and live in God's own country'.

Following his capture, Giuseppe was transported to one of Britain's twenty-nine Indian POW camps: Camp 22, Wing 4, Bangalore. Although housed in masonry buildings, the climate was harsh and the mainly vegetarian diet inadequate. As a result, he lost 30 kilos. As evident from photographs in the International Committee of the Red Cross archives, prisoners, their faith deepened by their plight and aided by local missionaries, observed many religious activities. Later, for many years, Giuseppe sent donations to the Salesians of Don Bosco for the impoverished local villagers who had helped him. A treasured photograph of the *Our Lady of the Prisoner* monument at Camp 1 (see Figure 2.7), painstakingly embroidered on his handkerchief with threads unpicked from his uniform's seams (see Figures 2.8 and 2.9), would later hang on Giuseppe's living room wall. Such self-made substitutes for Catholic prayer cards were common among his incarcerated compatriots.

Figure 2.6 Giuseppe Roncari's family home in Cerro Veronese, 1971. Courtesy of the Roncari family.

Leaving from Bombay to Australia on the troop ship *Mariposa* in 1944, Giuseppe was sent to Cowra POW Camp in New South Wales. Assigned to a rural control centre, he left camp on 4 August, two days prior to the infamous Cowra breakout when 1,001 Japanese POWs attempted an unsuccessful group escape. His POW service and casualty form places him at Dunedoo, east of Dubbo, and moving between Liverpool and Cowra before a more permanent assignment along with eighty-two others working on a St Ives government farm.[58] His work included salvaging and maintaining army vehicles and installations, before reassignment with two others to a private farm. Unlike in India, food was plentiful. A lamb was slaughtered weekly and the meat was stored in a Coolgardie safe, with leftovers for sheep dogs. Alexander notes that:

> There was an abundance of food here and he [also] set up a vegetable garden for the farm ... but he used to be watched by the old grandfather because the men in the house there had gone off to the war and they had not returned ... he would sit on the veranda

Figure 2.7 Giuseppe Roncari's photograph of the monument to *Our Lady of the Prisoner*, Bangalore Camp, Group 1, India, 1940 (printed from negative). Courtesy of the Roncari family.

Figure 2.8 Giuseppe Roncari unpicked the threads from the seams of his uniform to embroider this image of the monument to *Our Lady of the Prisoner* while at the Bangalore Camp, circa 1940. Courtesy of Alexander Roncari.

with a double barrel shotgun across his knees watching these prisoners so they wouldn't escape from the farm which was a long walk from anywhere.

Giuseppe's eventual repatriation on the troop ship *Ormonde* was as late as December 1946.

The second phase of Giuseppe Roncari's return to postwar Australia onboard the *Surriento* in June 1949 was sponsored by Johnny Cornale (an Italian-Australian farmer he had worked for while awaiting repatriation).[59] Like many European migrants of his generation his main concession to cultural assimilation was anglicizing his name; he identified as Joe from thereon. Through the Catholic Church, he found work at Wee Warrah sheep station at Willow Tree in northern New South Wales, sending (one year later) for his wife Angelina (Angela) as cook (see Figure 2.10) and

Figure 2.9 A poster appealing for the safe return of the two Roncari brothers taken prisoner during the Second World War, undated, circa 1940. Courtesy of the Roncari family.

sponsoring four others, including his brother Gugliemo and nephew Angelo. The couple started married life in a two-room weatherboard cottage on that property. Leafing through a copy of the *Glasgow Cookery Book*, gifted by the station owner's wife to her mother, Tosca described her approximation of British dishes, like sheep's head pie and lemon meringue pie, 'a family favourite'.[60] Angela's work assignments influenced more intimate changes in their cultural routines, including the institution of afternoon tea.

Joe's recruitment by the Snowy Mountains Authority (SMA) in 1954 inserted him into a new network of 120 work camps associated with dams, power stations, and tunnel and aqueduct infrastructure in the alpine region of Victoria and New South Wales (see Chapter 4). His technical skills were sharpened through forms of industrial discipline quite different from the farm work for which he had been socialized. These activities reverted to his private life. A pay rate higher than even in Sydney, because of the associated risks, brought the family to Cooma, the SMA headquarters, where they settled with other opportunity-seeking immigrants at the boundary of Cooma North – the company town. Unlike for Australian or foreign staff and workers recruited by either the SMA or international contractors, independent workers like Joe fended

Figure 2.10 Joe Roncari greets Angelina on her arrival in Sydney, 31 August 1950 (left), and Joe and Angelina at Warrah, circa 1950 (right). Courtesy of the Roncari family.

for themselves. He moved from the back room of a shared home at Culey Avenue in Cooma South to an adjacent plot at 22 Bent Street (see Figure 2.11). There, with a plan drawn by a local builder and help from his friend Charlie Sylvestro, Joe built his first, double-fronted weatherboard home. Although externally appearing no different from other low-cost homes along the street, a prominent Italianate fountain with a gargoyle head waterspout sculpted by his friend Angelo Rosetti proclaimed his Italian identity in aesthetic adaptations to the Australian house. Alexander observes that it was 'kind of flash at the time'. Similar decorative fountains had been erected by Italian POWs and internees in the wartime camps; tentative and temporary gestures that inserted urban Italian features into Australia's rural farmlands, but also demonstrated their affinity for embellishing the most ordinary constructions as assertions of their geocultural identity.

Such aesthetic cues were legible to the many Italians in Cooma: seasonal workers arriving via the camp network, sponsored immigrants like Joe, but also several hundred Italian joiners and carpenters brought over by contractor Legnami Pasotti to build the company head office and housing. Friday nights were *filo* nights when, before television was introduced in 1956, two or three families gathered for prayer, singing and storytelling. Inflections in their accents gave Australian places new meanings. Oral histories passed on to the next generation were the connective glue to villages transformed by war, families left behind, and the hostilities and generosity encountered in Australia. Alexander observes that the older generation were god-fearing, and his experiences were no different from those of immigrant children in his school. Their house interior was decorated with paintings of the obligatory Last Supper and photographs of various popes. The back garden had an orchard and a vegetable garden, which were essential for their food supply, and a separate rentable room with a

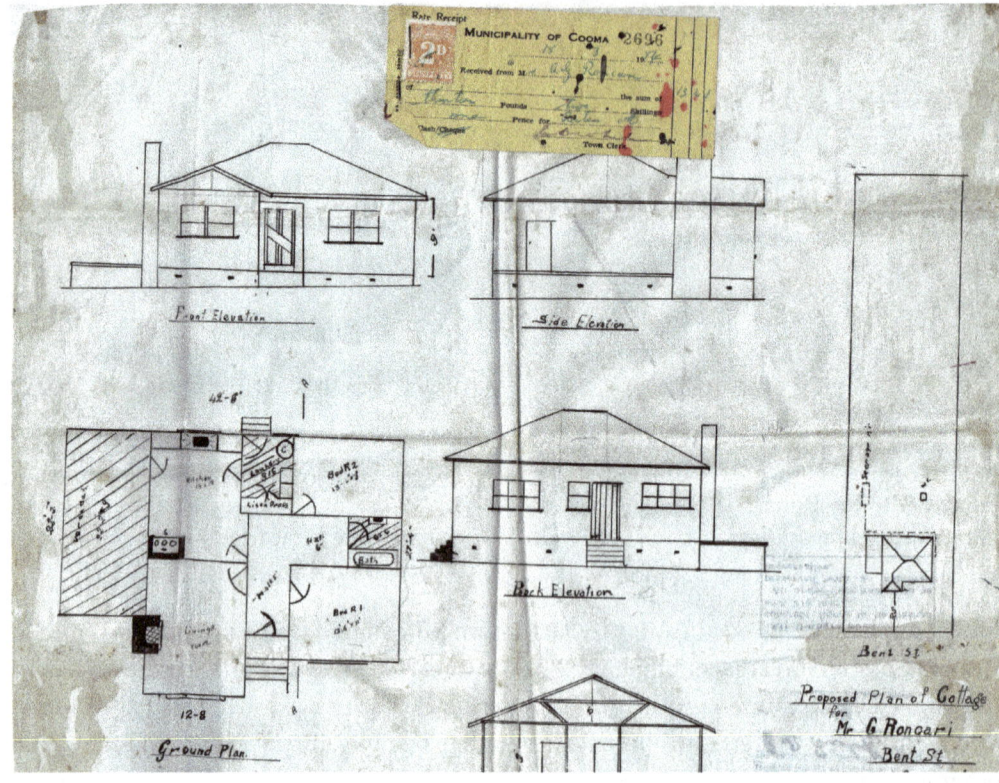

Figure 2.11 The Roncari home at 22 Bent Street Cooma. Plan drawn by builder Rodney Parkes, 1954 (above) and photograph, 1950s (below). Courtesy of Alexander Roncari.

kitchen, which gave Angela an additional income source. Both their families' peasant backgrounds – Joe's as itinerant tenant farmers from a *contrada*, leased from a landlord, and Angela's as serfs on a count's estate – aided in their self-sufficiency. Alexander laughs that his father submitted half a kilo of butter for his grade five certificate. Together, Joe and Angela, like many rural European immigrants, filled the yawning skills gap between the fast-vanishing smallholdings and industrial farming that was rapidly transforming postwar Australia.

Extant skills as well as those acquired on the job sometimes influenced an immigrant's work choices. Joe, having worked briefly as a cobbler after repatriation, retrained in smithery and was employed in chiselling massive tunnel drill-heads and bending steel for reinforcements in dam walls. He worked first at a tented camp at Guthega, then at Island Bend and Jindabyne, before being stationed at the base workshops at Polo Flat. His particular technoaesthetic talent was in turning steel offcuts into decorative features after the ironwork of his Veronese hometown. At the Cooma cemetery, from among several graves for workers who died in industrial accidents on the Snowy Scheme, some display headstones engraved by Angelo Rosetti and decorated with hexagonal rebar crosses fashioned by Joe. This intimate practice of care for the men with whom they shared the risks and austerities of industrial work lives contrasted sharply with the anonymity that the sheer magnitude of the hydro scheme imposed on its immigrant workforce. Their actions also alert us to the social costs and human sacrifices that inevitably underwrite any tale of immigrant success. Joe would later in life suffer from nerve deafness because of his work as a smithy. He also, perhaps because of these shared experiences, built close relationships that outlasted the Snowy work camps. Once the Snowy Scheme approached completion in 1963, he, along with eight other by then naturalized Italian families, migrated interstate from New South Wales to Victoria and settled in Dandenong, an outer suburb near farmlands with several farm equipment manufactories. Experience gained on the Snowy Scheme translated (for them) into fresh opportunities.

This brings us to a third interpretation of the machine analogy, as applicable to immigrant industry – immigrants' efforts at modifying the assimilatory and culturally Anglo-Australian, formal architecture and urban or suburban places that absorbed them. Joe commissioned, built and added to his second, cream-brick-veneer double-fronted home at 5 Belmont Avenue in a cookie-cutter working-class suburb, employing a local builder C.L. Moon (see Figure 2.12). This he commenced and largely completed before he brought his family over from Cooma, driving them interstate in the family car, cramped with all their worldly belongings, and sadly leaving their dog behind. Although in many respects a typical suburban home, Joe decorated the low front wall with a fence-topper fashioned from the metal pressings of twisted-steel factory offcuts (see Figure 2.13). They were also used to fence off the rear vegetable garden in an ingenious reuse of industrial waste products. Although not part of the SMA staff – from the Cooma North company town, but a labour-migrant at its

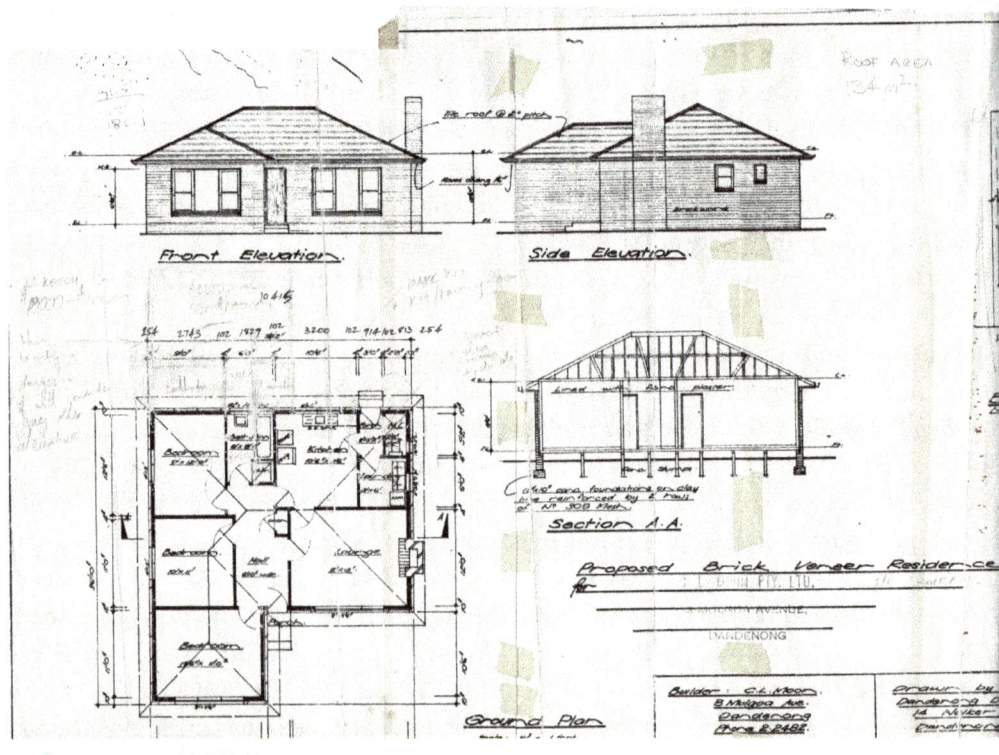

Figure 2.12 The Roncari home at 5 Belmont Avenue, Dandenong. Plan drawn by builder C.L. Moon, 1963 (above). Courtesy of Alexander Roncari. Photograph of the Roncaris' former home, 2022 (below). © Anoma Pieris.

fringe – Joe and his family embraced the industrial scheme's mediation of their Australian identity. The base of the family's first Christmas tree at their new Dandenong home featured a nativity with a Snowy Mountains backdrop (see Figure 2.14).

Figure 2.13 Decorative detail at 5 Belmont Avenue, Dandenong, 2022. © Anoma Pieris.

Figure 2.14 The Roncari family, left to right: (back row) Ronald, Alexander (Sandro) and Tosca; (front row) Angelina (Angela), Joe and Frank, circa 1960 (left), and their first Christmas tree at Dandenong showing a crib with a snowy mountain backdrop, 1963 (right). Courtesy of the Roncari family.

CONCLUSION

The camps witnessed three types of settlers: military recruits loyal to Britain, interned enemy aliens and labouring POWs, and, finally, the short-term labour-migrant settlers brought in to populate Australia. Joe Roncari identified with two of these groups. Notably absent from this grouping were the racially nonwhite internees who had been incarcerated alongside Europeans during wartime, such as Japanese internees, Formosans, Koreans and other racialized people of colour who, once repatriated after the war, were excluded from the country until immigration restrictions were relaxed in the early 1970s. In Roncari's example, as it was for many other working class non-anglophone white immigrants, racialization was graduated by class relations, and culturally British hierarchies and prejudices regarding Europeans and their different linguistic and social and cultural practices, physical features and religious faiths, more so than the more obviously racist black–white binary. The latter distinction that had solidified through violent forms of exclusion and repression of Indigenous Australian and Asian populations in the previous century resurfaced to blur these earlier nuanced distinctions once regional Asian and Pacific Islander immigration was permitted. Perceptions of the immigrant groups' relative modernity formed the outer core of racialized cultural differentiation, and in this, at least, European immigrants had the distinct advantage of coming from places that Australia deemed progressive.

The federally funded industries discussed in the next three chapters were among several major infrastructure projects that both continued the initial wartime impetus but also diverted it to a new purpose of postwar nation-building. Italian POW circulation beyond camp confines carved pathways travelled by subsequent European immigrants familiarizing Australians with ethnocultural differences within whiteness through industrial and farming practices that changed the physical landscape. Both these and previous nineteenth-century nonanglophone settlers had already made their mark, infusing this landscape with the peasant knowledges that industrialization obscures and that Australia as a settler colony that had dispossessed traditional custodians had no continuing legacy of. Their enterprise would soon transform Australian agriculture by introducing orchards, olive groves and vineyards. Likewise, immigrant entry into suburban areas changed the city's aspect through architectural adaptations including the transformation of localities and shopping strips (see Chapter 8) and through different modes of landscaping and land use. Far from the unidirectional assimilation expected of incomers, these individual interventions in otherwise foreign and often hostile environments presaged new kinds of rootedness and a more plural identity politics.

Anoma Pieris is Professor of Architecture at the Melbourne School of Design. Her most recent publications include the anthology *Architecture on the Borderline: Boundary Politics and Built Space* (2019) and *The Architecture of Confinement: Incarceration Camps of the Pacific War* (2022), co-authored with Lynne Horiuchi. She was guest curator with

Martino Stierli, Sean Anderson and Evangelos Kotsioris of the 2022 Museum of Modern Art exhibition *The Project of Independence: Architectures of Decolonization in South Asia, 1947–1985.*

ACKNOWLEDGEMENTS

Thanks to Alexander, Tosca and Ronald Roncari for sharing their father's story and their family documents and photographs, and to Alexander for corresponding and clarifying many details.

NOTES

1. Jupp, *Immigration*, 95.
2. Australian Bureau of Statistics, '4102.0 – Australian Social Trends, 1996, Population Growth'; Department of Home Affairs (Australia), 'Historical Migration Statistics'.
3. Greenberg, *Australia Land of Tomorrow, Circa 1948*, Emigration Poster.
4. Selenitsch, *flotsamandjetsam*.
5. Le Corbusier, *Towards a New Architecture*, 240.
6. Ibid., 242–43.
7. Crawford, *Building the Workingman's Paradise*, 11–12.
8. DeMars, 'Social Planning for Western Agriculture'; Eckbo, *Landscape Architecture*.
9. Crawford, *Building the Workingman's Paradise*.
10. Harrison, *Growing a Global Village*.
11. 'Migrant Hostels "Must Not Be Made Too Comfortable"', *The Argus*, 22 January 1953, 3. Retrieved 7 December 2023 from http://nla.gov.au/nla.news-article23223433.
12. 'Bitter Press Attack on Conditions at Migrant Hostels', *Northern Star*, 16 July 1951, 5. Retrieved 7 December 2023 from http://nla.gov.au/nla.news-article96560467.
13. Siobhan McHugh, Oral History Transcripts, Mitchell Library, State Library of New South Wales, 5.0 Jonathan Baska.
14. Gunew, *Haunted Nations*.
15. In reference to institutional cultures discussed by Goffman, *The Presentation of Self*.
16. 'Site Guide', Bonegilla Migrant Experience.
17. Pennay, 'Remembering Bonegilla', 44–47. Bonegilla migrant camp was administered by the army until 1949 and later in the 1960s was then co-located with army facilities.
18. Williams, *War Clouds over Benalla*.
19. Tatura Wartime Camps and Irrigation Museum (TWCIM): Wasli and Leokadija Denisenko.
20. 'Australia Migrants Who Started the Riots? From a Sydney Correspondent', *The Bulletin*, 82 (4250), 29 July 1961, 4. Retrieved 7 December 2023 from http://nla.gov.au/nla.obj-684514639.
21. NAA: 443 1952/15/2726, E.J. Parks to Secretary Department of Immigration 14 June 1949.
22. 'DP Camp at Rushworth', *Shepparton Advertiser*, 21 December 1949, 1. Retrieved 7 December 2023 from http://nla.gov.au/nla.news-article169564518; 'Migrant Camp Ends at Rushworth', *Shepparton Advertiser*, 19 June 1953, 2. Retrieved 7 December 2023 from http://nla.gov.au/nla.news-article173892234.
23. TWICM: Folder on Rushworth Migrant Camp, 'Migrant Centre Head Retires: Benalla Loses Valued Citizen, 1963'.

24. Pennay, 'Remembering Bonegilla', 44–47 and 49.
25. Pieris, 'Chapter 2: A Network of Internment Camps', 43–83, in Pieris and Horiuchi, *The Architecture of Confinement*, discusses this in greater detail.
26. Pennay, *The Army at Bonegilla*, 2, 4.
27. 'You Can Make a Room in a Nissen Hut Look Like This', *Good Neighbour* (ACT: 1950 – 1969), 1 August 1951, 1. Retrieved 7 December 2023 from http://nla.gov.au/nla.news-article176526247; NLA: 'A Migrant Centre Saved Greta from Ghost Town', *Muswellbrook Chronicle*, 26 August 1949, 1. Retrieved 7 December 2023 from http://nla.gov.au/nla.news-article107734917.
28. Keating, *A History of the Army Camp*.
29. Pieris, 'Chapter 2: A Network of Internment Camps'.
30. Hammond, *Walls of Wire*, 116.
31. Knee and Knee, *Walked in*, 42–54.
32. NAA: 443 1952/15/2726, Rushworth Holding Centre – Acquisition and alterations to buildings etc., February–November 1949.
33. Ibid.
34. NAA: 443 1952/15/2726, E.J. Parks to Secretary Department of Immigration.
35. Pennay, *Receiving Europe's Displaced*, 20.
36. NAA: 443 1952/15/2726, T.H.E. Heyes, response, 22 June 1949.
37. TWCIM: Lurline Knee interviews (LK): Ferdinand Schmertz [Schmerc].
38. TWICM-LK: Stanley Spodar, April 1990.
39. TWCIM-LK: Ferdinand Schmertz [Schmerc].
40. TWICM: Assimilation Activities in Immigration Centres 14/9/53.
41. Hammond, *Walls of Wire*, 116.
42. Dellios, *Histories of Controversy*, 8, 173
43. 'Welcome to Migrant Boys', *The Age*, 27 March 1948, 4. Retrieved 7 December 2023 from http://nla.gov.au/nla.news-article206877694.
44. Pennay, *Receiving Europe's Displaced*, 19.
45. Pennay, 'Remembering Bonegilla', 50.
46. Pieris, 'Chapter 4: Land and Labour', 116–43 in Pieris and Horiuchi, *The Architecture of Confinement*; Director General of Manpower, *Control of Manpower in Australia*, discusses this in greater detail.
47. Australian Federal Election Speeches, John Curtin, 26 July 1943. AWC: Agency CA 497, 1942–45.
48. NAA: A659, 1945/1/3162, AWC – Report of activities July 1943–February 1945, 84, 13.
49. The US Lend Lease programme authorized defence equipment production for export to the Allied nations and secured the necessary equipment and services for their operation through reverse lend-lease aid.
50. Report on Directorate of POWs and Internees (Australian Army Headquarters, DPWI), 1939–51 ORMF0024 (Official Record) (hereinafter RDPWI), part ii, chap.1, 101–3.
51. RDPWI, part iii, chap.2, 226–28; Director General of Manpower, *Control of Manpower in Australia*, 213–14.
52. RDPWI, part iii, chap.2, 229–30.
53. Ibid., Appendices. Schedules of control centers and hostels.
54. Pennay, *The Army at Bonegilla*, 11.
55. Keating, *A History of the Army Camp*, 29.
56. Northam Army Camp, Heritage Association Inc, 'Storylines/POW'.
57. Alexander Roncari, interview with the author via Zoom, 1 October 2021; Alexander, Tosca and Ronald Roncari, interview with the author, Korumburra, 19 March 2022.
58. NAA: MP1103/1, PWI64923; MP1103/2, 64923 Prisoner of War/internee, Roncari Attilie; NAA: A446, 1955/43091, application for naturalization.

59. NAA: 9245788, 14, Incoming passenger list to Fremantle, 'Surriento' arrived 17 June 1949.
60. Glasgow and West of Scotland College of Domestic Science, *Glasgow Cookery Book*, 96 and 169.

BIBLIOGRAPHY

Archival Records

Tatura Wartime Camps and Irrigation Museum (TWCIM).

Publications

Australian Bureau of Statistics. '4102.0 – Australian Social Trends, 1996, Population Growth'. Retrieved 25 February 2023 from https://www.abs.gov.au/ausstats/abs@.nsf/2f762f95845417aeca25706c00834efa/e2f62e625b7855bfca2570ec0073cdf6!OpenDocument.
'Australian Federal Election Speeches, John Curtin 26 July 1943'. Retrieved 23 February 2023 from https://electionspeeches.moadoph.gov.au/speeches/1943-john-curtin.
Crawford, Margaret. *Building the Workingman's Paradise: The Design of American Company Towns*. New York: Verso, 1995.
Dellios, Alexandra. *Histories of Controversy*. Melbourne: Melbourne University Press, 2017.
DeMars, Vernon. 'Social Planning for Western Agriculture', *Task* 2 (1941), 4–9.
Department of Home Affairs (Australia). 'Historical Migration Statistics'. Retrieved 25 February 2023 from https://data.gov.au/data/dataset/historical-migration-statistics.
Director General of Manpower. *Control of Manpower in Australia: A General Review of the Administration of the Manpower Directorate, February 1942–September 1944*. Sydney: Government Printer, 1944.
Eckbo, Garrett. *Landscape Architecture: The Profession in California, 1935–1940, and Telesis*. Gainesville: Regional Oral History Office, Bancroft Library, University of California, 1993.
Glasgow and West of Scotland College of Domestic Science. *Glasgow Cookery Book*. Glasgow: John Smith and Son, 1951.
Goffman, Erwing. *The Presentation of Self in Everyday Life*. New York: Doubleday, 1956.
Greenberg, Joe. *Australia Land of Tomorrow, Circa 1948*. Emigration Poster, Museum Victoria Collections, item SH 9905561948.
Gunew, Sneja. *Haunted Nations: The Colonial Dimensions of Multiculturalisms*. New York: Routledge, 2003.
Hammond, Joyce. *Walls of Wire: Tatura, Rushworth, Murchison*. Tatura, Vic: Joyce Hammond, 1990.
Harrison, Charles. *Growing a Global Village: Making History at Seabrook Farms*. New York: Holmes and Meier, 2003.
Jupp, James. *Immigration*. Melbourne: Oxford University Press, 1998.
Keating, Christopher. *A History of the Army Camp and Migrant Camp at Greta, New South Wales, 1939–1960*. Sydney: Uri Windt, 1997.
Knee, Lurline, and Arthur Knee. *Walked in: Seven Internment and Prisoner War Camps in the Tatura Area during World War 2*. Tatura: Tatura & District Historical Society, 2008.
Le Corbusier. *Towards a New Architecture*. New York: Dover Publications, 1986.
Lozanovska, Mirjana. *Migrant Housing: Architecture, Dwelling, Migration*. New York: Routledge, 2019.
Northam Army Camp, Heritage Association Inc. 'Storylines/POW'. Retrieved 7 December 2023 from https://northamarmycamp.org.au/storylines/pow/the-italian-pow-experience/.
Pennay, Bruce. *The Army at Bonegilla, 1940–71*. Albury and Wodonga, Vic: Parklands, 2007.
———. 'Remembering Bonegilla: The Construction of a Public Memory Place at Block 19', *Public History Review* 16 (2009), 43–63.

———. *Receiving Europe's Displaced: Bonegilla Reception and Training Centre, 1947–53*. Wodonga, Vic: Parklands Albury-Wodonga, 2010.

Pieris, Anoma, and Lynne Horiuchi. *The Architecture of Confinement: Incarceration Camps of the Pacific War*. Cambridge: Cambridge University Press, 2022.

Selenitsch, Alex. *flotsamandjetsam* (exhibition). Place Gallery, Melbourne. Retrieved 7 January 2018 from https://www.placegallery.com.au/2012/artists/alex_selenitsch/alex_selenitsch.htm.

'Site Guide'. Bonegilla Migrant Experience website. Retrieved 16 January 2024 from https://www.bonegilla.org.au/Portals/8/Downloads/BME_Site_Guide_June_2023.pdf.

Williams, Doug. *War Clouds over Benalla: The History of No. 11 Elementary Flying Training School R.A.A.F. Station Benalla, 1941–1945*. Deniliquin: Deniliquin Newspapers Pvt. Ltd., 2014.

Chapter 3

Unfinished Histories of Nation Building
Racialization, Space of Labour and Industry at Port Kembla Steelworks

Mirjana Lozanovska

Current labour scholar Bradley Bowden singles out activist and labour historian W.G. Spence as capturing the particularity of Australian labour history in 1909 when he stated that 'white man gave no consideration to the black man's rights' who 'dispossessed of "enormous areas" of land lay the basis for both the exploitation of the land's resources and the Aboriginal people as the basis of a profitable economy'.[1] Bowden claims that: 'Upon this all else was built, including a union movement of unusual character whose initial mass following lay in mining and pastoralism.'[2] In fact, mining and pastoralism intersect with colonizing military strategies and mediate both colonial-settler and labour practices. This chapter focuses on the deployment of postwar immigrant labour at the Broken Hill Propriety (BHP) Steelworks and the subsequent growth of the industrial town of Port Kembla, and argues that Australia's nation building economies are contingent on these foundational histories. Its examination of labour histories and geographies brings the exploitative practices to the foreground.

At the site of Port Kembla, now a coastal town 80 km south of Sydney, the entangled histories of colonizing strategies and industrial entrepreneurial practices evolve into strange and often shocking parallels between the subjugation of peoples and the exploitation of the land, flora and fauna. Iron, coal, mining and steel industries are intrinsic to Port Kembla economies of the nineteenth and early twentieth centuries when extractive industries were established in the Illawarra.[3] Coal mines such as Mount Keira and Bulli were opened in the mid-1800s.[4] After purchasing 400 acres of land in 1921 from the 'Five Islands Estate', the Hoskins Company moved its operations to Port Kembla[5] and formed Australian Iron and Steel Ltd (AI&S), which then merged with BHP in 1935 and acquired more land for future expansion.[6] The 'Garden of Illawarra', as it was referred to in the promotional material, was rendered into land holdings and then radically altered by extractive industries, amongst other colonial practices. Functional structures materialized as underground mining tunnels and railway lines establishing Port Kembla as a heavy industrial town.[7]

Extractive industries on the site of Port Kembla continued into the early twentieth century, and this included the dredging of the large and striking water catchment of Tuckalong, also known as Tom Thumb Lagoon, to make way for spatial expansion. More than 5,500 piles were used for the construction of new manufacturing technologies and increased productivity of existing technologies. A new section of the steelworks, the tin mill, was built, comprising the hot strip mill (1955), the new merchant rolling mill (1949), and the new tinplate and cold strip mill (1957). To facilitate these and escalate productivity in existing areas of steel manufacturing, a battery of forty-eight coke ovens (1950) was added to the existing line of seventy-two ovens and was followed by a further twenty-four ovens (1953). Increasing productivity required new blast furnaces (No 3 1952, No 4 1959), new open-hearth furnaces (two in 1956, two in 1959) and a new sinter plant (1957). In the ten years between 1950 and 1960, the BHP Steelworks expanded along the Port Kembla foreshore and pierced inland through to the residential suburb of Cringila, where many of the immigrant workers lived.[8] Pedestrian bridges and a network of subterranean tunnels joined the chimneys, ducts and pipes to produce a cacophony of machinic landscapes (see Figure 3.1).[9] The new basic oxygen steelmaking plant (Basic Oxygen Steelmaking – B.O.S, 1972) was one of the largest industrial buildings in Australia at the time.

Thousands of immigrant workers were recruited to service this industry. By 1966, of the nearly 15,000 employed by AI&S steel industry, over 9,000 were immigrants.[10] Of Wollongong's urban population of 200,000 at the end of the 1970s, 53% were immigrants or the children of immigrants.[11] Thousands departed from war-torn Europe, from economically underdeveloped homelands and later from the Vietnam War. Emigration was an opportunity, but forced migration and migration due to severe economic stagnation carry the burden of a shared sense of loss though displacement. Labour migrants were submerged within the interior workings and environments of the steelworks.

This chapter tackles the postwar immigrant labour histories at the Port Kembla Steelworks by drawing upon labour history and participant ethnographic data to examine how racialization and ethnicization structures work in the postwar nation building period (see Figure 3.2).[12] The structure of the chapter is divided into three sections. First, 'Labour History' will examine the industrial history and the immigrant recruitment policy that impacted on the Port Kembla Steelworks in the postwar period (1945–79). A sociohistorical framing will have a bearing upon this analysis to uncover the central influence of industry on government as well as racialized discrimination within the union, and to draw attention to the perspective of immigrant workers. Second, 'Space of Labour' will focus on the interior of the steelworks industry and its environments, connecting the migrant workers and their labouring bodies to the processes of work, as impacted upon by new management methods. Linked to this will be an analysis of the industrial landscape as it intersects with labour history (see

Figure 3.1 Immigrant workers leaving the Port Kembla Steelworks at the end of their work shift, 1955. Courtesy of the National Archives of Australia, NAA A12111, 1/1955/16/72

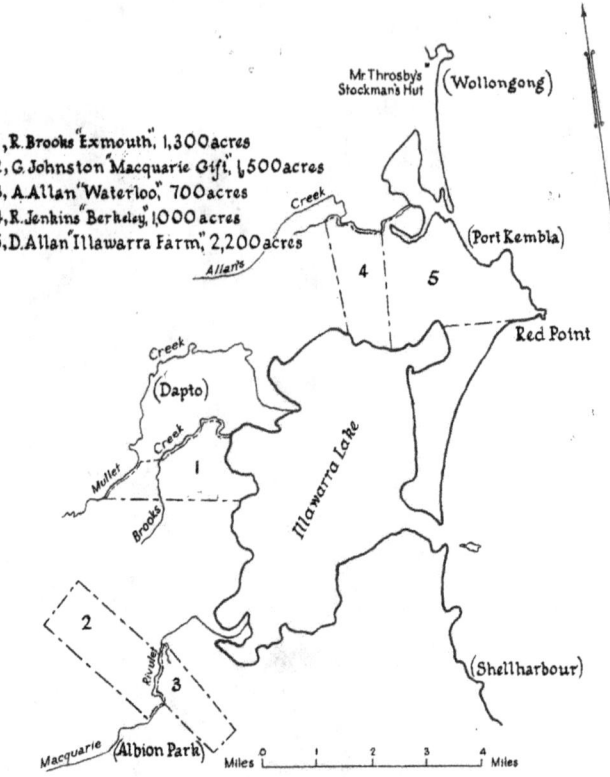

Figure 3.2 Map showing the five land grants offered by Governor Macquarie in Illawarra in 1817. In Bernard Thomas Dowd, *The First Five Land Grantees and Their Grants in the Illawarra* (Wollongong: Illawarra Historical Society, 1977 [1960]). Reproduced with permission. Courtesy of the Illawarra Historical Society

Figure 3.2). And the third section, 'Spatial Histories of Racialization', will review early histories of colonizing strategies (1817 Land Grants) and settler industries, and their impact on the land. This will draw attention to three sites significant to Indigenous Australians (Aboriginal and Torres Strait Islander First Nations/Peoples) – Dhgillawarah, Coomaditchie and Tuckalong – and how the Wadi Wadi, the custodians of this land, navigated the Kembla area. The physical sites illustrate intersections of racialized strategies with the spatial materialization of colonial industry. This focus on strategies of racialization and ethnicization as integral to Australia's industrial history deepens the historical grounding of the first two sections of the chapter.

APPROACH AND METHODOLOGY

Despite four decades (from the 1980s to 2020) of job losses and artificial intelligence (AI) technology advances that have descaled operations and the number of workers, the physical presence of the steelworks has not been diminished. It remains foundational to Port Kembla's identity as a place. In the 1960s the industrial infrastructure stretched along the coastline, dividing the Pacific Ocean from Port Kembla's civic centre and the housing in which many migrant workers were accommodated on arrival and thereafter lived. On-site material and spatial inscription – structures and landscapes, some operational, others as industrial ruins – trace a material architectural history and make evident the historical continuity of the steelworks in Port Kembla. The distinct approach here is not to identify the industrial typologies or stylistic chronology as an empirical inventory of industrial architecture, but rather to analyse representations of its physicality as it intersects historically with the larger histories of Australia's immigration recruitment campaign. The aim is to uncover the places in which postwar immigrants worked and their symbolic location in Australian politics, and thus to examine industrial architecture from the perspective of immigrant subjectivity.

The second section turns from the larger sociopolitical history towards migrant subjectivity. 'Space of Labour' is understood as simultaneously situated within the operations of the steelworks to which immigrants were allocated and in the microspaces in which each immigrant's subjectivity was shaped. Descriptions of such spaces of labour detail the dust, the toxic environment, the high temperatures, the noise, the pungent odours and the precarious nature of this machinic space.[13]

For this study, specific histories of immigrant labour are drawn from interviews and workshops conducted by the author in 2020 and 2021, with ethnic minority citizens who worked at BHP Port Kembla in the period from 1945 to 1979. These comprised fourteen individual semi-structured interviews conducted remotely via Zoom, two group workshops organized through the Macedonian Welfare Association (MWA) and the Multicultural Communities Council of Illawarra (MCCI, henceforth referred to as the Men's Shed), comprising seven participants each and conducted on site in Port Kembla, as well as a tour of the BHP Steelworks with twenty participants.[14] The interviews were digitally recorded and the workshops and the tour were documented by a professional film crew. Findings add the voices of the workers to documentation – archival and historical data, architectural plans, maps and visual data (steelworks, Port Kembla and Wollongong) – as well as to key studies of immigrant labour history and postwar immigration to Australia.[15]

A critical review of the historical construction of Port Kembla is the focus of the third section of the chapter. Focusing on a spatial history, it asks what had the site of Port Kembla been for the Wadi Wadi, the Indigenous custodians of this part of the Dhawaral Country? How can we learn about the Wadi Wadi understanding of this site? Documentation of the Indigenous Australians of Dhawaral Country, incorporating Port Kembla – even if fragmented and partial – includes significant histories that complicate and contest a dominant growth historiography. Material is drawn from archival collections, especially Michael Organ's large volume of collated documentation on the Indigenous Australians of Dhawaral Country. Consistent resistance to evacuations from Dhgillawarah (also known as Red Point), ongoing engagement with new colonial economies, and coexistence with colonial settlers build a contested history of the site of Port Kembla and its steelworks.[16]

In contrast to normative history, dominated by narratives of economic growth and nation building, a spatial history draws attention to a continuity of racialized strategies and exploitation of land and peoples that is embedded within the site of Port Kembla and its steelworks. It is an unfinished history because racialized strategies continue to structure the labour economies of Australia, and also as a retrospective intellectual activity that examines the particularities of a site's geographies and histories to uncover its multiple realities.

LABOUR HISTORY

An aerial photograph of 1960 included in the BHP publication *Seventy-Five Years of BHP Development* and captioned 'Port Kembla Steelworks today . . . scene of Australia's great industrial growth' illustrates the geometric linearity of the coke ovens structure, the machinic expression of the blast furnaces and the large cylindrical gasholder volumes, and in the distance, black chutes of the sinter plant at the harbour edge and the new hot strip mills shed in the foreground.[17] It was a symbol of modernity and nation building. Manufacturing in gigantic plants was very much a statement of the new postwar nation. The industrial landscape of the BHP Steelworks in Port Kembla presents a vast brown-grey terrain incised by tracks, here linear, there circular, here ordering, there chaotic, stretching over what might have once been a creek, its scale outlined as it meets the turquoise colour of the ocean, a terrain that is not domestic or suburban, not civil, commercial or urban, not natural or cultivated. While closer views will show its numerous and massive structures, ducts, pipes, towers, cylindrical volumes and gigantic sheds, the stuff of industrial heroics, in this wide panoramic aerial perspective (see Figure 3.3), structures are diminished and dispersed. The scale of the BHP Steelworks in Port Kembla does not resonate with the idea of architectural monumentality as object and geometric form or as a cohesive architectural image.

Industry and manufacturing landscapes on the edges of regional centres, such as Port Kembla, reinforce a postwar nationwide industrial decentralization strategy, their messy built landscapes and heavy manufacturing infrastructure demonstrating the flux of economic priorities.[18] In 1957, a few years prior to this photograph (see Figure 3.3), the general manager of BHP wrote in his report, 'Australia's two integrated steelworks at Newcastle and Port Kembla employ 6,580 immigrants', with 35% from the United Kingdom and the remaining 65% a combination of displaced persons (DP) and assisted migrants.[19] Statistics are not definitive, but if collated across sources, they do indicate the scale of immigrant labour: immigrants represented 70% of all additional labour of the BHP/AI&S workforces in the period from 1945 to 1960.[20] By

Figure 3.3 BHP Steelworks, Port Kembla, 1960. Photo: © *Seventy-Five Years of B.H.P. Development in Industry*, reproduced with permission

1963, BHP employed 14,400 immigrants, of which 10,560 were employed in Newcastle and Port Kembla Steelworks.[21] Until 1949, the majority of immigrants came from anglophone countries (Britain and Ireland), with thousands employed in the Bulli and other coal mines in the Illawarra providing the major coal source for the Port Kembla Steelworks.[22] The contribution of net immigration to population growth increased to around 45% in the mid-1960s, and continued to rise to 54% by 1980. In contrast, the British-born immigrant workforce at BHP dropped to 12% in 1963 and dropped thereafter, altering the ethnic and racial composition to nonanglophone-dominant.

In their significant book *A Divided Working Class*, labour history scholars Constance Lever-Tracy and Michael Quinlan examine and reveal Australia's discriminatory policies, legislation and practices affecting immigrant workers in the postwar period. Compiling the Monthly Workforce Statements from AI&S/BHP Port Kembla, their analysis shows the following:

> The AI&S Port Kembla operation, which expanded most rapidly to become by far the largest steelworks, had the most numerous and diverse non-Anglophone workforce. Between 1947 and 1975 total employment at this steelworks rose from 3,665 to 20,715 while steel production grew almost tenfold. By 1966 immigrants constituted just under half the total workforce and 61.7 per cent of all waged employees. Approximately 17.7 per cent of immigrant employees were British-born, the remainder coming from more than 70 countries.[23]

Lever-Tracy and Quinlan provided the breakdown of the country of origin of the Port Kembla workforce between 1966 and 1982, as detailed in a table of waged employees.[24] This shows the changes and fluctuations of its composition, reflecting ethnic recruitment hierarchy and strategic targeting of source countries. Immigrant workers recruited as DPs directly after the war were employed at the Port Kembla Steelworks in smaller numbers – by 1966 a total of 737 – from the Netherlands, Germany, Poland and other Northern and Eastern European countries. Following a transnational agreement between Australia and Yugoslavia in 1967, Yugoslavian immigrant workers became an immigrant labour majority at the Port Kembla Steelworks in the mid-1960s (double the number from Italy and 1,000 more than from the United Kingdom). Yugoslavian immigrants remained the highest number in 1973 (3,400), and again in 1977 and 1982. Such a flow contradicts the usual argument for emigration for economic betterment as Yugoslavia enjoyed a high economic standard at the time, as illustrated in Yugoslavian publications on industry, education and social standards.[25] Although census statistics do not specify this, a large number of the immigrants from Yugoslavia in Port Kembla were most likely from the Socialist Republic of Macedonia, one of the poorest republics in the Federation. This migration wave was reinforced by the earlier settlement of ethnic Macedonians in Port Kembla and the Illawarra in the 1920s, as documented in oral history accounts in the bilingual *Kompas* journal developed by the Macedonian Welfare Association in Port Kembla.[26] By the 1960s, people like the Šavkulevski family established boarding houses in Cringila (a suburb adjacent to the steelworks), where many single young men and men separated from their families lived.[27] To support such an interpretation, in the early 1980s, Macedonian was the second most-spoken language after English in Port Kembla and Wollongong.[28]

The Port Kembla Steelworks industry benefited from an unexpected alignment between the gigantic BHP corporation and the powerful Federal Ironworker Association of Australia (FIA), which was successfully negotiated by Australia's first Minister of Immigration, Arthur Calwell.[29] The biggest problem for BHP was labour shortage and instability; strikes were rife before the war and the communist-aligned FIA had strengthened its hold.[30] A change to its right-wing faction supported this postwar agreement.[31] The alignment came with restrictive conditions for the immigrants. By 1949, Calwell's immigration policy included two years of contracted labour and a promise to the FIA that migrants would be allocated the jobs no one else wanted and that all migrants employed at BHP would become FIA union members.[32]

In the 1940s, BHP also gained membership of the Commonwealth Immigration Planning Council (CIPC) and actively participated in immigration programs in the postwar period.[33] BHP was instrumental in three major immigration recruitment strategies. First, with direct links to the CIPC, BHP argued against a family migration policy (1954) and thereby shaped an immigration policy contingent on single, young and able-bodied men.[34] Second, further correspondence between BHP management and the CIPC sets a second plan in the 1950s for a mass immigration of 'unskilled' labour immigrants. The third is the strategy to source these 'unskilled' labour immigrants from Southern European countries, based on the view of BHP that they were readily available, eager to migrate and less reluctant to undertake hazardous, dirty and demanding jobs. Because they could not speak English and had limited job market knowledge, the company anticipated greater stability from such workers.[35] In this postwar mass immigration recruitment campaign, Southern Europeans were ranked lowest in the hierarchy of workers. Recruitment and immigration strategies were influential in producing BHP's and Australia's divided working class along the lines of ethnicity and race in the postwar period.[36]

Spanning almost four decades, between 1945 and 1979, Port Kembla witnessed the arrival of thousands of immigrants recruited to facilitate the production of steel and to generate what is known as the long economic boom in postwar Australia.[37] Postwar industrial growth of BHP Steelworks and its auxiliary partners is contingent on transnational non-anglophone mass immigration.

SPACE OF LABOUR

In *The Diasporic Condition*, Ghassan Hage speaks about 'reciprocity', stating that: 'Migration is, among many other things, a reciprocal relation.'[38] Migration scholars detail the ways in which the host and homeland countries both fail to be aware of the reciprocal dimension of migration: Lack and Templeton describe the negative impact of immigrant recruitment policy and national agenda on immigrants; Castles argues that the refusal of host nations to accept immigrants as residents caused severe problems (a point reiterated by Jean Martin for the Australian case); Zubrzycky discusses the lack of housing, services and inadequate conditions both inside and outside the industrial environment; Des Storer links lower-status work to social implications; and Ian Burnley details the negative hierarchy of employment and salary for nonanglophone immigrants.[39] The host countries believed immigrants would go away after they had served their labour contributions or, as in Australia, the wish was that immigrants would remain silent, invisible and assimilate. Postwar immigrant policy not only refused to acknowledge the immigrant homeland, culture and language, but also instituted that immigrants must leave their past behind. This was severely legislated in the first assimilation phase (1945–67); recent research surveys by migration scholars Dunn et al. have found its racist attitude sustained well into the twenty-first century.[40]

Reciprocity is contextualized within Hage's bigger project on developing an alternative to what he has called 'generalized domestication: a mode of dominating and exploiting nature and people', as is evident in processes and strategies of control, exploitation and extraction.[41] Hage brings the '"reciprocal" mode, where we experience our relation to what surrounds us as a gift' and the '"mutualist" mode, where we experience our lives and the life of whatever is surrounding us as mutually reinforcing' into the foreground, developing understanding of the multiplicity of realities.[42] The problem, Hage argues, is not that the reciprocal and the mutual modes can explain reality on their own as an alternative to 'generalized domestication', but that these bring an understanding of the entanglement of multiple realities to any one situation.

Recollecting their work experience in the Port Kembla Steelworks with their immigration to Australia, the participants in this study oscillated between, on the one hand, the sentiment of 'how lucky they are' to have migrated and proud of their contribution to building Australia, and, on the other hand, a sobering sentiment about the sacrifices they had made and the risks they undertook. An interface between immigrant labour and the processes of steel production requires entry into the depths of manufacturing interiors. In the industrial interior, architecture cannot be understood as abstract heroics of industrial structures, or its vast aspirational scale. The space of labour fractured into minuscule components as each immigrant's labour was divided and individualized within his or her allocation. Thousands of individual immigrant workers were submerged within a vast, chaotic, dangerous conglomeration of time and machine, each migrant body caught up in its own web of tasks, mediating machine, processes and oppressive environment. A view of the industrial interior foregrounds the entanglement of multiple realities that is disavowed by the dominance of 'generalized domestication'.[43] Participants spoke of the degrading reception they received at work in the steelworks:

> Discrimination very bad. Foreman – treat you really bad, they didn't say 'Sam' or 'Jorge' come here, they call you by whistling; 'not by name'. And it was very strong that word (hesitate to say it) 'wog'. Or they said, 'Eh you wog, come here'.[44]

Jose Acosta experienced this in the mid-1970s at the height of Whitlam's multicultural Australian era. Yet the infrastructure for this discrimination was already implicated in the postwar immigration recruitment policies in which BHP was an active participant.

At the end of *The Diasporic Condition*, Hage refers to the inequality within the dominance of 'generalized domestication' and differentiates between two types of inequality: 'distributional inequality' and 'extractive inequality'. The former may be understood as inequality of income differentiated by skills and abilities, inheritance and valorization, while the latter 'assumes a direct relation between, on one side, subjects doing the extracting and, on the other, subjects from whom things are being extracted'; in other words 'one part gets more at the expense of the other'.[45] Hage argues that situations such as the plight of Indigenous Australians cannot be explained as an either/or between these two inequalities; rather, these are at play in entangled ways.

Lever-Tracy and Quinlan's study comprehensively connects the history of postwar policies and realities of immigrant workers with 'distributional inequality' explained by the allocation of work, employer assumptions, categorization as 'unskilled', an unsupportive union and unequal pay.[46] Indeed, participants spoke of the ways in which they were able to navigate these inequalities towards a better situation.

For Italian immigrants, the auxiliary company Transfield was a better option. It was a company established in 1956 by Franco Belgiorno-Nettis (an electrical engineer) and Carlo Salteri (a mechanical engineer), who were sent to Australia by Società Anonima Elettrificazione Spa (SAE) in 1951. Transfield had major engineering contracts with BHP Steelworks and 500 men in the fabrication workshops and sleeping quarters.[47] In Australia, they worked with SAE's subsidiary company, Electric Power Transmission (EPT), to help build the country's first steel tower high-voltage transmission lines. Francesco Frino, employed by EPT in 1968, was then sent to Fremantle to build the first blast furnace at Kwinana in Western Australia. He recalls that he lived for eight months in a dormitory with four beds to a room and good food prepared by Italian cooks. He noted that many single men worked there, but that it was not popular. From 1972, Frino began work at the BHP Steelhaven fabrication workshop, where with welding qualifications he invented a piece for the metal inert gas (MIG) operation that would alleviate regular replacement of the nozzle. BHP paid Frino AU$50 took the sketch and incorporated it into the production, and they have the intellectual property.[48] Frino is disappointed. Migrants contributed not only to the production process but also to its technological improvement.

Carlo noted how better work in the 1970s helped him '[g]et more family life, social life'.[49] In the 1960s, postwar immigrants constructed forms of collective sociality around their ethnic communities. Dragan Grozdanovski, who retired after four decades at the BHP Steelworks (starting in 1963), and ventured into the Illawarra region to be immersed in its beauty, to camp and fish, stated 'I am not a lover of material wealth'.[50] He navigated the forces of dangerous work towards a good life.

However, Lever-Tracy and Quinlan's most important argument is that the postwar era divided nonanglophone immigrants from the Australian working class, a division not made on the basis of skills and abilities, but as a national imperative for the accumulation of labourers to work in the worst jobs, thus continuing a racial and ethnic strategy throughout Australia's recruitment history of immigrant labour. Which of the conditions of postwar immigrant labour may also be considered as 'extractive exploitation' or as a blurring between distributional and extractive inequality?

One participant, Saliba, recalls that in the late 1960s, double-decker buses coming from the port in Sydney entered the BHP Steelworks in Port Kembla directly with hundreds of newly arrived immigrants on a daily basis (see Figure 3.4). Their recollection of the process is as follows:

> There would be a stack of envelopes in the hands of a BHP staff member, and these were handed individually to each of the 'skilled' employees. A different style roll call of job allocation for 'unskilled labourers' comprised a loud announcement: 'Coke ovens!' followed by reading out a list of names. This mass of newly arrived workers were then herded to the Coke Ovens. This was followed by another loud announcement, 'Sinter Plant' and a list of names read out.[51]

This different style of roll call immediately conscripted workers from the point of arrival to the subterranean spaces of the industrial landscapes. At the centre of this vast change of work ethics was a hierarchical ethnicization of immigrant labour implemented via the classification of *unskilled* labour. Germans and Dutch were employed in *skilled* trades and white-collar or supervisory work.[52] British migrants were *skilled* tradesmen and professionals. The immigration policy that ranked immigrants from Southern Europe (and later those from Turkey, Vietnam and other Asian countries) as *unskilled* legitimated the allocation of these workers in the most arduous and dangerous operations. In combination with the experience of language difficulty, breakdown of family, brutal masculine culture, the process of immigration also rendered their bodies into a commodity. In the postwar period, the migrant male body was the only part of their migrant subjectivity that was perceived as useful to industry and government; it stripped them from a category of human being and at times rendered them as an anonymous extractive resource.[53] A distinct layer of discrimination that unleashed additional behavioural practices and conditions of exploitation was masked by the category of 'unskilled'.

The worker, the thousands of workers, bring a human corporeal rather than a machinic and production focus to the industrial interior. While their youthful, healthy, able, male and strong bodies were the reason they were recruited to BHP and allowed to migrate, immigrant workers were also aware of their lack. Each immigrant worker spoke about the disadvantage of language – 'no English', they said. Their voices were both absent from the nation's economic and industrial agendas and literally silenced in the steelworks' noisy interior. Diverse languages had been elided in the four decades of the White Australia Policy prior to their arrival. The immigration recruitment policy was dismissive of their homeland except as a source of labour.[54] What would they have said in their own languages?

Unfinished Histories of Nation Building

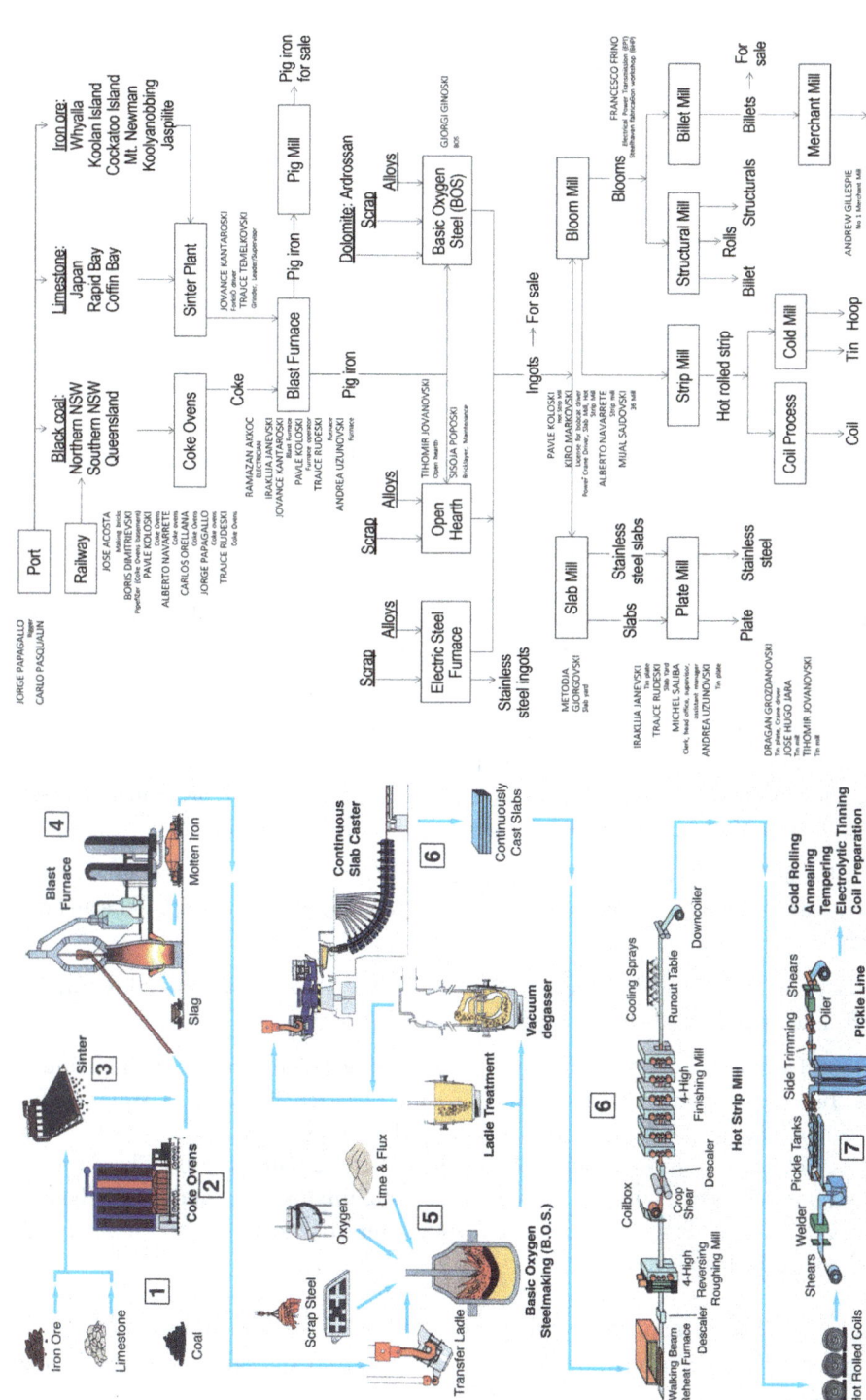

Figure 3.4 A diagram showing the steel production process but omitting the role and labour of the workers. © At Work with Our Environment (BHP), reproduced with permission (left). Process diagram of work linked to the individual worker (right). Drawn for the author by Alexandra Florea, 2022, based on participant information from the author's interviews with former migrant workers in 2020 and 2021

Meanings and realities of the worst jobs that no Australian would want evolved to produce a diverse linguistic terrain. Participants in the Macedonian Welfare Association workshop described the work as Гадна Работа, that is, horrible, dirty work:

> In the Hot Strip Mills – spray everywhere, poisonous vapour – oil, hot acid. Picker line, apply acid for cleaning the steel sheets; terrible to breath, noxious, 'lime water'. 12–13 lines of production; 4 to cut the sheets and pack in boxes – strapline. All under one roof.[55]

> In the Sinter Plant – smoky, noisy, very hot; red dust that stuck to your clothes. Could not wash it off. Safety glasses, wear mask; Conveyors – sinter – hot rocks. Very hard labour, pick and shovel from floor onto conveyors; white burns around eyes, recalls friend, Iliya Klinevski worked in the sinter plant for 20 years.[56]

> Work in the Coke Ovens – wooden clogs, lost eyelashes, eyebrows, hair burnt. Dusty, steamy, smell – of coke. Како трендафил [Like a rose].[57]

> Battery – a gallery of batteries. On the top of the batteries was very hot. The batteries are heating the ore.[58]

This was reiterated in the Men's Shed workshop:

> You are working on the ovens. Hard to work, heat from the ovens, walk on the top of the ovens, it was brick – hot. Clean up dropping of coke, open the hole, with shovel return the coke into the oven, cover it up. At that time, no safety gear – only wooden clogs provided.[59]

> I started working at No. 1 Battery Coke Ovens, and No. 2 shut by then, No. 3 completely shut, No. 4 Battery Working, then No. 5 and 6 new one. Hot 750 degrees. Seal had to put it around the hole. Always steam – 51 ovens steam pipes boxes –2–3 m high (small battery). Open at the top. Very hot on the floor, steam at the top [see Figure 3.5].[60]

> Supervision at Coke Ovens: woven asbestos cover head; heat resistant coat (down to ankles). He was in there for 30 seconds – come out – another guy suited up. Reheated steel ingots.[61]

> In all the departments of BHP, the Coke Ovens was the worst place. You did not want to go there. Not by choice – only if you got sent there. It was dirty.[62]

> Until 1982 I worked above, then below – *underground*, in the basement on the monitors, pumps. Terrible environment – fat and water, dirty oils, stench, acid, hot. Water sprayed to cool the steel at a speed of 250 kms/hour . . . What was your induction process to this work? . . . You rely on instincts, and physical coordination, natural skills. There were no windows, but lit by electric lights. It really reeks, awful mixture of odours, musty heat oil, animal fat. Uniform!? Pants and shirt . . . In 2001, after 21 years at the steelworks, I had a stroke and finished work.[63]

The *space of labour* is a space in which migrant bodies are not merely inserted but also embedded within its atmospheric and environmental spatial conditions. The atmosphere permeates their bodies as they breathe, hear, smell, feel: the *speed* in which conveyor belts, machinery and components moved; the *odours*, noxious gases, that filled the spaces, especially in the basement or up on the crane and control structures

Figure 3.5 BHP Steel Mill, Port Kembla, 1959. Photo by Mark Strizic. Courtesy of Monash Gallery of Art, MGA 2008.124 © The Estate of Mark Strizic.

near the roof; the *heat*, with temperatures escalating so that immigrant men removed their shirts or added jumpers to alleviate heat and danger; the *dust*, from the red ore that could not be washed off, to the fine invisible metal that workers inhaled; the *noise*, at very high atmospheric decibels, the screeching of metal blades that caused the loss of hearing.[64] To leave work at the end of their shift, migrant workers had to wrest their bodies from the oppressive and compressive interior, and this often involved a physically and psychologically abusive cycle (drinking and gambling).

Many participants spoke about the skills they brought into Australia that remain unacknowledged and the necessary resourcefulness, as well as their plan to gain training and upgrade their allocation.[65] The worst jobs could mean risk to workers' lives. Work injuries were frequent and meant no compensation, no work and no money. The worst jobs also meant constant risk to your life; their most valuable resource was learning how to stay alive: 'if the molten steel spilled, you run'. Their capacity to learn new tasks in horrendous environments was juxtaposed with the often-repeated phrase 'no training, no induction, no safety gear'.

Participants were not keen to discuss injuries, illnesses or deaths; these were still raw, unprocessed zones of shame and grief. Injuries were often casually noted – 'that's how I lost my hearing'. In the 1960s and 1970s, there were 'ambulance stations' all over the steelworks with queues of people waiting to be seen. Jorge Papagallo summed it up as follows: 'I am happy, look, in one piece. Obviously working hard down there. I can say I am OK, still alright. I lost a lot of friends down there. I lost about 18–20 working mates.'[66] Many also noted the 'crane chasers'. Nadia Colarusso's, father, Carlo Pasqualin, had arrived in 1954 and was a crane chaser at the Port:

> In 1969, 17 years after his arrival, my father had an accident at the Port. He slipped and fell. He died on 3 March 1970 . . . I think he (over)worked – he worked a lot. I know, because the year he died 1970 he had paid off the house. He died with no debt (took mortgage in 1954) . . . Did we report the accident – and get compensation? Father dead. For BHP, he was a foreigner, 'just a migrant' – no work, no money. Men worked. No debts, widow's pension. No support from BHP. No compensation offered, did not go to court.[67]

Dragan Grozdanovski reiterates: "Crane Drivers – all died before their time. Sat in cabins, high up near ceiling (at the time, no doors) (Figure 3.7). Fumes, vapours (acid, hot oil), gases, rose upwards. Пред време изумреа, and names them; Cvetko Ohridsko, Andrew Žabjani, Lazec and Ivan Ohridsko."[68] Women, like Borjanka Temelkovska, risked becoming destitute if their husbands fell ill:

> My husband became ill, his back ached, but it was internal. He got redundancy but no compensation. He left after 30 years of service with no money; and died three years later in 1992 . . . He was 62 years old. Many died, and many died young. The Kembla Grange cemetery is full of those that met their fate . . . After my husband died I did not receive any assistance and had to work. What did I not do? На лопата на метла на све работав . . . I worked with a shovel in the Sinter Plant – the conveyor moves along, you pick up fallen material, and put it back on the conveyor belt . . . after my husband died, I was hoisting buckets, climbing ladders, drilling with jackhammer – very hard jobs . . . the foreman wanted me to resign, but I did not want to stay at home.[69]

To many participants, their homeland was present as a memory and was later activated by return visits. Reflective of his decision to emigrate, Jorge Papagallo said 'it was a huge loss, to separate from your family – mother, father, brothers and sisters; it was the biggest sacrifice' (see Figure 3.6).[70] Young single men fell into depression:

> Many times I would come to the Pacific – crying, homesick, very unsatisfied. The heat, dust, red; lonely, very hard; conveyors, noisy; the dust stuck to you, even when you washed clothes, it did not wash off. I was sad about this work. Relief only at the cinema, billiards, 3 packs [of] cigarettes per day (Benson Hedges, Kent, 20 cigarettes per packet), my hands were shaking. Life must continue.[71]

Immigrant workers sometimes gave up: 'I wanted to leave. I was working in the Coke Ovens, wooden clogs, I lost my eyelashes and eyebrows; and my hair burnt.' The immigrant worker's supervisor, Heinz Heinrich (from Germany) warned him to give notice. He did not . . . life got worse.[72]

The breakdown of immigrant families was frequent and severe in the postwar period. A large majority of the able-bodied young male immigrants who entered the steelworks were married, but their families remained at the homeland until enough funds were accumulated to pay for their migration. The distance and separation caused a brutal disruption and often damage to the family, which continued into subsequent generations.[73] It was well known that immigrant workers left their work at BHP Steelworks within the year of arriving.[74] Those who remained provided the usual explanation that they did it for their children. But this response flattens subjectivity and life at the level of economics. Migrant subjectivity evolves within the context of immigrant labour, constructed under the conditions at the BHP Steelworks and the diminishing of symbolic/ontological being and personhood, alongside escape habits, gambling, alcohol, drugs and sex workers. What, on reflection, do they recollect from this period in their

Figure 3.6 Jovanče Kantaroski with his mother in the village Brusnik, SR Macedonia, Yugoslavia prior to his departure, January 1970. Courtesy of Jovanče Kantaroski/Јованче Кантароски

Figure 3.7 Dragan Grozdanovski with friends in Port Kembla, soon after he started working at the BHP Steelworks, Port Kembla, 1963. Courtesy of Dragan Grozdanovski/Драган Гроздановски

lives? Sisoja Poposki who had remained quieter than the others in the MWA workshop, offered a sobering response:

> Ми се плачи. I want to cry. И плачам, кога ќе се сеќавам, и плачам. дури сега. озбилно ти велам – од жешки работи, од тешки работи, од тежина, од прашина, сее. Од трчај, буфтај, џабе. И тоа е.[75]

Others added: 'It was dangerous everywhere. Lucky I am still alive. Maybe move on it is dreadful/fills me with dread. There was money but it was very hard work. That's why we had to pass by the pub – I felt dreadful – to calm down. I could not go home.'[76]

Immigrant labour is underscored by transnational and global economies. The transnational dimension and the question of reciprocity is explored in a 1974 film on Macedonians in Australia (with a focus on Port Kembla) entitled *Avstralija, Avstralija* by the well-known director Stale Popov from the Socialist Republic of Macedonia. While the opening scene on the beach is not an unusual reference to the Australian continent bordered by seas and oceans on all sides, its dramatic intensity is created by the sound of seagulls, which escalates to a shrieking cacophony that competes with the roar of the ocean. Echoes of Alfred Hitchcock's *The Birds* soon fade away as this film is focused on the terrifying human story of immigration. The next scene, heralded by Indigenous sound and music, captures succinctly the plight of Indigenous Australians via their housing and the casual play of football, dramatically contrasted to a game of lawn bowls where the players are dressed in white laboratory coats; this creates a poetic, if not an informative framing of Australian society. In one scene, back in a mountainous village in Macedonia, the villagers are dressed in their Sunday best black clothing and wait at their front door or the main street. A van arrives and the people gather around; a coffin is pulled out of the van and left on the ground. This transnational delivery of a coffin (of a person who died at the Port Kembla Steelworks) presents reciprocity as an uncanny resonance of the linguistic trope 'return to sender'. A past steelworks worker, who following their retirement and loss of their partner withdrew from the present time to find belonging into temporal spaces of nostalgia:

> After twenty-one years of work at the steelworks, the support I received was my super of $5,000. I am very sad, I miss Macedonia, where everything is familiar. Here 'нее твоје' (not yours). It is good but not dear to you: Осеќаш туѓина. Feel estrangement.[77]

Immigrant labour and lives fall into the chasm between stagnant, undeveloped and corrupt economies of the homeland and rapacious economies of advanced societies that promote high living standards. Neither the sending nor the receiving nations (Yugoslavia and Australia in this case) felt a moral obligation to the emigrant/immigrant. In the economic equation underpinning their agreement, the immigrant was not a particularity, a particular subject as understood by the people receiving the coffin in the village, but an abstract entity constructed within state laws and a necessary but abstract loss within transnational economic agreements. In the period from 1947 to 1975, the workforce at the Port Kembla Steelworks alone had grown from 3,665 to 20,715; by 1966, immigrants constituted over 60% of all waged employees and 82% were from nonanglophone countries.

Nonanglophone immigrants were subjected to backbreaking work in which their lives were at constant risk. Migrants were subjected to three scales of force outlined below, all of which defined the parameters of the space of labour. Migrant subjectivity was born out of *geopolitical* inequalities and became the currency of exchange of transnational economies, industrial capital and immigrant recruitment strategies. In the postwar period, the space of labour materialized as an intense and unbearable environment of noise, toxicity, dust and odour in the depths of *the interior* of heavy manufacturing. Migrant bodies were subjected to extreme conditions and excessive physical demands against which their permeable bodies had no protection. Their *bodies* were joined to the machinery – the conveyer belt, the steel-cutting machine and the crane – and were subjected to its mechanized speed and operational complications. Each scale – *the geopolitical, the architectural and the body* – is a human scale because each intersected with the migrant. Migrant bodies were not merely inserted into the space of manufacturing; they were shaped and deshaped by the political and physical machinery of operation. Hage points to 'extractive inequality' as 'the essence of capitalism' and in the postwar era, immigrant workers were capitalism's operational units – mobilized and dispersed to advance industrial economies.[78] A gap between the subject as emigrant and the subject as immigrant is experienced ontologically, as a hidden psychic landscape of immigrant subjectivity. Migrant subjectivity was set on a perilous path to navigate the forces that erased his or her subjectivity and the innate desire to exist and to be.

Participants only quietly and tentatively spoke of the fall into a slavery to money and their tone was one of shame. Their sense of searching for 'reciprocity', as Hage explains, results in 'a very frustrating and paradoxical situation where the immigrant plays a game of reciprocity without a reciprocating party'.[79] This imaginary of reciprocity of the migrant subject is not because the migrant fantasizes about their contribution, but because the immigrant hopes for a moral recognition as a subject who is not merely lucky to have immigrated, but as one who has contributed to the making of the nation.[80] Money was referred to as both the rationale and compensation to their hardship. Money, it appears, evolved into a strange substitute for reciprocity; it was the only 'return' for their contribution. It also appeared very difficult for the participants to reconcile their suffering in exchange for the money gained.

The sites of the BHP Steelworks and Port Kembla are part of a longer history of racialized strategies of exploitation of the land and the Indigenous Australians, prior to Australia's post-Second World War mass immigrant labour recruitment campaigns. While in Australian scholarship and research, histories of colonization and its impact on Indigenous Australians and lands are separated from histories of immigration, this study asks what a site-based analysis can uncover about the steelworks and Port Kembla. In the following section, the chapter shifts from a sociopolitical history of immigration to a spatial history of racialization and exploitation in order to examine earlier strategies of Australia's racial politics, and the *a priori* construction of the grounds on which postwar Port Kembla was imagined and built.

SPATIAL HISTORIES OF RACIALIZATION: THE WADI WADI IN PORT KEMBLA

Looking seawards, out from Dhgillawarah, the dramatic coastal headland, it is said the Wadi Wadi – the Indigenous custodians of the lands on which Port Kembla was constructed – sighted a strange 'monster with white wings', the ship that was travelling up and down the eastern coast of Australia in 1770, surveying the land.[81] Dhgillawarah was to become a contested site, defended and resisted by the Wadi Wadi peoples against British colonial military and industrial interests as well as their strategies of forced eviction, domination and erasure.[82] According to the Illawarra Aboriginal Land Council, this place – as both an ancestral site of the Dreaming as well as a place of forced eviction – should be the start of any narrative about the Aboriginal peoples in Wollongong.[83]

Dhgillawarah, Coomaditchie and the lands and waters of Tuckalong Lagoon had provided an abundance of food resources for the Wadi Wadi and other Indigenous Australians as well as a site for ceremonial gathering,[84] and they uncover a spatial history of racialized strategies of exploitation. Referring to the two-part concept of inequality, Ghassan Hage argues that in Australia, 'we still have a colonial situation and an extractive order of inequality . . . with the state being both party to this subjugation and dispossession and an active participant in the colonizing assemblage'.[85] However, this is also a reminder that 'we have a postcolonial society of citizens governed by a postcolonial and managerial state that relates to all the inhabitants of Australia, its Indigenous peoples included', which means we also have distributional inequality.[86]

The Wadi Wadi along with the Dhawaral to the north and Wandidian to the south were coastal-dwelling hunter-gatherers and thrived 'on a rich diet of seafood, local animals such as kangaroo, wallaby and possum, and a wide variety of plant life'.[87] Many creeks emanated from the escarpment and flowed east across the plain into coastal lakes or into the sea. Crustacea, fish, roots, tortoises and water birds would have been gathered.[88] Fats, grease and fish oil, with a coating of sand was used as a barrier against mosquitoes and flies, and also served as a thermal layer, while many plants were used for medicinal and ceremonial purposes. The lands gave rise to an abundant economy that was not mediated by the use of money, wealth or property.[89] Colonial operations and activities, including i) land grants, ii) industries (informal and organized), and iii) the Aborigines Protection Board (APB), effected the appropriation of lands, the destruction of flora and fauna, and the subjugation and control of Indigenous Australians.[90] Industries – pastoral, cedar cutting and manufacturing – proceeded after the offer of land grants to five colonists in 1817. By the mid-1800s, the ecological damage to the land and waterways was irreparable and had set the foundation and trajectory for the site of the Port Kembla Steelworks. The APB was key to the control of the Wadi Wadi and other Dhawaral inhabitants and by the 1900s sharpened their authoritarian practices.[91] Land appropriations, as well as coerced labour and indentured servitude, was enshrined in British legislative acts and formed part of the new economic regimes.[92]

The Indigenous spatial history of Port Kembla, which is fragmented and partial, complicates and contests a historiography dominated by narratives of colonial economic growth. Before and after the early 1900s, many Indigenous inhabitants of Dhgillawarah fought for title of the land and the right to continue to live there. In 1927, Joseph Timbery (an Aboriginal man) had written to the local paper, the *Port Kembla Pilot*, to inform them 'that his tenure is all right and will not be required to remove residence'.[93] He had previously requested security of land tenure from Central Illawarra Council.[94] Residents on Dhgillawarah lodged applications to secure land titles, battling against a series of claims, including a golf club. The NSW APB wrote letters in support of the Aboriginal land title applications, first to the Central Illawarra Council (1928) and then to the Department of Defence (1929), and these were reported in the *South Coast Times*, stating the community lived on fishing, and some 'men were receiving the basic wage, but living in humpies'.[95] The site of the Dhgillawarah/Wadi Wadi clan and the five islands is significant to Indigenous Australians and is central to their spiritual beliefs. Moreover, Dhgillawarah was socioeconomically and politically significant as a site from which these Indigenous Australians welcomed other clans and protected their Country (see Figure 3.8).[96] The five islands that can be observed from Dhgillawarah comprise one of the origin stories for this part of the Illawarra.[97]

Two forms of distributional and extractive inequality were instrumentalized from the very early periods of British colonization. Cedar-getting was an early colonial industry and boats sailed right into Lake Illawarra, exploiting the land prior to 1815, with resulting erosion that caused it to silt up. At the same time, several stockmen took their cattle to the land of 'Five Islands' on the Illawarra pastures after discovering an inland track.[98] By 1817, Governor Macquarie offered five land grants to colonists appropriating land in the order of 5,700 acres around the lake.[99] To the Indigenous Australians, news of the arrival of the first fleet in Sydney in 1788 had spread along the south coastal areas as 'when the sky fell down', and they feared, 'the landscape and all of its Dreamtime associations would be transformed. Everybody would be killed'.[100] From a thriving set of clans in the 1820s (Organ estimates several thousand in the Illawarra), the Indigenous Australian Wollongong population dwindled to ninety-three by 1846. The Port Kembla Steelworks was later built on the site of one of the five land grants.

In 1881, the first jetty was erected north of Dhgillawarah with a port opened two years later to service the Mount Kembla coal mine. The NSW government tried to force out the Indigenous Australians living in these areas in 1900, 1901, 1904, 1909 and 1914, ultimately resulting in the APB directing them to Aboriginal reserves.[101] Again in 1942, when the site was declared a military command centre, the Department of Defence forced Indigenous Australians off the site and subsequently burnt

Figure 3.8 Watercolour and pencil drawing of 'The Five Islands' by Edward Close, circa 1820. Courtesy of the Mitchell Library, State Library of New South Wales

their houses.[102] During the early 1950s, Indigenous Australians regained use of the area.[103] The Aboriginal Welfare Board (formerly the APB) applied more direct pressure and by 1957 assisted in the evictions of the local Wadi Wadi into Housing Commission houses. In 1967, residents again applied to the Defence Department to extend their land title to the area behind Coomaditchie, but this was instead turned over to sand mining (probably for the steelworks).

Many families then set up camp nearby around Coomaditchie Lagoon and among the sand dunes along Port Kembla beach, a site to which the Indigenous Australians who did not agree to go to the reserves were relocated.[104] Heather Ball was two years old when she moved with her family into one of six little weatherboard houses at Coomaditchie, with seven more homes promised to replace those pulled down at Dhgillawarah in 1942.[105] However, the seven additional houses promised for the Coomaditchie reserve never materialized.[106]

Evident in these operations is a 'governmental assemblage' that on the one hand promotes fairness, citizenship, a respect of the law as well as the protection of nature, but on the other hand also instigates dispossession, excessive violence and facilitates the destructive extraction of resources (see Figure 3.9).[107] Colonialism, Hage argues, is

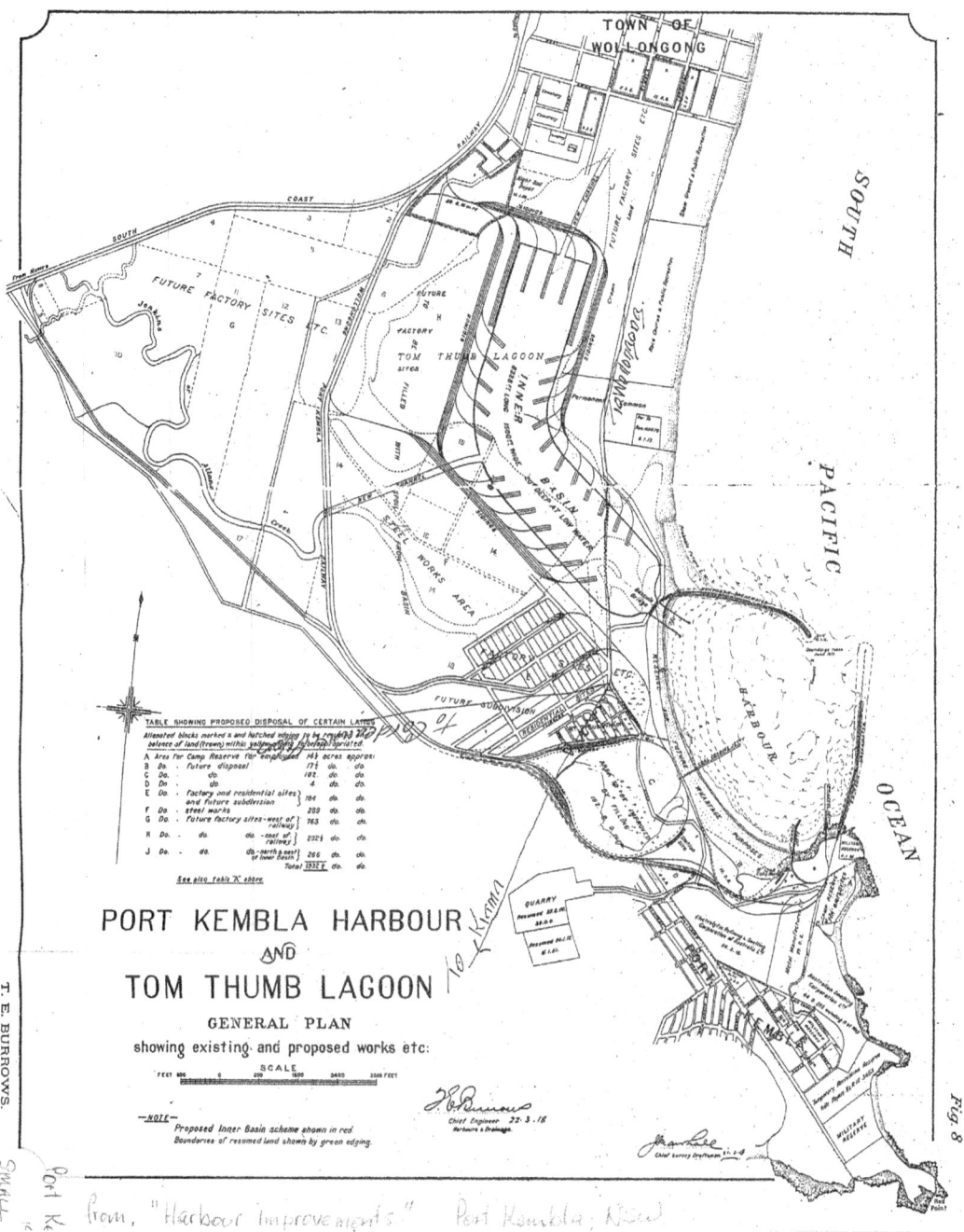

Figure 3.9 Public Works Department (PWD) plan showing the proposed development of Port Kembla Harbour, including the Inner Basin. The lagoon and adjacent lands had been the sites of Indigenous Australian industriousness and livelihoods, 22 March 1918. Courtesy of Wollongong City Libraries and the Illawarra Historical Society

not an event in history, but a continuing structure of inequality.[108] While spaces, sites, places and people are exploited in human history, there exists a divide between a normative type of exploitation and 'unchecked savage accumulation', where an excessive capitalism produces racial and ecological destructive operations, which becomes part of what Hage calls 'modes of exterminatory tendency.'[109]

In Port Kembla, the 'governmental assemblage' is evident not in one event, but in the recurring appropriation and devalorization of lands as ongoing and repeated actions of extractive capital and the forced evictions of Indigenous Australian families. The spatial strategies at Tuckalong Lagoon that manifested in a deep port harbour disclose the 'governmental assemblage' as an alliance between legislative acts (the 1898 Port Kembla Harbour Act), government monetary investment (NSW authorized expenditure of £200,000) and industrial operations. But the cost of the development of Port Kembla facilities in 1898 and 1937, including the 'breakwaters, jetties, haulage and shipping appliances and land', amounted to £1,052,048.[110] By 1918, the NSW government regained more of the 'Five Islands Estate'[111] and in 1948 a further 175 acres were reclaimed by AI&S from Tuckalong Lagoon as a site for the mill and auxiliary equipment.[112] Indeed, as steelworks historian Helen Hughes observes, 'the whole area was tidal and had to be raised twenty feet, with piles as deep as ninety feet reaching through silt and gravel to bedrock. By 1950 the concrete foundations were being poured, and early in 1951 the mill began to take shape above the ground'.[113]

Spatial strategies such as mining, dredging, cedar-getting and dairy farming are not merely topographical inscriptions, but intensive ecologically and spiritually irreparable incisions. Two of the 1817 land grants (to Robert Jenkins and David Allan) bordered on the estuary and the waterways. As early as 1904, the ABP forced Indigenous Australian families from the Tuckalong Lagoon into state-sponsored reserves.[114] A site-based analysis of Port Kembla uncovers a much longer history of spatial strategies of racialization and exploitation, and also a continuity of dispossession, disavowal and exploitation of the Wadi Wadi peoples. Another different set of strategies of racialization and ethnicization in the form of postwar Australian immigrant labour and its histories inscribes the site of the steelworks from the late 1940s into the 1980s.

CONCLUSION

The 1940s and the 1950s brought the British and Australian racialized, colonial and extractive exploitations of Indigenous lands and peoples to a historical interface with Australia's postwar ethnicized immigrant labour strategies. It is not a historical accident or coincidence that in 1942 the Wadi Wadi were evicted from Dhgillawarah by the Australian Defence Department and by 1947, DPs recruited on a two-year work contract were accommodated in migrant camps on military sites in the Illawarra.[115] In the 1950s, Indigenous Australians continued to resist eviction and some settled in Coomaditichie, an area where many postwar immigrants, like Nadia Colarusso's family, also settled.

In her important work *Haunted Nations: The Colonial Dimensions of Multiculturalism*, migration theorist Sneja Gunew argues that the partitioning of Indigenous Australian and nonanglophone Australian immigrant histories in research has disavowed intersections and skewed discourse about Australia and who is Australian.[116] The Australian *evasion* of the race discourse spreads across the entangled and yet obstinately separated fields of multiculturalism, postcolonial theory and colonialism.[117] A decolonizing historiography can only emerge if research embarks on a more situated knowledge.

An architectural lens embedded in spatial histories uncovers that industrial Port Kembla is not merely superimposed on the sites of the Dhawaral peoples. Rather, the industrial transformation of sites involves both structural and infrastructural exploitation, and shows that eviction from Dhgillawarah, neglect at Coomaditchie, mining of the Illawarra escarpment and dredging of Tuckalong Lagoon are ongoing and persistent practices. A spatial history of the industrial architecture and landscapes as constructed on sites of land grants, dairy farming and Tuckalong Lagoon provide a two-way lens: one looks retrospectively at the foundational colonial trauma and the other looks inwards, into the interiors of industrial sites as spaces of immigrant labour. This two-way 'sectional lens', vertical and horizontal, and its spatial approach uncover Port Kembla as a site of longer ongoing histories which entangle the substratum of Indigenous Australian country and its occupation with the multiple geographies and interior psychic landscape of immigrant transcultural displacement.[118]

Postwar immigrant workers were submerged within this industrial architecture and infrastructure, in a kind of subterranean spatial field. Nation building, driven by a renewed and insatiable industrial and economic growth policy – 'a need to plunder' – intertwined with a modernizing narrative, extracted young, able-bodied men (and later women) from nations with fledgling political economies and submitted them to the worst and life-threatening work environments. Increased severity of exploitation in the 1960s drew in hundreds of thousands from Southern Europe (Italy, Yugoslavia and Greece), more immigrants from Turkey and, again in the 1970s, immigrants from Vietnam (and other troubled Asian nations). Their settlement participated in the civil remaking, modernization and expansion of Port Kembla and Wollongong as a multicultural and cosmopolitan place. In the early 1980s, the *Port Kembla Ironworker*,[119] the magazine of the powerful union of the Federation of Ironworkers, with an immigrant, Nando Lelli, for the first time in a senior position, included translations of sections in the languages of the workers – Italian, Macedonian, Portuguese, Turkish, Serbian and Vietnamese – a testimony to the ethnicization underpinning postwar mass immigrant labour.

Mirjana Lozanovska is Professor in Architecture and Director of the Architecture Vacancy Lab at Deakin University. Her work investigates the creative ways that architecture mediates human dignity through multidisciplinary theories of space. Her books include *Migrant Housing: Architecture, Dwelling, Migration* (2019) and *Ethno-architecture and the Politics of Migration* (2016). Her creative works include *Venetian Blinds* (European Cultural Centre, Venice 2021), and, with David Beynon, Cameron Bishop, Diego Fullaondo and Anne Scott-Wilson, the exhibition *Iconic Industry* (2017, National Wool Museum, Geelong). She was co-editor of Fabrications: *Journal of the Society of Architectural Historians Australia and New Zealand* from 2018 to 2021.

NOTES

1. Cited in Bowden, 'The Rise and Decline of Australian Unionism', 51; Spence, *Thirty Years in the Life of an Australian Agitator*, 11.
2. Bowden, 'The Rise and Decline of Australian Unionism', 51.
3. Piggin and Lee, *The Mount Kembla Disaster*.
4. Elford and McKeown, *Coal Mining in Australia*, 169, 173.
5. Hoskins moved from Lithgow Valley to Port Kembla in 1928; Australian Iron and Steel, Turnbull and BHP Ltd., *Commemorating*, 13, 15.
6. Reynolds, *A History of the Land*, 25.
7. Port Kembla is officially a suburb of the town of Wollongong.
8. In the postwar period the growth of the Port Kembla Steelworks surpassed that at Newcastle in the northern part of New South Wales.
9. Australian Iron and Steel, Turnbull and BHP Ltd., *Commemorating*, 19, 63, 67; Hughes, *The Australian Iron and Steel Industry*, 158.
10. Lever-Tracy and Quinlan, *A Divided Working Class*, 193.
11. Burnley, *The Impact of Immigration on Australia*, 107
12. NAA: Department of External Affairs [II], Central Office; A1066, G45/1/1, Calwell, Arthur. 'Statement to the House of Representatives by the Minister for Immigration', 1945.
13. Lewis and Matters, 'In the Belly of the Monster'; Morrisey and Jakubowicz, 'Migrants and Occupational Health'; Cochrane, 'Anatomy of Steel Works', 65–66; UoW: Federated Ironworkers Association of Australia. Port Kembla Branch, *Port Kembla Ironworker*, September 1984, 15; November 1984, 4,13; January 1985, 8–9.
14. Nadia Colarusso, interview with the author, via Zoom, 16 February 2021; Francesco Frino, interview with the author, via Zoom, 22 February 2021; Metodija Gjorgovski, interview with the author via Zoom, 15 February 2021; Dragan Grozdanovski, interview with the author, via Zoom, 16 February 2021; Michel Saliba, interview with the author, via Zoom, 9 December 2020; Jovanče Kantaroski, interview with the author, via Zoom, 15 February 2021; Borjanka Temelkovska, interview with the author, via Zoom, 16 February 2021; Kiro Markovski, workshop with the author, MWA Port Kembla, 24 March 2021; Sisoja Popovski, workshop with the author, MWA Port Kembla, 24 March 2021; Jose Acosta, Ramazan Akkoc, Carlos Orellana, Jorge Papagallo, Trajče Rudevski, workshop with the author, MCCI Mens Shed, Coniston, 5 April 2021.
15. Ellis, Greg. 'Memories Flood Back on Steelworks Tour'. *Illawarra Mercury*, 6 April 2021, 6. This ethnographic data highlights immigrant labour in the 1960s, a period that has attracted less historical research to postwar refugees and assisted migrants. See Balint and Simic, 'Histories of Migrants and Refugees in Australia', 378–409.
16. Organ, *Illawarra and South Coast Aborigines 1770–1850*, xxxix.
17. The Broken Hill Proprietary Company Ltd., *Seventy-Five Years of B.H.P.*, 32.
18. Panoramic pictures of the BHP Port Kembla Steelworks (ibid. 32, 79); after purchasing AI&S in 1935, BHP acquired nearby mines, incising the region further afield. See Lee and Hagan, *A History of Work*, 6.
19. NAA: A2169, McLennan, Ian M. 'The Place of Iron and Steel Industry in the Australian Economy', Report June 1957, *Commonwealth Immigration Advisory Council – Agenda, Notes and Minutes of 32nd, 33rd and 34th Meetings Held during 1957*, 284.

20. Hughes, *The Australian Iron and Steel Industry*, 190.
21. The data, sourced from the BHP archives (1963), are cited in Lever-Tracy and Quinlan, *A Divided Working Class*, 191.
22. Hagan and Wells, *A History of Wollongong*; Lee and Hagan, *A History of Work and Community in Wollongong*.
23. Lever-Tracy and Quinlan, *A Divided Working Class*, 193.
24. Ibid.
25. Kalezić, *Socijalistička Republika Makedonija Denes*.
26. Mendo Trajcevski, 'Flight to Australia', in Mendo Trajcevski (ed.), *Компас/Kompas: Macedonian Community Magazine* (March 2009), 4–21; Mendo Trajcevski, 'When the Men Left for Australia', in Mendo Trajcevski (ed.), *Компас/Kompas: Macedonian Community Magazine* (March 2009), 22–35; Mendo Trajcevski, 'Where We Come From', in Mendo Trajcevski (ed.), *Компас/Kompas: Macedonian Community Magazine* (March 2005), 4–11; Mendo Trajcevski, 'Spase Markovski, Jovan Gagovski', in Mendo Trajcevski (ed.), *Компас/Kompas: Macedonian Community Magazine* (March 2005), 4–11.
27. Walker, 'First Accommodation', 21.
28. Burnley, *The Impact of Immigration on Australia*, 107.
29. Lever-Tracy and Quinlan, *A Divided Working Class*, 172.
30. Hughes, *The Australian Iron and Steel Industry*, 136–46.
31. Lever-Tracy and Quinlan, *A Divided Working Class*.
32. Ibid., 172; Eklund, *Steel Town*, 167.
33. Lever-Tracy and Quinlan, *A Divided Working Class*, 190.
34. Ibid.
35. Ibid., 45.
36. Ibid., Chapter 2, 'Immigration and Modern Capitalism', 39–116.
37. Jupp, *Immigration*, 75.
38. Hage, *The Diasporic Condition*, 55.
39. Lack and Templeton, *Bold Experiment*; Castles, Booth and Wallace, *Here for Good*; Martin, *The Migrant Presence*; Zubrzycki, *Settlers of the Latrobe Valley*; Storer, 'Migrant Families in Australia'; Burnley, *The Impact of Migration on Australia*.
40. Dunn et al. 'Constructing Racism in Australia'.
41. Ibid., 188.
42. Ibid.
43. Ibid.
44. Jose Acosta, workshop with the author, MCCI Mens Shed, Coniston, 5 April 2021.
45. Hage, *The Diasporic Condition*, 189.
46. Lever-Tracy and Quinlan, *A Divided Working Class*, 39–53, 167–236; Collins, 'Immigration and Class,' 1–27.
47. Nadia Colarusso, interview with the author, via Zoom, 16 February 2021.
48. Francesco Frino, interview with the author, via Zoom, 22 February 2021.
49. Carlos Orellana, workshop with the author, MCCI Mens Shed, Coniston, 5 April 2021.
50. Dragan Grozdanovski, interview with the author, via Zoom, 16 February 2021.
51. Michel Saliba, interview with the author, via Zoom, 8 December 2020.
52. Burnley, 'The Wollongong Experience', 105–14.
53. Lever-Tracy and Quinlan, *A Divided Working Class*, 189.
54. Ibid., 49.
55. Dragan Grozdanovski, interview with the author, via Zoom, 16 February 2021.
56. Jovanče Kantaroski, interview with the author, via Zoom, 15 February 2021.
57. Sisoja Poposki, workshop with the author, MWA Port Kembla, 24 March 2021.

58. Trajče Rudeski, workshop with the author, MWA Port Kembla, 24 March 2021.
59. Jose Acosta, workshop with the author, MCCI Mens Shed, Coniston, 5 April 2021.
60. Jorge Papagallo, workshop with the author, MCCI Mens Shed, Coniston, 5 April 2021.
61. Michel Saliba, interview with the author, via Zoom, 9 December 2020.
62. Ramazan Akkoc, workshop with the author, MCCI Mens Shed, Coniston, 5 April 2021.
63. Metodija Gjorgovski, interview with the author, via Zoom, 15 February 2021.
64. See Lefebvre's concept of the social and spatial body: Lefebvre, *The Production of Space*, 169–71.
65. Passenger cards of immigrants interviewed state 'unskilled' or 'labourer'. But many had trade certificates, and some in time underwent examination at Wollongong Technical School and went to Sydney to have these translated.
66. Jorge Papagallo, workshop with the author, MCCI Mens Shed, Coniston, 5 April 2021.
67. Nadia Colarusso, interview with the author, via Zoom, 16 February 2021.
68. Dragan Grozdanovski, interview with the author, via Zoom, 16 February 2021.
69. Borjanka Temelkovska, interview with the author, via Zoom, 16 February 2021.
70. Jorge Papagallo, workshop with the author, MCCI Mens Shed, Coniston, 5 April 2021.
71. Jovanče Kantaroski, interview with the author, via Zoom, 15 February 2021.
72. Jovanče Kantaroski, interview with the author, via Zoom, 15 February 2021.
73. Lozanovska, 'Port Kembla Steelworks'.
74. Lever-Tracy and Quinlan, *A Divided Working Class*, 196–97
75. Sisoja Poposki, workshop with the author, MWA Port Kembla, 24 March 2021.
76. Kiro Markovski, workshop with the author, MWA Port Kembla, 24 March 2021.
77. Metodija Gjorgovski, interview with the author, via Zoom, 15 February 2021.
78. Hage, *The Diasporic Condition*, 189.
79. Ibid., 55.
80. Ibid.
81. Herbert, Reginald. 'Reminiscences of the Moruya Area', *Moruya Examiner*, 26 January 1888, cited in Organ, *Illawarra and South Coast Aborigines 1770–1850*, 344.
82. Organ, *Illawarra and South Coast Aborigines 1770–1850*; Organ, *Illawarra and South Coast Aborigines 1770–1900*; Donaldson, Bursill and Jacobs, *A History of Aboriginal Illawarra*, vols 1 and 2; Wesson and Gahan, *A History of Aboriginal People of the Illawarra*.
83. John Peterson Heritage Consulting, 'Concept Study for Establishing a Heritage Centre of Human Migration'.
84. See the following map: Illawarra Aboriginal History Poster, Early Contact Map, New South Wales Environment and Heritage. Retrieved 2 January 2024 from https://www.environment.nsw.gov.au/resources/cultureheritage/illawarraAboriginalHistoryPoster.pdf. Dhgillawarah goes by several names: Illowra, Ti Tree Hill (1920s), Red Point, and Hill 60. Tuckalong is also known as Tom Thumb Lagoon.
85. Hage, *The Diasporic Condition*, 190.
86. Ibid.
87. Organ and Speechley, 'Illawarra Aborigines', 13.
88. Wesson and Gahan, *A History of Aboriginal People of the Illawarra*, 10.
89. Organ and Speechley, 'Illawarra Aborigines', 9.
90. NLA: NSW Aborigines' Mission. 'Report of the Aborigines' Protection Board for 1894'. *The New South Wales Aborigines' Advocate: A Monthly Record of Missionary Work amongst the Aborigines, Issued Under the Auspices of the NSW Aborigines' Mission*, 42 (30 December 1904), Leichhardt, NSW: T.E. Colebrook; Peckham, Ray. 'Activists for Indigenous Rights in the Mid 20th Century', NLA: Interview with Rob Willis, part of the *Oral History Project, 2012*. National Library of Australia. Retrieved 2 January 2024 from https://nla.gov.au/nla.obj-213880846/listen.

91. Eklund, *Steel Town*, 117–27.
92. Winter, 'Coerced Labour', 3.
93. Report on Central Illawarra Council meeting, *Illawarra Mercury*, 10 June 1927, cited in Organ, *Illawarra and South Coast Aborigines 1770–1900*, 235.
94. Ibid.
95. 'Report on Aborigines at Hill 60', *South Coast Times*, 13 December 1929, cited in Organ, *Illawarra and South Coast Aborigines 1770–1900*, 238.
96. Wesson and Gahan, *Aboriginal People of the Illawarra*, 46, 51–52.
97. Organ and Speechley, 'Illawarra Aborigines', 11.
98. NLA: Report, *Sydney Gazette*, 18 March 1815. In these early times, Port Kembla was also a great wheat producing area of New South Wales. See Davies, Borrie and the Department of Social Studies, *A Social Survey*, 1.
99. Grants four and five, between Illawarra Lake and Tom Thumb's Lagoon, were gifted to Robert Jenkins ('Berkeley', 24 January 1817) and David Allan, including Red Point area ('Illawarra Farm', 24 January 1817). In 1828, William Charles Wentworth purchased and changed the name of the property to 'Five Islands Estate'. See Dowd, *The First Five Land Grantees*.
100. Organ and Speechley, 'Illawarra Aborigines', 17–18.
101. NLA: 'Aborigines' Protection Board', *Sydney Morning Herald*, 5 February 1898.
102. Donaldson, Bursill and Jacobs, *A History of Aboriginal Illawarra*, vol. 2, 46.
103. Ibid.
104. Ibid.
105. Ibid., 47.
106. 'Coomaditchy Homes for PK Aborigines', *South Coast Times*, 12 March 1962, cited in Organ, *Illawarra and South Coast Aborigines 1770–1900*, 261–62.
107. Hage, *Is Racism an Environmental Threat?*, 53–63.
108. Ibid., 58.
109. Ibid., 54, 107.
110. Davies, Borrie and the Department of Social Studies, *A Social Survey*, 1.
111. Reynolds, *A History of the Land*, 7–8.
112. Ibid., 28.
113. Hughes, *The Australian Iron and Steel Industry*, 157.
114. Wesson and Gahan, *A History of Aboriginal People of the Illawarra*, 7, 10.
115. In 1943 Australia's first Minister of Immigration, Arthur Calwell, directed the nation towards a mass immigration campaign. See Chapters 1 and 2 in this volume.
116. Gunew, *Haunted Nations*.
117. Ibid.
118. Hage, *Is Racism an Environmental Threat?*, 58.
119. UoW: Federated Ironworkers Association of Australia. *Port Kembla Ironworker* (Wollongong: Port Kembla Branch, September 1984).

BIBLIOGRAPHY

Archival Records

National Archives of Australia (NAA)
University of Wollongong (UoW)

Publications

Australian Iron and Steel, Clive Turnbull and BHP Ltd. *Commemorating the Official Opening of the Hot Strip Mill and Other Major Plant Extensions at Port Kembla, New South Wales on Tuesday, August 30, 1955*. Melbourne: BHP, 1955.

Balint, Ruth, and Zora Simic. 'Histories of Migrants and Refugees in Australia', *Journal of Australian Historical Studies* 49(3) (2018), 378–409.

Berger, John, and Jean Mohr. *A Seventh Man: The Story of a Migrant Worker in Europe*. Cambridge: Granta Books in association with Penguin, 1975.

BHP Steel & External Affairs & Communications Department. *At Work with Our Environment: The Port Kembla Steelworks*. Port Kembla, NSW: External Affairs & Communications Department, Flat Products Division, BHP Steel, 1996.

Bowden, Bradley. 'The Rise and Decline of Australian Unionism: A History of Industrial Labour from the 1820s to 2010', *Labour History: A Journal of Labour and Social History* 100(1) (2011), 51–82.

The Broken Hill Proprietary Company Ltd. *Seventy-Five Years of B.H.P. Development in Industry*. Melbourne: BHP, 1960.

Burnley, Ian. H. *The Impact of Immigration on Australia: A Demographic Approach*. Melbourne: Oxford University Press, 2001.

Castles, Stephen, Heather Booth and Tina Wallace. *Here for Good: Western Europe's New Ethnic Minorities*. London: Pluto Press, 1984.

Cochrane, Peter. 'Anatomy of Steel Works: The Australian Iron and Steel Company Port Kembla, 1935–1939', *Labour History* 57 (1989), 61–77.

Collins, Jock. 'Immigration and Class: The Australian Experience', in Gillian Bottomley and Marie de Lepervanche (eds), *Ethnicity, Class and Gender in Australia* (Sydney: Allen & Unwin, 1984), pp. 1–27.

Davies, V., W.D. Borrie and the Department of Social Studies. *A Social Survey Undertaken by the Department of Social Studies, Sydney University for the Rotary Club of Port Kembla*. Sydney: Sydney University, 1949.

Dowd, Bernard Thomas. *The First Five Land Grantees and Their Grants in the Illawarra*. Wollongong: Illawarra Historical Society, 1977 [1960].

Donaldson, Mike, Les Bursill and Mary Jacobs. *A History of Aboriginal Illawarra Volume 1: Before Colonisation*. Yowie Bay: Dharawal Publications, 2015.

——. *A History of Aboriginal Illawarra Volume 2: Colonisation*. Yowie Bay: Dharawal Publications, 2017.

Dunn, Kevin, James Forrest, Ian Burnley and Amy McDonald. 'Constructing Racism in Australia', *Australian Journal of Social Issues* 39 (2004), 409–30.

Elford, Harold S., and Maurice Robert McKeown. *Coal Mining in Australia*. Melbourne: Tait Publishing Company, 1947.

Eklund, Erik. Carl. *Steel Town: The Making and Breaking of Port Kembla*. Melbourne: Melbourne University Publishing, 2002.

Evans, Raymond, Kay Saunders and Kathryn Cronin. *Race Relations in Colonial Queensland: A History of Exclusion, Exploitation and Extermination*. Brisbane: University of Queensland Press, 1993.

Federated Ironworkers Association of Australia. *Port Kembla Ironworker*. Wollongong: Port Kembla Branch (September, November), 1984; (January) 1985. (University of Wollongong Archives.)

Gray, Stephen. 'The Elephant in the Drawing Room: Slavery and the Stolen Wages Debate', *Australian Indigenous Law Review* 11(1) (2007), 30–54.

Goodall, Heather. 'Land in Our Own Country: The Aboriginal Land Rights Movement in South-eastern Australia, 1860 to 1914', *Aboriginal History* 14(1/2) (1990), 1–24.

Gunew, Sneja. *Haunted Nations: The Colonial Dimensions of Multiculturalism*. London: Routledge, 2004.

Hagan, Jim, and Andrew Wells. *A History of Wollongong*. Wollongong, NSW: University of Wollongong Press, 1997.

Hage, Ghassan. *Is Racism an Environmental Threat?* Cambridge: Polity Press, 2017.

———. *The Diasporic Condition: Ethnographic Explorations of the Lebanese in the World*. Chicago: University of Chicago Press, 2021.

Haskins, Victoria. '"& So, We Are Slave Owners!": Employers and the NSW Aborigines Protection Board Trust Funds', *Labour History* 88 (2005), 147–64.

Hughes, Helen. *The Australian Iron and Steel Industry, 1848–1962*. Parkville, Vic: Melbourne University Press, 1964.

John Peterson Heritage Consulting. 'Concept Study for Establishing a Heritage Centre of Human Migration'. Report Completed for the Port Kembla Community Investment Fund. Wollongong: Multicultural Communities Council of Illawarra (MCCI) and Illawarra Migration Heritage Project (IMHP), 2020. Retrieved 10 January 2023 from https://mhpillawarra.com.au/?p=97.

Jupp, James. *Immigration*. Melbourne: Sydney University Press with Oxford University Press, 1991.

Kalezić, Danilo (ed.). *Socijalistička Republika Makedonija Denes* [*The Socialist Republic of Macedonia Today*]. Skopje: Samoupravna Praksa, 1984.

Kidd, Rosalind, and Australians for Native Title and Reconciliation. *Hard Labour, Stolen Wages: National Report on Stolen Wages*. Rozelle, NSW: Australians for Native Title and Reconciliation, 2007.

Lack, John, and Jacqueline Templeton (eds). *Bold Experiment: A Documentary History of Australian Immigration since 1945*. Melbourne: Oxford University Press, 1995.

Lee, Henry Patrick, and Jim Hagan. *A History of Work and Community in Wollongong*. Rushcutters Bay, NSW: Halstead Press in association with Wollongong University Press, 2002.

Lefebvre, Henri, *The Production of Space*. Oxford: Blackwell, 1991

Lever-Tracy, Constance, and Michael Quinlan. *A Divided Working Class. Ethnic Segmentation and Industrial Conflict in Australia*. London: Routledge & Kegan Paul, 1988.

Lewis, Susan, and Paul Matters. 'In the Belly of the Monster: Researching Workers' Health at the Port Kembla Furnaces', *Australian Left Review* 1(91) (1985), 17–21.

Lozanovska, Mirjana. 'Port Kembla Steelworks, Australia: Post-War Immigrant Histories of Architecture, Urbanism and Heritage', in Julia Gatley and Elizabeth Aitken Rose (eds). *Ngā Pūtahitanga/Crossings: Proceedings of Society of the Architectural Historians Australia and New Zealand (SAHANZ)* 39 (2023), 315–30.

Martin, Jean I. *The Migrant Presence: Australian Responses 1947–1977*, vol. 2, Hornsby, NSW: Allen & Unwin, 1978.

Moore, Clive. 'South Sea Islander Mortality, 1860s–1900s, and Mackay's Islander Hospitals: Why Reparations Are Required'. Tabled in Queensland Parliament by MP Stephen Andrew, Member for Mirani, 30 September 2022, 1–35.

Morrissey, Michael, and Andrew Jakubowicz. 'Migrants and Occupational Health: A Report'. *Social Welfare Research Centre Colloquium, July 1980*. UNSW: Social Welfare Research Centre.

Organ, Michael K. *Illawarra and South Coast Aborigines, 1770–1850*, vol. 1. Wollongong: Wollongong University Printery, 1990.

———. *Illawarra and South Coast Aborigines, 1770–1900*, vol. 2. Canberra: Report to the Australian Institute of Aboriginal and Torres Strait Islander Affairs, 1993.

Organ, Michael, and Carol Speechley. 'Illawarra Aborigines', in Jim Hagan and Andrew Wells (eds), *A History of Wollongong* (Wollongong, NSW: University of Wollongong Press, 1997), pp. 7–22.

Piggin, Stuart, and Henry Lee. *The Mount Kembla Disaster*. Melbourne: Sydney University Press in association with Oxford University Press, 1992.

Quinlan, Michael. Garry. 'Immigrant Workers, Trade Union Organization and Industrial Strategy', Ph.D. Dissertation. Sydney: University of Sydney, 1982.

Reynolds, Donald K. *A History of the Land Purchased for the Building of Port Kembla Steelworks*. Wollongong: BHP Flat Products, 2001.

Southern, Jack L.N. *A Railway History of the Illawarra: The History of Rail Transportation at Australian Iron and Steel Pty Ltd, Port Kembla, New South Wales Together with an Account of the Development of Railways and Shipping Ports in the Illawarra Region*. Melbourne: Broken Hill Proprietary Co. Ltd, 1987.

Spence, William. Guthrie. *Australia's Awakening: Thirty Years in the Life of an Australian Agitator*. Sydney: Worker Trustees, 1909.

Storer, Des. 'Migrant Families in Australia: A Review of Some Social and Demographic Trends of Non-Anglo Saxon Migrants 1947 to 1981'. Melbourne: Institute of Family Studies, 1981.

Trajcevski, Mendo (ed.). Компас/*Kompas: Macedonian Community Magazine*. Port Kembla: Macedonian Welfare Association, 1996–2000.

Walker, Meredith. 'First Accommodation for Migrants Arriving in Wollongong Post World War 2'. *Migration Heritage Project, Wollongong's Migration Heritage Thematic Study, 'Places Project'*, 2007. Retrieved 10 January 2023 from https://www.mhpillawarra.com.au/pdf/places_accommodation_essay.pdf.

Wesson, Sue, and Kate Gahan. *A History of Aboriginal People of the Illawarra 1770 to 1970*. Hurstville, NSW: Department of Environment and Conservation, 2005.

Winter, Sean. 'Coerced Labour in Western Australia during the Nineteenth Century'. *Australasian Historical Archaeology* 34 (2016), 3–12.

Zubrzycki, Jerzy. *Settlers of the Latrobe Valley: A Sociological Study of Immigrants in the Brown Coal Industry in Australia*. Canberra: Australian National University Press, 1964.

Chapter 4

Company Town
Housing Labour Migrants on the Snowy Hydro Scheme

Anoma Pieris

In early 2019, before the pandemic restricted interstate travel, I made my second of several research trips to Cooma, the former headquarters of the Snowy Mountains Hydro Electric Scheme (1949–74) (hereinafter 'Snowy Scheme'); a town whose public park is flanked by a row of international flags of the thirty or more countries with which Snowy workers identified. I had previously toured the Monaro region's dams and reservoirs, captivated by their iridescent beauty and intrigued by inundated and relocated townships like Adaminaby and Jindabyne (see Figure 4.1). Seduced by these impressive, vast water bodies with their brutally magnificent concrete dam backdrops, I never questioned the attendant environmental and human costs. Like Australia, several former British colonies pursued technorationalist developmental goals during the postwar decades. The Bhakra Nangal Dam (1951–63), funded by the union (federal) government and famously described by Indian Prime Minister Jawahar Lal Nehru as among the 'Temples of the New Age', symbolized the self-determination of the decolonizing decades.[1] The Soviet-built Aswan High Dam, which controversially inundated Egypt's historical sites at Abu Simbel and Philae, was accompanied by heightened Cold War tensions relating to political alignments and development aid. These transformative infrastructure projects promised long-term benefits to growing populations of flood management, irrigation and clean energy.

By harnessing the Snowy River's power and resources, Australia demonstrated the nation's growing authority in managing and transforming the bountiful resources seized through colonization.[2] Initiated six months after legislation of Australia's *Citizenship Act* (1948), differentiating Australian (as former British subjects) from British immigrants, the Snowy Scheme declared the former dominion's greater

Figure 4.1 Jindabyne Reservoir, 2015. © Anoma Pieris

self-sufficiency and deepened its alignment with the United States.³ Many of these mid-twentieth-century schemes were influenced by the US-New Deal infrastructure projects built by its Bureau of Reclamation, such as the Tennessee Valley Authority (1933) with direct links to the Snowy Scheme. The Snowy Mountains Hydro Electric Authority (SMHEA, hereinafter 'SMA' or 'the Authority') was conceived with comparable ambitions along similar lines. The (at the time) AU$820 million Snowy Hydro megaproject was distributed across over 1.2 million acres (1,978 square miles) of alpine territory, across the state border between New South Wales and Victoria. The scheme's network of sixteen dams, eight power or pressure stations, and twelve transmountain tunnels, and its contribution to reducing Australia's two most populous states' coal-fired power dependency made it pivotal for postwar industrial growth (see Figure 4.2).⁴ Brad Collis's definitive book *Snowy: The Making of Modern Australia* captures the project's singular national significance.⁵ Among its many innovations was rock-bolting for tunnel walls and the transistorized computer Snocom.⁶ Publicity for mandatory seatbelts, introduced on all SMA vehicles in 1960, encouraged their implementation throughout Australia.⁷ 'The Snowy' was 'catalytic for preparing a generation of Australian engineers', trained by multinational contracting companies.⁸ Cooma's Snowy Hydro Discovery Centre and the Khancoban Visitor Centre display its technoscience. The Snowy Mountains Engineering Company (SMEC), established

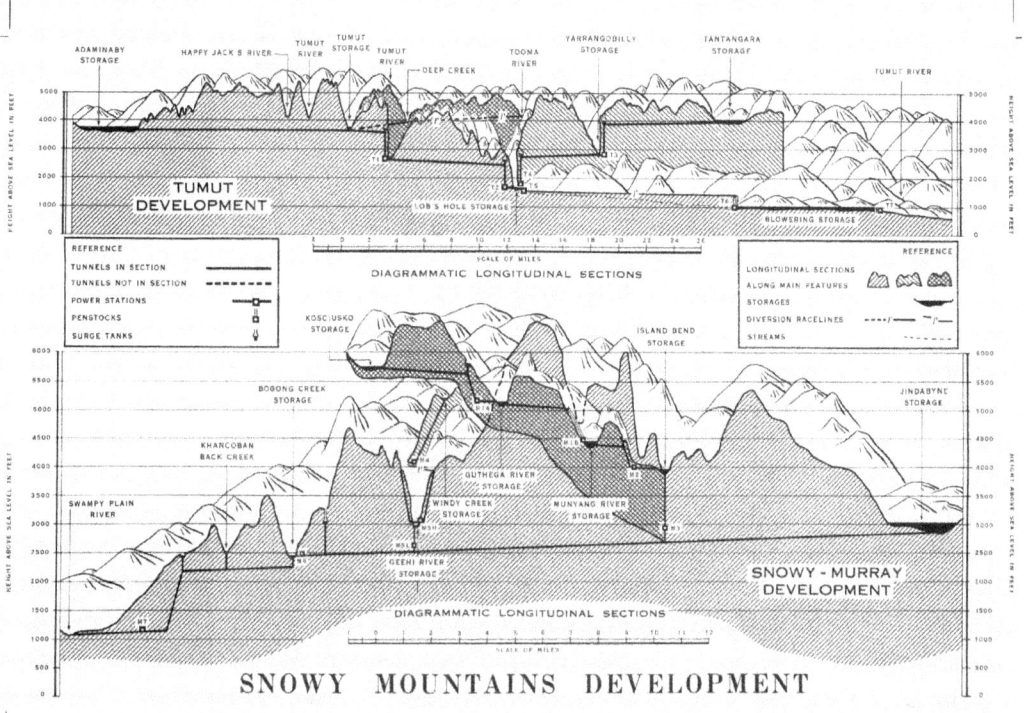

Figure 4.2 A diagram of the Snowy Mountains Development, 1953. Courtesy of the National Archives of Australia, A1200, L16067

in 1970, internationalized its scope to servicing Australian aid projects overseas.[9] The AU$5.1 billion contract for Snowy 2.0, awarded in 2019 to an Italian, American and Australian partnership WeBuild, extends its legacy.[10]

The Snowy workers, signified by the Cooma town colours, are subsumed into this developmental narrative. Of the 100,000 employed over the scheme's lifetime, 60% were nonanglophone European immigrants, including displaced persons (DPs) from the war. These, the largest workforce employed in any industrial site at the time, substantiate its extraordinary dependency on exogenous contractors and labour streams. Their stories, surfacing in tandem with Australian policies of multiculturalism during the 1970s, have been incorporated as Snowy heritage.[11] Siobhan McHugh's *The Snowy: The People Behind the Power* humanizes the immigrants, and includes women on the scheme, noting in particular the intermediary role of Irish immigrants whose country had remained neutral during the war.[12] This chapter partly references her archived oral transcripts collected in the 1980s.[13] Ivan Kobal, a Slovenian chainman, has written *The Snowy: Cradle of the New Australia* and *Men Who Built the Snowy*, asserting the role played by male labour-migrants. *Snowfraus: The Women of the Snowy Mountain Scheme* gives voice to the endurance of the few women on the scheme.[14] These persistent, multivocal and intersectional retellings of the Snowy story, addressing gender, class and ethnocultural particularities of industrial experience, highlight mid-twentieth century nonanglophone labour-migrant contributions to nation building.[15] They differentiate continental European immigrant experiences from postwar British immigrant histories along axes of preferential treatment of some and discrimination of others; a prevalent distinction within racially white Australian populations, between those who inherited imperial settler colonial entitlements and those who did not. The revisionist lens, in part, addresses sentiments voiced by some European immigrants that their role was insufficiently recognized.[16]

These authors pay less attention to the environmental and Indigenous Australian (Aboriginal and Torres Strait Islander First Nations/Peoples) histories of the Monaro that might challenge the Snowy Scheme's progressive teleology and the immigrants' eagerness to be represented as equal pioneers within it.[17] Nineteenth-century settler histories scrutinized by authors Eve Pownall and W.K. Hancock have likewise given way to its developmental rhetoric.[18] The immediate corollary of the idea of migration as the forced displacement of the European DPs and dispossession of Australian Indigenous peoples attaches to these many unravelling strands. Considering these nuances in the scheme's representations, and on who constitutes an immigrant or who is being displaced, Australia's alpine region is imprinted by multiple conflicting environmental epistemes. A deeper temporal understanding of the region's transformation and its striated cultural geography adds to the scheme's complexity. There are competing and entangled historical claims on the Monaro.

We need to be wary of the rhetoric of the mid-twentieth-century era. Both Australian governments and publics after the Second World War displayed unquestioning faith in technorationalist thinking. Such sensibilities were energized by the US-led reconstruction in Europe and Asia. Related policies have been brought into disrepute in critiques of the environmental and social cost of feted megaprojects, most recently in Jonathan Peyton's *Unbuilt Environments* focusing on British Columbia.[19] While conscious of the need to resettle dispossessed communities, few, if any, dam builders addressed the long-term environmental consequences of resource optimization or heeded the resultant erasure of Indigenous Australian heritage. Since the 1993 Mabo decision,[20] native title claimants across Australia view such developments as amplifying the violent dispossession of Indigenous Australian lands. But, as argued by Gelder and Jacobs in 'Uncanny Australia', Indigenous Australian groups are not uniformly anti-development. Many actively engage in pastoralism and mining.[21] Some may do so as the only available means for economic integration or by choice. Others advocate for environmental recovery by invoking geocultural provenance and millennia-old, symbiotic custodianship. Historically, and alongside struggles for political self-determination, these populations from whom lands were so brutally taken have striven to maintain cultural differentiation even when assimilating into these development goals.

Using Indigenous Australian dispossession as its starting point, this chapter weaves a story of white settlement in the Monaro region, and the unsettlement caused by the changing water courses in fulfilment of Australia's industrial ambition for its alpine resources. I use the term 'development ecology' to describe the enmeshment of human expertise and labour in their utilitarian reconception for agro-industries and power generation, and recreational tourism. This multilayered excavation of the region's historical stratums is influenced in part by conceptualizations of the Anthropocene epoch during which human activity has irrevocably altered the environment and the climate.[22] Paying less attention to the Snowy Scheme's engineering achievements, but focusing on its human dimension, this ecology encompasses its construction phases and material culture: the ephemeral campsites and prefabricated accommodation that housed the largely immigrant workforce. The chapter ends with a discussion of Cooma North, the company town. The timeline in the chapter stops with the 1970s, before the dissolution of the White Australia Policy (WAP) reopened the nation to immigrants of colour.

PREPARING THE GROUND

The industrial schemes of the mid-twentieth century advanced a form of developmental colonization in what was believed to be the sparsely populated Monaro alpine region, an Indigenous Australian name describing a high plateau. The highest peak of the Dividing Range, the source of the Snowy, Tumut, Murrumbidgee and Murray Rivers, was named Mount Kosciuszko (initially anglicized as Kosciusko) by Polish explorer Paul Strzelecki, after a Polish general and military engineer Tadeusz Kościuszko in 1840. A recent proposal in 2019 to reclaim its Ngarigo (Ngarigu) identity through dual naming as *Kunama Namadji* (snow and mountain) challenges the teleology of *terra nullius* that justified claims by colonial graziers and pastoralists and later by industries servicing metropolitan needs.[23]

Until the late nineteenth century, the Indigenous Australian Monaro peoples made ritual pilgrimages for annual intergroup feasting on Bogong moths (*Agrotis infusa*), tracking pathways through and across the mountainous alpine landscape. As recounted in Josephine Flood's *Moth Hunters*, the moth's spring migration to aestivate in caves in high-altitude regions created concentrations so numerous that they provided the several Monaro 'tribes' with an important protein-rich food source.[24] In order to attend the annual feasting, upland and coastal peoples crossed tribal boundaries, conducting numerous social ceremonies at each intergroup encounter – preceding the sometimes gruelling ascent to mountain tops.[25] Tindale's map of the area shows the upland custodians of the lands through which the Tumut, Murray and Snowy Rivers flowed as the southern Ngunawal, Walgalu, Djilamatang and Ngarigo respectively.[26] The downriver coastal groups were the Krauatungalung and Bidawal of East Gippsland. As reported by a member of the Acclimatisation Society,[27] they came from Eden, Bega, Braidwood, Tumut, the Upper Murray and Gippsland, wending their way to the table lands, and from there to the foot of the main range. 'Here a halt was made to observe certain formalities before commencing the feast of several months duration, usually November, December and January.'[28]

The performative migratory rituals and ceremonies produced a socially embodied, intimate cartography of the Monaro landscape. These rituals extended to caring for all aspects of the natural environment, as conveyed in Jakeline Troy and Linda Barwick's interpretation of the 'Song of the Women of the Menero Tribe', a Ngarigo ritual invoking the snow's return to sustain the alpine ecology.[29] Following the Bundian Way, a route westwards and inland from Twofold Bay in Eden, John Blay notes the seemingly impossible terrain.[30] Regional place names including the major sites associated with the Snowy Scheme, such as Adaminaby, Thredbo and Tumut, are believed to be Indigenous Australian resting places (or camping grounds). Cooma is said to mean large lake or sand bank;[31] Cabramatta – the head of the waters – and Bombala – where the waters meet. However, given the extent to which place names may be corrupted through anglicization, their provenance and meaning is often unclear. Rivers appear not to have singular identities, but are named after local features, and custodianship extends into the coastal waters. Collective custodianship and care of the land contrasted with its exploitation for individualized ownership.

The first settlers employed (and sometimes forced) Indigenous Australian trackers to show them the pathways to the basalt-rich, fertile valleys inhabited by their peoples and later occupied by the Snowy Scheme. These they claimed as pastoral lands, dispossessing their Indigenous Australian occupants and setting up small townships connected by dirt roads. Kiandra was briefly associated with gold mining. Many were on former Indigenous Australian camping grounds. The place names of the Monaro persisted, reduced to unintelligible syllables. More critically, pastoralists occupied vast acreages and brought in hoofed livestock, destroying the carefully managed endemic fauna and flora – the Indigenous Australians' food supply. Frontier wars over the fast-dwindling resources persisted until the late nineteenth century, when the Monaro tribes who had survived genocide, intertribal conflict and white settler diseases were concentrated in the Delegate, Walgalla Lake and Lake Tyers (in Victoria) Aboriginal reserves, or camped on the fringes of the Snowy River floodplain.[32] The government acting through the Aborigines Protection Board forced the numerically depleted Monaro peoples into relationships of dependency, while pastoralism and overgrazing domesticated and leached the alpine landscape. Symbiotic and sustainable collective practices that characterized Indigenous Australian land use receded before resource exploitation for personal gain.

Racial attitudes of white settlers towards Indigenous Australians passed through hostility to indifference by the end of the nineteenth century. Their institutionalization, removal of mixed-race children, and dispersal as domestic servants and station hands further depleted their numbers. The surviving population moved from reserve to reserve, adopting seasonal work as evasive strategies.[33] The Monaro became a colonial settler domain.

TAMING THE LAND

Settler occupation advanced initially as squatting runs (snow-leases) – fixed acreages of freehold land leased from the Crown for depasturing animals. Some 130 properties were documented in the Monaro Squattage District by the mid-nineteenth century.[34] Competing settlers battled for possession of the most desirable acreages, and the monopolies of several hundred thousand acres sustained by some individuals stretched from Cooma to Bombala.[35] Perceived only as pastoral lands, the Monaro townships rarely grew beyond a main street and a few residential blocks, their leasing from the Crown further substantiating the region's availability for development by the Snowy Scheme. In *Searching for the Snowy*, George Seddon describes this period as the heroic age of colonial expansion, immortalized in Banjo Paterson's *The Man from Snowy River*.[36] The 1890 poem's evocation of a stockman's pursuit of wild brumbies naturalizes the folk hero stockman's intimacy with the Australian outback.[37]

The Snowy River flowed from the Australian Alps through the Monaro Table Lands and East Victorian Uplands down to the Gippsland Plains and thence to the Bass Strait. It would swell to a mighty torrent with the winter snow melt. The need to harness the river and discipline the wilderness for agro-industries and hydropower generation was a recurrent focus in the political debates of the late nineteenth century.[38] The seeming wastage of its waters prompted the first proposals for diverting the Snowy River inland in 1884, followed by a 1904 legislation granting the Commonwealth water rights. The proposal was to trap the river's headwaters and divert them to two power stations positioned to distribute hydropower to Australia's most populous southeastern states – Victoria and New South Wales – depriving the downstream towns of Orbost and Dalgety of their supply. Two world wars interrupted, but also helped justify the proposition when it was broached again in the late 1940s.

Among the several arguments that supported the shift away from the coastal coal-fired steam turbines to hydropower generation was the vulnerability of coastal power plants to enemy attack. There was an added need to reduce interstate power dependencies. Invocation of national defence gave greater legitimacy to an expensive and long-term project. Collaboration with the United States Bureau of Reclamation (USBR) extended relationships strengthened by joint wartime operations in the Pacific, but also foregrounded successful public–private partnerships. Closely modelled after the US-Tennessee Valley Authority (TVA), the SMA was created as a statutory authority, established by a 1949 Act of Federal Parliament and led by Commissioner William Hudson, an Aotearoa New Zealand engineer and expert on dam construction.[39] The SMA had a degree of autonomy from the relevant state governments' public works departments, giving Hudson the freedom to commission multinational and Australian contracting companies.

The act of taming the river: diverting it west through the Great Divide to irrigate the Murrumbidgee and Murray valleys, assumed an instrumentality and developmental rationale. Adaminaby, Jindabyne and Talbingo were sacrificed for its diversion, being inundated and relocated to the banks of Eucumbene, Jindabyne and Talbingo (Jounama Pond) reservoirs, respectively. Localities previously associated with tenacious settler populations were identified as dam, reservoir or power-station sites. The SMA published the scheme's progress annually; its productivity measured in dam heights and storage capacity, tunnel lengths and diameters, power stations' kilowattage and pumping stations' pumping head.

The physical transformation of the alpine terrain in the interests of drought security and additional power generation provoked opposition on several fronts.[40] In a 1952 lecture at the University of Sydney, geologist W.R. Browne conjectured the 'Kosciusko' plateau 200–300 years in the future as a deforested wasteland with an intermittently flowing river choked with the debris and silt of the Snowy Scheme. Diligent archaeologists would be unearthing relics in the mud-buried cities of Jindabyne and Adaminaby.[41] There was growing environmental awareness during the prewar decades. The *Kosciusko State Park Act* (1944) and Trust (funded by snow leases) protecting 1,300,000 acres and a newly established Soil Conservation Service both emphasized protection of catchment areas.[42] William Hudson sought the expertise of New South Wales (NSW) soil conservation pioneer E.S. Clayton for the more pragmatic purpose of preventing the silting-up of dams, due to soil erosion by bulldozing. The SMA introduced fire prevention services and employed scientists to study erosion, siltation and soil conservation with the aim of repairing and preventing further damage. There were efforts at reforestation with snow gum woodlands. Downstream, however, the river's diversion had already endangered local wildlife (freshwater fish) habitats. The raised water table pushed salt to the surface, affecting grazing lands.[43]

The battles over the Monaro's conservation pitted scientists against bushwalkers and graziers: Hudson and Clayton against the Kosciusko Park Trust; and the high-altitude snow leases on which the Trust depended were terminated as an environmental threat. The Trust countered in 1963 by designating a 'primitive area' closed to road and engineering works. This was the closest the environmentalist came to preserving Indigenous Australian heritage, albeit for the recreational pleasure of 'skiers, walkers and all citizens'.[44] Despite this protracted environmental tug of war and the Snowy Scheme's many critics, it was received, when completed, as a major national achievement; blessed by visiting dignitaries like Queen Elizabeth II and the Duke of Edinburgh and other members of the royal family. The scheme was distributing hydropower at a comparably reduced cost to the largest concentration of consumers in the country, had increased irrigated land area benefiting agroproduction and had attracted immigrant workers essential for populating Australia. Moreover, provision of detailed environmental impact assessments by industrial infrastructure projects was not legislated for in Australia until the 1970s.[45]

The SMA invested heavily in publicity campaigns to stimulate public acceptance and thereby ensure continued government funding for each successive phase of the scheme. Pamphlets in nontechnical language documenting progress were produced periodically for the general public. The Eucumbene Observation Building & Tea House was designed in 1958 by SMA architects with Sydney practice Fowell, Mansfield and Maclurcan as a stopover point for bus tours and 'follow me' car convoys. An 'alpine way' across the Dividing Range was reminiscent of the TVA's scenic highways at the US dam sites.[46] The Monaro took on a progressive new identity as a place for recreation: bushwalking, mountaineering, skiing, and imported trout and salmon fishing. These in turn had environmental impacts like deforestation for the increased uptake in downhill skiing, first introduced in the 1860s, but growing in popularity following the appointment of the Norwegian contractors Selma Engineering Pty Ltd for the first Guthega Dam project.[47] Blended activities combining recreational and industrial tourism also ensured the economic viability of local settlements beyond the lifetime of construction, once workers had left and they turned to other economic stimuli. These future-oriented transformations assumed and extended historical settler privileges over the alpine terrain, but recast them through a new lens of national productivity. Colonial settler histories were subsumed into this dominant developmental legacy.

UNSETTLEMENT AND REPOSSESSION

The communities uprooted due to inundation of historical towns at Adaminaby, Jindabyne and Talbingo gave up generational land claims on spacious country properties for the constrained sites of the new town grids. Timber double-framed houses with tiled roofs were cut off at the foundations and trucked to the new site, often leaving fireplaces behind. Materials from some buildings were salvaged to build new ones like the Adaminaby church and courthouse. The spectacular wholesale removal of the Adaminaby bank building, conveyed in numerous photographs, became feasible by removing the strong room.[48] Although younger residents enjoyed the new town's amenities, older residents were unsettled by the associated loss of community place-memories. If they were unable to reoccupy their former homes, Adaminaby residents sold their houses to the SMA to be allocated to Jindabyne new town. Removalist Eddy Doherty, who moved fifty houses there over six months, recounted financial disputes between the residents and SMA.[49] Many complained about proximity to neighbours, including Noel Potter, a long-time Indigenous Australian resident of Adaminaby.[50] Rooms were partitioned and views were blocked.[51] The shire provided loans that bridged any gaps between the selling and buying price.

Alice Kidman describes a drought-time boat trip out on the lake when submerged buildings began to surface, recollecting her sadness upon seeing the drowned church where she was married. Douglas Stewart's poem 'Farewell to Jindabyne' lamented its drowning in the copious currents of the Snowy, the Thredbo and the Eucumbene (see Figure 4.3).[52] The SMA's actions in contrast suggested 'forced official forgetting', according to historian Peter Read.[53] He observes that the Authority changed the reservoir's name from Lake Adaminaby to Lake Eucumbene, commemorating the related

Figure 4.3 Scenic Jindabyne and the valley of the Snowy River, with the camp for 'new Australians' in the foreground, 1950. Courtesy of the National Archives of Australia, A11016, 19

river, and proposed renaming the old town Coolawye. A second proposal to rename it Chifley after the then Prime Minister was vehemently opposed.[54] Read argued:

> The Snowy Mountains Authority, through signs expressed in words, machinery, manpower, and the crushing moral weight of its propaganda, attempted to mediate the collective remembrance of the loss of the town as less catastrophic than the residents first perceived it to be. The Authority cast it as a town not destroyed but submerged, lost or moved through changeover and smooth transfer.[55]

The plight of the uprooted settlers attracted more attention than the dispossessed Indigenous Australian communities whose dispersal and diminished numbers affected any place claims, nor were there mechanisms for asserting them. But they were not entirely absent from the Monaro. Commenting on the reckless driving of the Norwegian workers at the Guthega Dam site, which commenced in 1949, hydrographer Johnny Abbots Smith observed that vehicle wrecks were as numerous as Aboriginal campsites.[56] During the early years of the Snowy Scheme, small groups of Indigenous Australians from the regions' reserves may have wondered back to former seasonal camping grounds, in place-practices inhibited by the advancement of the scheme.

THE SNOWY HYDRO WORK CAMPS

The mountains were being dissected and documented in preparation for construction through a different kind of geographical knowledge from that of either Indigenous Australians or the settlers. They were being reconfigured as part of a development ecology – a vast network of dams and tunnels governed by a disciplinary logic that would constrain the fire hazards, floods and droughts that imperilled the region's agro-industries. Invited to join the scheme's survey branch by its founder H.F. Eggeling, former military surveyor Major Hugh Clews led a team of fifty surveyors on reconnaissance surveys of the Snowy terrain, often advancing on foot. In the first eight years of the scheme since his appointment in 1950, Clews' team comprising largely of 'Balts' (Lithuanians, Latvians and Estonians), the first postwar immigrants to Australia, were joined by Polish, German, Yugoslav and Hungarian surveyors, chainmen and foresters, who documented Guthega, Geehi, Lobs Hole, Dry Dam, Kings Cross, Kenny's Knob, Three Mile, Tumut Pond, Indi, Scammels Spur and Cowombat Flat.[57] German surveyor Wally Wassermann noted that unlike Europeans, the army-trained Australian and New Zealand surveyors had little construction or project-related surveying expertise. Aerial photogrammetric surveys, using Royal Australian Air Force (RAAF) planes and some private operators (a wartime innovation), were used for the initial mapping. Their data was verified by controlled surveys.[58]

Reconnaissance surveys involved hydrographers to measure water flow (stream gauging, flood incidences, meteorological conditions, rainfall, drought, snowfall, etc.), followed by geologists drilling at selected points for surface mapping, and engineers and soil conservationists assessing site conditions. Finally, diamond drillers and excavators began earthworks and tunnelling (see Figure 4.4). Marking frameworks and control points for dams and pressure tunnels, and for generators, turbines and valves, required a high degree of accuracy. Wasserman notes that the discovery of the solid rock surfaces needed to anchor each dam necessitated several trial site investigations. Investigative work involved climbing steep inclines, through narrow ravines, avoiding falling trees, landslides and snow falls in different types of weather, and on muddy or icy roads recently bulldozed for access. Wassermann noted: 'All the men who were in charge were hard men ... you did not last long in the mountains if you were not really tough. The mountains, the isolation, no women, everything ... [and, moreover] Not everyone could stand having 10 people around them talking in 5 different languages.'[59]

Having bulldozed vehicular access roads through perilous mountainous terrain to work camps erected or dismantled in tandem with the project's phases, surveyors, engineers and workers carved out a subterranean geography of tunnels and dams above and beneath the forest floor. Workers' experience of the Monaro geography thus occurred at these many levels, sometimes deep in dimly lit cavernous interiors or elevated on pylons stringing high-tension power lines. They were distributed across the camp constellation, moving from one to another for different phases of the scheme.

Figure 4.4 Construction work on pressure tunnel Tumut 1 Power Station, 1958. Courtesy of the National Archives of Australia, A1200, L25102

Each camp cluster was related to a specific dam or tunnel project. There had been over 120 camps by the scheme's end aiding in the transformation of the multilayered terrain (Figure 4.5). These were connected to works townships at Island Bend, Cabramurra, Eucumbene, Jindabyne, Geehi and Khancoban. Cooma North, the SMA company town (see Figure 4.6), was the scheme's administrative nerve centre networked with extant, expanded or newly created townships at Cabramurra and Khancoban, and Adaminaby, Jindabyne and Talbingo. The base workshops at Cooma's Polo Flat contained both heavy and light earth-moving and constructing equipment, vehicular transport, fabrication and machine shops, and mechanical services needed for a scheme of this scale. Prefabrication workshops were also located at Jindabyne. The Bombala railway line ran through Cooma.

The SMA's field construction division built the infrastructure that networked the project, and its architects designed many SMA facilities. Due to the magnitude of the contracts and insufficient Australian capacity, many overseas contractors from the Netherlands, Norway, France, Belgium, Switzerland, Britain and the United States joined Australians in constructing parts of the scheme or providing essential equipment. The first Guthega Dam and Munyang powerhouse were designed and constructed by the Norwegian company Selmer Engineering Pty Ltd. The USBR designed the dams, tunnels and power stations of the Upper Tumut Project, training Australian

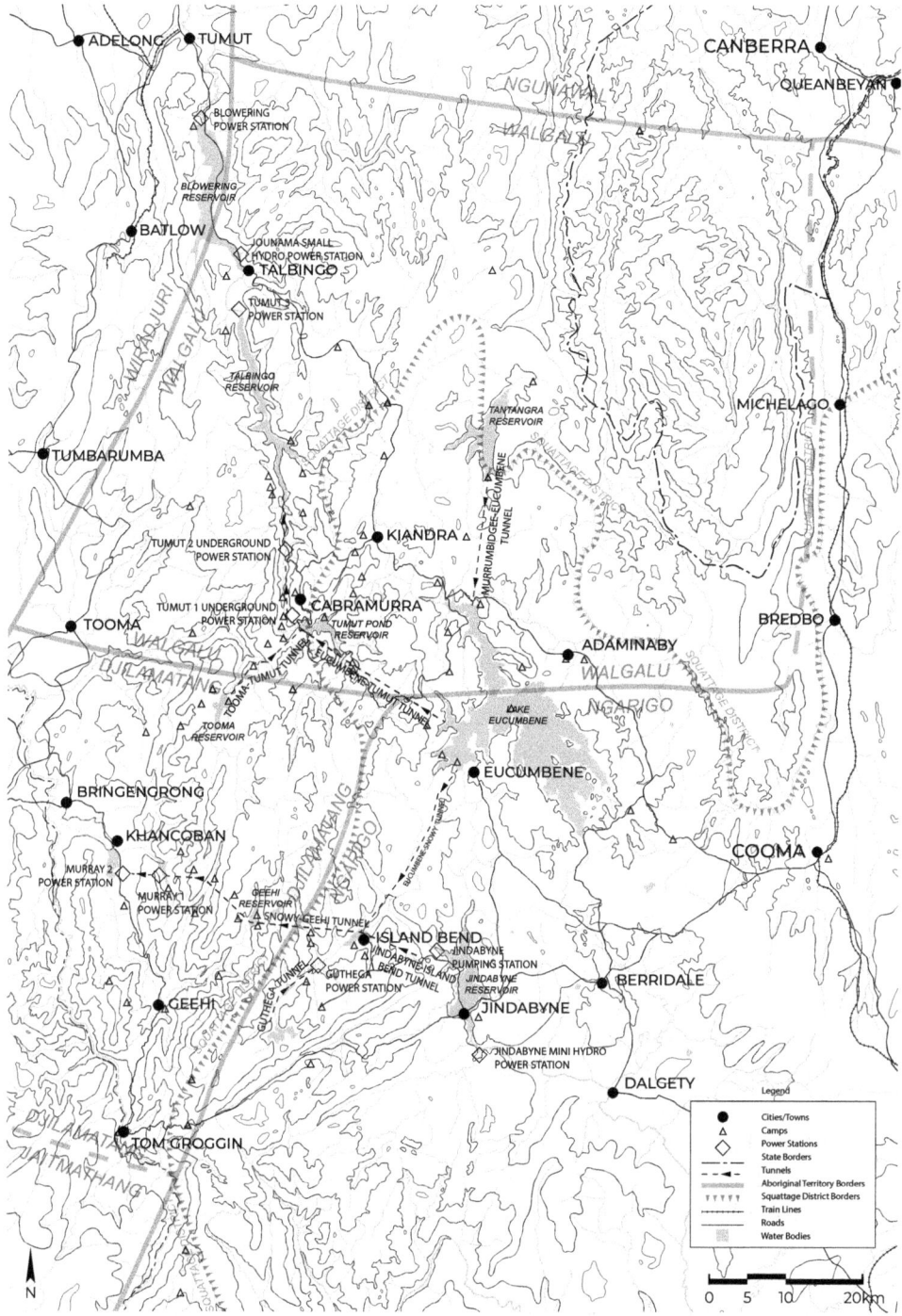

Figure 4.5 Snowy towns and work camps showing multiple overlays. Drawn for the author by Brian Duong, 2022. Based on Brad Collis, *Snowy: The Making of Modern Australia* (Melbourne: Coretext, 2015), 97; conjectured tribal boundaries and squattage districts as depicted in Michael Young, *The Aboriginal People of the Monaro* (Sydney: NSW National Parks and Wildlife Service, 2000), maps 8 and 22; and State Library of NSW: General map of the Snowy Mountains area, Maps 1965

Figure 4.6 Cooma North housing, 1951. Courtesy of the National Archives of Australia, A11016, 591

engineers in the United States to mediate its direct involvement in an international project.⁶⁰ The major contractor, Kaiser-Walsh-Perini-Raymond, a joint venture between four US companies, had built the Boulder Dam, the Grand Coulee Dam and the Niagara Falls' twin tunnels in the United States.⁶¹ Utah Australia Ltd and Brown and Root Sundamericana Ltd won the Murrumbidgee-Eucumbene contract. Others included a French consortium under Études and Enterprises; Dumez France-Australia and the Australian Theiss Bros. While the overseas contractors came with core employees, they drew on staff and labour from among Australian and immigrant workers assigned to or attracted to the scheme. Government organizations played a more minor role – state departments of works, roads and forestry, the local shire, and the Commonwealth Department of Works – so that the public works hegemony that dominated state projects was absent.⁶² Numerous smaller Australian companies built support facilities like factories, labour accommodation and offices. They included Williams and Co., Wallace, James and Co., and Fripp and Williams from Wollongong, Vandyke Bros, Hutchison Bros, Econo Steel, and Architon Construction Co. of Sydney who built cottages and barracks.⁶³ Stephansdach Holzbau also built greenhouses and recreation buildings.

The early and more remote camps were tented facilities, later supplemented by snow huts, transportables and more permanent structures with amenities. But generally, they remained rough, all-men environments. Frank Rodwell describes his work camp at Cooma as thirty, two-bed, 10 × 8 foot tents with wooden floors, boarded halfway up the sides, each with a canvas fly stretched on top and lit by a kerosene lamp.[64] There were four corrugated fibro igloos serving as kitchen, mess and two dormitories. Toilets and washrooms were at one end, with limited-capacity hot showers and wood-fired coppers for washing clothes. In the freezing winter months workers would sleep fully clothed. The issue of two blankets for each person hardly sufficed. Rodwell's *Homes on the Range* identifies 'survey camps, drilling camps, horse camps, (very temporary) flying camps, summer camps, winter camps, road camps and contractor camps'.[65] The several international contractors with staff housing in Cooma North and workers stationed at tented or temporary camps near the dams, tunnels or power station constructions comprised several thousand souls. A new ecology of temporary shelters – canvas tents, fibro igloos, 700 demountable houses transported from centre to centre, twenty-man barracks and 8 × 8 foot-squared snow huts mushroomed across the Monaro.[66] Houses would be constructed in two parts at the Cooma workshops and trucked on low-loaders to town or campsites. Some, Rodwell notes, were 'neat as a pin'; a few were 'pig sties'. The movement of heavy equipment, and industrial activities such as excavations, explosions and drilling pervaded the Monaro soundscape, as did the foreign languages spoken by contractors and workers. Accommodation was divided quite early into 'Aussie' and what were pejoratively described as 'Wog' camps.[67]

THE IMMIGRANT WORKFORCE

These were the temporary and sometimes perilous conditions under which impoverished single men from a war-devastated Europe risked pacifying the alpine wilderness for Australia's industrial gain. Many of them came directly from Europe's concentration and refugee camps, and found themselves in the company of their wartime enemies. Australia received 170,700 DPs initially from Eastern European countries and Germany, and later from Southern Europe.[68] Those who were recruited from European cities were surprised at the primitive camp conditions and the vastness of the bush landscape. Conscripted to work on government projects, as a condition of their entry, they passed through reception and holding centres like Bonegilla, Benalla, Greta, Parkes and Cowra to the work camps on the scheme. Among the anglophone immigrants who formed 41% of the immigrant intake between 1947 and 1951 were many Irishmen.[69]

The postwar relaxation of immigration policies, giving greater access to non-British Europeans, saw the entry of sufficiently large numbers of racially white, but linguistically and culturally nonanglophone immigrants who, as stated earlier, comprised 60% of the scheme's 100,000 strong workforce. These nonanglophone immigrants, identified by locals as New Australians, or pejoratively as Balts, Wogs and Reffos came through various pathways, aside from migrant camps and hostels: through direct recruitment by the SMA, or international contractors and also individually, having entered the country previously through camps or sponsorship. Because foreign workers remained a dominant and visible majority within the scheme's workforce, and the work regimes and practices of international contractors governed the various phases of a project's execution, the scheme's delivery was perceived as an extra-Australian endeavour even though Australian experts, workers and contractors played a part in its success. The term 'New Australians' was used to differentiate nonanglophone immigrants from those whose culture and language was British. McHugh's oral history collection, dating from the 1980s, captures immigrant perceptions of Australia. Despite the high risks and primitive conditions, people were motivated to work, and the Snowy benefited from the sheer contrast between Australia and postwar Europe.[70] Lack of English was not a deterrent to employability, and living conditions were better than Europe's DP camps.

Arriving in Australia after more than five years spent constructing hospitals in Normandy, as a German prisoner of war (POW) from the Russian front, and following this, picking cotton in the United States, Polish-born Heinz Geromin worked first at Sue City, then Jindabyne, with approximately fifty compatriots and eleven Irishmen. He self-deprecatingly attributed Australia's need for 'square heads' to the German 'spirit' (work ethic).[71] Arrested by the Gestapo on his wedding day, Belgrade-born Duška Miloradović (Duke Milford) worked as a DP in Germany before migrating to Australia. He came via Queensland's cane fields to Happy Jack's camp.[72] Ukrainian DP Sándor Berger passed through concentration camps at Auschwitz, Ohrdruf and a subcamp of Buchenwald before arriving in Australia. He worked in five Snowy camps.[73] Jan Kilma fled postwar Czechoslovakia through the Iron Curtain in his Czech army uniform, with forged documents. Captured at the German border by US counterintelligence, he passed from Landsburg DP camp to Bonegilla. Located far from the turbulent aftermath of the European theatre of the war, many Australians were unaware of and uninterested in these immigrant traumas.

Employment of Germans was part of SMA policy from the very start because of their superior education, particularly in surveying. SMA assistant engineer Roy Robinson recruited 640 tradesmen (out of 3,000 applicants), eighty engineers and forty to fifty surveyors directly from Berlin, Hamburg and Hanover.[74] They were screened for Nazi affiliations by a joint US–British military organization, which graded individuals from A to C according to their perceived levels of risk. Some with affiliations who had helped the international authorities were permitted entry (two were in fact deported). Collis mentions tattooed ex-Waffen SS in Guthega camp.[75] Australia emulated Britain and the Soviet Union's desire for German scientific expertise.[76] The first fifty German camp fitters arrived by air and the remainder later by sea. Karl Rieck was photographed at Island Bend camp with several of them wearing the waistcoat and trousers of the German carpenter's guild.[77]

Many Australian ex-servicemen, who found city life difficult after years in the field, came looking for something that resembled army life. Experience in the artillery led Bill Cameron straight to surveying.[78] Johnny Abbots Smith recalls a celebratory

Anzac Day dinner at Spencer Creek when soldiers who had fought on two sides of Tobruk laughed at the senselessness of war.[79] Aubrey Hosking, having got his first taste of engineering as a prisoner of the Japanese in Asia, studied civil engineering at the University of Western Australia and joined the SMA in lab investigation.[80] Sent for a year's training to the USBR hydro projects, he was among one hundred Australians trained there by 1961. US work practices rubbed off on the trainees and he observed that 'the Snowy was carried forward on a wave of enthusiasm, start to finish'. '[G]etting away from the public works mentality' was 'a breakthrough'.[81]

Anecdotal evidence suggests racialized graduation of labour. McHugh observes that different nationalities may have been attracted to specific tasks, based on previous skills or the timing of their arrival in relation to the scheme's progress.[82] Germans were skilled carpenters, mechanics and electricians. There were Dutch supervisors and inspectors. Italians, renowned for their stone masonry, built the tunnels and retaining walls, often arriving in the summer following winter in the Queensland cane fields.[83] Italian contractor Legnami Pasotti flew in 300 Brescian carpenters and joiners. Yugoslavs were recruited as miners or semi-skilled tradesmen; Czechs and other Eastern European nationalities tended towards hydrography, requiring long hours of skiing, although surveyors were drawn from many nationalities. Dangerous high-wire work fell to southern Italians and Spaniards, due to their smaller stature. Irishmen were typically plant operators and construction workers.[84] The contractors learned from experience not to concentrate nationalities, to make the most of existing skills and to be cautious of former high-ranking army officials who might abuse their authority.[85] Many trained professionals were relegated to manual labour, causing frustration and tension in the workforce.[86] Australians, McHugh notes, worked on dams and roads and as bulldozer drivers and were conspicuous in their absence underground. Once the Authority shifted its employment practice from day labour to contract labour in the early 1950s Australian inspectors were trained to supervise the various contractors on the scheme. 'Wife starvers' (men unwilling to pay spousal maintenance) in Sydney were often 'believed to have gone to the Snowy'.[87]

Casualties and fatalities are mentioned in many oral histories (this is discussed in greater detail in the Conclusion). Some 121 deaths were incurred during construction on steep terrain, navigating precarious roads in extreme weathers, rock falls during blasting in subterranean confined spaces or stringing high-voltage cables, as well as injuries from cold, noise, bad air or misuse of equipment, not to mention the workers' own unwillingness to conform to regulations – to put on their safety harnesses or seatbelts. There were many lacerations and broken bones, splinters and razor-sharp cuts through bones and tissue.[88] These deaths prompted the introduction of safety officers, equipment, instruction booklets and seatbelts, which previously had not been mandated in Australia. Although cited as less than the US average at the time, casualty numbers offered sobering evidence of what McHugh terms the human 'price of progress'.[89] Key among the issues that amplified the danger was competition between shift workers incentivized by bonuses.

The roughness of the all-men camp environments softened with the arrival of married women on the Snowy Scheme. Eva Grunnsund, whose father worked for Selmer Engineering, found the Norwegian-style self-built family home at Berridale old-fashioned, the location 'remote' and the amenities 'primitive'.[90] It was one of twelve weatherboard dwellings built for the Norwegian company. Northerners assimilated easily, unlike Southern Europeans, and enjoyed competitive skiing, introducing cross-country skiing to Australia. The arrival of married women associated with the international contractors and, later, workers' wives also diffused ethnocultural and class tensions because they had more time to socialize and went into town for shopping. Australians were also attracted to the scheme. The Authority's first architect employed by the Sydney office was a woman, Valerie Havyatt, who designed worker housing.[91] Georgina McQuade, the accommodation officer at Cabramurra, was named 'Duchess' because of her extravagant wardrobe.[92] The Cabramurra doctor Ina Berents spoke of the difficulties of reaching snowbound patients or injured men. By 1952, there were 108 women on SMA staff and around 200 wives.[93] Immigrant doctor Jonathan Baska mused that it was a:

> tremendous experience in relation to my professional field and in personal relationships and observation of people in not normal circumstances, emotions, excitement, loneliness, alcoholism – people's strengths and weaknesses. Women isolated, worried, the difficulty that there was little social life. All these left an impression that lasted a lifetime. And you learned something you don't forget about the field of humanity that things are possible if you have a will.[94]

Because Australian workers were a (dominant) minority and contractors were mainly foreigners, the Snowy immigrants did not fuse into the desired 'New Australian' identity, the government's recommendation for creating a harmonious postwar white society. Their resistance to the forms of acculturation demanded of nonanglophone immigrants was aided by the international networks and plural cultural characteristics that infused the physical and social infrastructure of the Snowy Scheme. This was most evident at Cooma.

THE COMPANY TOWN

Cooma (established in 1849), a sleepy country town 117 km south of the nation's capital Canberra and made up of tight-knit and generational grazier families was transformed by the SMA's arrival.[95] The Authority initially conducted its operations from Alexandria, in suburban Sydney, occupying the old church and army drill hall at Cooma as a temporary office and store until the new head office was built there in 1952.[96] The town evolved rapidly into the nexus of the dormitory and tented camp network. Cooma local Dee Simpson recollects the mighty Antars carrying giant turbines, and big cement trucks passing through Cooma to the Polo Flat industrial yards and the work sites.[97] The town was transformed into a hive of activity.

The influx of large numbers of foreigners, both overseas contractors and New Australians, placed tremendous pressure on the local way of life and racialized social divisions along new axes of language, culture and mistrust born out of wartime hostilities.[98] The locals frowned on intercultural relationships. They did not mix with foreigners. They were suspicious of 'townies'. Pejorative terms were freely used. Rod Bridge's war-veteran father was suspicious of anyone who did not speak British-English, in particular Germans, who were ubiquitous on the scheme.[99] The separation between Cooma South and North was marked.

Beyond this climate of mutual distrust was a new form of identification related to industries. The scheme's workers were part of a consolidated community – the Snowy People – answering to William Hudson and the SMA, and living, for the most part, in the company town and its constellation of camps. Divisions within the SMA community were graduated by a class structure based on 'wages' (daily wage workers) and 'staff' (on a monthly salary). Although divisions between Australians and so-called 'Wog' labourers persisted, the presence of international contractors provisionally deferred the racialization occurring elsewhere in Australian society. Intergroup cohesion during the early years of the scheme splintered into various national groupings as numbers increased in tandem with assisted-passage agreements and fulfilment of immigrant quotas.[100] Cooma was an international settlement, where the government's larger project of assimilating newcomers was held in abeyance in the interests of industrial efficiency.

SMA housing policies reinforced the class rather than the racial hierarchy. Cooma North with its well-laid out suburban streets and two-to-three-bedroom bungalows stepping down the incline were allocated to professionals, engineers and administrators who drew a monthly salary and attendant benefits. Cooma East across the railway line that connected the residential to the industrial factories at Polo Flat was dedicated to daily-wage-worker housing. Rows of small two-room, fibro cottages packed together like sardines resembled a caravan park. Bruce Bashford observed that if you misbehaved, you would be sentenced to a period in East Camp.[101]

The continental cultures of the majority of workers altered the tempo of Cooma. On the one hand, they boosted the region's economy, with the fortnightly injection of wages frequently spent on drinking or entertainment in Cooma and the smaller townships. New venues and new entertainments attracted custom from as far away as Canberra.[102] Locals whose highlights had been woolshed dances, country fairs and church found their town host to three hotels (pubs) and five nightclubs. On pay day, these twenty-four-hour establishments would have hundreds fighting to get in and orchestras were sometimes brought in from Sydney.[103] Pino Frezza recalls singing Italian songs while Eric Pauls played for the Maori Esquires at the Lido restaurant.[104] They introduced metropolitan musical trends: cha-cha and The Beatles. The explosion in entertainment expanded to illicit gambling activities, topless dancers and sex workers, to which the SMA responded with retrenchments, although certain contractors turned a blind eye. Six to eight Sydney women were brought up by procurers to

Cooma, periodically, in caravans, and premises were rented for their business in some contractors' camps. Their presence became apparent when a line of waiting men stood patiently outside. Drunken brawling, intergroup rivalries, petty theft, indeed all the vices of any township were augmented by the predominance of single men without family responsibilities. The vice squad would arrive once a month, to the misfortune of any who got caught.[105]

Possibly because of the clear designation and availability of sex services, the few women on the Snowy claimed they never feared molestation, although townspeople remained mistrustful of intercultural relationships. Some women noted the contrast between well-dressed and polite, continental Europeans and untidy and casual Australian men who came courting. While it is possible that certain Snowy workers were more sophisticated than Australian country folk, we cannot generalize their relative merits. Immigrants assigned to hard manual labour sometimes exaggerated their pasts to impress their host countrymen, while others were frustrated because their professional qualifications were not recognized. In this respect, the Snowy contractors proved more willing to find compatible assignments. And the Americans, often portrayed as ruthless taskmasters, employed workers on the basis of willingness and ability rather than qualifications. The greatest incentive was undoubtedly the pay – up to five or ten times what could be earned in Sydney.

As the humdrum nerve centre of the entire scheme, the company town, a place temporarily transformed by industry, was the humane counterpart of the totalitarian military environments described in Chapter 2. Like Earl Draper's housing for the TVA, its intention was to raise a particular grade of worker's standard of living, albeit not across colour lines unlike in the United States.[106] Among the rare exceptions are a few Lebanese immigrants including Abdullah Khoury, who worked on the scheme during the late 1950s.[107] Despite these racial caveats, Cooma witnessed a form of hitherto unprecedented internationalization in Australia. Moreover, the international contractors contributed to community services that benefited the townsfolk. Money raised at the 1958 Festival of the Snows and a contribution from the US Kaiser Corporation gave the town its Festival Swimming Pool.[108] The Australian Architon Construction Co. built local schools and shopping centres in the region. Sydney practice Fowell, Mansfield and Maclurcan built several SMA buildings. But quite apart from enhancing civic amenities, the scheme tested innovations in modern town planning.

The aforementioned new plans for Jindabyne (by R. Keith Harris) and Adaminaby and Khancoban (by Denis Winston) saw Sydney architectural practitioners experimenting on greenfield sites.[109] The SMA retained consulting architects (Fowell, Mansfield and Maclurcan) and appointed an aesthetics committee (Denis Winston, D.G. Maclurcan and engineer Ivor Pinkerton). SMA architects (including one woman and several draftspersons) designed the buildings and layouts built by independent contractors for the SMA.

While barrack, tent and hut accommodation prevailed in temporary satellite work camps, not least because they were pragmatic responses to a highly dispersed and phased construction programme, Cooma North, with curvaceous lines and cul-de-sacs, was modelled after postwar suburbs. Like Earl Draper's plan for Norris that amalgamated three naturalistic landscape traditions – the British, the American and Draper's own rural aesthetic[110] – its domestic plan and layout clearly superseded the utilitarian antecedents of company housing (see Figure 4.7). Detached homes built after SMA type plans tumbled down the inclines of the loosely configured street grid, each with its own front garden and back yard; an embodiment of the dream homes that had enticed immigrants to Australia. But, more importantly, they illustrated postwar Australian experimentation with precut and prefabricated construction technologies as a solution for growing housing needs.

A tour of Cooma North's residential streets offers new insights into the scheme's tangible heritage. Up and down streets with euphonious Indigenous Australian names, we can still identify the various SMA housing types from A to K (see Figure 4.8).[111] The transportable comes with hooks for lifting it into place. The most elaborate among them, the American A-Type, is elevated on a basement, like homes in the United States, and is clustered at the northern end of town. Housing contractors included Williams, Wallace, Vandyke, Carson, Fripp & Williams, the Italian firm Legnami Pasotti and the Dutch firm Civil and Civic.[112]

Several international contractors established their reputations on wartime ingenuity. The US Kaiser Engineering Company, which brought American staff to the scheme, had built Liberty ships, tankers and baby aircraft carriers at the US Portland and Richmond shipyards.[113] Wolff and Zimmer of Portland, Oregon, designed 105 houses at its Sue City camp.[114] Dutch engineer Gerardus Jozef (Dick) Dusseldorp[115] survived forced labour in Berlin, a Nazi camp in Krakow and famine in Utrecht to join Bredero's Bouwbedrijf, a Dutch building company, after the war. In collaboration with the Royal Dutch Harbour Co., Bredero formed Civil and Civic (later the Lendlease Corporation) in 1951, to erect 200 houses for the SMA in Cabramurra and Cooma East. Dusseldorp used his European connections to procure plumbing from England, roofing from Belgium and prefabricated building frames from Finland, and to bring over thirty-five Dutch tradesmen. The firm put down roots and later partnered with well-known architects Harry Seidler (interned in England and then Canada as an enemy alien during the war), Robin Boyd and others to produce distinctive Modernist project homes.[116]

The Italian firm Legnami Pasotti Società per Azioni was already renowned for its modular timber systems in Italy, developed during fascist rule, when modern technological innovations were promoted alongside Italian colonial experiments in East Africa. Pasotti exhibited a prototype prefabricated single-family home in Milan in 1945.[117] After the war, the firm introduced the *Garda* houses with interchangeable prefabricated components generating nineteen variations. By 1952, Pasotti was working in Australia, building 1,000 houses with the Queensland Housing Commission at Carina before moving to Cooma. The firm's Pasotti D-Type cottages had a distinctive chimney shape and exterior opening for removing ash.

Figure 4.7 Cooma North housing layout, 1952. Drawn for the author by Brian Duong, 2022, based on National Library of Australia, SMHEA map, G9871.N33, 1952, and Google Earth and other sources

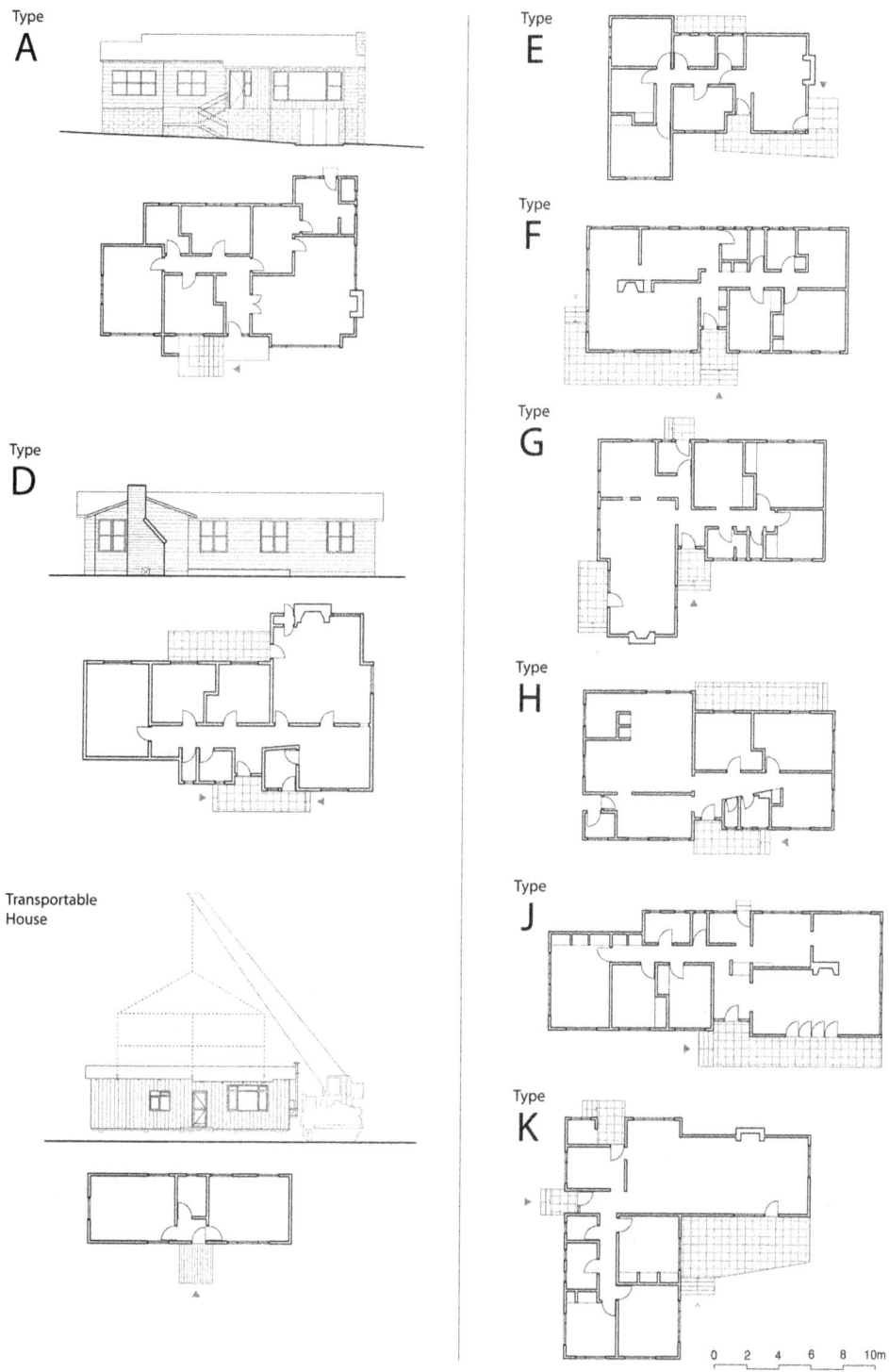

Figure 4.8 House plans for prefabricated dwellings in Cooma North. Drawn for the author by Dhanika Kumaheri, 2022. Based on Snowy Mountains Hydro-Electric Authority Building Manual, 1953. National Library of Australia, Nq 728.099447 B932.

Italians, like the Germans, were employed in large numbers: from the migrant camps, as individually sponsored immigrants and as staff of an international contractor flown in directly from Italy. Their country's early capitulation somewhat softened their public reception, although they too fell into the category of Southern Europeans most frequently identified as 'Wogs'. Their wartime presence as POW workers discussed in Chapter 2 may have also familiarized their presence in some NSW towns, although nowhere in the Monaro region. Pasotti brought 300 Italian joiners and carpenters to Cooma under engineer G. Ciotti, the majority of them young men in their early twenties.[118] In addition to 132 staff cottages, Pasotti constructed a 224-person hostel, a staff dining hall, but most importantly the Snowy head office complex, jointly constructed with Civil and Civic, with later additions by the Authority and Architon Construction Co. (see Figure 4.9).[119] The building is depicted in period photographs as a magnificent 51,000 square foot, three-storey timber-framed structure, deemed the largest in Australia. Pasotti engineers tested a prototypical building section at the company's factory in Brescia, and prefabricated timber components and materials were shipped to Australia.[120]

Although the multistorey SMA Head Office and other construction-related buildings were dismantled when the scheme was completed, the auxiliary community facili-

Figure 4.9 SMA Head Office, Cooma North (snow scene), 1954. Courtesy of the National Archives of Australia, 1954. A11016, 5588

ties like schools, churches, a swimming pool and former SMA housing remain in an altered form. Housing is particularly significant because of its ubiquity. Sold off and absorbed into the town's residential housing stock during the 1970s, they exemplify the Snowy Scheme's still-tangible domestic heritage. Whereas elsewhere in Australia, adaptation to an anglophone culture's house forms was instrumental in immigrant assimilation, these purpose-built Cooma North houses blending cultural preferences with utility are lasting testaments to postwar prefabrication technologies. When construction ended, and locals bought these properties, there was a reverse assimilation into immigrant-constructed and culturally inflected models of Snowy housing. Some SMA employees who remained in and were absorbed by the local community kept the memory of those exceptional decades alive. Others carried it with them to the metropolitan centres closest to the Snowy – Sydney, Melbourne and Canberra. The human story of the Snowy became diffused.

CONCLUSION

This chapter has located and elaborated on the contributions to Australia's feted Snowy Hydro Scheme of the majority nonanglophone workers who arrived in Australia after the Second World War – workers who were either compelled or chose to work on this major and risky infrastructure project. Their experiences are integral to a developmental ecology that superseded other epistemes of the Monaro region, erasing some and subsuming others while repackaging how the immigrant contribution is received. This chapter's main innovation has been to present the immigrant traces in the Monaro's transformations as a critical slice of the region's ecology rather than a minority pioneering narrative that echoes a progressive teleology.

In hindsight, the Snowy Scheme's celebratory discourses, including immigrant labour contributions, must be attenuated by a new awareness of Indigenous Australian dispossession and environmental costs, which are no longer negligible in present-day industrial projects. Immigrant workers employed for the scheme are unwittingly implicated in the dereliction of care towards the alpine landscape; their contribution to mid-twentieth-century nation building extends and amplifies damaging settler legacies. We could also argue that due to their circumstances and working conditions, labour migrants were absorbed into Australia's development ideologies and only later repositioned themselves as equivalent pioneers in nation building. For the most part, labour migrants took immense pride in their contributions, often commenting on their inadequate representation in official Snowy histories. Their relative anonymity and the sublimation of hardships and sacrifices in projections of the scheme's achievements are absences that revisionist histories have sought to fill. Because their work environments were temporary and because, like Giuseppe Roncari (see Chapter 2), they left the Monaro region following the end of their contracts, these endeavours were poorly acknowledged.

While the scheme was undergoing construction, for the reasons elaborated in this chapter, Cooma North was a separate international settlement distinct from any other in postwar Australia; linguistically and culturally partitioned from the town's settler colonial legacies and physically separated as SMA territory. If the TVA is celebrated for its New Deal social ideals of statist development and democratic planning, the SMA can be viewed as convening the many forces that opened up isolationist 'white' Australia, reintroducing a different kind of cultural complexity to the Monaro. This change is best captured in the celebratory images of the Festival of the Snows with its floats by the different contractors and its audience of workers from different nationalities (see Figure 4.10). Not a birthplace of multiculturalism, as later claimed for the region, but of internationalization, linking everyday cultural practices to their far-away geographies – scenarios where those international experiences and expressions were not censored. These relations were reinforced by the international contractors' presence and a town they created with shops, services, schools and other multilingual environments that familiarized foreign ways of inhabiting a parochial Australian community. However, there is no escaping the fact that the Snowy workers were white. No Asian contractors

Figure 4.10 Festival of the Snows – Cooma International Club float moves along a Cooma Street during the grand procession, 1958. Photo by Don Edwards, courtesy of the National Archives of Australia, A12111, 1/1958/17/9 [7422998]

or labourers were included in the workforce due to continuing restrictions on regional immigration until the dissolution of the White Australia Policy in 1973.

The Snowy's immigrant workers resisted acculturation. Their resistance was enabled by the nominal separation and the collective enterprise of the postwar industrial environments and workforce. The scheme's overdependence on immigrants stimulated worker tactics of self-preservation, assisted by the international character of the Cooma North community. But while the developmental ecology of the Snowy Scheme was robust and longlasting, the heterogeneity of its workforce was temporary and fragile, marking a period of transition before their dispersal home or through absorption into Anglo-Australian society.

ACKNOWLEDGEMENTS

Thanks to Patrick Swain for his tour of Cooma and for sharing domestic building plans, and to Laura Greco for information on Legnami Pasotti.

Anoma Pieris is Professor of Architecture at the Melbourne School of Design. Her most recent publications include the anthology *Architecture on the Borderline: Boundary Politics and Built Space* (2019) and *The Architecture of Confinement: Incarceration Camps of the Pacific War* (2022), co-authored with Lynne Horiuchi. She was also guest curator with Martino Stierli, Sean Anderson and Evangelos Kotsioris of the 2022 MoMA exhibition *The Project of Independence: Architectures of Decolonization in South Asia, 1947–1985*.

NOTES

1. Nehru, 'Temples of the New Age', 3.
2. Pieris, 'Subaltern-Diasporic Histories of Modernism'.
3. NAA: A1559, 1948/83, 'Nationality and Citizenship Act of 1948'.
4. 'History', Snowy Hydro.
5. Collis, *Snowy: The Making of Modern Australia*.
6. 'History', Snowy Hydro.
7. Milne, *Fitting and Wearing of Seat Belts in Australia*, 4.
8. 'Snowy Mountains Hydro', National Museum of Australia.
9. Ringer, *The Spirit of SMEC*.
10. 'Snowy 2.0'.
11. Ashton, 'The Birthplace of Australian Multiculturalism?', 384–85.
12. Siobhan McHugh, 'Life and Death on the Snowy', *Irish Times*, 16 October 1999. Retrieved 12 December 2023 from https://www.irishtimes.com/news/life-and-death-on-the-snowy-1.239667.
13. McHugh, Oral History Transcripts, Mitchelle Library, State Library of New South Wales (hereafter MLOH 287, McHugh).
14. Kobal, *Snowy; Men Who Built the Snowy*; McGoldrick, *Snowfraus*. See also Unger, *Voices from the Snowy* and many others.

15. Crenshaw, 'Demarginalizing the Intersection of Race and Sex'.
16. MLOH 287, McHugh, 3.40. Heinz Geromin.
17. Young, *The Aboriginal People of the Monaro*.
18. Pownall, *The Thirsty Land*, 22; Hancock, *Discovering Monaro*.
19. Peyton, *Unbuilt Environments*.
20. The Native Title Act 1993.
21. Gelder and Jacobs, 'Uncanny Australia', 179.
22. Horn and Begthaller, *The Anthropocene*.
23. Wheaton, Claire, and Simon Lauder, 'Mount Kosciuszko and the Push to Give Our Highest Peak an Indigenous Dual Name', *ABC South East NSW*, 15 June 2019. Retrieved 12 December 2023 from https://www.abc.net.au/news/2019-06-15/inside-the-push-to-dual-name-mount-kosciuszko/11207722. Note that this is under consultation.
24. Flood, *Moth Hunters*.
25. Young, *The Aboriginal People of the Monaro*, 193–95.
26. NLA: Norman B. Tindale, Map showing the distribution of the Aboriginal tribes of Australia. MAP G8961.E1. Adelaide Govt. Photolithographer, 1940.
27. Young, *The Aboriginal People of the Monaro*, 56, cites a 1949 letter on the migration from R. Forrester Payten to A.S. Le Souef, both members of the Acclimatization Society.
28. Young, *The Aboriginal People of the Monaro*, 194.
29. Troy and Barwick, 'Claiming the "Song of the Women of the Menero Tribe"'.
30. Blay, *On the Track*, 120–33.
31. Reed, *Aboriginal Place Names*.
32. Miller, *Snowy River Story*, 226.
33. Young, *The Aboriginal People of the Monaro*, 339.
34. Hancock, *Discovering Monaro*, 47.
35. Ibid., 91.
36. Seddon, *Searching for the Snowy*, xxii.
37. NLA: Patterson, Banjo. 1890. 'The Man from Snowy River', *The Bulletin* 11(53), 26 April 1890, 13. Retrieved 12 December 2023 from http://nla.gov.au/nla.obj-443549096.
38. Byrne, 'Schemes of Nation', 33 and 97.
39. Miller, *Snowy River Story*, 4–5.
40. McMahon and Petheram, 'Australian Dams and Reservoirs within a Global Setting'.
41. Hancock, *Discovering Monaro*, 164, quoting Dr W.R. Browne, 21 August 1952, David Memorial Lecture in the University of Sydney, *Australian Journal of Science*, Supplement, XV, 3, December 1952.
42. Hancock, *Discovering Monaro*, 165–67.
43. MLOH 287, McHugh, Hnenhe, Klaus. No tape.
44. Although recognized as citizens in 1948, Indigenous Australians did not receive voting rights until 1962.
45. Environmental Protection (Impact of Proposals) Act 1974; Currie, Black and Duffield, 'Sustainability Assessment of Two Australian Hydro Megaprojects', 256.
46. Restaurant, Adaminaby Dam, NSW, from Cross-Section no. 81, July 1959, Faculty of Architecture, Building and Planning, University of Melbourne, Folder 4, 1959, CSE00271, series 12. Retrieved 12 December 2023 from https://www.csec.esrc.unimelb.edu.au/CSES0012.htm.
47. Hancock, *Discovering Monaro*, 138.
48. MLOH 287, McHugh, 72B Eddie Doherty.
49. Ibid.
50. MLOH 287, McHugh, 14.36. Puddin [Noel] Potter.
51. Ibid., 67A Alice Kidman.

52. Stewart, 'Farewell to Jindabyne', 30.
53. Read, 'Remembered Dead Places', 36.
54. Ibid., 35–36.
55. Ibid., 36.
56. MLOH 287, McHugh, 2.38 Johnny Abbots Smith.
57. Gough, *The Major*, 18; 'Major Clews', Snowy Hydro. 'Balt' was often used pejoratively.
58. MLOH 287, McHugh, 35.69A Wally Wassermann.
59. Ibid.
60. Byrne, 'Schemes of Nation', 175.
61. NLA: 'US Firm Wins Snowy Job', *Newcastle Morning Herald and Miners' Advocate* (NSW: 1876–1954), 10 April 1954, 1. Retrieved 12 December 2023 from http://nla.gov.au/nla.news-article134904934; NLA: 'American Companies Get £ 25 m Contract for Snowy Mountains Power, Irrigation', *Weekly Times* (Melbourne, Vic: 1869–1954), 14 April 1954, 6. Retrieved 12 December 2023 from http://nla.gov.au/nla.news-article224912208.
62. 'The Snowy Waters: A Vast Engineering Enterprise'.
63. NAA: CP608/1 Bundle 1, Snowy Mountains Hydro-Electric Authority – Summary Showing Value of Commitments for Property, Stores and Materials, Contracts, Construction Plant and Equipment for Permanent Plant as at 1 February 1952.
64. Rodwell, *Homes on the Range*, 6.
65. Ibid., 4.
66. Ibid., 3.
67. Ibid., 2.
68. Jupp, *The Australian People*, 102–3.
69. Ibid., 99.
70. MLOH 287, McHugh, 5.0 Jonathan Baska.
71. Ibid., 3.40 Heinz Geromin; McHugh, *The Snowy: The People behind the Power*, 184.
72. Ibid., McHugh, 18.24 Dusca Miloradovic (Duke Milford).
73. Persian, *Beautiful Balts*, 94–95; Berger, *I Protest*, 38.
74. MLOH 287, McHugh, 22.18 Roy Robinson.
75. Collis, *Snowy: The Making of Modern Australia*, 107.
76. Ibid., 107–8; Department of Foreign Affairs and Trade (DFAT), '280 Cabinet Submission by Dedman and Calwell, Agendum 1266A'.
77. 99/101/2–4 Photograph (1 of 12), black and white, group of eleven men standing on veranda of single men's barracks at Island Bend, paper, photographer unknown, Victoria, Australia, 1951. Powerhouse collection. Gift of Mr Karl Rieck, 1999. Photographer unknown.
78. MLOH 287, McHugh, 32 Bill Cameron.
79. Ibid., 2.38 Johnny Abbots Smith.
80. Ibid., McHugh, 63A Aubrey Hosking.
81. Ibid.
82. McHugh, *The Snowy*, 39–40; MLOH 287, McHugh, 8.12 Allen Clarke.
83. MLOH 287, McHugh, 8.12 Allen Clarke.
84. McHugh, *The Snowy*, 40.
85. MLOH 287, McHugh, 8.12 Allen Clarke.
86. Collis, *Snowy: The Making of Modern Australia*, 201. Collis mentions a Polish criminologist at Island Bend and a Latvian doctor at Kenny's Knob, both employed as labourers, and an Estonian senior employment officer, Ksenia Nasielski, who spoke five languages, but did not qualify for a house with a veranda.
87. MLOH 287, McHugh, 58A Bev Wales.
88. MLOH 287, McHugh, 5.0 Jonathan Baska.

89. McHugh, *The Snowy*, 'Chapter Thirteen: The Price of Progress', 229–51.
90. MLOH 287, McHugh, 46 Eva Grunnsund.
91. McHugh, *The Snowy*, 42; Hanna, 'Absence and Presence', 167.
92. MLOH 287, McHugh, 23.28. The Duchess.
93. 'Feminoddities', *SMA Magazine*, 1, 4.
94. MLOH 287, McHugh, 5.0 Jonathan Baska.
95. Ibid., 8.12 Allen Clarke.
96. Ibid., McHugh, 2. 38 Johnny Abbots Smith.
97. Ibid., McHugh, 8.13 Dee Simpson.
98. Ibid., McHugh, 15.31 Rod Bridges.
99. Ibid.
100. Ibid., McHugh, 2.38 Johnny Abbots Smith.
101. Ibid., McHugh, 14.36 Bruce Bashford.
102. Ibid., McHugh, 15.31 Rod Bridges.
103. Ibid., McHugh, Pino Frezza (no tape).
104. Ibid., McHugh, 15.2 Eric Pauls.
105. Ibid., McHugh, 58A Bev Wales.
106. African Americans were employed at 12% of their ratio in the general population. See Huxley, *TVA*, 56.
107. 'From Lebanon to Sydney via the Snowy Mountains', *ABC Radio*, 24 September 2014.
108. NLA: 'Kaiser Donates £5,000 towards Cooma Pool', *Canberra Times*, 3 September 1958, 8. Retrieved 12 December 2023 from http://nla.gov.au/nla.news-article103119735; Back to Cooma, Reunion Easter 2016, Souvenir Booklet, 23 March 2016.
109. NAA: A5628 C1962/244 Preparation and Publication of Article on Snowy Mountains Scheme by Royal Australian Institute of Architects in Their "Journal" Architecture in Australia, Peter Keys and Tony Moore, 'Case Study: Development of the Snowy Mountains'.
110. Crawford, *Building the Working Man's Paradise*, 195–96.
111. Thanks to architect Patrick Swain for a Cooma town tour in 2021.
112. NLA: Cooma Headquarters Township 1952, Snowy Mountains Hydro-Electric Authority, MAP G8971.N33, 1952.
113. NLA: Buttrose, Charles. 'Henry Kaiser Comes to the Snowy', *Daily Telegraph*, 17 April 1954. Retrieved 12 December 2023 from http://nla.gov.au/nla.news-article248870417.
114. 'Portland Architects: Wolff and Zimmer', in *Twenty Northwest Architects*, Exhibition, University of Oregon, Museum of Art, 1962, 33. NAA: A5628 C1962/244, Peter Keys and Tony Moore, 'Preparation and Publication of Article on Snowy Mountains Scheme by Royal Australian Institute of Architects in Their "Journal" Architecture in Australia, Peter Keys and Tony Moore, 'Case Study: Development of the Snowy Mountain Scheme', 12.
115. Larry Schlesinger, 'Lendlease's Dick Dusseldorp: From Nazi Labour Camp to Listed Giant', *Financial Review*, 3 September 2018. Retrieved 12 December 2023 from https://www.afr.com/property/residential/lendleases-dick-dusseldorp-from-nazi-labour-camp-to-listed-giant-20180702-h1252g.
116. 'Concrete Nation', *Plus.One, Architecture and Design*. See also Clark, *Finding a Common Interest*; O'Callaghan, *Designer Suburbs*, 85–88; Wilton, *Internment*.
117. Greco, 'Modern Dwellings after World War II'.
118. NAA: SP1122/1, 1951/24/344, [box 24]. Air France flight arriving Brisbane 13 July 1951 proceeding to Sydney per TAA flight 13 July 1951 (aircraft flight file – includes [the] passenger list of Italian Nationals selected by Legnami Pasotti Ltd for employment Snowy Mountains Hydro-Electric Commission).

119. Rodwell, *Homes on the Range*, 15; 'Modern Townships for Snowy Mountains Workers', *Sydney Morning Herald*, 12 January 1954, 11.
120. NLA: 'Italians to Build for C'Wealth', *Barrier Miner* (Broken Hill, NSW: 1888–1954), 21 December 1950, 6. Retrieved 12 December 2023 from https://trove.nla.gov.au/newspaper/article/49580006.

BIBLIOGRAPHY

Archival Records

McHugh, Siobhan. Oral History Transcripts, Mitchell Library, State Library of New South Wales (MLOH 287, McHugh).
National Archives of Australia (NAA)
National Library of Australia (NLA)

Publications

Ashton, Paul. '"The Birthplace of Australian Multiculturalism?" Retrospective Commemoration, Participatory Memorialisation and Official Heritage', *International Journal of Heritage Studies* 15(5) (2009), 381–98.

Berger, Sandor. *I Protest: A Complete Collection of Letters & Articles which the Author Penned and Sent to the Press Etc., on Various Current Controversial Subjects in the City of Sydney, NSW, Australia, in 7 Years between 1954 and 1961 under the Name: 'Sandor Berger'* [by] Alexander Mountain. Sydney: Sandor Berger, 1962.

Blay, John. *On the Track: Searching out the Bundian Way*. Sydney: NewSouth Books, 2015.

Byrne, Graeme. 'Schemes of Nation: A Planning History of the Snowy Mountains Scheme'. Ph.D. dissertation. Sydney: University of Sydney, 2000.

Clark, Lindie. *Finding a Common Interest: The Story of Dick Dusseldorp and Lend Lease*. Cambridge: Cambridge University Press, 2002.

Collis, Brad. *Snowy: The Making of Modern Australia*. Sydney: Hodder & Stoughton, 1990.

'Concrete Nation', *Plus.One. Architecture and Design*, 24 July 2020. Retrieved 12 December 2023 from https://www.architectureanddesign.com.au/features/comment/concrete-nation.

Crawford, Margaret. *Building the Working Man's Paradise: The Design of American Company Towns*. New York: Verso, 1995.

Crenshaw, Kimberle. 'Demarginalizing the Intersection of Race and Sex: A Black Feminist Critique of Antidiscrimination Doctrine, Feminist Theory and Antiracist Policies', *University of Chicago Legal Forum* 1 (1989), 139–67.

Currie, Glen, John Black and Colin Duffield. 'Sustainability Assessment of Two Australian Hydro Megaprojects', *Journal of Megainfrastructure and Sustainable Development* 1(3) (2019), 255–80.

Department of Foreign Affairs and Trade (DFAT). '280 Cabinet Submission by Dedman and Calwell, Agendum 1266A, Employment of German Scientist and Technical Personnel in Civil Industry in Australia, 6 December 1946'. Retrieved 25 February 2023 from https://www.dfat.gov.au/about-us/publications/historical-documents/Pages/volume-10/280-cabinet-submission-by-dedman-and-calwell.

Environmental Protection (Impact of Proposals) Act 1974. 2023. Australasian Legalities Institute website. Retrieved 19 February 2023 from http://www.austlii.edu.au/au/legis/cth/consol_act.

'Feminoddities'. *SMA [Snowy Mountains Authority] Magazine*, 3 June 1952.

Flood, Josephine. *Moth Hunters of the Australian Capital Territory*. Downer, ACT: J.M. Flood, 1996.

Gelder, Ken, and Jane. M. Jacobs. 'Uncanny Australia', *Ecumene* 2(2) (1995), 171–83.

Gough, Noel. R. *The Major: Lt. Col. Hugh Powell Gough Clews*. Melbourne: Noel. R. Gough, 2004.

Greco, Laura. 'Modern Dwellings after World War II: An Italian Experience of Wooden Prefabrication by Legnami Pasotti', in Joao Mascarenhas-Mateus and Paula Pires (eds), *History of Construction Cultures*, vol. 2 (London: CRC Press, 2021), pp. 185–190.

Hanna, Bronwyn. 'Absence and Presence: A Historiography of Early Women Architects in New South Wales'. Ph.D. dissertation. Sydney: Faculty of Built Environment, University of New South Wales, 1999.

Hancock, W. Keith. *Discovering Monaro: A Study of Man's Impact on His Environment*. Cambridge: Cambridge University Press, 1972.

'History' 2020. Snowy Hydro website. Retrieved 19 February 2020 from https://www.snowyhydro.com.au/about/history/.

Horn, Eva, and Hannes Begthaller. *The Anthropocene: Key Issues for the Humanities*. Abingdon: Routledge, 2019.

Huxley, Julian. *TVA: Adventure in Planning*. Cheam: Architectural Press, 1943.

Jupp, James (ed.). *The Australian People*. Sydney: Angus & Robertson, 1988.

Kobal, Ivan. *Men Who Built the Snowy*. Cammeray, N.S.W.: Saturday Centre Books, 1982.

——. *The Snowy: Cradle of a New Australia*. Rydelmere, NSW: I. Kobal, 1999.

'Major Clews' 2022. Snowy Hydro website. Retrieved 19 February 2022 from https://www.snowyhydro.com.au/wp-content/uploads/2022/04/Our-proud-history_Major-Clews_fact-sheet-3_APR-22.pdf.

McGoldrick. Kirsty. *Snowfraus: The Women of the Snowy Mountain Scheme*. East Roseville, NSW: Kangaroo Press, 1998.

McHugh, Siobhan. *The Snowy: The People behind the Power*. Melbourne: William Heinemann, 1989.

McMahon, Thomas, and Cuan Petheram. 'Australian Dams and Reservoirs within a Global Setting', *Australasian Journal of Water Resources* 24(1) (2020), 12–35.

Miller, Claire. *Snowy River Story*. Sydney: ABC Books for the Australian Broadcasting Corporation, 2005.

Milne, Peter. W. *Fitting and Wearing of Seat Belts in Australia: The History of a Successful Countermeasure*. Canberra: Australian Government Publishing Service, 1985.

Native Title Act [The] 1993. 2019. Federal Register of Legislation website. Retrieved 19 February 2019 from https://www.legislation.gov.au/Details/C2017C00178.

Nehru, Jawaharlal. 'Temples of the New Age', *Jawaharlal Nehru's Speeches*, vol. 3, *March 1953–August 1957*. New Delhi: Government of India, 1960.

O'Callaghan, Judith. *Designer Suburbs: Architects and Affordable Homes in Australia*. Sydney: NewSouth Publishing, 2012.

Persian, Jayne. *Beautiful Balts: From Displaced Persons to New Australians*. Sydney: NewSouth Books, 2017.

Peyton, Jonathan. *Unbuilt Environments: Tracing Postwar Development in Northwest British Columbia*. Vancouver: University of British Columbia Press, 2017.

Pieris, Anoma. 'Subaltern-Diasporic Histories of Modernism', in Vikramaditya Prakash, Maristella Casciato and Daniel. E. Coslett (eds), *Rethinking Global Modernism*. (New York: Routledge, 2021), pp. 251–271.

'Portland Architects: Wolff and Zimmer', in *Twenty Northwest Architects*, Exhibition. Eugene, OR: University of Oregon, Museum of Art, 1962.

Pownall, Eve. *The Thirsty Land: Harnessing Australia's Water Resources*. London: Methuen, 1967.

Read, Peter. 'Remembered Dead Places', *Public Historian* 18(2) (1996), 25–40.

Reed, Alexander. W. *Aboriginal Place Names*. Chatswood, NSW: William Heinemann, 1967.

Ringer, Ronald. E. *The Spirit of SMEC: Snowy Mountains Engineering Corporation*. Sydney, NSW: SMEC Holdings Limited, 2012.

Rodwell, Frank. *Homes on the Range*. Cooma: F. Rodwell, 1999.

'Snowy 2.0'. WeBuild website. Retrieved 16 January 2024 from https://www.webuild-group.com.au/en/what-we-do/projects/snowy20/.

Seddon, George. *Searching for the Snowy: An Environmental History*. St Leonards: Allen & Unwin, 1994.

'Snowy Mountains Hydro'. National Museum of Australia website. Retrieved 19 February 2020 from https://www.nma.gov.au/defining-moments/resources/snowy-mountains-hydro.

'The Snowy Waters: A Vast Engineering Enterprise', *The Round Table* 49(193) (1958), 37–42.

Stewart, Douglas. 'Farewell to Jindabyne'. *Overland* 30 (1964), 30–33.

Troy, Jakeline, and Linda Barwick. 'Claiming the "Song of the Women of the Menero Tribe"', *Musicology Australia* 43(2) (2020), 85–107.

Unger, Margaret. *Voices from the Snowy*. Kensington, NSW: NSWU Press 1989.

Wilton, Janis. (ed.). *Internment: The Diaries of Harry Seidler, May 1940–October 1941*. Sydney: Allen & Unwin, 1986.

Young, Michael. *The Aboriginal People of the Monaro*. Sydney: NSW National Parks and Wildlife Service, 2000.

Chapter 5

Woomera
A Landscape of Displacement and Renewal

Andrew Saniga

INTRODUCTION

During a 2002 fieldtrip to Woomera, the base village for Australia's rocket and missile-testing facility in the South Australian desert, I visited the Woomera History Museum and was struck by a display of hundreds of shortwave radio 'QSL' cards mounted on the wall. They are an internationally recognized letterform of confirmation that an amateur shortwave radio station's transmission has been received.[1] Rich in colour with a variety of graphics, photographs and texts, hundreds of period postcards received from different nations formed a striking frieze upon the wall. Prominent within the display was a QSL card received from Kaunas in Soviet-occupied Lithuania. Then I saw a card displaying a hammer and sickle, on another the place name 'Krasnoyarsk Siberia', and then a representation of Lenin in profile. This handful of QSLs transgressing the Iron Curtain seemingly posed a rhetorical question of Woomera's participation in the Cold War, a unique role underpinned by values of national and Commonwealth security (see Figure 5.1). As one narrator aptly put it: 'Woomera owes its origins to fear. Fear of annihilation.'[2] Yet the QSL cards seemed to challenge the officialdom and 'fear'. Back in Melbourne and upon searching in Peter Morton's historical tome *Fire across the Desert* (1989), I would soon discover that European immigrants were among the labourers sent to build Woomera in the post-Second World War years.[3] Yet there was nothing in the History Museum that told their story.

In this chapter I give voice to the 400 or so European immigrants sent to help build the joint UK–Australian Long Range Weapons Establishment (LRWE). They were employed as labourers by the Commonwealth Department of Works and Housing (CDWH) in the late 1940s.[4] I explore their cultural makeup and their experiences via archival research, interviews and site documentation. In terms of environmental,

Figure 5.1 Two QSL cards linking Woomera with the Soviet Union via amateur shortwave radio, 2002. Courtesy of Roger Henwood, Australian Government Department of Defence Corporate Services & Infrastructure Group, Woomera, used with permission

social, political and workplace contexts, the European immigrant workers' experiences had much in common with their non-European workmates who were greater in number. Yet their story is also uniquely defined by endurance and recovery, characteristics accentuated through the difficulties they faced as immigrants seeking new lives after the Second World War.

EMIGRATING TO A REMOTE LANDSCAPE

The LRWE began on 1 April 1947, driven by the pursuit of international security and defence. The United Kingdom sought to develop capacity for its own nuclear deterrent after the United States sought to terminate international atomic collaboration with the allies it had formed during the Second World War.[5] The Australian government deemed partnering with the United Kingdom in weapons testing, including nuclear weapons, was a commitment that the nation needed to make. The United Kingdom would supply technology and Australia would test it within the country's vast open spaces that were relatively free of settlement or inhabitants. The LRWE[6] was an enormous investment that produced a missile and rocket testing range within the Woomera Prohibited Area (WPA). The WPA occupied a significant portion of the northwest part of its host state of South Australia. Its remarkable infrastructure extended beyond military and space research hardware and included a modern township with state-of-the-art planning and design. Marooned 500 kilometres northwest of Adelaide and deep within South Australia's arid region, Woomera Village provided a uniquely salubrious suburban lifestyle in the unlikely setting of a treeless, stony (gibber) and waterless plateau. Remote, microclimatically extreme and stretched in terms of all manner of resources, a 173 kilometre-long pipeline, completed in mid-1949, carried potable Murray River water to Woomera: an artificial lifeline to an establishment built to endure its environment.

Defying the odds also led to audacious acts with the potential to impact on Indigenous (First Nations) people, mainly in terms of Woomera Village and the Range's launch and testing facilities occupying the land of the Kokatha people. Weapons testing resulted in the firing of missiles and rockets hundreds of kilometres to the northwest, necessitating the clearing of people from the potential fall zones of spent rockets. The job of the Native Patrol Officers, W.B. MacDougall (appointed 4 November 1947) and later Robert Macaulay (circa 1956), was to scout large areas of territory – eventually including extensive areas of Western Australia and the Talgarno Prohibited Area – to warn any Indigenous people of impending dangers and to move them away from the firing trajectories.[7] MacDougall would soon voice firm opposition to the radical forms of displacement that the LRWE began to perpetrate, and broad objection came from sectors of society in far-off cities.[8] However, the value of building Woomera for the sake of national security prevailed even if the various defence programmes waxed and waned, sometimes with breathtaking demises.[9]

Woomera finds parallels in other postwar infrastructure projects that were of an extraordinary scale, like the Snowy Mountains Hydro Scheme (see Chapter 4), where the value of industrial capitalism also triumphed over the certainty of environmental impact. As landscape historian and theorist George Seddon noted of the Snowy scheme: 'Without those values, it is virtually incomprehensible; with them it seems necessary, almost inevitable.'[10] Woomera's existence, in principle and realization, extended national military mythologies. Yet it also came with important distinctions that pitched military innovation against remote, Indigenous landscape and a pioneering spirit. As one resident of Woomera from 1962–77 recounted:

> Everywhere the incredible age of this country seemed to dominate one's consciousness, and the children grew up in two contrasting worlds – the modern world of rocketry inside the village and the ancient land outside.[11]

What is striking about Woomera is its incredible reach across all manner of dimensions – political, social, economic, environmental, cultural and more. This is accentuated by Woomera's remoteness, physically and conceptually – one minute endorsed and purposeful, the next aimless and lost. These extremes often surprise and astound, as is evident in the voices of thousands of past residents who, in recounting via online platforms – especially Facebook – reminisce and lament the halcyon days gone by, the remarkable and unique lifestyles of a population that peaked at around 6,800 people yet today is under 200. Woomera 'actually' owes much to the military imperative and financial backing legitimized by Australia's partnership with the United Kingdom, which played directly into the hands of postwar optimism. Australia was progressing, shaking off years of war and economic depression. As Kathleen Tymukas, an ex-Woomerite who was also married to Kostas, one of the Lithuanian immigrants involved in this account, put it: 'Australia was advancing, we were "becoming something" . . . it was a complete change.'[12]

Herein lies the first of many contradictions that define Woomera – a combination of the industry of war and a progressive and optimistic spirit – an unusual 'theatre' of the Cold War. Into this theatre landed a founding cohort of around 406 European immigrant workers who were sent to work for the CDWH in Woomera between April 1948 and mid-1949. They had fled the atrocities and hardships of the Second World War, only to be tasked with helping to build a huge outdoor weapons testing laboratory. As survivors on a path towards a new life free from communism and Russian oppression, the unlikely vacuum of the Australian desert became the kernel of their new life amid uneasy echoes of the previous one.

Woomera's earliest immigrant workers were of diverse cultures and personal trajectories and were predominantly displaced persons (DPs), but also included eleven Polish ex-servicemen who had emigrated to Australia as part of the Polish requisitioned resettlement scheme.[13] Collectively, as immigrants from Central and Eastern Europe, they helped create an international 'feel' that was extended by immigrants from the United Kingdom and elsewhere. In June 1949, the CDWH secured 99 Maltese tradesmen selected as part of a joint Australian and Maltese government agreement granting assisted passages as 'British Subjects'.[14] However, immigrants like those from the United Kingdom and Malta were essentially different from the group who I will consistently refer to as the 'European immigrants': the DPs' emigration was assisted by the International Refugee Organization (IRO) resettlement scheme and had come about because of their refusal to return to their homelands where they would have been required to live under Stalinist communist rule. They were obliged to fulfil a two-year work commitment to the Australian government as payment for their passage to Australia. The European immigrants' political leanings that had formed in direct response to political upheaval related to the Second World War had the tendency to place them in stigmatized workplace and social relations.

LABOUR AND 'LIFESTYLE'

Labour shortages were acute when the CDWH began establishing Woomera in 1947. In early 1948 the Director General of the CDWH conveyed to the Department of Immigration that the LRWE project was at a critical stage and deserved the highest priority, but had struggled due to difficulties in sourcing labour.[15] By August 1948, European immigrant workers accounted for under 10% of a 900-strong workforce (see Figure 5.2a).[16] Most had come to Australia aboard the *General MB Stewart* (February 1948) and the *General WM Black* (April 1948), with a smaller number having arrived in late 1947 aboard the first ship transporting DPs to Australia, the *General Stuart Heintzelman* (see Figure 5.2b). The logistics of sourcing the earliest immigrant workers was complicated by the fact that many had already been deployed to work assignments elsewhere in South Australia to places like Berri, Renmark and Iron Knob.[17] A considerable escalation in the deployment of European immigrant labourers occurred between October 1948 and June 1949 when nearly 300 more were sent, a significant number of these having arrived on the *Protea* (December 1948). Around forty-five immigrant labourers of the founding 406 did not last long: they were either 'adversely recorded' or dismissed within days or weeks of arriving in Woomera.[18]

The ongoing immigrant labour workforce as of mid-1949 numbered 361, most of whom were men aged in their twenties and thirties, with only a small proportion in their forties or teens (see Figure 5.2c). Two women, who will be introduced later on, were part of the founding cohort. Polish, Lithuanians and Latvians were the most well represented, with fewer from Estonia, Yugoslavia, Czechoslovakia and Ukraine (see Figure 5.2d). Most of the European immigrants were spread across one of the four main construction worker camps (see Figure 5.2e). Their proportion of the total approximated workforce of 2,280 engaged in the construction of the LRWE as of June 1949 was approximately 16%, but they made up a significantly higher proportion of 30% of the CDWH's workforce.[19] Many of the civilian construction workers were returned servicemen who had picked up trades through the Commonwealth Reconstruction Training Scheme.[20] The European immigrants in many cases worked alongside them, but were formally designated as day labourers. The Director General of the CDWH had been told of their potential capabilities, but was cautioned over the unlikelihood of there being any skilled workers acceptable to workers' unions.[21] At this time, the immigrant workers received wages of £7.10.0, which included special living allowance minus 16/6 per week for 'keep', which was considered reasonable by those in charge, given that few out-of-pocket expenses were expected to be incurred.[22]

The special living allowance certainly was for 'special living' – another contradiction in terms. As Estonian Guido Laikve put it: 'We became bushmen, in the desert... it had nothing to do with reality. It was really, totally different living.'[23] In mid-1948, the only evidence of settlement was the fledgling construction workers' camps where one's world of work was separated by the finest of lines. Occasionally, drovers passed through hailing from the neighbouring large pastoral stations – The Pines, Arcoona, Roxby Downs, Andamooka and Purple Downs – often with Indigenous stockmen, who at this time were essentially working for their keep.[24] A photograph from the collection of Bronislaw Blazejowski (of the Polish Air Force resettlement scheme) of fellow immigrant workers approaching two stockmen on horseback, one of whom may have been an Indigenous stockman, is particularly salient – the displaced Europeans meet the displaced Indigenous (see Figure 5.3 – above). Blazejowski (1923–1991) was based at Koolymilka on the banks of Lake Koolymilka, which was some 50 kilometres northwest of the main site of Woomera Village. Koolymilka grew into an independent settlement close to where trials were being conducted on the Range. Like all the construction workers' camps, it was essentially militaristic and unforgiving (see Figure 5.3 – below). In the context of extremes, there were small acts of reprieve:

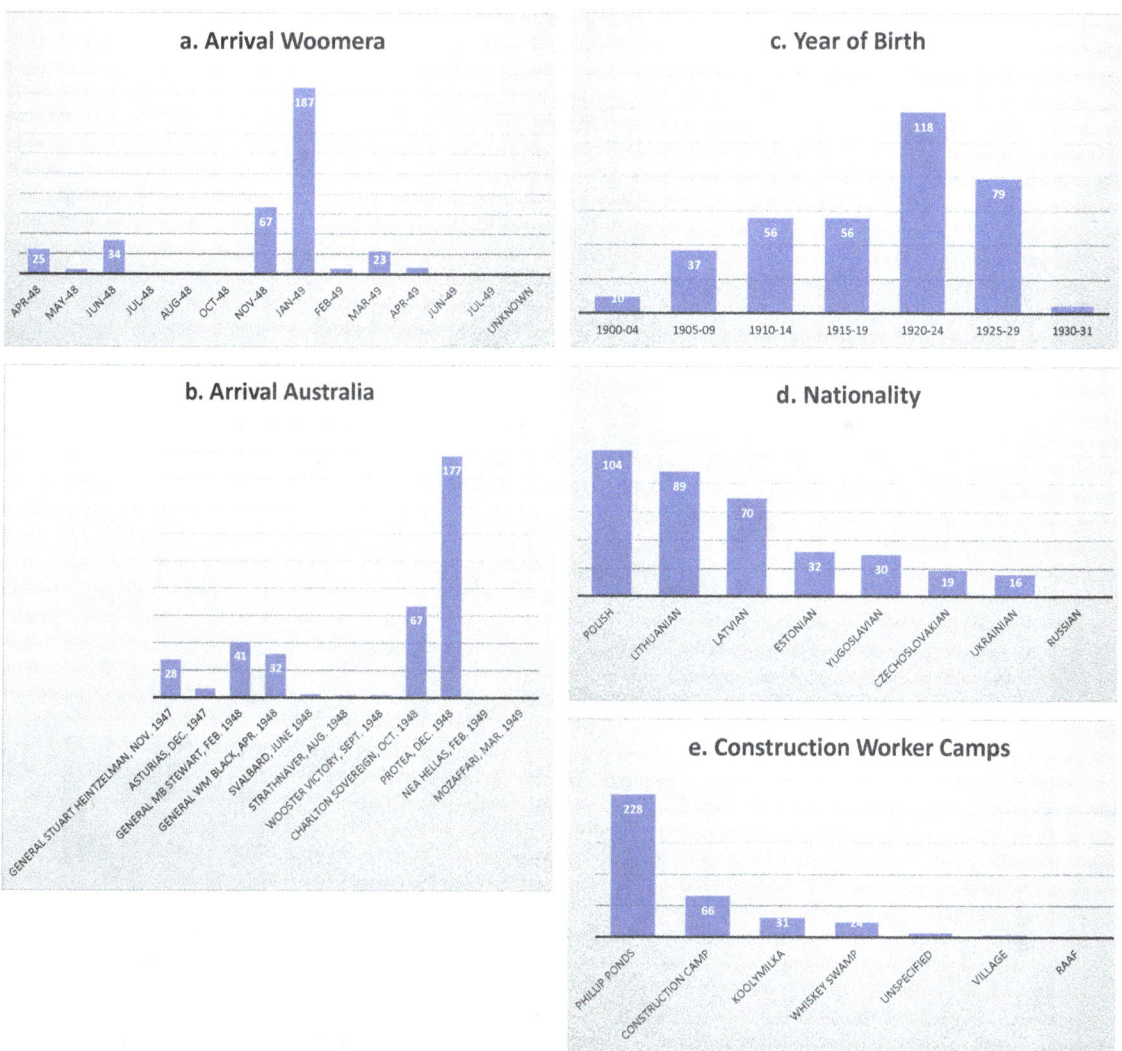

Figure 5.2 Details of European immigrant personnel recorded at Woomera from mid-1948 to mid-1949. Compiled and developed primarily on basis of: NAA: D1918 S1493–5-2, Commonwealth of Australia Attorney General's Department File of Papers, 'Nominal Roll of D.P's at Woomera', 1949. Charts generated by Andrew Saniga, 2023

This had an appearance for all the world like a concentration camp, and it housed the largely migrant group of souls who carried out the labouring tasks in the Range area. It is doubtful if any Australian migrants ever served their Antipodean apprenticeship under more adverse circumstances. It appeared to be darker shades of the Foreign Legion. A visit to their weekly cinema night, organized by the humanity of the area padre, was always a night to remember.[25]

The construction workers' camp at Phillip Ponds initially took most of the immigrants, but in time it was superseded by the camp at Woomera West. Both coexisted

Figure 5.3 CDWH workers meet stockmen from a pastoral station neighbouring Woomera on the lands of the Kokatha People, mid-1948 (above). Canvas tents at Lake Koolymilka construction workers' camp at night, date unknown (below). Photographs by Bronislaw Blazejowski. Courtesy of Louise Blazejowska

with the Royal Australian Air Force base camp adjacent to the aerodrome. Like Koolymilka, 'Captain Bennett's Camp' at Whiskey Swamp was around 50 kilometres away from Woomera and close to where the bomb ballistics range was established in 1948. Most of the immigrant workers were flown in to Woomera aboard military planes in the summer months, descending into scorching heat, beating sun, dirt and incessant flies. Piercing winds blew day and night – twelve blankets in winter and still one was cold – everything was infused with dust, even the food.[26] Living in canvas tents along with a few corrugated iron buildings on concrete slabs that housed messes, ablution blocks, kitchens and the like, all spread across bare, open sites meant little respite from the elements. Commencing two years of work in these conditions exacerbated a sense of displacement, especially for those who had spouses and children in far-off places. For those who appreciated the arid environment, often the novelty did not take long to wear off. The content of Lithuanian Jonas Mockunas' diary entries transition from lengthy observations of the desert's unusualness and interest – plants, animals, patterns and cycles – to a lonely weariness:

> These are long and boring days of solitude. Five months have already passed here. I have planned to stay for another 3 months. The desert has become very tiresome, but what is there to do? You have to bear it.[27]

Still, a sense of empowerment was evident in Woomera's European immigrants despite feelings of disillusionment, frustration and lack of self-determination that some have branded common in immigrants' experiences.[28] A growing confidence may have been enabled via military-style resourcefulness mixed with pioneering individuals. The surveyor Len Beadell who charted roads and the centreline of Woomera's vast Range used innovative techniques in tough conditions. His Land Rover was painted in a manner of a large-scale stadia mark, functioning as a surveyor's staff when viewed over long distances. Lithuanian émigré Česlovas Dubinskas would later develop his own ways of overcoming surveying challenges, using explosives to create distant waypoints in order to establish sightlines that would otherwise not have been possible due to the vegetation.

The European immigrants were exposed to colourful characters and work environments that quickly hurled them into Australian idioms around a sense of mateship.[29] Mockunas was located at Bennett's Camp, to which other immigrant workers would travel so that they could visit compatriots while watching films for free.[30] Innovations at Bennett's extended to the construction of Australian Rules Football ovals with goalposts of the same sectional steel as the poles used for the communications lines that workers were simultaneously constructing.[31] Recreation and work came in other forms. As fate would have it, these early years were also unusually wet, with heavy rains filling large salt pans at Lake Richardson (near to Phillip Ponds camp) and Lake Koolymilka. This periodic feature of the arid landscape further combined with a spirit of resourcefulness, enabling swimming and even boating. Photographs in Blazejowski's collection depict him with Polish friend Jerzy Borejko (1922–1993) and fellow immigrant 'bush carpenters' constructing pontoons, moorings, ramps and other water-based recreational accoutrement on Lake Koolymilka (see Figure 5.4 – above). Blazejowski and Borejko established families in Sydney and remained friends for life, such was the long-term influence of the camaraderie that was generated while living in the LRWE's camps.

Innovation also came from the top-down. The Workmens' Framed Tent, designed by CDWH Chief Executive Engineer J.J.W. Gray around mid-1949, was unique to Woomera and was intended to make living conditions more bearable. The design was functional and pragmatic in the extreme: a gable-roofed structure of timber, corrugated iron and metal flywire gauze with pre-existing canvas tent suspended from its beams and pitched upon a timber platform that sat directly on the ground (see Figure 5.4 – below). The Minister for Supply and Development, Senator John Armstrong, praised the result: 'The workers were excellently housed in wooden huts with tents inside, which would give warmth in winter and coolness in summer ... The dwellers themselves had devised ingenious ways of making the interiors as comfortable and attractive as possible.'[32] Whether the design alleviated temperatures within is disputable, but the Workmens' Framed Tent certainly gave occupants a break from the nuisance of flies and possibly helped shield inhabitants from the dust.

Ultimately, discomfort could be more acute as a product of the apparent randomness of the system of allocating tentmates. For some, the result proved formative in terms of lasting friendships that were forged out of hardship. For others, the process was not always mutually amenable, with language often at the heart of the problem. Latvian Alberts Veigurs' diary entry conveys this well: 'I ended up with an Australian Brit. It would have been good if he had been a bit more talkative, but here Australians all are unusual, it's hard to understand them, what they think about us.'[33] Other immigrants like Mockunas were less forgiving and viewed their time in Australia as provisional: 'I hope to work here for 6 or 7 months and return to the city having saved £300. Then, if there is still no opportunity to return home to Europe, to build some sort of home.'[34]

Social and cultural assimilation and life in immigration camps elsewhere in Australia have been discussed in preceding chapters in this book as well as in recent publications.[35] Language difficulties and the push for programmes for learning the English language after hours were not unusual to Woomera.[36] Alcohol and gambling played a significant role in creating an oppressive environment.[37] Transgressive forms of socialization could bridge cultural divides, fracture relationships or result in personal demise, as occurred to Guido Laikve's tentmate who consistently lost all his earnings to illegal gambling, despite Laikve's best efforts to provide salvation.[38] A headline in the *Smith's Weekly* entitled 'Big-Time Gambling on S.A. Rocket Range' cited an Estonian immigrant's claims that 'games were loaded against players, especially displaced persons who understood neither the games nor the language'.[39] In the face of such adversities, immigrants' recollections convey a sense of camaraderie and mutual support among them that was previously forged within the communities within DP camps in Europe and even aboard ships en route to Australia. Cultures mixed, but there were also actions that kept cultural 'silos' firmly in place. A group of well-organized Lithuanians in

Figure 5.4 Immigrant 'bush carpenters' at Lake Koolymilka with Bronislaw Blazejowski (left) and Jerzy Borejko (with saw strapped to waist), circa 1948 (above). Photograph in Bronislaw Blazejowski collection. Courtesy of Louise Blazejowska. Clothes hung out to dry in front of the Workmens' Framed Tent, which was a type of prefabricated hut designed by Department of Works and Housing Chief Engineer J.J.W. Gray, circa 1949 (below). Photograph by Lance Kain courtesy of Avriel Kain's personal collection

Woomera submitted articles to the Australian Lithuanian national community newspaper *Mūsų Pastogė* (*Our Shelter*), agitating for the maintenance of ethnicity and for humanitarian support for compatriots left in Germany.[40] This core group also happened to have elevated themselves in the CDWH's hierarchy of work, from blue-collar labouring tasks to white-collar professional and subprofessional desk jobs within the Drawing Office. While issues of language, assimilation and the simultaneous maintenance of cultural identity simmered more broadly across Australia, Woomera revealed nuanced tensions around 'New Australians' within workplaces and professions that were further problematized by strains of the Cold War and left and right-leaning politics.

IMMIGRANT WORKERS FOR THE DEPARTMENT OF WORKS AND HOUSING

The LRWE and all its infrastructure and facilities required enormous amounts of labour and capital investment. The CDWH designed it to include schools, churches, medical services, houses and apartment blocks, shopping and civic centres, recreational grounds and facilities including a swimming pool.[41] An arboretum and research station, conceived and designed by arboriculturalist and landscape architect R.H. Patterson, completed innovative work.[42] It provided the town's generous civic plantings of trees and shrubs in parks, private gardens and streetscapes. A green belt partially encircled the village (see Figure 5.5). Introduced plantings were kept alive by a grey water irrigation system fed by Woomera's sewerage treatment plant that Latvian civil engineer Arvids Blūmentāls more than likely helped design and implement in 1948–49. Patterson's experimental research established appropriate plant species for Woomera's conditions. Among the local and international species tested was Russian Rye. In this regard, the extent to which Patterson may have been influenced by Woomera's immigrant workers can only be speculated upon. However, in discovering Patterson writing in more depth about related cultural practices, it would appear that he may have learnt from the knowledge bases and practices of Woomera's significantly Baltic immigrant workforce when he wrote: 'This grain is used for the making of black bread in the Baltic countries, and after the harvesting of the grain, the remainder is cut and stored as a winter feed for cattle.'[43]

Patterson's links to European immigrants are implicit in his writing, but there are also instances of rapport between Australians and European immigrants that are more explicit. Those leading the CDWH's building programme were well-seasoned military-trained people who as well as running a structured and organized unit also commanded respect in unique and spirited ways. Between 1947 and 1951, the CDWH was led by Project Officer A.D. Bouch working alongside Brigadier E.M. Neylan, who was Range Superintendent and leader of the military workforce from September 1948 to May 1951. Bouch had experience of developing military infrastructure during the Second World War[44] and was a Squadron Leader within an RAAF airfield construc-

Figure 5.5 Woomera nearly fifteen years in the making. The experimental arboretum is in the foreground, much of Woomera's early facilities and housing is in the middle ground, and in the distant background the treeless gibber plain of the pre-existing arid landscape, date unknown. Courtesy of Roger Henwood, Australian Government Department of Defence Corporate Services & Infrastructure Group, Woomera

tion unit[45] sent to the Mindoro island of Leyte as part of the war effort in the Philippines.[46] By 1946, Bouch was formally an engineer with the Department of Works and after consulting on a range of projects in regional New South Wales (NSW), he was assigned to Woomera.[47] Neylan and Bouch were known as highly approachable and charismatic in many levels of the Woomera social and military hierarchy, including its emerging civilian population. The popular view was that Bouch was admired by his men.[48] He extended his benevolence to some of the immigrant workforce, for example, in formally recognizing Latvian civil engineer Aleksandrs Dančauskis, who risked his life attending a fire that had threatened to destroy the CDWH's drawing office.[49] Immigrants who were suited to a culture of military service and could rise to the challenge of tough conditions in a male and military-dominant environment were enabled in a workplace led by Bouch, particularly if they had experience in building infrastructure and public works.

Latvians Sergejs Bergtals (born 1912) and his brother Nicolajs (1914–74) are a case in point. They arrived in Australia on 28 November 1947 aboard the *USAT General*

Heintzelman. In Latvia, Sergejs was a captain and master mariner and Nicolajs was an architect who had experience as works supervisor with the Latvian Department of Works (1934–38) and then with the drawing office (1939–43). In Bremen, after the war, they had jointly supervised a 200-strong Latvian gang in the reconstruction of shipping docks from 1946 to 1947.[50] Arriving in Woomera in May 1948, Sergejs ended up in a supervisory role, a 'ganger' on aerodrome construction, with at least ten displaced persons (DPs) under his command.[51] Nicolajs arrived in July 1948 and was immediately deployed to the CDWH's Drawing Office, probably at Sergejs' recommendation, and was also afforded ganger status, although working as an architectural draftsman.[52] Ultimately, the Bergtals' transition to a life in Australia was not smooth, partly because of alcohol but also due to minor dealings with the law.[53] This is despite their skills and the opportunities afforded to them by Bouch. Other European immigrants, namely Dubinskas and Lithuanian compatriot Jonas Meškauskas, referred to the supportive and constructive Bouch as their 'patron':

> Almost all technical staff were dismissed, even one engineer, a former Japanese war prisoner, but Jonas and I stayed on. This engineer was very angry, but the director explained to him that he left only people who could work on-site and in the drawing room, even though the authorities had ordered the migrants to be dismissed first.[54]

The full extent to which European immigrants benefited from the value that Bouch may have bestowed upon them is not known. What is clear from stories such as those of the Bergtals brothers is that individuals' successes and failures often came with a good dose of the cavalier. In this highly distinctive social, cultural and political context, Woomera's immigrant workers began to confront their new lives in complex ways.

POLITICAL IDENTITY AND SECURITY

Ethnicity and politics were in turn connected with international relations, the Cold War and the perceived threat of communism. Australia as a nation was coming to terms with its emerging value and role in an international arms race and defence research.[55] Across Australia, spotfires of resistance and objections aimed at the LRWE came from diverse fields and usually from afar in Australia's capital cities.[56] Cold War politics had a significant impact and sat uneasily with public and unionist perceptions, particularly those linked with communism and communist states. When interviewed regarding his displacement to Australia, Guido Laikve was unequivocal in terms of wartime experiences and subsequently life at the dawn of the Cold War, stating:

> Our focus of hate was Soviet Union and communism . . . Since we went through the whole thing from the beginning there was always something military happening, some bombs, some fire, some whatever happening, no food and no place to sleep and things like that. So, we were quite prepared to take a lot of punishment or quite of lot of changes. In fact, what we had in Woomera was a great advantage over what we had during the war. There

is food on the table all the time and a bed you can sleep on and being able to do all kinds of things and participate.⁵⁷

Debate in Woomera concerning politics, unionism, communism and the building industry's role in construction of the LRWE began to emerge in March 1947, well before European immigrant workers had arrived on site. The Adelaide United Trades and Labour Council and the Building Trades' Federation both agitated for better conditions, workers' rights and, to varying extents, objected to defence activities on a number of grounds, including the heightening of Australia's vulnerability as a target by foreign forces, along with the impact on the region's Indigenous population.⁵⁸ Under the conservative government of Robert Menzies, the labour unions struggled for influence and were invariably caught up in stirrings relating to communism, Russia, the arms race, defence and Cold War rhetoric. The arrival of immigrant workers from mid-1948 fuelled tensions owing to their tendencies to be politically conservative and with a hatred of communist ideology and practices.⁵⁹ Jealousies had erupted between Australian workers and the European immigrants over handouts they received, along with suspicions that they were 'quislings and fascists', 'pro-Nazi Balts', 'unpredictable' and temperamental with inclinations to disrupt the stability of the work camps and workplaces.⁶⁰ Such tensions were common in the capital cities and surfaced in veiled ways within the popular media.⁶¹ In Woomera, tensions were heightened because it was a most active site of industry of the Cold War. An article in the *Tribune*, the Communist Party of Australia's newspaper, further railed against the Balts for being anti-communist:

> Balt migrants who lately fought for Hitler running around with cameras, fights between the arrogant Balts and Australian workmen, poor working conditions, gambling rackets and non-unionism on the field are some of the facts previously disclosed in the current union dispute with Rocket Range authorities.⁶²

Woomera's European immigrant workers were aware of international politics and the need to publicize the global situation and the impact of the Cold War. In July 1950, a protest was organized in Woomera in support of the suffering of Lithuanian people remaining in Soviet-occupied Lithuania. Participants listened to a lecture delivered by Algis Kružas and twenty-four individuals signed a protest letter asking the Australian Prime Minister to support the Lithuanian Liberation Action.⁶³ In March 1953, an article entitled 'Communists in Woomera' published in *Mūsų Pastogė* reported on an event that had seen the local workforce cast 107 votes for the registration of a communist candidate at Woomera's polling station. The anonymous Lithuanian authors claimed that this had caused 'a great deal of noise across Australia' and articulately outlined issues that are in line with latter-day historians' assessments:

> The results of the vote showed that there are, however, communists in Woomera who can be dangerous to Australia's security interests by living and working in a special area of secret testing. That fact was also vividly commented on by the British and US press. It

was even stated that such facts do not allow the British and US governments to cooperate properly on some sensitive military issues with the Australian government, as it is unable to form the conditions appropriate for its security. There had been sharp controversy about this in the Australian parliament. As usual, the relevant Australian authorities have stated that, despite that fact, Australian security matters and secret protection measures are at the right level.[64]

The US Embargo of 1948–49 saw relations between Australia and the United States deeply strained along security lines. The US's distrust of Australia was in part linked to suspicions regarding the Australian government's attitude towards communism, a situation that was improved when conservative Prime Minister Robert Menzies came to power in 1949. In addition, the United States did not trust Australia's ability to secure defence technology secrets as cases of espionage had tarnished the nation's record. The founding of the Australian Security Intelligence Organisation (ASIO) on 16 March 1949 was in response to this and the organization immediately attempted to establish systems and processes to quash security threats, furthering the role that the Commonwealth Investigation Service had been providing.[65] At this time, practically all immigrants at Woomera were from Soviet-occupied countries, with only one Russian-born immigrant worker, Anton Scharkejewic, who changed his name to 'Ivan Lipin' in July 1955. The culture of security that emerged at Woomera and in Woomera-related government departments played directly into the psyche of the European immigrant workers that had been shaped by wartime experiences. Kostas Tymukas had a deep respect for the *Official Secrets Act* and was very reticent to discuss with his family his work with the CDWH at Woomera and at a related testing base of Maralinga. His resolve in confidentiality was based on the convergence of life experiences. Displacement from his Soviet-occupied homeland, as well as fear of communism and oppression, resulted in a strong interest in the history of war and the Soviet Union, including current affairs favouring more 'right-wing international relations'.[66]

At a national level within defence industries and forces, extra precautions were required to control perceived risks when employing European immigrants.[67] At Woomera, security restrictions for the entire workforce took the form of guarded checkpoints and Woomera-specific passport controls monitored by the LRWE's Security Office and its personnel. The use of cameras was heavily restricted and partially explains a paucity of visual records from the period. A culture of fear emerged that was previously unfamiliar to many in the Australian nonmilitary workforce, but less so for the immigrants from Europe. They had faced years of restrictions, interrogation, covert operations and overt oppression. Woomera's fledgling Security Office proceeded with uncertainty concerning roles and procedures for screening, monitoring and protocols that invoked bureaucratic red tape in handling anything that involved European immigrant workers. Dubinskas recalled:

> Once a theatre group of Woomera performed a comedy. Among other jokes, the actors spoke like this: 'Who's the stupidest in Woomera?' Answer: 'Security Chief.' That was

true. One time, two security guards came to the drawing room and started interrogating a Latvian engineer, because a book with ancient symbols of Baltic tribes had been found. The Nazis had stolen this sign for their own affairs (Hakenkreutz). It was hard to convince them that it was an old Latvian (Baltic) symbol. Disappointed, the security guards went out.[68]

The nominal roll of European immigrant workers that was produced between April and June 1949 by Security Officer G. Phillips of the LRWE included comments indicative of the Security Office's assessments and the Commonwealth Investigation Service's charter: identifying those who had corresponded with the Soviet Union and directing their removal from Woomera; identifying those with notable war service records; and intercepting mail from potentially suspect sources, such as correspondence with bookshops that may have been involved in transmitting communist literature.[69] The monitoring verged on the petty and ludicrous: 'Speaks good English, writes it very descriptively, spent 3 weeks Xmas leave with Pastor Traeger at Whyalla. Has corresponded with Traeger's daughter.'[70] Reverend F.H. Traeger of the Lutheran Manse, Whyalla, had Germanic heritage and was also concerned about European immigrants' spiritual needs, extolling their worthiness as both future Australian citizens and religiously devout individuals.[71] Monitoring was also inconsistent: two European immigrant women were not included in the Security Office's head count.

Against the backdrop of spurious security checks and suspicions by the authorities, European immigrants also faced victimization, bullying and racism that were a result of stigmatizing their identities. Dubinskas recounted a case where a nonspecified Ganger supervising immigrants constructing a new rail line from Pimba, Woomera's nearest settlement 5 kilometres to the south, threatened to deport European immigrants or to hand them over to the Russians. One Lithuanian whose victimization was so severe was reported to have become suicidal.[72] In response, Dubinskas, who had secured a place in the CDWH's Drawing Office, shepherded him away from his appointed labouring job and instead to work as a chainman (see Figure 5.6).

Security officers became involved at all levels and were often at the heart of inane transactional procedures and correspondence. European immigrants working within the CDWH's Drawing Offices in both Woomera and Adelaide were exposed to segregation rules and were continually monitored.[73] European immigrant workers had limited access to the Main Office and the secure areas and storage units.[74] Systems for establishing degrees of sensitivity of CDWH information emerged when a local security officer in Woomera established that European immigrants working as surveyors and supervisors had access to 'secret plans'.[75] Security restrictions impacted on workforce shortages, exacerbated by strains in Australia's labour market at that time. To avoid losing valued employees, Project Officer Bouch and colleague A.J. Stevenson needed to navigate protocols vigorously and were careful to oblige and cooperate with all the security officers' demands by providing information regarding the procurement and responsibilities of European immigrant workers.[76] The way forward was cumbersome. For example, so that immigrant engineers, surveyors and drafts-

Figure 5.6 Workers constructing the Pimba to Woomera rail line endured exposure to heat, wind and dust, while undertaking backbreaking manual labour under gangers who were capable of bullying and victimization, 1949. Courtesy of the National Archives of Australia NAA D874 NB47

men could continue their work on engineering of roadways and rail line, kerbs and channels, drainage, sewerage pipelines and the like, Bouch wrestled with 'de-grading committees' that oversaw the security clearance of documents. A telegram (quoted verbatim below) was highly indicative of the complexities:

> Security refuse allow New Australian surveyors and draftsmen have access plan SA1653/C of Tech Area Services Layout although no legend attached [stop] Causing complete stoppage [deleted text] survey and drafting work Tech Area sewerage [stop] This means new Australians useless for Tech Area survey or drafting work [stop] Please take action degrade plan SA1653/C immediately [stop] Letter following.[77]

Letters also indicate that, in the context of security threats, skilled immigrant workers were expendable upon the procurement of Australian workers qualified to take their place.[78] In one trail of deliberations, it was proposed that women could be a possible option for replacing immigrants' roles in completing menial tasks, 'for which ordinary Australian citizens simply will not offer at the present time'.[79] As European immigrant workers completed their two-year work obligation in Woomera, some stayed on as tradesmen or independent contractors, often carting quarried stone. Other European immigrants, like the builder M. Matulevičius, came to Woomera after fulfilling their two-year work obligations elsewhere, their knowledge of profitable business opportunities in Woomera stemming from connections within Adelaide's Lithuanian community. Matulevičius completed many of Woomera's early buildings, including the cinema.[80] Regardless of the circumstances, European immigrants' engagement was complicated whenever attempts were made to offer them work within the Restricted Area.[81] For the CDWH, this led to further red tape. Project Officer Stevenson, who like Bouch was known to be supportive of immigrants in the Design Office, had to articulate suitable locations for immigrant workers, concluding these to be 'Workshops, Hostels and Arboretum Sections' and other locations outside of the Range or any Technical Areas.[82] Ultimately, these deliberations were part of a larger challenge facing the Australian population, namely that of accepting unfamiliar cultures into their established systems of employment and professions.

PROFESSIONAL RESPECT, FUTURES UNEARTHED

Across Australia as a whole, the initial contribution that European immigrant workers could make was deemed by the Australian government to be as unskilled workers with private employers or government departments and allocated in a relatively unsystematic manner.[83] Egon Kunz and others have explained how the broad attribution of the status of 'labourer' had acute psychological impacts, resulting in feelings of resentment, bewilderment, degradation, affront, dismay and insecurity.[84] Professionals with tertiary education were downgraded, while the unskilled or those with partially complete educations could find themselves in trades or other technical occupations.[85] Skilled or professional immigrant workers were often left powerless and subjected to professional jealousies, British bias, and degrees of ignorance from Commonwealth or state authorities, professional organizations, private employers and universities.[86] The path towards a profession often came at a high price in terms of the strain of studying while working full time and often supporting family members.[87] Sheer hard work and determination drove immigrants like Bronislaw Blazejowski who after arriving in Australia in December 1947 first traversed numerous labouring assignments: Tasmania's Hydro-Electric Commission, the LRWE in Koolymilka and lastly the Snowy Mountains Hydro Commission. He and his mother then settled in Sydney in March 1950 whereupon he commenced a medical degree which he completed in 1956. All this was achieved in under a decade. In fact, immigrants' successful work trajectories could be dramatically varied: rising up through factories or other unskilled labour; jostling for cadetships and semi-funded training opportunities; and seizing work or business opportunities, whether self-instigated or serendipitous.

The situation in Woomera in many ways reflected national trends but it was also distinctive because of the nature of the operation and the people involved. The CDWH faced difficulties in satisfying its workforce in terms of engineers, architects, surveyors and draftsmen within Woomera's Drawing Office. The demands were high due to the sheer scale of the operation in siting and engineering roads, railways and aerodromes along with the footprint of the entire village of Woomera and its crucial network of sewerage and drainage infrastructure. By December 1948, a select few immigrants had begun 'performing higher grade duties' while officially being engaged and paid as day labourers, a situation of inequity that Bouch and others in the CDWH were keen to address by way of negotiating employment rates and status and other awards issues.[88] Consignment lists identified in advance any European immigrant worker who had potential. For example, Kostas Tymukas was recorded as 'Labourer (Useful civ[il] engineering)'[89] and compatriot Jonas Meškauskas as: 'Maybe suitable for supply lines but more suitable for survey work.'[90] In such cases these skilled workers were still sent as labourers, but 'on the understanding that they will be re-classified as suggested on each form if satisfactory [to Woomera's Project Officer]'.[91] Engineers were well represented among the initial transports, which supports the claim that engineers were part of the overrepresented Latvian intelligentsia of postwar Latvian refugees.[92] The CDWH's Drawing Office immigrant workers were skewed towards Latvians and Lithuanians with smaller numbers of Poles and Estonians.

Chainmen were assistants to surveyors. They helped with measuring distances, held the surveyor's staff, drove pegs into the ground or generally assisted by clearing vegetation and the like.[93] Such tasks did not require formal training, but it seemed prudent to assign the role of chainman to any immigrant workers with even an inkling of what was entailed in surveying or engineering. Three of the earliest chainmen in mid-1948 all had traces of experience: Jerzy Gabriel Szymming (Polish) was a trained land surveyor; Juozas Backaitis (Lithuanian) a photographer, factory worker and tracer (of drawings); and Vilis Taube (Latvian), whose severely interrupted vocational development due to the war included student of economics (University of Latvia), clerk in printing office (in Germany), electrician (in Czechoslovakia), draftsman redrawing title plans (for Polish Army) and student of civil engineering (Hamburg DP University).[94] Taube was able to 'graduate' out of the field and into a desk job in the CDWH's Drawing Office. In mid-1949, the CDWH had fifteen chainmen who were European immigrants.[95] A number of others followed.

Estonian Guido Laikve (born 1931) established a lifelong career in the architecture profession via initial footholds he secured within the CDWH in Woomera. Guido was seventeen years old when he and his brother Erich (aged twenty) arrived in Woomera in January 1949.[96] Erich was given electrical work because of his previous training, but the younger Guido was deployed to tough labouring jobs until a serious workplace accident (in which he nearly lost his eyesight) resulted in him being given easier duties in the camps and messes, including entertainment (he was an accomplished saxophonist). In May 1950 Guido took up work as a chainman while also commencing studies in surveying and engineering by correspondence with the Sydney Office of the British Institute of Engineering Technology (Australasia). Laikve became a junior engineering land surveyor with the CDWH at Woomera (see Figure 5.7 – below). After moving to Adelaide in 1951, Laikve secured a position in the survey and town planning section of the South Australian Housing Trust (SAHT) where Latvian civil engineer Aleksandrs Dančauskis from Woomera already held a commanding position. Ultimately, it was employment within the SAHT that provided a catalyst for Laikve to pursue professional training in architecture, resulting in a rich and illustrious career, first in Adelaide then from 1970 in Canada, where he was still residing in 2024.

Bouch's support of transitioning European immigrants into staff appointments was an attempt to afford recognition of their professional or technical standing during a phase when their obligation to the Australian government was as unskilled labourers. His early attempts were not successful because of the conditions of their immigration, along with security procedures which ruled out European immigrants from anything other than subordinate and highly restricted roles. This would not dissuade the CDWH from making repeated attempts at promoting immigrants to staff positions, as eventually occurred in March 1950 for Arvids Blūmentāls (upgraded to Civil Engineer Grade II), Aleksandrs Dančauskis (upgraded to Civil Engineer Grade II), Kostas Tymukas (upgraded to Civil Engineer Grade II) and Vilis Taube (upgraded to Engineer Surveyor Grade I).[97] The tenor of Bouch's recommendation for Taube's 1948 promotion (albeit unsuccessful at that time) gives a sense of the importance of surmounting procedural logistics in return for securing the skills of European immigrants:

> Mr. Taube is giving excellent service as an engineering Surveyor. On arrival at Woomera he was attached to the Dept. of Air Surveyors as a chainman, but was quickly placed in charge of a survey party. Since the departure of the Dept. of Air Surveyors some two months ago, Mr Taube has been responsible for the setting out of airstrip, drainage, taxiways, railway, technical area bldgs. Etc. he is giving excellent service and is well thought of by Supervising Surveyor Ballam. Age 34, good appearance, single and speaks fair English. Recommended for appointment as Engineering Surveyor.[98]

Arvids Blūmentāls (1912–67) was born in Riga, Latvia, and graduated in civil engineering at the University of Latvia in 1944. His curriculum vitae suggests that he was well accustomed to public works departments, having worked first for the Government Railroad Department (circa 1938–39), Chief Designer for three years for the Department of Works, Riga, during German occupation (1941–44), and Chief Structural Engineer for the Department of Wooden Construction.[99] Just prior to being 'deported' to Germany in August 1944, Blūmentāls designed a sewerage mains and treatment plant for a town with a population of 50,000 people. After arriving in Australia aboard the *General WM Black*, he was sent in June 1948 to work at Woomera. Within two months of his arrival, the CDWH organized for his wife, Millija Erna Blūmentāls (1915–2014), to be brought to Woomera to work as a waitress, an indication of his value to the CDWH.[100] There was only one other woman known to have been sent to Woomera

Figure 5.7 The Phillip Ponds construction workers' camp where Guido Laikve was based with bare, dusty and stone-laiden gibber plain in foreground, circa 1949–50 (above). Courtesy of the Tymukas Family. A rare photograph of a survey team in Woomera with Guido Laikve believed to be on the far right holding a surveyor's staff, circa 1950 (below). Courtesy of Andrew Domaševičius-Žilinskas

in the period from mid-1948 to mid-1949: Viltis-Lodze Petruškevičienė, who arrived within months of her husband Jonas Petruškevičius, although more would follow.[101] Millija and Viltis-Lodze would have lived within the fortified women's compound that Laikve recalled existed at the Phillip Ponds construction workers' camp (see Figure 5.7 – above). After the failed attempt to promote Arvids Blūmentāls to a staff position in December 1948, he remained a ganger until the repeat attempt in March 1950, this time to Civil Engineer Grade II, at which stage Bouch heralded Blūmentāls as 'one of the mainstays of the construction section'.[102]

By August 1950, there were approximately ten New Australians working in the Drawing Office in Woomera West, many of whom had come through the ranks under the supervision of Blūmentāls.[103] Alongside him was Latvian Civil Engineer Aleksandrs Dančauskis (1908–97), who arrived in Woomera in January 1949 and within a short period of time became Manager of the Engineering and Planning Office in Woomera.[104] Dančauskis had graduated in civil engineering from the University of Latvia in 1943, a year earlier than Blūmentāls. At the end of 1950, while still working in Woomera, he was accepted as an Associate of the Institution of Engineers, Australia, with his formal membership being processed when he transferred to the CDWH's Adelaide offices in early 1951, reputedly making him one of the earliest of the Baltic engineers to have his qualifications recognized in Australia. Kunz noted that the Institution was distinctive as body that 'from the outset followed a different policy, used different methods, and exhibited a strikingly different attitude to foreign engineers from that of the generally unsympathetic Australian professionals in [other professions]'.[105]

Woomera's immigrant engineers were afforded work experience that was out of reach of European immigrants elsewhere in Australia. During Blūmentāls' time in Woomera, the sewerage treatment plant was constructed. Given his credentials and Bouch's praise of his engineering services Blūmentāls probably helped bring to fruition the plant's innovative production of grey water for irrigating Woomera's civic landscapes. In August 1951, Blūmentāls took up a position of Engineer Grade 2 with the CDWH in Papua New Guinea (PNG) as designer of sewerage treatment and drainage works. Between 1963 and 1965, he took on Acting Sewerage Engineer appointments in PNG, while Millija worked as an 'accounting machinist'. Arvids and Millija returned to South Australia in November 1966, possibly due to health reasons, as Arvids died less than a year later at the age of fifty-three. They had spent nearly twenty years actively engaged in Commonwealth public service, yet because many of these years were spent in PNG, currently they are considered a mystery by some in Adelaide's Latvian community.[106] It is unclear how Millija lived her life after Arvids' death, although she died in Adelaide relatively recently in 2014.

Alongside the individual successes of Blūmentāls and Dančauskis, a group of Lithuanians also made an enduring mark on the CDWH, both in its Woomera and Adelaide offices. From arrival in Australia to the binding comradeship forged in Woomera's construction workers' camps and workplaces alike, their story of establishment in Australia is marked by deep social and cultural connections that live on in their descendants today.

Lithuanian Kostas Tymukas' migration to Australia meant leaving the family farmhouse in the village of Kašeliškiai, a separation that became one of his greatest challenges throughout his life. The Lithuanian community in Australia fulfilled a vital connection with his cultural roots. Tymukas (1920–1982) came to Australia with a Diploma in Civil Engineering, hard-earned under difficult circumstances and unconventional means due to variable periods of living under political occupation, first by the Soviet Union, then Germany and then by Soviet troops in 1944. Upon fleeing to Germany, he took up work as a civil engineer in Graz (Austria), then as a mathematics teacher in a DP camp. Photographs aboard the *Charlton Sovereign* show Tymukas among young and adventurous albeit also undernourished-looking youths, including Algimantas Žilinskas (1924–1996) and Jonas Meškauskas (1909–1989).

Žilinskas' early years were marked by an international upbringing, first in Šakiai, Lithuania, and then in Argentina. His mother's death when he was about five years old caused upheaval in the family. His father, Kazys, placed him in the care of his grandparents at Kvetkai until their eventual reunion four years later in Buenos Aires. There he lived with his father and stepmother until 1938. The family returned to Lithuania just months prior to the outbreak of the Second World War when Lithuania's forced occupation led him to participate with his father in resistance activities. After a period on the run from the Gestapo, and three years in DP camps in Germany, Žilinskas acquired multiple skills by resourcefully gaining tertiary technical studies in Lithuania and in Germany at the Technische Hochschule Karlsruhe, resulting in him being classified as a 'draughtsman's apprentice' upon emigration. When he came to Australia, he was a worldly twenty-four year old who spoke numerous languages and had survived many wartime challenges, including serious military oppression. He would have viewed life in Woomera's supposedly high-security environment, and the government's fear of espionage, with a degree of jaded acceptance.

When Česlovas Dubinskas (1906–1993) arrived in Woomera on 11 January 1949, he was assigned to a large military tent where Tymukas, Žilinskas and Meškauskas also resided (see Figure 5.8). This proved formative, not only in terms of lasting friendships but also because all of Dubinskas' tentmates had secured positions in the CDWH Drawing Office – Tymukas in engineering, Žilinskas in drafting and Meškauskas as an engineering surveyor. Dubinskas and Meškauskas were roughly fifteen years older than Tymukas and Žilinskas, and all had grown up in rural or regional settings in Lithuania. When Dubinskas fled Russian occupation in October 1944, he left his wife and two children behind, losing contact with them until the mid-1970s, when his wife, Stefanija, eventually came to Australia. Kathleen Tymukas described Dubinskas as a deeply thoughtful and spiritual person who was continuously troubled by the trauma of war, separation and displacement. As Dubinskas put it, his spirituality was 're-flected in my beloved family, and especially my spiritual suffering'.[107]

Meškauskas' story is less clear. As a Lithuanian by nationality but born in Tiltgali, Latvia, little could be uncovered regarding his formative years in Europe or his emigration to Australia. He was social and charismatic, at ease in Woomera's messes and bars as well as accommodating and popular in large social settings. His work placement documentation stated his suitability for survey work and that he had training in civil engineering, water supply and irrigation construction.[108] Dubinskas explained

Figure 5.8 Jonas Meškauskas, Algimantas Žilinskas, Jerzy Szymming and Kostas Tymukas outside canvas tent accommodation at Phillip Ponds construction worker's camp, circa 1949–50 (left); Kostas Tymukas (to the right) and Algimantas Žilinskas (middle) at work in the Drawing Office of the Commonwealth Department of Works and Housing, Woomera, circa 1949 (right). Courtesy of Andrew Domaševičius-Žilinskas

that Meškauskas became a leader in the Drawing Office, guiding and advising immigrant colleagues and newly graduated Australian engineers alike. Together the European immigrants formed a tight-knit group, predominantly Lithuanian in makeup, but inclusive of other like-minded people from the Drawing Office such as the Polish-born Jerzy Szymming (1912–69). The Latvian engineers in the Drawing Office, Dubinskas claimed, were less collegial – one was particularly authoritarian – representing what he believed to be a generalized tendency of his Latvian 'brothers' to 'gain an advantage by criticising or cursing others whilst at the same time praising themselves'.[109] He also acknowledged that it was natural for immigrants to be self-promotional and to attempt to 'serve Australians in positions of authority'.[110]

Dubinskas' book *I Was Always with You: Memories* (1992), which he wrote in the Lithuanian language and had published in Lithuania just months prior his death, provides invaluable insights into life in Woomera and the internal politics and experience of working in the public service from an immigrant's perspective. He clearly knew the importance of artfully managing professional relationships, averting conflict by knowing one's place, exercising diplomacy when things went wrong and winning people over from a subordinate position. Despite the militaristic and highly structured environment, Dubinskas and Meškauskas lived in Woomera for ten years and developed remarkable freedoms and influence: a Jeep that gave mobility for both work and recreation; the ability to shepherd other European immigrants away from difficult or oppressive work situations; access to senior and staff messes and bars where they could mix with professional and qualified staff; and, more broadly, degrees of respect, both socially and in the workplace. All the workers for the LRWE and the

CDWH relied on the messes for food, entertainment and informal social interaction. The messes were spaces of assimilation in many respects, although the military's caste system ultimately determined access to the Senior (Officers') Mess, the Staff Mess and the Junior Staff Club (aka 'The Jazza').[111] The civilian population was deployed in parallel with the military hierarchy along the lines of salaried professionals, tradesmen and foremen, and labourers and industrial workers respectively.[112] Dubinskas and Meškauskas were entitled to use the Staff Mess in Woomera West and the Officers' Mess when in Koolymilka, and could invite guests from the lower ranks. Dubinskas tactfully reflected on discrimination and class distinction when he wrote: 'The English were kind, though they regarded themselves as our superiors.'[113] They subsequently faced moments of discrimination:

> When the building work on the Catholic Church began, Jonas and I designed the access roads, footpaths, square, and provided all kinds of technical assistance without any payment. We also helped to transport sand and gravel for construction on Saturdays. We bought two 'stations' and received a promise that our names would be engraved under them. However, the chaplain (military) forgot to do this. Every Sunday we made a donation for the maintenance of the church. When the church was consecrated, many priests, even a bishop, came. The local Catholic newspaper published the names of the donors and helpers, however our names were absent. One Irishman who did not attend church, but donated £50, was publicly acknowledged as the finest Catholic.[114]

Freedom from oppression, a likely product of distancing from their pasts in both geographical and environmental senses, made it palatable for Dubinskas and Meškauskas to stay in Woomera after practically all their compatriots had left. They lived in the CDWH's Staff Quarters at Woomera West, within 100 metres or so of the Drawing Office and messes. When trees and shrubs became available to residents in April 1951, they developed a garden adjacent to their quarters that gave them the opportunity to nurture plants, entertain guests and even to establish a beehive among other activities (see Figure 5.9). Dubinskas' writings indicate that he was very aware of the microclimate of Woomera; the way things grew and other aspects of gardening and living in the desert. Climbing plants cloaked their quarters, providing relief from the desert sun, a kind of 'cultivated resistance' against the austerity of the desert encampment. They even developed flower gardens around the Administration Building, to which they directed their assistants to tend. The Arboretum's activities included the use of fertilizers that had incorporated 'broken down sludge from the Sewage Treatment Works at Woomera'.[115] In Dubinskas' account, he described how they used sludge with great success. In humble ways, their garden helped transform the perception that the desert could only be a barren place:

> The flowers grew beautifully because we used sludge from the sewers, which was a very good fertilizer when it dried. We gave flowers to the Anglican chaplain to decorate the church. Farmers from Woomera and the surrounding areas visited our gardens and marvelled that plants in the desert grew so well.[116]

Figure 5.9 Česlovas Dubinskas and Jonas Meškauskas (in the doorway) in the garden they created adjacent to their rooms in the Commonwealth Department of Works and Housing's Staff Quarters at Woomera West, date unknown (above); two unidentified colleagues of Dubinskas and Meškauskas in the garden showing a degree of cultivation of garden beds, specimen planting and lawn, date unknown (below). Courtesy of the Tymukas family

CONCLUSION

The largest cohort of European immigrant workers had served their two-year work obligation by 12 June 1951 and most departed. A census on 21 October 1952 (again for security reasons) revealed only four immigrant workers still remaining in Woomera's drawing office: Č. Dubinskas, P. Mazins, J. Meškauskas and J. Szymming, with a number of others having been relocated to the CDWH's Adelaide office and still working on Woomera-related projects.[117] There were discussions at this time around the prospects of recruiting engineers and architects primarily from the UK, without discounting recruits sought from the Continent, but mainly from the Netherlands, Northern Italy, Scandinavia, Germany and Switzerland.[118] Despite the essential service that the predominantly Eastern European immigrants had provided, no evidence has been found that indicates that the CDWH actively sought further recruits from the Department of Immigration or of Eastern European descent, although European immigrants still came to Woomera of their own volition seeking work for good money. Some also came on holidays to reunite with family or friends who had settled in Woomera, and some ended up staying on.

This was the case with Yugoslavians Rosa and Slavo Lazic, who in 1952 went to holiday with friends and stayed until Christmas 1983, a thirty-year 'visit' that came with 'stability and quality of life most people could only dream about'.[119] One of their close friends was Velimir Tadic, aka Tarzan, who arrived in 1958. At a seventy-fifth anniversary celebration of Woomera that I attended in 2022, my queries about recollections of European immigrants almost always started, and ended, with the exclamation: 'Oh, I remember Tarzan!'[120] Tarzan's notoriety stemmed mainly from the fact that he worked at Woomera's swimming pool and had a strong and memorable presence, but also from his popularity as a troubadour. When interviewed for the local newspaper in 1965, he said he liked Woomera and his job and would stay, especially since he had no relatives in Australia and had 'nowhere else to go'.[121] There is an uneasy sentiment embedded in such accounts, made even more poignant given that Woomera today is a shadow of its former self.

Much of Woomera's housing and infrastructure has been dismantled, resulting in an erosion of the physical manifestations of all those who made it (see Figure 5.10). The gardens that Dubinskas and Meškauskas developed at Woomera West have been completely erased. Ironically, this same site where they resided eventually became the site of the Woomera Immigration Reception and Processing Centre (1999–2003) that saw the incarceration of 'unauthorized arrivals' to Australia – a latter-day (circa 2000) episode in Australia's 'unauthorised arrivals' that arguably reached even greater public notoriety than the earlier European immigrants.

The QSL cards from the Soviet Union that sparked my enquiry led me to unearth a complex if difficult history linked to European immigrants' displacement from their homelands and their unerring bid for self-determination. Yet the gravity of their flight from Europe persists. When I interviewed Guido Laikve in February 2022, Russia had invaded Ukraine the previous day, causing Guido visible distress. However, from the few personal accounts I could find, there were stories defined by a sense of hope often embedded in the creation of new lives, establishing families and a legacy of contributions to building a nation during a period of heightened cultural evolution for Australia. Crucial to Kostas Tymukas' new life was the family he and his Australian-born wife Kathleen (née O'Donohue, 1929–2023) created with their six children. Tymukas died at the relatively young age of sixty-two due to an illness suspected by his family to be related to exposure to radiation while working in Maralinga west of Woomera, where nuclear tests had been staged. This was a tragic outcome after years of contribution to public works. Kathleen's reflections on the 'boom times [when] Australia was advancing and becoming something' seem a fitting way to conclude:

> And those people who went to Woomera, and did all these things, a lot of Australians wouldn't have done it. But they had the opportunity to *do something* and they adopted this country. It was *amazing* ... They took it in their stride, but that wasn't going to be their future. That was just the interim, before they actually started life.[122]

Figure 5.10 The remains of the Pimba to Woomera rail line bridge. Gangs of European immigrants helped build the rail line and some men succumbed to victimization and bullying due to race and politics. The rail line had been closed for decades before this bridge crossing was severely damaged following flooding rains of January 2022. The bridge culvert and rail line are still evident, albeit in ruinous states. Photograph by Rudi Saniga

Andrew Saniga is Associate Professor of Landscape Architecture, Planning and Urbanism at the University of Melbourne. His research includes a history of landscape architecture in Australia and his writings have documented and explained key designers and projects with an emphasis on the mid-twentieth century. His book *Making Landscape Architecture in Australia* (2012) won the Victoria Medal from the Australian Institute of Landscape Architects. *Campus: Building Modern Australian Universities* (2023), a book he co-edited with Robert Freestone, is a collaborative history that sheds light on the origins and evolution of campus design in Australia from the Second World War to the current day. Andrew teaches design and history of landscape architecture, and is a registered landscape architect with the Australian Institute of Landscape Architects. He is also a member of DOCOMOMO International.

NOTES

1. The 'QSL' abbreviation is derived from the three-letter code for 'acknowledge' used in amateur shortwave radio communications.
2. Bardwell, *Woomera: The Silent Partners*.
3. Morton, *Fire across the Desert*, 99–100 and 128–29.
4. A very small number of European immigrants were designated employees under the Department of the Interior for a few months but were subsequently reclassified under the CDWH. In this chapter they are discussed in the context of the CDWH.
5. Instrumental in this was the McMahon Act passed in August 1946, as discussed in Morton, *Fire across the Desert*, 8.
6. The LRWE subsequently came under a range of different titles, including the Weapons Research Establishment (WRE), among others.
7. For a detailed account, see, Davenport, *Cleared Out*. The exact way in which rocket-firing trajectories interacted with the lands of different groups of First People's is difficult to ascertain. However, referring to *The AIATSIS Map of Indigenous Australia* (1996) created by David R. Horton, the groups potentially impacted in the main consisted of the following (in order from southeast to northwest): Kokatha; Nakako; Pitjantjatjara; Ngatatjara; Mardu; and, Nyangumarda.
8. Morton, *Fire across the Desert*, 69–96; Davenport, *Cleared Out*, 23–33.
9. The Blue Streak missile programme was perhaps most infamous in terms of the economic shock waves it caused. See the extensive account given in Morton, *Fire across the Desert*.
10. Seddon, *Searching for the Snowy*, xxv.
11. Pauline Windeyer, cited in Morton, *Fire across the Desert*, 235.
12. Kathleen Tymukas, interview with the author, via Zoom from Adelaide, 8 October 2020.
13. For the historical context, see Artymiuk, *Destination Australia*. The Polish ex-servicemen were: Bronislaw Blazejowski; Jerzy Borejko; Czeslaw [Mieczyslaw] Dabkowski; Stanislaw Konopka; Roman Kosiarski; Stanislaw Kowalczyk; Aleksander Lange; Jerzy Marzec; Karol Metamonski; Adam Mrozowski; and Edward Oleszkiewicz, who was profiled in 'New Australian's Fine War Record', *News*, 23 January 1950, 16.
14. NAA: D156, 1948/1945, W.T. Haslam, Minute paper, 22 June 1949.
15. NAA: A434 1948/3/4846, Director General DWH, Letter, 17 March 1948; NAA: A434 1948/3/4846, T.H.E. Heyes, Letter, 20 April 1948.
16. Morton, *Fire across the Desert*, 121.
17. See: NAA: A434 1948/3/4846, T.H.E. Heyes, Memorandum, 20 April 1948; NAA: D156

1956_114 Part 1_26, F.K. Dwyer, Letter, 5 April 1948; NAA: A434 1948/3/4846, W. Funnell, Letter, 8 April 1948.
18. NAA: D1918 S1493-5-2, Commonwealth of Australia Attorney General's Department File of Papers, 'Nominal Roll of D.P's at Woomera', 1949.
19. Proportions calculated on the basis of total workforce numbers given across various military divisions and CDWH personnel in Commonwealth of Australia, *The Joint United Kingdom-Australian Long Range Weapons Project*.
20. NAA: D156 1948/1945, H.T. Scattergood, Letter, 14 July 1949.
21. T.H.E. Heyes, Memorandum.
22. W. Funnell, Letter.
23. Guido Laikve, interview with the author, via Zoom from Toronto, Canada, 25 February 2022.
24. Marshall, *Raparapa*.
25. Chambers, *Woomera: Its Human Face*, 28.
26. Lance Kain, Letter, undated but circa 1950 (courtesy of Avriel Kain).
27. Jonas Mockunas, Diary entry, 25 April 1949 (translation by Jonas Mockunas, January 2022).
28. Panich, *Sanctuary?*, 88.
29. Jaronis, Liudas. 'Woomera through Lithuanian Eyes', *Australijos Lietuviu*, 20 December 1948(8), n.p.
30. Dubinskas, *I Was Always with You*, 39.
31. Morton, *Fire across the Desert*, 320.
32. NLA: 'Woomera Rocket Platform Nearly Complete'. *Advertiser*, 3 June 1949, 1.
33. Veigurs, Alberts. Diary entry, 25 January 1949 (translation by Valda Veigurs, October 2022).
34. Mockunas, Jonas. Diary entry, 25 April 1949 (translation by Jonas Mockunas, January 2022).
35. For a recent valuable contribution, see Fitzpatrick, *White Russians, Red Peril*.
36. NAA: A437 1949/6/21, Director General DWH, Letter, 10 December 1948; Hammerton, *Water South Australia*, 229; NAA: A434 1948/3/4846, Hansard Extract, 'Guided Weapons Testing Range', Department of Immigration, 29 June 1949.
37. NAA: D156, 1948/1945, People of Malta, Letter, 26 July 1949.
38. Laikve, 'Guido Einar Laikve', 2013, 125–33.
39. NLA: 'Big-Time Gambling on S.A. Rocket Range', *Smith's Weekly*, 4 June 1949, 5.
40. NLA: 'Remia Ligonius' [Support Patients], *Mūsų Pastogė*, 31 May 1950, 4 (translation by Andrew Saniga, 2021.) See also 'Gelbekime Vokietijoje Pasilikusius TBC Ligonius' [Let's Save the TBC Diseased Who Remain in Germany], *Mūsų Pastogė*, 16 August 1950, 4 (translation by Andrew Saniga, 2022). The protagonists cited were: A. Alyt, S. Balsys, P. Bareišis, J Daunoravičius, Č. Dubinskas, L. Jaronis, J. Juodsnukis, J. Kairys, A. Kružas, J. Meškauskas, J. Naujokaitis, J. Paluobis, V. Petruškevičienė, J. Petruškevičius, K. Tymukas and A. Žilinskas.
41. Garnaut, Freestone and Iwanicki, 'Cold War Heritage', 549.
42. Patterson, *The Climate, Soils, Plant Ecology*.
43. NAA: UNESCO/NS/AZ/145, R.H. Patterson, report to UNESCO, Arid Zone Programme, 10 September 1953, 9.
44. NLA: 'R.A.A.F. Awards Service in Radar Recognised', *The Age*, 6 March 1946, 2.
45. NLA: 'Airfield Construction Work of R.A.A.F. Unit', *Kalgoorlie Miner*, 19 December 1944, 2.
46. NLA: 'R.A.A.F. Unit on Mindoro Race Against Time to Provide Airstrips', *The West Australian*, 18 December 1944, 5.
47. NLA: 'Coolah's Water Supply Visit of Departmental Engineer', *Mudgee Gaurdian and North-Western Representative*, 18 April 1946, 24.
48. Morton, *Fire across the Desert*, 116.
49. NAA: D156 1950_1265_4, A. Dancauskis [sic], personal statement, undated, 14; NAA: D156 1950_1265_2, F.L. Loder, Memorandum, 25 August 1950.

50. NAA: D156 1956_114 Part 1_6, Stanley A. Clem, Letter, 13 December 1948.
51. These were: Latvians S. Dzenis, J. Latvelis, A. Melnsils and J. Skila; Lithuanians A. Janilionis, V. Meskelis and E. Staugas; Polish A. Kapala, J. Prokopenko and P. Zajac; and Yugoslavian C. Stjepanovic.
52. NAA: D156 1956_114 PART 1_1 [48/371/198], A.D. Bouch, Letter, 20 December 1948; NAA: D156 1956_114 PART 1_1_A , J.J.W. Gray, Minute paper, 24 December 1948.
53. NLA: 'Stole Cement from Employers', *Advertiser*, 16 March 1951, 14.
54. Dubinskas, *I Was Always with You*, 36.
55. For a detailed account, see Morton, *Fire across the Desert*, 96–114.
56. James, *Cosmopolitan Conservationists*, 49–50.
57. Guido Laikve, interview with the author, via Zoom from Toronto, Canada, 25 February 2022.
58. Morton, *Fire across the Desert*, 118.
59. Karnups and Zembergs, cited in Putniņš, *Latvians in Australia*, 30–31. See also Kunz, *Displaced Persons*; Fitzpatrick, *White Russians, Red Peril*, 69; Morton, *Fire across the Desert*, 99–100.
60. Ibid., 128–29.
61. NLA: Ellis, A. Les. 'New Australians' Language', *Advertiser*, Adelaide, SA, 19 June 1950, 2; Tymukas, Kostas. 'Letter to the Editor', *Advertiser*, no date, n.p.
62. NLA: 'Balts, Cameras, Fights on Rocket Range', *Tribune* [SA], 3 September 1948, 1.
63. NLA: 'Protesto Minėjimas Woomeroje' [Commemorating the Protest in Woomera], *Mūsų Pastogė*, 12 July 1950, 4 (translation by Andrew Saniga, 2021).
64. NLA: 'Komunistai Woomeroje' [Communists in Woomera], *Mūsų Pastogė*, 25 March 1953, 2 (translation by Andrew Saniga, 2021); Morton, *Fire across the Desert*, 103–8. Morton's analysis of security, communism, international politics and the American Embargo of 1948–49 suggests the accuracy of the Lithuanian authors' claims.
65. Morton, *Fire across the Desert*, 98 and 107.
66. Peter Tymukas, letter to the author, 8 October 2020.
67. NAA: D156 166_168_17, F.K. Schneider, Memorandum, 20 April 1950.
68. Dubinskas, *I Was Always with You*, 37.
69. NAA: D1918 S1493-5-2, Commonwealth of Australia Attorney General's Department File of Papers, 'Nominal Roll of D.P.'s at Woomera', 1949; NAA: S/238/48, Salisbury, Memorandum, 31 August 1948. The nominal roll of DPs was forwarded to the Deputy Director of the Commonwealth Investigation Service, Adelaide.
70. Ibid.
71. NAA: A434 1948/3/4846, A.L. Nutt, Letter, 10 February 1949; NAA: A434 1948/3/4846, Reverend Traeger, Letter, 17 November 1948.
72. Dubinskas, *I Was Always with You*, 33.
73. NAA: D156 166_168_15, G.H.J. Phillips, Letter, 17 October 1952; NAA: D156 166_168_13, W.T. Haslam, Memorandum, 21 October 1952. Haslam noted that the seven alien employees involved were: T. Krastins, A. Dančauskis (ex-Woomera), V. Kmitas, K.T. Tymukas (ex-Woomera), A. Berzins, J. Krievs and A. Springis; NAA: D156 166_168_21 and NAA: D156 166_168_21, Schedule of Aliens Employed in Staff Positions by the Department of Works, South Australia.
74. NAA: D156 1950_1265_4, A.D. Bouch, Statement, undated.
75. NAA: D156 166_168_33, A.D. Bouch, Letter, 9 August 1950.
76. NAA: D156 1956_114 Part 1_18, T.R. Henderson, Letter, 21 September 1948; NAA: A434 1948/3/4846, Director General DWH, Letter, 18 October 1948; NAA: D156 166_168_33, A.D. Bouch, Letter, 9 August 1950; for the case of securing the employment of immigrant workers in the DWH Adelaide Office, see NAA: D156 166_168_19, W.T. Haslam, Letter, 2 October 1952. These were: A. Berzins, A. Dančauskis, V. Kmitas, T. Krastins, J. Krievs, A. Springis and K. Tymukas.

77. NAA: D156 166_168_34_1, A.D. Bouch, Telegraph, 9 August 1950.
78. NAA D1918 S1493-5-2: Commonwealth of Australia Attorney General's Department File of Papers, 'Nominal Roll of D.P's at Woomera'; For further references to the 'replaceability' of migrant workers, see also NAA: D156 166_168_25, G.H.J. Phillips, Letter, 30 September 1952.
79. NAA: D174 SA5136, Minute Paper, 21 March 1950.
80. Dubinskas, *I Was Always with You*, 34.
81. NAA: D156 166_168_27, A.J. Stevenson, Letter, 5 May 1952; NAA: D156 166_168_1, I.C. Holloway, Letter, 21 September 1955; see the files in NAA: D174 SA5163, item number 985287.
82. NAA: D156 166_168_4, A.J. Stevenson, Letter, 9 November 1953.
83. Kunz, 'The Engineering Profession', 23, paraphrasing Australia, *Department of Immigration, Statistical Bulletin*, No. 1, January 1952; Hammerton, *Water South Australia*, 234.
84. Kunz, 'The Engineering Profession', 23–24; Kunz, *Displaced Persons*, 159, 165.
85. Kunz, 'The Engineering Profession', 22.
86. Ibid., 24.
87. Jędrzejczak, *Love's Cadenza*, 268–298.
88. NAA: A437 1949/6/21, Director General DWH, Letter, 10 December 1948; NAA: D156 1956_114 PART 1_1_A, J.J.W. Gray, Minute paper, 24 December 1948.
89. NAA: D156 1956_114 Part 1_13_A, A.N. Jowett, Letter, 11 November 1948.
90. NAA: D156 1956_114 Part 1_16_M, Industrial Section DWH, Letter, 8 November 1948.
91. NAA: D156 1956_114 Part 1_13_A, A.N. Jowett, Letter, 11 November 1948.
92. Putniņš, *Latvians in Australia*, 16.
93. Jędrzejczak, *Love's Cadenza*, 270, 273.
94. NAA: D156 1956_114 Part 1_6, Vilis Taube, Curriculum Vitae, 11 December 1948.
95. These were: Estonian V. Selter; Latvians I. Adams-Adomsons, U. Buss, V. Dzirnis-Dzirne, R. Hartmanis, A. Labans and V. Strazds; Lithuanians P. Bareišis, Č. Dubinskas, J. Kairys, A. Kružas, J. Merkevičius and K. Žilinskas; and Polish S. Korzyniewski and A. Lange. See NAA: D156 1956 114 PART 2 47 E, 'Classification of the New Australian Personnel, 14 June 1949.
96. Heino Laikve (father of Erich and Guido) arrived in Australia four months after his sons and was deployed to Woomera in July 1949.
97. NAA: D174 SA5163, Superintendent LRE Range, Letter, 15 March 1950.
98. NAA: D156 1956_114 PART 1_1, A.D. Bouch, Letter, 20 December 1948.
99. NAA: D156 1956_114 Part 1_6, Arvids Blūmentāls, Curriculum Vitae, 18 December 1948.
100. NAA: D1918 S1493-5-2, Commonwealth of Australia Attorney General's Department File of Papers, 'Nominal Roll of D.P's at Woomera'; NAA: D156 1956_114 PART 1_11_A, W.T. Haslam, Memorandum, 21 December 1948.
101. For instance, Estonian Walborg Hakki arrived in Woomera in September 1951 to work as a nurse for the Department of Health, having served for two years as a nurse at the Woodside Army Camp (South Australia). In July 1953 she married Estonian Hans Salupalu, who had come to Woomera to work as a motor mechanic in February 1950.
102. NAA: D174 SA5163, Superintendent L.R.E. Range, Letter, 15 March 1950.
103. These were: Estonian V. Selter; Latvians U. Buss, V. Dzirnia-Dzirne, R. Hartmanis, A. Labans and V. Taube; Lithuanians C. Dubinskas, A. Janilionis and J. Meskauskas; and Polish A. Lange.
104. Andersons, 'Aleksandrs Dančauskis', 293.
105. Kunz, 'The Engineering Profession', 24.
106. Aldis Putniņš, personal communication, Adelaide, 22 January 2022.
107. Dubinskas, *I Was Always with You*, 44.
108. NAA: D156 1956_114 Part 1_16_M, Industrial Section DWH, Letter, 8 November 1948.
109. Dubinskas, *I Was Always with You*, 32–33, 43.

110. Ibid., 43.
111. See a fuller explanation in Morton, *Fire across the Desert*, 240–41; Chambers, *Woomera: Its Human Face*, 20 and 22.
112. Morton, *Fire across the Desert*, 239.
113. Dubinskas, *I Was Always with You*, 37.
114. Ibid., 34.
115. Patterson, *The Climate*, 10.
116. Dubinskas, *I Was Always with You*, 34.
117. NAA: D156 166_168_21, 'Schedule of Aliens Employed in Staff Positions by the Department of Works, South Australia'.
118. NAA: A451_1950_5708, A.F. Spratt, Letter, 12 June 1951.
119. Lazic, Peter. 'Blast from the Past in Memory of Slavo and Rosa Lazic', *Gibber Gabber*, 17 June 2022, 10–11.
120. Caz Harding, conversation with the author in Woomera, 17 April 2022.
121. NLA: '"Tarzan" Tadic Troubadour', *Gibber Gabber*, 16 December 1965, 4.
122. Kathleen Tymukas, interview with the author, via Zoom from Adelaide, 8 October 2020.

BIBLIOGRAPHY

Archival Records

Australian Lithuanian Archive (ALA)
National Archives of Australia (NAA)
National Library of Australia (NLA)
Woomera History Museum (WHM)

Publications

Andersons, E. (ed.). 'Aleksandrs Dančauskis', in *Latvju Enciklopēdija 1962–1982* [*Latvian Encyclopedia 1962–1982*], vol. 1. Rockville, MD: Amerikas Latviešu Apvienības Latviešu Institūts, 1983, 293. (Translation by Aldis Putniņš, 24 January 2022.)
Artymiuk, Lucyna. *Destination Australia Polish Soldier Migrants (1947–48)*. Melbourne: Polish Museum and Archives in Australia Inc., 2019.
Bardwell, Harry (ed.). *Woomera: The Silent Partners* [film documentary]. Sydney: ABC Commercial, 1988. (Transcribed by Andrew Saniga.)
Chambers, Edward. W. *Woomera: Its Human Face*. Henley, SA: Seaview Press, 2000.
Commonwealth of Australia. *The Joint United Kingdom-Australian Long Range Weapons Project in Australia*. Canberra: Department of Supply and Construction, 1949.
Davenport, Sue, Peter Johnson and Yuwali Nixon. *Cleared Out: First Contact in the Western Desert*. Canberra: Aboriginal Studies Press, 2010.
Dubinskas, Česlovas. *Aš Visą Laiką Buvau Su Jumis: Atsiminimai* [*I Was Always with You: Memories*]. Kaunas: Gabija, 1992. (Translation by Dr Edita Meškauskaitė and Andrew Domaševičius-Žilinskas, 2021.)
Fitzpatrick, Sheila. *White Russians, Red Peril: A Cold War History of Migration to Australia*. Carlton, Vic: La Trobe University Press in conjunction with Black, 2021.
Garnaut, Christine, Robert Freestone and Iris Iwanicki. 'Cold War Heritage and the Planned Community: Woomera Village in Outback Australia', *International Journal of Heritage Studies* 18(6) (2012), 541–63. DOI: 10.1080/13527258.2011.621439.

Gaynor, Andrea. *George Seddon: Selected Writings*. Carlton, Vic: La Trobe University Press, 2019.
Grayden, William. *Adam and Atoms*. Perth: Frank Daniels, 1957.
Hammerton, Marianne. *Water South Australia: A History of the Engineering and Water Supply Department*. Netley: Wakefield Press, 1986.
Jackson, John. B. *The Necessity for Ruins and Other Topics*. Amherst: University of Massachusetts Press, 1980.
James, Peggy. *Cosmopolitan Conservationists Greening Modern Sydney*. North Melbourne: Australian Scholarly Publishing Pty Ltd, 2013.
Jędrzejczak, Waclaw. J. *Love's Cadenza A Migrant's Story 1939–1956*. Hectorville, South Australia: Waclaw J. Jędrzejczak, 1999.
Kunz, Egon. F. 'The Engineering Profession and the Displaced Person Migrant in Australia', *International Migration* 7(1–2) (1969), 22–30.
——. *Displaced Persons: Calwell's New Australians*. Sydney: ANU Press, 1988.
Laikve, Guido. 'Guido Einar Laikve'. *Memoirs Malutunglad V*. Toronto: Tartu College, 2013.
Marshall, Paul. (ed.). *Raparapa: Stories from the Fitzroy River Drover*. Broome, WA: Magabala Books, 2011.
Morton, Peter. *Fire across the Desert: Woomera and the Anglo-Australian Joint Project 1946–1980*. Canberra Airport, ACT: Defence Science and Technology, 1989 [2017].
Pálsson, Gísli. 'Situating Nature: Ruins of Modernity as *Natturuperlur*', *Tourist Studies* 13(2) (2013), 172–88. DOI: 10.1177/1468797613490374,
Panich, Catherine. *Sanctuary? Remembering Postwar Immigration*. Sydney: Allen & Unwin, 1988.
Patterson, R.H. *The Climate, Soils, Plant Ecology, Aboricultural Activities and Vegetative Development L.R.W Project Areas North West Arid Interior South Australia*. Canberra: Department of Works, 1953.
Putniņš, Aldis L. *Latvians in Australia Alienation and Assimilation*. Canberra: ANU Press, 1981.
Seddon, George. *Searching for the Snowy: An Environmental History*. St Leonards, NSW: Allen & Unwin, 1994.
Southall, Ivan. *Woomera*. Sydney: Angus & Robertson Ltd, 1962.
Wohltmann, Michael. *Looking Back to See the Future*. Clarence Gardens, SA: Digital Print Australia, 2022.

Chapter 6

Noncompliance and Agency in Migrant Family Life
Greta and Benalla Migrant Camps

Alexandra Dellios

The people who lived in Australia's postwar migrant camps faced official constraints to their daily working and family lives. We know this from both the archival material and from the personal testimonies shared and published over the last forty years. However, something else happens to the picture if we skew the lens and look beyond their victimization or their unfair treatment at the hands of government authorities and a system that dehumanized them, and if we focus instead on how families creatively navigated constraints and enacted changes to the built environment of the camp and the departmental ethos that underpinned it. This chapter contains individual stories of family life within regional migrant camps, particularly Benalla (VIC) and Greta (NSW), delving deeper into the camp experiences introduced in Chapter 2. The framework for analysing these testimonies borrows loosely from the sociological concept of 'bounded agency' used in education and vocational studies. The term seeks to understand the experiences of people within a given social context by accounting for the ways in which people influence but are not wholly determined by their environments. Of course, factors like gender, class and race also play a part in the amount of influence one can exert over their social environments, and this too is part of the analysis. The interrelationship between structure and agency is pertinent to this study of migrant lives within a highly regulated and bureaucratic space (the migrant camp) and one that is often discounted the trauma of their premigration lives and the specific needs of their settlement.[1] The stories unpacked in the following discussion are drawn from published and unpublished testimony, digital storytelling and oral histories, as well as archival material from government departments.

This chapter makes one thing clear: people improvised and found makeshift or unsanctioned ways to live better lives in the camps. Alongside their efforts and sometimes in response to their demands, the Commonwealth and specifically the Department of Immigration (DOI) and the Department of Labour and National Service (DLNS) responded with slow and incremental changes to the safety and comfort of the camps.[2] By focusing on migrant activities, on their demands, daily practices and ways of living – the home and family life, including childrearing, feeding and building comfort, and its relationship to formal and informal work – this chapter acts as a corrective to historical narratives about the postwar migration scheme. A holistic analysis of migrant family life in regional postwar Australia should integrate both emotional and material factors. While the agency of displaced persons (DPs) and assisted migrant families living in camps were constrained and regulated, their recollections of life within the camp resists their classification and homogenization as 'factory fodder', a faceless workforce. These accounts provide insight into prevailing beliefs about maintaining individual dignity and the social aspirations of non-Anglo migrant peoples in postwar Australia.

In her history of the DOI, Ann-Marie Jordens referred to the agency of migrants, and particularly migrant women, within the camps, as taking the form of 'noncompliance'. She dismissed the notion that noncompliance is a 'weapon of the weak' or the ineffective reaction of a 'victim' and argued that it can 'be a powerful spur to administrative reform and sometimes even cultural change'.[3] Her 1997 book *Aliens to Citizens* drew on archived correspondence from DOI social workers and camp administrators recounting the situation facing women with children in the camps, and provides a useful entry point into the official archive and the position of the DOI across this period. While often intractable and bound by sometimes callous policy, they were capable of responding to the demands of migrants within individual camps.

However, and where possible, acts of noncompliance and the reality of daily life in the camps are best captured by migrant voices themselves, which in some cases provide a less benign reading of policy change and bureaucracy than that provided by Jordens.[4] In an effort to privilege migrant voices and in lieu of the original aims of migrant oral history to engage in 'ordinary people's history', I have drawn heavily on two newly released migrant-initiated storytelling platforms. The first is hosted and facilitated by the ex-resident group Benalla Migrant Camp Inc., which collects and showcases online the testimony of former residents of Benalla, alongside donated photographs from their family collections; the second is Alek Schulha's epic attempt to capture the stories of Greta residents in his self-published 2020 tome *Beneath the Shadows of Mount Molly Morgan*. Both were facilitated by social media platforms such as Facebook and the connection and sharing they enabled. They are rich examples of community-initiated public history archives made by former residents of Australia's postwar migrant camps. Both are still growing. As community-built and managed archives, underpinned by the desire of former residents to tell their own stories, these platforms for migrant storytelling are ripe for historical analysis, but have not yet received much academic attention.[5]

Upon migration to Australia, DPs (refugees arriving under Australia's scheme with the International Refugee Organization between roughly 1947 and 1952) and then assisted migrants (arriving from European countries with whom Australia signed migration agreements), were summarily classified as 'unskilled labour', regardless of their qualifications. Within the industrializing nation state, they were placed, without consideration for their family circumstances or past experiences, into a system that directed them towards labour-hungry industries. In the early years of the postwar immigration scheme (before 1952), these industries were mainly regional or rural due to government subsidies relating to the decentralization of industry (see Chapter 1). The Commonwealth's short-lived push to regionalize industry shaped the early mobility of migrant labour. The continuum of camps and hostels in which they lived reflects this reality. Their living arrangements were linked to industry and short-term work contracts. While most migrants accepted available placements, many resisted; others chose to leave their allocated jobs and take their chances in the major cities, before or after the term of their two-year contracts with the Commonwealth government had expired. They did this despite the risks. In the early years of the scheme, two-year work contracts were strictly applied, including the stipulation that migrants must remain in the employment (and accommodation) allocated to them by authorities and report any changes in their circumstances to a local Commonwealth Employment Office. They could be subject to deportation if they repeatedly refused offered employment or left their allocated employment without Departmental consent.[6]

Return migration rose steadily in the postwar era. It reached a peak in the mid-1960s, when it became a subject of concern for the government.[7] Sociologists attributed high rates of return migration to the nonrecognition of skills and qualifications as well as the poor standards of care offered in work and accommodation.[8] Despite these undesirable circumstances, some of the most prominent voices in the collective memory of Australia's migrant camps come from those who made migrant camps their home for an extended period, beyond two years. Notably, these 'public memory advocates' are more likely to be those who lived in the camp as children, as the drive to collect these stories only began in earnest from the 1980s. Many of the first generation of DPs who arrived as adults are now deceased.

The stories of those who passed through the camp system quickly, in addition to the stories of those who left Australia entirely, are not easy to access. The second generation, especially children of DPs, have sought to collect and self-publish recollections (online and in published formats). They are not uniform recollections, and I have attempted where I can to offer a diversity of experiences. Nonetheless, there are a few commonalities across recollections that will be explored in subsequent sections: family separation, creative building of informal economies of exchange and work, and the pressures (as well as the benefits) of childrearing in a semi-regulated but communal setting.

FAMILY SEPARATION: NAVIGATING LONG-TERM STAYS AND BEING MOBILE

Families were formed, reformed and divided during and after the Second World War, and within the 700 DP camps spread across Germany and Southern Italy.[9] Often, if the family consisted of a male 'breadwinner', they were separated again in Australia, under the terms of the two-year work contract. Temporary family separation was a near-universal experience for DPs in Australia from 1947 to 1952.[10] It is important to note that as a matter of policy, British dependants were not separated from their breadwinners, with the authorities blithely assuming migrants from the British Isles expected and required a higher level of care.[11] Historians Kevin and Agutter argue that the Commonwealth's two-year work contract can be understood as part of a 'continuum of unfree labour', coerced rather than forced, but still jarringly familiar to those who had endured forced labour during the Second World War. The application and implications of the work contract had gendered dimensions too, and women were vulnerable to different types of exploitation in the camps and in the workplace, as well as having access to different forms of agency, as will become clear in the following discussion.

People found ways to deal with the family separation engendered by the work contract, whether through weekly or monthly visits or repeated requests for new placements or accommodation. For example, Schulha's book recounts the story of Nevina Andrean, whose family migrated in 1951 after living in five different refugee camps in postwar Italy. According to the story, the family made efforts to stay together in Australia, flipping the script by stating that the Department 'complied' with Nevina's mother's demands:

> Officials complied with a request from her mother that living in Bonegilla was too far from her husband. The children were missing him too. Subsequently the family was moved to their *seventh* camp at Cowra, which was closer to Wollongong [where her father was living and working at the water board]. They lived in a Nissen hut on top of a hill.[12]

A few months later, they moved to their eighth camp, Greta (in a remote town in the Hunter Region of NSW, some 400 km from the Cowra camp), although the circumstances are unclear. 'I thought that it was just another camp. We had been in so many that they all looked the same', Nevina said. However, Greta was one of the larger postwar processing and holding centres, consisting of both Nissen huts (labelled Silver City) and wooden barracks (Chocolate City). It housed over 170,000 DPs and assisted migrants from 1949 to 1961. Like the Bonegilla and Benalla camps, Greta was a former Department of Defence training facility. From 1947, it underwent a massive building programme to accommodate the influx of new migrant arrivals, although much of this construction was based on army principles of organization and did not consider the needs of families or young children. Things like facilities to sanitize bottles or childminding centres came later, after residents made their demands known; in the early years of the postwar immigration scheme, migrant family units were separated in the camps and housed in rooms according to gender.

Sixteen new kitchens were constructed, and improvements and repairs were made to the roads, sewage and drainage systems. By 1952, Greta contained a library, a theatre, at least one play centre and primary school in both Chocolate and Silver City, a post office, a Commonwealth Employment Office (where people were allocated jobs), two ovals, several church halls, a small hospital and recreation halls. At least three Bedford buses carried camp residents across various stops in Chocolate City and Silver City. A former child resident recalled that 'it took about 20 minutes from one end to the other [by bus]. A lot of children used to ride on the bus'.[13] When it came to getting around the camp, children also noted the sense of freedom that a bicycle could give them. For them, Greta was a city to be explored (see Figure 6.1). However, to some adult DPs, as was noted in Chapter 2, it felt uncomfortably familiar to the IRO refugee camps in Western Europe they had just left.

Residents could also use nearby Greta Railway Station or Maitland Railway Station to travel further afield. Others recall their fathers catching 'the coal trains' in order to commute from their work at BHP in Newcastle to their families in Greta.[14] Those who worked in Sydney travelled to and from the camps by train. Nina Drobot recalls that her father Peter (a Russian DP who migrated in 1949 in his late thirties) visited the family at Greta every weekend and cried about having to leave his family for the long journey back to Sydney, Chullora, where he worked on the railways and lived in a tent. He would wonder 'if it was worth it as he boarded the train at Greta Railway Station every weekend to travel back to Sydney'.[15] They endured this situation for two years, until his work contact was fulfilled. The government's planned expansion of regional railways in the postwar era was fuelled by migrant labour and it in turn assisted their ability to move across regional Australia during the sometimes lonely years of their work contracts. Maria Zintschenko, who arrived in Australia as a young child with her Polish parents and lived first in Bonegilla, then Rushworth and finally Benalla camp, recalled that 'many of the men in the camp' worked on the railways; her father 'would go off Monday morning and come back Friday afternoon'.[16]

The accessibility of the railway line and the pushback from separated families did not result in universal free movement – I do not wish to imply that mobility was an easy and harmonious option. Many were unable to visit family on the weekends because their work allocations were too far away. Those who were allocated work on the Snowy – such as Adam Graf from the Netherlands, who was 'involved in the tunnelling process', one of the most dangerous jobs of the Snowy scheme – only occasionally returned to Greta every few months. Lucy Sidorko's father was away in the cane fields in Cairns for twelve months in 1949–50 before he was able to return and visit his family in Greta. In addition to trains, at least one account mentions that some buses transported male workers whose 'dependants' were living at Greta to BHP Steelworks in Newcastle and to the brick works and dam construction sites at Scone.[17]

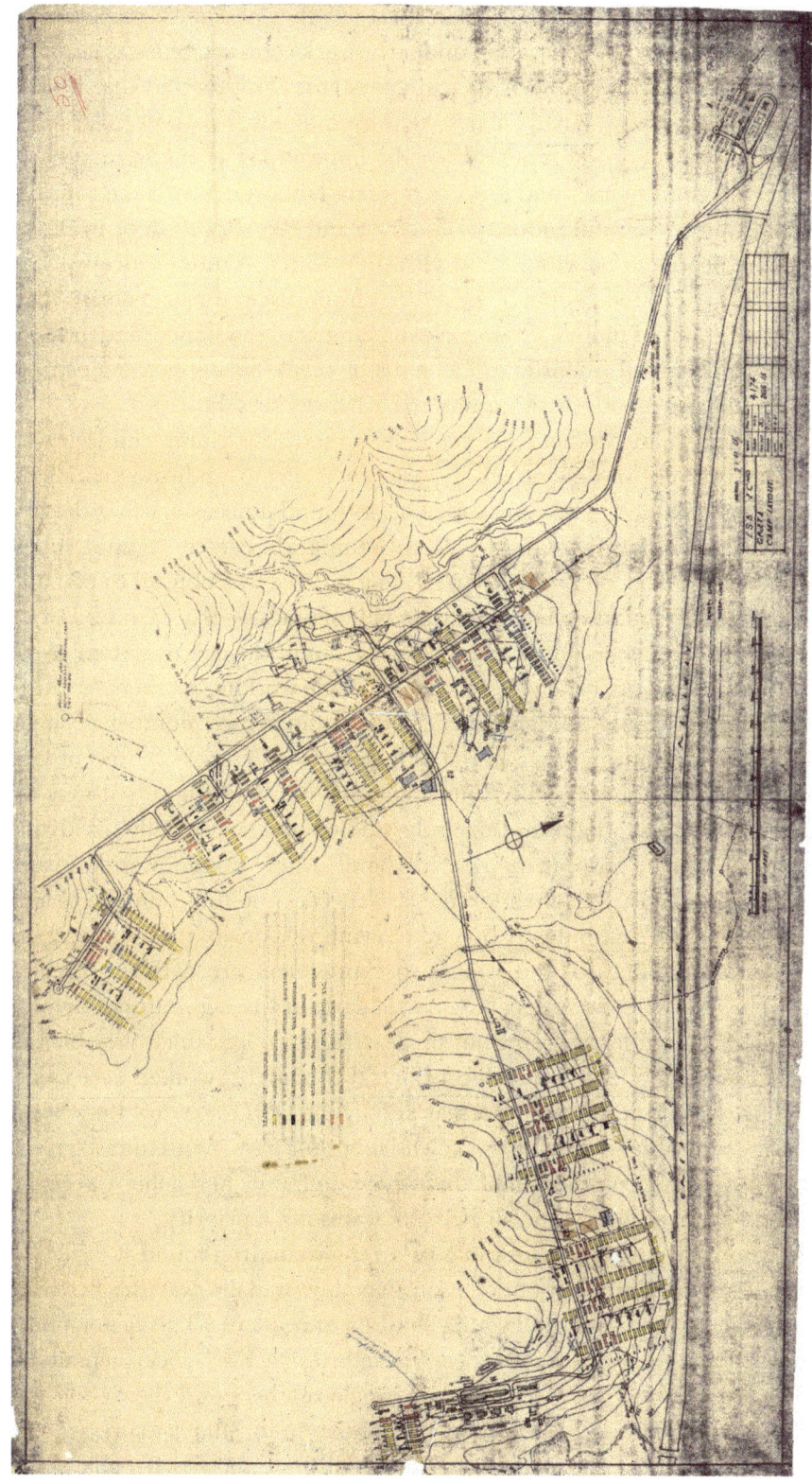

Figure 6.1 Greta Camp layout. Courtesy of the National Archives of Australia, NAA A12872, 1949

In her account penned in the 1980s, historian Catherine Panich empathized with the family lives destroyed by separation under the work contract. She was a small child when her own family moved out of the camp system. She reflected that it was only after leaving that they were 'finally able to take an individual path in Australian society, without the restrictions of indenture or the impositions of communal life'.[18] The continual movement, the back and forth of migrant labourers across the country, was the result of government and industry directives and the allocation of work, as well as the desire of people to be with family. Historian Karen Agutter evocatively argues that the 'endless parade of people being shifted from place to place' meant that DPs were on a 'continuum of mobility'.[19] In a clear example of resistance, one that extends beyond noncompliance, Jordens cites incidents of wives leaving holding centres and 'squatting' in their husbands' work camps or DLNS workers' hostels.[20]

While only pregnant women and married women with young children were exempt from the two-year work contract, departmental memos indicate that all women were officially encouraged to take up work. Others found it necessary in order to cover the costs of accommodating a family within the migrant centre. Agutter states that 'for the dubious privilege of [family] separation a refugee was obliged to pay up to £3 a week', a charge that amounted to more than half of one's weekly earnings. In theory, this was meant to operate as an incentive to move out of the centre system as soon as possible, but it had the opposite effect for many single working mothers.

Benalla Migrant Camp is infamous for housing the highest number of single-parent families, and for housing them in the long term (see Figure 6.2). Recent research into the difficulties facing so-called 'unsupported' mothers (those without a male breadwinner) has shone a light on this understudied and structurally disadvantaged cohort within the wider postwar migration scheme. Many women were pressured by DOI social workers to place their children into state care and thus fulfil the obligations of their work contract unhindered by child caring responsibilities. Tellingly, social workers' reports from across the period also express concern over the 'breakdown' of families. However, they were speaking particularly of the high rates of divorce and the institutionalization of children from nuclear families, for which they blamed the family separation engendered by work contracts.[21] Unmarried women were valued (by migration officers recruiting them overseas and by the DOI once they were here) only insofar as they were able to provide unskilled labour for in-demand industries – as domestics or factory workers – and their right to retain family and achieve resettlement with their emotional and social needs being met was not a priority.

Those who resisted the pressure to give up their children found it difficult to afford to move out of camp accommodation. Notably, Benalla was the first camp to provide a creche for the babies and young children of residents. This factor, combined with the availability of work in two nearby factories seeking cheap female labour, meant the camp became the place to which single mothers and their children were 'shunted' by the DLNS and the DOI. Social workers in the 1950s expressed concern about the concentration of migrant women's labour that allowed Benalla to become

Noncompliance and Agency in Migrant Family Life 173

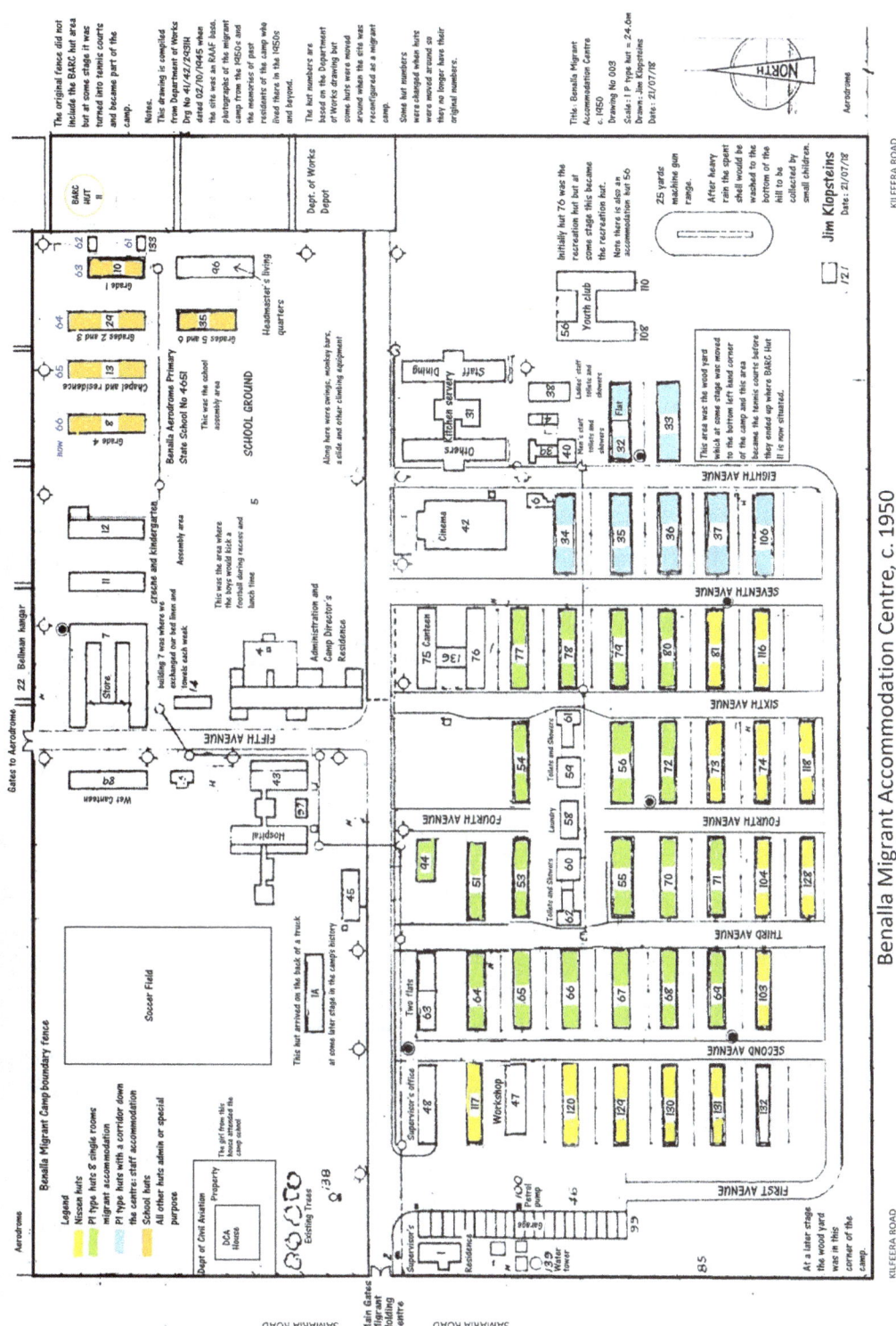

Figure 6.2 Benalla Camp layout, circa 1950. With permission from Jim Klopsteins.

an 'experiment' in the concentrated accommodation of single mothers. They labelled these women and their children 'problem cases' who were resistant to assimilation.[22] Social workers saw Benalla as a temporary solution. They underscored the need to 'teach and marry off' the women for their 'long-term benefit' – an approach that went out of favour among social workers by the late 1950s, and, in any case, appeared to have no effect on the long-term population of Benalla camp.

As author, former long-term resident of Benalla and heritage advocate Helen Topor has publicly argued:

> Their unwillingness to [relinquish their children], and their inability to marry (either because they lacked the documents verifying their marital status) or their reluctance to marry, put pressure back on the government to fund child-minding services so these women could work. The provision of government-sponsored childcare has been documented as a radical departure from prevailing cultural norms. It demonstrated the effectiveness of involuntary non-compliance to force structural change. It was a pioneering move.[23]

As Topor stresses in her testimony, in their noncompliance these women were pioneers, slowly but surely compelling bureaucrats to enact changes to the limited services on offer. That said, she also recognizes that the 'camp's long-stayers epitomize a sad and difficult Catch-22': they found they were unable to afford to pay off rent debts to holding centres; their pay, whether from nearby factory work or the camp's kitchens, barely covered their family expenses, and so they stayed in the camp system. In total, Topor's family – including her German-born mother and two younger siblings but not her Polish father – stayed in the camp system for seventeen years. Public historian Bruce Pennay, in his commemorative book on Benalla, notes that these families experienced a 'broadly unhappy dispersal' from their spartan but familiar Benalla camp home after it was closed by the DOI in 1967.[24]

Another point becomes clear from the testimony: it was not only single-parent households that stayed in the camp system for years, nor was Benalla the only camp with long-term residents. There are also examples of nuclear families who also stayed in the camp system beyond the terms of their two-year contracts. Countless recollections mention the necessity of 'extra work' or 'odd jobs' to save enough money to move out of the camps – this informal economy will be explored in more detail below. Others mention that movement into a home (or even makeshift and self-built sheds) was only possible if two families shared the costs and moved out together.[25] Another possibility presents itself: some families, including single-parent households, preferred the communal environment of the camp. At the very least, the camp was shielded from mainstream (and often xenophobic) Anglo-Australian society, especially if one found employment within the camp itself. All of this is to say that a range of factors kept some families living in camps well beyond the ending of their two-year work contracts.

Former residents recall both pushing against the inconveniences of camp life and using them to their advantage. Migrant storytelling reveals that the mobility necessitated by labour allocations and accommodation could be both a positive and negative aspect of the postwar migrant camp system. Voy Ilic, whose family originally hailed from the former Yugoslavia, lived at Greta for ten years, a time he has 'mixed feelings' about. The Ilic family's first home in Australia in 1949 was Bathurst migrant camp (200 km from Sydney), where they stayed for a week before Voy's father was sent to work in the State Dockyards in Sydney. The rest of the family was transferred to Greta, where the huts 'seemed similar' to Bathurst. Within Greta, five-year-old Voy, his mother and his three younger siblings were transferred multiple times to different huts across both Silver and Chocolate City. New additions to the family (his mother gave birth to two more babies) and employment opportunities within one of the many camp kitchens prompted these internal movements.

Due to his extended stay and movements across Greta camp, Voy is able to recall small or incremental changes to the camp's built fabric (for example, the rectangular huts in Chocolate City were painted a light blue-green in 1955) as well as the features of the landscape that shaped his activities – living in U block in Silver City, for example, meant he was only 100 metres from Greta Northern Railway Line. 'I loved watching the trains go by', he recalls.[26] Voy's father travelled by train from Sydney to visit his family in Greta; it was the same line Voy would use to get to high school in East Maitland from 1957, while still living at Greta camp. Living in close quarters to other families grappling with their wartime trauma, he references the Second World War-induced post-traumatic stress disorder (PTSD) displayed by many DPs at the camp, as well as his witnessing of domestic violence and child abuse. Schulha has publicly discussed his research around the issue, citing the strain that separation placed on relationships, the jealousies incited by living in close quarters with other separated families, and the widespread but undiagnosed influence of PTSD. Women and children bore the brunt of the abuse, and their isolation and language barriers compounded their vulnerabilities. Like many abuse survivors, they felt unable to report it to the authorities for fear of being disbelieved or, worse, sent back to Europe. 'I have a large file containing cases heard in Maitland Court involving such cases during the camp years', Schulha recounts. Some of these tragic cases, traced through court records and newspaper reports, will be given in his next book on Greta.[27]

Voy's contemporary, Christine Schaller, whose German family stayed at Benalla camp for only six months in 1955, commented that: 'It could get really rough at the camp – working fathers were away for weeks on end and when they came back, fights and drunkenness were the order of the day.'[28] Accordingly, in Voy's account, the extended bouts of separation from his father were not always negative occurrences. For some families, separation afforded dependants a break from 'an oppressive family situation', as Voy described it.[29] For her part, Topor explains that 'we came to Benalla to get away from my father', who was a fearsome presence in her childhood.[30] In other words, in some cases migrants were able to manoeuvre and use seemingly restrictive directives from camp and DOI officials to their advantage. Others, like Nevina's family mentioned above, successfully requested transfers in order to reunite families temporarily separated by work.

Reporting on Greta Migrant Camp in June 1949, the *Newcastle Morning Herald* shared the voices of migrant residents, providing its largely Anglo-Australian readership a rare glimpse into DP aspirations for settlement, the deleterious effects of the contract system on their sense of independence, as well as the wasteful dismissal of premigration qualifications:

> In the words of Mr. Adam Dukars, a Latvian economist who works in the quartermaster's store of the Centre [Greta] and whose lawyer wife works as a domestic: 'Everyone wants to start a new life in Australia. When our two years' contract is over, we look forward to a home and independence again in Australia . . . As for the migrant camps, we are used to camps in Germany. But what I look forward to is my independence again' . . . Saturday is a big day at the camp, when some lucky husbands are able to come from Sydney and other places to see their families . . . Merle, aged two and a half . . . She often asks when her father, who is away working, will come home.[31]

As was noted above, the extant testimony rarely contains the views of those who passed through the camps quickly; most of those I have cited thus far come from families that stayed in the camp system for at least a few months, if not years, a choice that was not always under their control. In addition, Australia's migration histories rarely contain accounts of those who became disillusioned with Australia and moved on to other countries. Among the reasons why an individual or family might choose to emigrate again was the Australian government's and industry's refusal to recognize migrants' overseas qualifications. Some chose to spend years regaining their qualifications in Australia; others never practised in their field again.

A young William Mader and his Hungarian parents arrived in Australia and were accommodated in Greta in July 1949. As William recalls: 'The camp itself looked very much like war-time camps in Europe, with its wooden huts arranged in rows.'[32] The family quickly became frustrated: they could not find jobs in their respective professions (engineering and the visual arts). Mr Mader was 'forced' to become a weaver at Burlington Mills, Rutherford (only 14 km from Greta), where William also worked briefly (see Figure 6.3). After the devastating Maitland floods of 1955, the

Figure 6.3 Inside Burlington/Bradmill Industries Mill at Rutherford, weaving ribbons, circa 1950. Courtesy of the National Archives of Australia, NAA, B4498 102E9

family moved to Sydney. There his father 'took on menial work in a factory in the city's northern outskirts', during which the 'family's disillusionment with Australia was complete', and they applied to emigrate to the United States instead. 'Within two weeks after arriving, my parents found jobs in their actual professions.' However, the transnational connections of heavy industry helped William to find work in the United States too: 'I went by train to Greensboro, North Carolina, to work as a clerk at Burlington Industries headquarters, thanks to a recommendation by my American boss at Burlington Mills in Maitland [NSW].'[33]

THE DEPENDENCE OF INDUSTRY

The relationship between migrant camps and nearby industry is most apparent in the relationship between Burlington Mills and Greta. A comparable example for Benalla would be the two factories of Latoof and Calill clothing and Renold Chains; both were dependent on migrant labour. These industries directly appealed to Commonwealth employment officers in nearby migrant camps to source their workforce.

Burlington Mills (Aust) was a joint venture involving Burlington Mills (USA) and Bradford Cotton Mills (Aust) Pty Ltd, the latter established in Sydney in 1927. They established a mill in Rutherford in 1945, leasing the land (an area of 120 acres) from the Federal Government until the mid-1950s, after which it purchased the site. Rutherford, in Central Maitland, is a half-hour train ride (or a 15-minute bus ride) from Greta. This factory became known as 'Bradmill' Industries from the late 1960s, when it expanded its acquisitions.[34] Bradmill produced a range of textiles, including 'high-fashion sheer fabrics to heavy gauge belting ducks'.[35] It was a major employer of migrant labour and many were resident at Greta camp. Its workforce peaked in 1972 with over 1,600 employees. Its success encouraged the local Maitland Council to invest in the region's textile industry – another two factories were established in the Rutherford area, funded by the Council and leased to tenants. The decline of Maitland's textiles industries began in the early 1980s, and the Bradmill factory finally closed in 2000, but fond community memories of working at the Mills remain strong, as demonstrated in recent efforts to commemorate and exhibit working life at Bradmill.[36]

Latoof and Calill, which produced women's and children's clothing, has a shorter history. The factory opened in 1945 with an initial workforce of 300 'girls' (see Figure 6.4).[37] It hired mostly migrant women who lived at the Benalla camp. The company first occupied Austral House in Bridge Street Benalla and once the new factory site was built, they moved to Coster Street, opposite Benalla Hospital and close to the migrant camp. It closed in the late 1960s – as Sabine Smyth, the instigator of Benalla Migrant Camp Inc., reflects, 'Latoof and Calill really came and went with the influx of migrants'.[38] Its physical remnants – the factory had a beautiful Art Deco style façade – have been the focus of some heritage attention from former residents. The 'bare and run-down' factory hosted a small exhibition and anniversary event in

Figure 6.4 Women workers outside the Latoof and Callil factory in Benalla, circa 1950. Courtesy of Sabine Smyth, Benalla Migrant Camp Exhibition

2015. However, the building was demolished a few years later and was subdivided for housing.[39]

Renold Chains, Benalla's other major employer of migrants, is best understood in reference to the Commonwealth's postwar push for decentralization, which had waned by the late 1950s. In 1953, when Renold Chains began marketing its manufacture of a new motorcycle chain, the Minister of State Development C.P. Stoneham 'paid a very high tribute to the courage and efficiency of Renold Chains (Aust) Pty Ltd' and said 'the factory had played a major part in the scheme of decentralization'.[40] These two factories made Benalla, in the mid-twentieth century, a centrally located hub of Victorian industries, a far cry from its reputation as a sleepy regional town today, known more for its street art and murals than for its industry.

MULTIETHNIC, MULTINATIONAL?

Residents and the Australian press would refer to migrant camps like Bonegilla as a 'little Europe'.[41] And yet, the support that migrant families received from Departmental social workers was always framed in reference to aiding assimilation. Assimilation, as loosely articulated government doctrine, shaped mainstream perceptions about the 'success' of the immigration scheme. The main argument of the above-cited *Newcastle Morning Herald* article was the 'problem' of migrant languages at the camp and in their migrant-dominated workplaces – that the lingua franca among the diverse DP cohort was *not* English, but more often German, Polish or Ukrainian, depending on the numbers in the camp at any one time (and from the mid-1950s onwards it was more likely to be Greek or Italian). From a migrant perspective, this was one of the positive aspects of camp life. Maria Zintschenko remembers that her Polish parents appreciated the strength of the Polish community at Benalla and participated in Polish dance groups and staged plays throughout the early 1950s. Estonian and Ukrainian choirs, and Latvian and Polish folk dancing groups became an important part of the cultural life of these respective migrant cohorts in the camps. Government officials and DOI social workers were initially suspicious of the formation of 'national groups' within the camps, believing that they would hinder 'assimilation', but they nonetheless become a defining feature of many children's memories of camp life.

Jordens reports on the official discouragement of nationalistic organizations within camps and workplaces, but this was specifically reserved for those that became 'political'.[42] On-site camp administrators were weary that the national and interethnic tensions that erupted during the Second World War and were stoked again by the Cold War could erupt in the camps and in workplaces. However, on occasion, 'cultural' groups performing dances and songs were used by the Department as a means to 'sell' happy ethnics to regional Anglo-Australian populations. Dancing troupes were paraded in their national costumes at local fairs and festivals. Of course, the line between cultural and political identification is hazy – Karen Schamberger's research describes the type of anti-Soviet nationalism that emerged among those exiled from their Baltic homelands.[43] Jordens notes that in 1954, the Director of Scheyville Holding Centre disbanded a Boy Scout group 'because it developed into a national group'.[44] The personal accounts offer a less sinister perspective, particularly for those who were children while in the camp system. For children at least, camp life was like living in 'a continuous playground'.[45] This too underlines the mismatch between childhood memories of the camp and the memories of their adult parents who grappled with new and changing political realities in Cold War Australia.

Like many long-term residents, Voy and his family only left Greta when it closed in January 1960, at which point Voy was fifteen:

> During the early years from 1949 until 1953 when there was a large population [at Greta] it was interesting. From 1955 to 1960 it got monotonous and as boring as batshit. I badly needed to get out beyond those mountains surrounding the camp and extend my view of the world. I was growing up and felt claustrophobic and restricted in the camp confines.[46]

The claustrophobia of camp life was also frequently cited by teenage and adult residents, alongside (and in ambivalent fashion) memories of communal harmony and the relief of sharing similar experiences and languages. For those who had spent over a decade living in different camps throughout Europe and then Australia, it could take a long time to adjust to living outside a camp and without the camp community. Natalie, who was sixteen months old when her family arrived at Greta in 1950 and nearly twelve years old when they left in January 1960, argues that camp life 'was another life and in some ways a little unnatural as people were protected from the real world'.[47]

SOCIAL WELFARE, UNIONS AND SUPPORT FOR MIGRANT WORKERS

Migrants, and especially migrant women, also found little support through their trade unions in the early postwar years. Christine Schaller, who arrived from Germany with her family in 1955 and stayed for a short period in Benalla migrant camp, remembers a few encounters:

> I worked at Latoof and Calill for a while. Those sewing machines were big industrial ones and if you were no good at operating them, you got the sack straight away. The company would just go back to Bonegilla and get a new lot of workers. One of my friends once went to complain to the union man about something, so the union man went straight to management and told on her, and she got the sack too. It was all very strange, and we never had much confidence in the Australian Unions after that.[48]

Language issues hindered communication between workers and their unions, with the latter making little attempt to communicate with a growing migrant workforce in a language they could understand. Anna Lemega, whose family originally hailed from Czechoslovakia and who worked and lived across Europe throughout the 1950s, provides her perspective on working in the factories: 'I also worked at Latoof and Calill. I felt sorry for the women that worked at Latoof and Calill who spoke no English, the Australian bosses used to yell at them to work harder. They were often in tears. I could at least help myself and speak up.'[49] Non-English-speaking migrant women were concentrated in the clothing trade and, according to migrant rights activists emerging in the 1960s, they faced a 'double disadvantage' in the workforce. Only a few militant left-wing trade unions recognized the special needs of migrant workers at this time, let alone working migrant women.[50] But it is equally important not to overstate their subjugation or rely solely on a culturalist framework to explain the disadvantage they faced in both their ethnic communities and in their workplaces. Vera Kent, publishing in the mid-1970s, argued that migrant women remained largely ignorant about unionism, but she stressed their ability to show 'tremendous strength and solidarity'.[51] She references their fights against factory owners on the issue of overtime and their successes through the Arbitration Commission as an example.[52] But this was decades after the period with which this chapter is concerned. Furthermore, Eastern European DPs have been described by some historians as distrustful of organized action and unions, not only because of unions' discriminatory negligence of migrant workers, but also because of DPs' anti-communist tendencies.[53] While the clothing industry employed predominately migrant women, membership to the Clothing Trades Union was poor throughout the postwar period. Ultimately, this reflected both their premigration experiences and the structural constraints and Anglocentrism of the union itself. Within camp populations, networks of support were informal and communal, and this, more than unions, acted as a protection – that 'long-timers became friends and treated each other as family'.[54]

Interethnic communality within the camp also aided in creating informal and sometimes unsanctioned economies of exchange and work that operated within (or in close proximity to) the camp. Recollections of these sometimes profitable activities that improved the daily lives of migrants in the camp provide another example of migrant agency in the camp system.

INFORMAL ECONOMIES OF EXCHANGE AND WORK: SIDE JOBS AND SERVICES

Countless accounts mention migrants undertaking 'side jobs', 'odd jobs' or 'extra work' for 'extra money'. This work could be sanctioned (in the case of temporary fruit-picking assignments or seasonal farm work) or unofficial (operating clandestine businesses within the camp). According to ex-resident and chronicler of Greta, Alek Schulha, adults took on extra work – often in addition to their allocated employment in industry – solely because they 'wanted to get out of the camp' and get away from the communal showers, the poor heating and cooling, and the lack of privacy.[55] The need for extra income was acute for those with only one breadwinner in the family.

'Sanctioned' extra work has a presence in the official archive – in Departmental records of labour movements – and has been accounted for in the historical records. For example, when Zosia Cukier recalls that 'many women from the camp went to Maitland picking potatoes to earn extra money. Others went grape picking near Cessnock',[56] these routes are visible through the numbers (though not named people) recorded in Departmental memos between the camp administrators, the DLNS and respective employers. The agricultural industry historically (and currently) relies on seasonal workers from overseas, mainly the Pacific. For a period in the postwar era, they relied on the wave of migrant settlers. Unsanctioned work is less traceable, and I have no way of providing any estimates of how many people engaged in extra, 'unsanctioned' or side jobs. This work constituted an informal economy (which also recalls the piecemeal and informal work arrangements of Southeast Asian refugees in Melbourne from the 1970s, which will be discussed in Chapter 8). While this type of work was 'outside' the migrant's Commonwealth Employment Service (CES) recorded job, it was dependant on local economies – including the informal and marginal ones established by the concentrated presence of a large cohort of migrant peoples within the community, in camps and regional towns.

John Gebhardt remembers that his father Franek (a Polish DP who arrived in Australia in 1949 with his wife and mother) would travel back to his family at Greta camp on the weekends, where he repaired shoes to earn extra income for the family.[57] Similarly, Teodor Fergin, also originally from Poland, would, 'when time permitted, earn extra money as a barber and cobbler', offering his services to residents at Benalla camp. He would do this when he was not working as a labourer picking fruit or tobacco or as a kitchen hand in one of the camp's communal kitchens.[58] Clearly, many used the skills they were unable to use in their sanctioned contract work. Sophia Arendt notes that her father Bruno Golonski 'made lovely pull-along wooden toys to earn a bit of extra money' while living at Benalla.[59]

Extra work was especially welcome in single-parent households. Irena Slusarczyk was resident at Benalla with her mother and two younger brothers from 1952 to 1967. Prior to this, they had passed through Bonegilla, on their way to Bowning NSW, where her mother Tosia worked as a domestic. The family were then transferred back to Bonegilla before being sent for a short stint to Uranquinty camp, and then transferred back to Bonegilla again, all within a two-year period. They then stayed at Benalla until its closure in 1967, and Irene has generally fond memories of the camp, its safety and the freedoms the children enjoyed there. She recalls that 'a decision had been made to sew curtains for all of the rooms in the camp and mum was given the extra work, earning more money; a low amount but welcoming the extra shillings per pair of curtains and was happy to do so'.[60]

Others recall with fondness 'Hilde's Hairdressing' at Benalla camp, which short-circuited the need to go into town and attempt communication with an English-speaking local hairdresser. According to her friend Christine: 'Hilde was a fully qualified hairdresser but had to go back to an Australian Hairdressing College to get a new qualification.' Even after their family moved out of the camp, Christine would get her hair cut at Hilde's Hairdressing until Hilde started up her own salon in Nunn Street, Benalla. It appears there were a number of hair services operating at Benalla in the early 1950s, and while not all clandestine business were based on formally acquired skills, they thrived in the informal economy of the camp and proved necessary for the future prospects of many migrant families.

Irene Kornienko's (née Chlebnikowski) extended Ukrainian family migrated from a German refugee camp in 1949. The family was separated upon migration, with her father, grandfather and great-uncle allocated temporary work assignments in other parts of Australia, including army tank maintenance at the Army training facility of Puckapunyal in Central Victoria. Her mother and two younger brothers were accommodated first at Bonegilla, then Cowra and finally Benalla, where they stayed until February 1951, and were eventually joined by the rest of the family. Irene, who was born at Benalla, recalls:

> For extra money, my Great Uncle and Grandfather become the resident barbers [at Benalla]. They had little previous experience, so once again found themselves in a position where they had to refund money to their customers, because many were not happy, but they improved their skills with time and managed to save some extra money. So when their 2 year contracts finished they had collectively saved enough money to purchase a house in Melbourne, it was very small, so they built extra rooms to it and were able to rent those rooms out to other migrants.[61]

Information about this informal or clandestine network of work (and of support) is accessible in these types of anecdotal recollections. Some were more enterprising and long-term profitable than others, and the historiography around 'ethnic entrepreneurs' and small business has traced some of these successes, alongside a critique of capitalism and its perpetuation of class divides within ethnic communities in Australia. But these studies have largely considered small businesses in cities like Sydney or Melbourne.[62] Camp-based ghost economies left few traces, even as they had a major impact on the settlement experiences of DPs and assisted migrants in postwar Australian towns and cities.

One of the more frequently recollected personalities at Greta camp was Zenon Kmak, who was known among former Greta residents for his salami. He lived at the camp for nine months, working first as a member of the outdoor maintenance staff and then in nearby Singleton, cutting and carting timber for Jock Stevens, who had a contract to supply the camp with cut timber to use in the boilers. Zenon then found work at Burlington Mills (Bradmill). Throughout these jobs, Zenon also harboured other aspirations, and he experimented with making salami and building his own smokehouse with rented machinery. While still working at Burlington, he began to sell his salami from the back of his Ford Falcon station wagon to migrant residents at Greta camp. Elizabeth Matt, who spent six years of her childhood at Greta camp, evocatively recalls the impact of Zenon's business on camp life:

> He would set up his van outside the main gates and sell residents items like veal, pork mince, continental sausages, kielbasa, brawn, pork trotters and brown bread. At the same time the women would put in their orders for the following Saturday. As a result of the influx of 'migrant food', the smells wafted over the camp as borscht (Russian soup), goulash, gowompky (cabbage rolls), luski (noodles) and pierogi (Polish dumplings) were cooked on primus burners in nearly every barrack.[63]

After leaving Burlington Mills, Zenon went on to establish a successful butcher shop and had a large and loyal migrant clientele based at Greta migrant camp. Notably, the cooking of one's own food in accommodation huts was against camp regulations, and yet Zenon's business thrived off the back of migrant demand.

Other business ventures too were, if not contrary to camp regulations, definitely outside mainstream industry. Informal economies, or grey economies, thrive among disadvantaged, stigmatized or distrusted communities – they operate outside the normal distribution of goods and services, outside government taxation and monitoring. Charlie Wisniewski, Greta's head of security and official gatekeeper who was born in Poland in 1925 and migrated as a DP with his wife and children in 1950, was always looking to 'make a quick buck' in the camp.[64] According to his children, he charged forty pence per person to transport migrants to and from Greta railway station. He could carry six people in his small Morris Minor. Side jobs and ventures were common for those who held jobs on the camp staff. Charlie also 'became obsessed with greyhounds and greyhound racing' while at Greta. According to his daughter's account, 'while walking his dogs the camp director caught him and told him to get rid of all of them. He delayed their removal until he moved out of the camp'.[65] It was necessary to bend or break camp rules in order to maintain informal economies. Other long-term residents, like the Kozaczynski family, had three dogs and a few chickens, 'despite camp rules prohibiting the possession of animals. Most families had some animals or pets. Many residents also made gardens in and around their huts'.[66] For the Wisniewski family, after they left the camp in 1959 and even as Charlie took up a position at Burlington Mills, greyhound racing remained a sometimes profitable passion project.

There is a risk of approaching this type of freelance work with rose-tinted glasses. This was precarious labour in a political economy that afforded nonanglophone migrants little economic power. To avoid whitewashing their situation, we can approach this type of side or extra work as a form of cultural production, and an example of the bounded agency of migrant actors living within the camp space and working in adjacent industry.

The success of these side ventures was premised on the migrant camp population and despite its bounded limits, the camp and its residents had a clear effect on the tastes and desires of local and regional economies, which have been overlooked in much of the historical literature.[67] Some extra work depended on the transient, marginal and concentrated nature of the community within the camp and dissipated once the camp closed; others, like Zenon Kmak's salami or Kozaczynski's greyhounds, continued to change local economies as they and their families established themselves.

Another way in which the influence of the camp population on local economies can be seen is in the hiring of migrant workers in local Australian-owned businesses, primarily to act as interpreters for a new migrant clientele. Lucy Sidorko recalls:

> The employment office at the camp originally offered me the job as a nurse's aid in Toowoomba. My mother, who came with me to the employment office, started crying because she didn't want me to go. Had she not been there, I would've accepted the job. A few days later I got another call from the employment office offering the job at Hustlers [haberdashery, in nearby Maitland]. Because I spoke about six languages, my job was to help migrants from Greta Camp who had difficulty explaining what they wanted.[68]

Lucy stayed at Hustlers for four years. Her account, aside from indicating that individual migrants were afforded some choice in employment allocations, underscores the need from local businesses for both migrant clients and migrant staff. The camp population had an immediate impact on local food production. For those who stayed in the region, their personal gardens followed them once they moved out of the camps and into the local towns. They grew and distributed vegetables that were then uncommon in Australian cooking, including zucchinis, capsicums and garlic, as well as preserved and pickled vegetables like cucumbers. According to Margot Paez, at Benalla camp, migrant women spent a lot of their time growing and producing food, a labour of cultural production – despite their full-time working hours (in this case, as factory workers in Benalla's Latoof and Calill clothing factory or as nurse's aides in the hospital) and the obligation of evening English language lessons.[69] Gardens were a form of subsistence and supplemented or improved the camp-issued food from the communal mess halls. Countless accounts from long-term residents mention foraging, hunting, gardening and then cooking (on primus stoves) and eating meals in a family's hut. These acts, specifically the cooking and eating, run contrary to the historic image of migrants eating in communal mess halls, although the latter was commonplace for short-term residents.

As mentioned earlier, in the early years of Greta's existence as a migrant camp, it was an administrative requirement that all meals be taken in communal mess halls, and the cooking and eating of food within one's hut was discouraged, but this rule became untenable for long-term families, who pushed back against these restrictions until eventually the rule was abandoned.[70] Horst Farken, who arrived with his wife Rena and two children in the 1960s from Germany, recalls Rena's efforts to improve their meals at Benalla: 'We used to pick up the food from the canteen and then Rena used to spice it up and make it tasty back in our rooms on a little cooker.'[71] Horst recognizes too that conditions had gotten 'better and better' for migrants by the time they arrived in 1960, which was the result of resistance and complaints from migrants who came before them.

Even then, however, the food remained an issue. The creative practice of finding, adjusting and (re)cooking camp-issued food to suit different tastes stood out in the recollections of many. George Nikolsky, another former Benalla resident whose father and mother worked full-time at Renolds and Latoof and Calill respectively, recalls that the men 'would fish and hunt rabbits like most people, to supplement our food and survive. We also picked hops and tobacco at Myrrhee and we cut firewood, for extra money. Life was hard, but simple'.[72] These creative practices were part of building comfort in a spartan setting. Family survival, and the ability to leave the camp, relied on extra work and the informal economies that allowed them to thrive.

CONCLUSION

The individual and family stories presented in this chapter cover the breadth of experience of migrant camps like Benalla and Greta – from the melancholy and tragic through to the affirming and aspiring. Across these recollections, individuals and families act to alter their circumstances, no matter how restrictive the context. Migrant camps were not only nodes in a network that directed labour. We should resist the historiographical tendency to operationalize human beings – as faceless workers in a 'mass' migration scheme – when discussing migration, industrial labour and postwar reconstruction. The intimate angle facilitated by new and emerging storytelling platforms – those initiated by migrant and ethnic-minority community groups associated with the place of the migrant camp – do this work and offer a necessary corrective.

This chapter has accordingly integrated both emotional and material factors into an analysis of migrant family life in regional postwar Australia. Families found innovative ways to build comfort in the sometimes inhospitable and ex-military environment of the camp – to resist or adapt to (and indeed escape) the regimentation and communal living, to build alternative ways of wellbeing and safety in the camp. Sometimes their 'noncompliance' instigated changes to camp systems and the level of care provided, while in other cases change was slow and incremental, and families found creative ways to function – especially those stuck in the camp system for more than two years. Accounting for these stories, the subjectivity of migrants living and working within Australia's postwar migrant camps means recognizing this bounded agency and the impossible-to-ignore ghost economies and relational networks of exchange that these families built within Australia's migrant camps.

Alexandra Dellios is a senior lecturer in the Centre for Heritage and Museum Studies at the Australian National University. She is the author of *Heritage Making and Migrant Subjects in the Deindustrialising Region of the Latrobe Valley* (2022) and *Histories of Controversy: Bonegilla Migrant Centre* (2017), and is coeditor (with Eureka Henrich) of *Migrant, Multicultural and Diasporic Heritage: Beyond and between Borders* (2020). She is Chair of the Editorial Board for *Studies in Oral History*, a founding member of the Australian Migration History Network and an Executive Committee member of the Association of Critical Heritage Studies.

NOTES

1. Kamm and Gebhardt, 'Risk Patterns and Bounded Agency in Vocational Orientation', 11–31; Rubenson and Desjardins, 'The Impact of Welfare State Regimes on Barriers to Participation in Adult Education', 187–207.
2. Dellios, *Histories of Controversy*, 64–123.
3. Jordens, *Aliens to Citizens*, 60.
4. Ibid.
5. Nguyen, 'Refugees, Museums and the Digital Diaspora'; Pennay, 'Almost Everyone's Bonegilla', 1–19.
6. Dellios, *Histories of Controversy*, 23–63.
7. Castles, 'Italians in Australia', 346.
8. For further explanation of 'settler loss' and return migration rates, see Price, 'Australian Immigration: 1947–73', 308–9.
9. Persian, '"Chifley Liked Them Blond"', 80–101; Agutter, 'Displaced Persons and the "Continuum of Mobility"', 142; Jordens, *Redefining Australians*, 48; Dellios, *Histories of Controversy*, 24.
10. Dellios, 'Displaced Persons, Family Separation and the Work Contract in Postwar Australia', 427.
11. NAA: A4933, ID/1, 'For Standing Committee of Cabinet on Industry and Development: Immigrant Programme, 1950 – Employment and Accommodation of Migrant Workers'.
12. Andrean, cited in Schulha, *Beneath the Shadows*, 162.

13. Wally, cited in ibid., 99.
14. Graff, cited in ibid., 165.
15. Drobot, cited in ibid., 301.
16. Zintschenko, cited in *Benalla Camp Exhibition*.
17. Schulha, cited in Schulha, *Beneath the Shadows*, 113.
18. Panich, *Sanctuary?*, 183.
19. Agutter, 'Displaced Persons and the 'Continuum of Mobility'', 147.
20. Jordens, *Aliens to Citizens*, 63.
21. NAA: A2567, 1968/27, 'Bonegilla Migrant Reception and Training Centre – Czech Refugees, Report by Welfare Officer, E. Martek', 4 June 1969; NAA: A2567, 1968/27, 'Report by Welfare Officer, E Martek, 4 June 1969; NAA: A445 140/5/6, 'The Social Worker in Immigration – Social Workers' Reports', June 1952.
22. NAA: A445, 140/5/6 1951 and, A445/1, 276/2/10, 276/1/6, Hazel Dobson's social welfare reports, 'Widows and Unmarried Mothers with Dependent Children', March 1951.
23. Topor, *Benalla Migrant Camp*, 6.
24. Pennay, *Benalla Migrant Camp*, 13.
25. Gebhardt and Polack, cited in Schulha, *Beneath the Shadows*, 169.
26. Ilic, cited in ibid., 105.
27. Alek Schulha, 'Facebook Post: 29 August 2022', *Beneath the Mountains*.
28. Schaller, cited in *Benalla Camp Exhibition*.
29. Voy, cited in Schulha, *Beneath the Shadows*, 105.
30. Helen Topor, interview with the author, Canberra, September 2016.
31. 'Greta Has a Language Problem', *Newcastle Morning Herald*, 11 June 1949.
32. Mader, cited in Schulha, *Beneath the Shadows*, 119.
33. Ibid., 120.
34. Insite Heritage, *Aboriginal and European Heritage Assessment of the Proposed Resource and Recycling Facility*, 21–24.
35. Ibid., 22.
36. Sharpe, Donna. 'National Textile Exhibition', *The Maitland Mercury*, 7 January 2020. Retrieved 18 December 2023 from https://www.maitlandmercury.com.au/story/6568018/fond-memories-of-the-mill/.
37. SLV: Crown Apparel Company, 'Announcement: Benalla', State Library of Victoria Collections, Accession No: H92.250/960, 1945.
38. Smyth, cited in 'Old Factory Display', *Benalla Ensign*, 21 January 2015.
39. Smyth, 'A Last Look at Latoof and Callil Clothing Factory in Benalla'. Retrieved 18 December 2023 from https://vimeo.com/157685916.
40. 'Benalla's Largest Industry's New Product: Melbourne and Benalla Celebrations', *Benalla Ensign*, 19 November 1953.
41. *The Herald*, 2 October 1971, cited in Sluga, *Bonegilla, 'A Place of No Hope'*, 130.
42. The Australian Security Intelligence Organisation (ASIO) conducted extensive surveillance of politically active migrant workers at this time, especially those involved with left-wing trade unions or the Communist Party of Australia.
43. Schamberger, 'Weaving a Family and a Nation', 178–98.
44. Jordens, *Alien to Citizen*, 149.
45. Chyl (née Sujecki), cited in Schulha, *Beneath the Shadows*, 156.
46. Ilic, cited in ibid., 109.
47. Kennedy (née Golionc), cited in ibid., 187.
48. Gruzewski (née Schaller), cited in Benalla Migrant Camp Exhibition.
49. Lemega, cited in ibid.

50. Hearn, 'Migrants and Trade Unions', 65–70.
51. Kent, *Migrant Women Workers Kit*.
52. See also 'Women Workers Beat the Bosses', *Melbourne Times*, 18 June 1975.
53. Fitzpatrick, *White Russians*; Persian, 'Cossack Identities', 125–42.
54. Sidorczuk, cited in Benalla Migrant Camp Exhibition.
55. Alek Schulha, phone correspondence with the author, 14 September 2021.
56. Cukier, cited in Schulha, *Beneath the Shadows*, 145.
57. Gebhardt, cited in ibid., 169.
58. Fergin, cited in Benalla Migrant Camp Exhibition.
59. Golonski, cited in ibid.
60. Slusarczyk, cited in ibid.
61. Kornienko, cited in ibid.
62. Collins, *A Shop Full of Dreams*; Piperoglou, 'Migrant Labour and Their "Capitalist Compatriots"'.
63. Matt (née Lodo), cited in Schulha, *Beneath the Shadows*, 130.
64. Wisniewski, cited in ibid., 149.
65. Ibid.
66. Shearer (née Kozaczynski), cited in Schulha, *Beneath the Shadows*, 159.
67. Forsyth and Loy-Wilson, 'Introduction', 1–7.
68. Sidorko (née Kallaur), cited in Benalla Migrant Camp Exhibition.
69. Paez, cited in ibid.
70. NAA: A2567, 61/026, 'Removal of Food 1960–62 Memorandum'.
71. Horst and Rena Farken, cited in Benalla Migrant Camp Exhibition.
72. George Nikolsky on his parents, Pietr and Margaret Nikolski, cited in ibid.

BIBLIOGRAPHY

Archival Records

National Archives of Australia (NAA)
State Library Victoria (SLV)

Publications

Agutter, Karen. 'Displaced Persons and the "Continuum of Mobility" in the South Australian Hostel System', in Margrette Kleinig and Eric Richards (eds), *On the Wing: Mobility before and after Emigration to Australia* (Melbourne: Anchor Books, 2013), pp. 136–52.

Agutter, Karen, and Catherine Kevin. "From forced to coerced labour: displaced mothers and teen girls in post-World War II Australia." *Labor History* 64, no. 3 (2023): 256–68.

Benalla Migrant Camp Exhibition website. Retrieved 25 February 2019 from https://www.benallamigrantcamp.com.au/.

Castles, Stephen. 'Italians in Australia: The Impact of a Recent Migration on the Culture and Society of a Postcolonial Nation', *Center for Migration Studies Special Issues* 11(3) (1994), 342–67.

Collins, Jock. *A Shop Full of Dreams: Ethnic Small Business in Australia*. Leichhardt, NSW: Pluto Press Australia, 1995.

Dellios, Alexandra. 'Displaced Persons, Family Separation and the Work Contract in Postwar Australia', *Journal of Australian Studies* 40(4) (2016), 418–32.

——. *Histories of Controversy: Bonegilla Migrant Centre*. Melbourne: Melbourne University Press, 2017.

Forsyth, Hannah, and Sophie Loy-Wilson. 'Introduction: Political Implications for the New History of Capitalism', *Labour History: A Journal of Labour and Social History* 121(1) (2021), 1–7.

Fitzpatrick, Sheila. *White Russians, Red Peril: A Cold War History of Migration to Australia*. New York: Routledge, 2021.

Gibson-Graham, J.K., and Kelly Dombroski. 'Introduction – The Handbook of Diverse Economies: Inventory as Ethical Intervention', in J.K. Gibson-Graham and Kelly Dombroski (eds), *The Handbook of Diverse Economies* (Cheltenham: Edward Elgar Publishing, 2020), pp. 1–24.

Hearn, Julie. 'Migrants and Trade Unions', in Des Storer (ed.), *Ethnic Rights, Power and Participation Toward a Multi-cultural Australia* (Melbourne: Clearing House on Migration Issues, Ecumenical Migration Centre and Centre for Urban Research and Action Melbourne, 1975), pp. 65–70.

Insite Heritage. *Aboriginal and European Heritage Assessment of The Proposed Resource and Recycling Facility 11 Kyle Street, Rutherford, NSW*. Wangi Wangi, NSW: Insite Heritage, 2005.

Jordens, Ann-Marie. *Redefining Australians: Immigration, Citizenship, and National Identity*. Sydney: Hale & Iremonger, 1995.

——. *Aliens to Citizens: Settling Migrants in Australia: 1945–75*. St Leonards, NSW: Allen & Unwin in association with the Australian Archives, 1997.

Kamm, Chantal, and Anja Gebhardt. 'Risk Patterns and Bounded Agency in Vocational Orientation', *Studia Paedagogica* 24(2) (2019), 11–31.

Kent, Vera. *Migrant Women Workers Kit*. Melbourne: Centre for Urban Research and Action, 1975.

Nguyen, Anh. 'Refugees, Museums and the Digital Diaspora'. Melbourne Museum Public Lectures. Retrieved 18 June 2019 from https://www.youtube.com/watch?v=ItKr1KwG53o.

Panich, Catherine. *Sanctuary? Remembering Postwar Immigration*. Sydney: Allen & Unwin, 1988.

Pennay, Bruce. *Benalla Migrant Camp: A Difficult Heritage*. Benalla: Benalla Migrant Camp Inc., 2015.

——. 'Almost Everyone's Bonegilla: An Expanded Digital Archive on the Reception of Newly Arrived Migrants', *Journal of Australian Studies* (2022), 1–19.

Persian, Jayne. '"Chifley Liked Them Blond": DP Migrants for Australia', *History Australia* 12(2) (2015), 80–101.

——. 'Cossack Identities: From Russian Émigrés and Anti-Soviet Collaborators to Displaced Persons', *Immigrants & Minorities* 36(2) (2018), 125–42.

Piperoglou, Andonis. 'Migrant Labour and Their "Capitalist Compatriots": Towards a History of Ethnic Capitalism', *Labour History* 121 (2021), 175194.

Price, Charles. 'Australian Immigration, 1947–73', *International Migration Review* 9(3) (1975), 304–18.

Rubenson, Kjell, and Richard Desjardins. 'The Impact of Welfare State Regimes on Barriers to Participation in Adult Education: A Bounded Agency Model', *Adult Education Quarterly* 59(3) (2009), 187–207.

Schamberger, Karen. 'Weaving a Family and a Nation through Two Latvian Looms', *Immigrants & Minorities* 36(2) (2018), 178–98.

Schulha, Alek. *Beneath the Shadows of Mount Molly Morgan: History and Stories of Greta Camp 1939–1960*. Ashtonfield, NSW: Alek Schulha, 2020.

——. 'Post 29 August 2022'. *Beneath the Mountains* Facebook Page. Retrieved 30 August 2022 from https://www.facebook.com/profile.php?id=100063685683288.

Sluga, Glenda. *Bonegilla, 'A Place of No Hope'*. Melbourne: Melbourne University Publishing, 1988.

Topor, Helen. *Benalla Migrant Camp: Submission for Inclusion in the Victorian Heritage Register*. Benalla: Victorian Heritage Council Hearing BPACC, 10 and 11 February 2016.

Chapter 7

Design Experiments in Collective Housing
The Renewal of Commonwealth Migrant Hostels

Renee Miller-Yeaman

From the commencement of immigration recruitment programmes directly after the Second World War, political and public anxieties surrounding arriving migrants and refugees were directly linked to broader perceptions of housing in Australian society. Historian Ann-Mari Jordens argues in her book *On Accommodating Migrants* that due to a housing shortage stemming from the Great Depression after the war, 'the political acceptability of the immigration programme depended upon the ability of the government to prevent migrant home-seekers from competing with Australian-born for rented and privately-owned accommodation'.[1] Initial strategies included housing migrants from the British Isles with their sponsors and families, but gradually subsidized on-arrival accommodation was set up for all migrants arriving on assisted passage schemes. The need to provide initial accommodation contributed to a little-researched connection between immigration policy and housing agendas emerging from the Commonwealth Government from the Second World War onwards.[2] For the Commonwealth to implement and win public approval for its nation-building programme, centred on population and labour force growth through migrant recruitment, it needed to provide alternative accommodation for arriving populations. During the late 1940s and 1950s, Commonwealth on-arrival accommodation sites were set up across Australia and by 1951 the federally owned company Commonwealth Hostels Ltd, working with the Department of Immigration, took over the operation of all federally run hostels.[3] Migrant hostels were initially conceived by the Commonwealth Government as transitory accommodation and provision for assimilatory practices, and their physical, spatial and material character shaped this critical entry point into Australian citizenship. The changing landscape of on-arrival accommodation in turn reflected positional changes in the kind of hospitality extended to newcomers as it shifted from repurposed military camps discussed in previous chapters to hostel models experimenting with collective housing. The implementation of the federal government's immigration programme and its perceptions of housing were nevertheless underscored by political anxieties regarding racialized, cultural differences that surrounded arriving populations.

This chapter's central focus is on the Endeavour Migrant Hostel located in Randwick (now South Coogee), Sydney (see Figure 7.1). Opened by the Minister for Labour and National Service in March 1970, it belongs to a later generation of on-arrival accommodation and can be viewed as an experimental site for approaches to housing historically used for migrants and refugees. Accommodating up to approximately 1,000 people, the design's provision for temporary, collective living was aligned with dwelling arrangements seen in apartments rather than the ex-army barrack-and-hut facilities indicative of earlier camp and hostel incarnations. By exploring these new design strategies used to accommodate migrants and refugees entering the country, this chapter considers the postwar migrant influx as pivotal for design and social experimentation in housing.[4] Previous chapters have connected housing prefabrication and industry. This chapter looks at the architecture industry and profession's increasing engagement with public housing.

Figure 7.1 The Endeavour Migrant Hostel, Randwick (now South Coogee), Sydney, 1977. Courtesy of the National Archives of Australia, NAA: C5102, 15/64

The trajectories of Commonwealth migrant hostel sites are defined by constant experimentation with housing, from provisional practices to testing out new models for collective living within institutional frameworks. In this process of renewal – from emergency reception centres to a type of federal institution – the designs drew on diverse spatial models, from the abovementioned military barracks seen in the early migrant worker camps to later hotels and motels and contentiously, prisons, shifting across industrial, recreational and eventually punitive architectural typologies. Later incarnations of Commonwealth on-arrival accommodation, such as the Endeavour, can be viewed as test cases for different forms of housing provision in Australia, underscored by modern types of housing design that can arguably also be linked to institutionally informed domestic configurations. Arriving populations that did not have access to individual property or familial dwellings were introduced to broader constructions of Australian citizenship through these framings and forms of domesticity. In the direct aftermath of the Second World War, initial on-arrival accommodation experimented with spatial arrangements, often inherited from the military to 'warehouse' large groups of people, arriving predominantly from the British Isles and Europe, who would provide a crucial workforce for Australia's developing industries.[5] However, the Endeavour's completion and ensuing occupation coincided with the decline in the Commonwealth Government's recruitment drive to bolster its population and the beginning of resettlement services for refugees from non-European backgrounds.

THE ENDEAVOUR HOSTEL

During the 1960s, Commonwealth Hostels Ltd, in conjunction with the Department of Immigration and the Department of Labour and National Service, undertook a nationwide programme to improve migrant resettlement facilities. This programme included purpose-built housing designed by trained architects from within the Commonwealth Department of Public Works and prominent Australian firms.[6] This redevelopment programme to improve on-arrival accommodation in the 1960s was also linked to perceptions of housing from within Australia and more specifically to perceptions originating from outside Australia. The interdepartmental discourse surrounding the programme was grounded in policy that aimed to substantially bolster migrant recruitment from a competitive market in Europe due to its increasing political stability and economic prosperity.[7] Europe's postwar revival placed pressure on Australia to market itself as an advantageous destination and resulted in the Department of Immigration's acquisition of new sites and construction of modern hostels with improved and subsidized accommodation for migrants.[8] Although not the primary motivating factor in improving hostel accommodation, frequent protests from residents about the standard of food and facilities (see Figure 7.2) were equally crucial in the Commonwealth of Australia's need to improve the standard of accommodation and facilities of these sites.[9]

Figure 7.2 Residents lining up for meals at the Endeavour Hostel, 1971. Courtesy of the National Archives of Australia, NAA: A12111, 1/1971/22/23

The Endeavour Hostel was part of this broader programme of improving on-arrival temporary accommodation and design related to the Commonwealth's shifting agendas with accommodating incoming populations during the 1960s and 1970s. Broader political, public and frequently racialized tensions informed hostel design in relation to government-subsidized housing. The Endeavour had a Melbourne counterpart, the Enterprise Migrant Hostel (see Chapter 8), which opened later in the 1970s and was located in Springvale, which at the time was on the fringe of suburbia and near industries in southeastern Melbourne.[10] The Endeavour and the Enterprise share an almost identical design (see Figure 7.3). The Endeavour Migrant Hostel was an open but self-sufficient complex that included housing, dining, entertainment and childcare facilities. New migrants and refugees were accommodated in radially planned, rectangular, brick-faced housing blocks surrounded by sports fields, two basketball courts and landscaped gardens. Occupying a vast site, there were three accommodation complexes consisting of six radial housing blocks and a separate entrance building for the industrial kitchen and communal dining areas, childcare centre, recreation hall and an adjoining car park. This central amenity block also included a post office, a small kiosk and offices for administrative staff. Meals, as with other Commonwealth migrant hostels, were provided in a large, centralized dining hall. The Commonwealth Government regarded the hostel as a self-sufficient community requiring the appropriate amenities that had be developed in the early large hostels such as the Villawood

Migrant Hostel in western Sydney. Similar to all other major hostels, the Endeavour was not closed, and residents were free to come and go as they pleased and used the wider neighbourhood facilities such as schools and shops.

The Endeavour hostel exhibits novel planning arrangements rarely used in other public housing or private apartments in Australia during this period, in that it utilized clusters of radial planned apartment wings that make an imposing impression from the aerial photographs. Consequently, demonstrating the appropriation and amalgamation of design languages lifted from various dwelling types, where they converge into an institutional form that is also reminiscent of prison designs and evokes spatial languages of incarceration and confinement. An analysis of the Endeavour's design and the merging of spatial qualities related to the house – as inscribed by the apartment, the hotel and motel, and more institution-based accommodation – relays a tension between ideas of permanence and transience that arguably reflects anxieties around the forms of Commonwealth hospitality offered to incoming populations.

The emergence of Commonwealth migrant hostels as sites for design experimentation in housing is evident in both the built facilities and the aspirations for the new designs as described and circulated by the Australian Government publications. Sources for the chapter, including fragmented Commonwealth Government archives of architectural drawings, Public Works Committee reports and interdepartmental communication records, reveal the design strategies employed for the Endeavour. A

Figure 7.3 The Enterprise Migrant Hostel under construction, Springvale, Melbourne, 1970. Courtesy of the National Archives of Australia, NAA: B6295, 2416E

lineage of proposed and built on-arrival housing experimentations starts with research undertaken by the Department of Works and Housing's Commonwealth Experimental Building Station (CEBS).[11] The CEBS investigated prototypes to maximize efficiency in accommodating migrant workers in the 1940s. The Commonwealth used the later, new hostels, such as the Endeavour, with its innovative and collective living designs to promote Australia as a sought-after destination for resettlement to prospective migrants through publicity and immigration campaigns – offering hospitality through interpretations of collective and institutional living arrangements. The Endeavour's brief development was grounded in the aim to bolster migrant recruitment through providing more appealing on-arrival facilities and services and resulted in the Department of Immigration's acquisition of new sites and the construction of modern hostels through the Department of Works.[12]

In examining the final years of the Endeavour's operation, we witness the transition away from hostel accommodation to self-sufficient apartments with kitchens under the Migrant Transitory Flat Scheme reflective of broader changes in immigration programmes and policy. During the late 1960s and 1970s, the Australian government's objectives and policies regarding immigration and refugee resettlement were changing, in part due to the economic unrest beginning in the early 1970s as well as Australia's involvement in the Vietnam War.[13] In the late 1960s and 1970s, successive Commonwealth Governments debated the number of refugees arriving from non-European countries that Australia should resettle. Included in these debates were people leaving Pinochet's dictatorship in Chile and people arriving from mainland Southeast Asia during and after the Vietnam War.[14] Although the impetus behind the Endeavour's construction belongs to the earlier era of migrant recruitment, in the 1970s, Commonwealth hostels provided transitory accommodation for migrant and refugee families arriving not only from Europe but also from Turkey and South America and subsequently housed a small number of refugees from mainland Southeast Asia, along with evacuees from East Timor in the mid-1970s.[15]

The Endeavour's construction and enduring use is wedged between these shifting and overlapping immigration agendas and is a period of inquiry that is often overlooked in existing scholarship on migrant hostels. Increased interest in former migrant and refugee on-arrival accommodation sites as exemplifiers of new practices of placemaking are evident in the work of Australian historians such as Sara Wills, Alexandra Dellios, Glenda Sluga and Pamie Ching Tsz Fung.[16] Their primary focus has been in connection to social and political histories of these sites, with an emphasis on the early decades of the Commonwealth's immigration programme and its parallel provision of on-arrival accommodation. In architecture, the connection between migration and housing in Australia is an expanding field. Notably, with the work of Mirjana Lozanovska, where the intersection of house and home is revealed as fertile ground to explore how cultural difference manifests in architecture with formal and aesthetic choices and design fashions.[17] The emphasis in her work is on owner-occupied houses. Although she contends that the prevalence of house ownership in Australia has an assimilatory dimension to it, what this work highlights is that recently arrived, ethnoculturally marginalized migrants were nevertheless able to cultivate spaces in private houses through home-building and community-building practices not necessarily available or allowed in government-sponsored housing. Much of the research in this field is focused on houses owned by migrants rather than government-subsidized facilities that endorse temporary tenures and conditions of physical transience, such as migrant hostels and other forms of public housing. Arguably, government-sponsored domestic design experimentations can tie in with broader social agendas and consequently social engineering.[18] Indeed, how political aspirations influenced the design in the push for maximum utility in Commonwealth migrant hostels is a driving question for this chapter.

THE DEPARTMENT OF WORKS AND HOUSING'S COMMONWEALTH EXPERIMENTAL BUILDING STATION

During the 1950s and 1960s nation-building era, the domestic realm as produced through public housing was a site for innovation in construction technologies and programmatic arrangements, exemplified best by the urban renewal schemes undertaken by the Housing Commission of New South Wales (HCNSW) and, notably, the Housing Commission of Victoria (HCV). The HCV's schemes were centred on debates around 'slum' reclamation and subsequent high-rise flat construction, which adopted the British welfare system of the mixed estate.[19] The design construction for HCV tower blocks experimented with prefabricated concrete panels and industrialized constructed methods.[20] After the Second World War, the CEBS experimented with the design of housing incoming migrant populations. The station was set up in 1944 and was initially under the jurisdiction of the Department of Post War Reconstruction (1942–50) and then moved shortly afterwards to the Department of Works and Housing (1945–52) and relocated its base to North Ryde, Sydney.[21] Fundamental to its inception was the housing shortage that occurred during the Second World War and that continued into the 1950s.

After the war effort contributed to a shortage of traditional materials such as bricks and timber, the earlier incarnation of the CEBS aimed to develop technologies directly connected to housing, such as prefabricated mechanical equipment for low-cost concrete housing. The station was conceived and practiced with the cooperation of industry, the professions and a collaborative partnership with the then Council for Scientific and Industrial Research, which later became the Commonwealth Scientific and Industrial Research Organisation or CSIRO.[22]

In the CEBS records there is a selection of diagrams that show a variation on emergency accommodation for individual migrants. The aims of this research conducted in early 1949 were outlined as follows: 'Attached are sketches showing how the basic shells of permanent houses could be used economically to serve as hostels for single-male immigrants, and subsequently completed as permanent houses of normal standard.'[23] At this early stage of the postwar drive to populate, there was a recruitment emphasis on young men to generate a workforce for infrastructure projects and satisfy the emerging need for industrial labour. In the early migrant camp sites, genders were frequently segregated, and men were often separated from any accompanying partners and children. The CEBS plan for this adaptive reuse of housing advocated six basic house shells situated together, with four being occupied as dormitories, one consisting of part dormitories, part laundry, and the sixth as the dining hall and ablutions block. In this grouping of six shells the plan was for thirty-eight people. A notable feature of this adaptive plan was the efficiency in materials: most materials were to be reused in the second housing incarnation, with the only foreseeable waste being the plywood screens between sleeping areas. This dwelling strategy was not conceived as a replacement for the emerging camps and hostels that were being erected throughout Australia towards the end of the 1940s, as the project report states:

> It is not suggested that this type of development is suitable for the housing of all immigrants, but it is suggested that it is a practicable and economical way of providing for single men in areas where permanent housing will in due course be required, i.e. adjacent to larges factories, mines. etc.[24]

The programmatic divisions in this arrangement were also evident in the early built camps and hostels, which exhibited clearly defined divisions between dormitories and eating blocks that resembled army barracks in their plan configurations and that were frequently assembled from leftover army supplies and materials.

The CEBS project was advocated on the economic platform that 'completing the house shells at a later date for permanent occupation should not be greater than if carried out originally'.[25] This housing model generated a simple and innovative approach to adaptive housing solutions for large incoming populations and is a historical example of the adaptive housing discourse prevalent today in Australia.[26] In the early 1950s, the Department of Works and Housing and the Immigration Planning Council in consultation with Jack Cheesman, the then President of the Royal Australian Institute of Architects (RAIA), developed an adaptive house model for potential use at migrant workers' hostels.[27] The design is possibly a development on the CEBS protype and the search for a cost-effective housing model was in part due to the anticipation of future shortages of the Nissen huts if incoming migrant numbers increased.

This preliminary investigation by the Department of Works and Housing sought a model that was to be suitable for prefabrication abroad, included 'immediate and residual value for money expended' and, like the earlier CEBS model, could subsequently 'contribute to the pool of normal housing'. Two models were drawn up: the first, for decentralized accommodation, was a self-contained house that included a kitchen and bathroom along with the bedrooms. Described as a 'half-house', the second model was planned for accommodating migrants in existing hostels, where the kitchen, dining and bathroom facilities were centralized and communal. In 1951, the Cabinet approved a submission based on these prefabricated housing models to improve standards for migrant workers' hostels. Still, the emphasis was on improving the worker-hostels' conditions by any cost-effective method attainable.[28] The difficulty of locating contextual information, on either the earlier CEBS prototypes or their later development, apart from construction schedules, makes it hard to ascertain if these prototypes were constructed at any of the migrant workers' hostels.

When understood in the context of the Australian government's postwar immigration programme, this research to maximize the efficiency of migrant accommodation can be linked to wider political motivations. CEBS's prototype research was initiated at a time when a housing shortage crisis preoccupied the government at both a state and a national level, and housing featured heavily in the nation's reconstruction after the war.[29] This is emphasized through the establishment of the Commonwealth Housing Commission (CHC) and, in particular, the CHC's final report, which outlined the need for the federal government to participate in the issue of housing, partly as a continuance of wartime control.[30] In the first phases of the immediate postwar European migrant recruitment, there was a political need to reassure voters that incoming migrants would not compete with Australian-born citizens for housing.[31] The CBES's and then the Department of Works and Housing's experimentation with housing models that could be adapted to family use after the immediate influx of the temporary workforce dissipated indicates processes of multi-use, with the suburban home as the end point. In the later housing incarnations of migrant hostels such as the Endeavour, these concerns about reassuring the existing Australian-born population about housing competition decreased in intensity, owing in part to a general acceptance of the migration programme and arguably, an increase in housing options for the general population in the 1950s and 1960s.[32]

DESIGN EXPERIMENTATION IN TRANSITORY MIGRANT AND REFUGEE ACCOMMODATION

The Endeavour, referencing the first British colonial investigative ship to land on the east coast of Australia in 1770, is commonly recognized as a street name replicated in cities and rural towns across Australia. This name selection deliberately flagged the British colonial and, by extension, settler populations to incoming migrant and refugee populations during the 1970s and 1980s, when the Endeavour Hostel was in operation. Applying this administrative formula of selecting colonial objects and personalities to name infrastructure also signals that migrant on-arrival accommodation had, by this point, become a type of federal institution. The hostel was located on a portion of the former Commonwealth Rifle Range. When it closed in 1985, the land was returned to the Australian Army, which used the hostel as a training site for new recruits.[33] The institutional arrangement of dormitory-style accommodation with central amenities, with both shared bathrooms and dining facilities, lent itself to military interpretations of military, or university or college accommodation.

Prior to the Endeavour's erection, the main hostel that serviced Sydney's industrial southeast was the Bunnerong Hostel, built on land owned by the New South Wales Government that the Commonwealth needed to vacate by 1967. When the Endeavour closed, the remaining migrants were transferred to the Villawood/Westbridge hostel, located in western Sydney. By then, only ninety-three people remained of its approximate 750–1000 occupancy potential. Its closure saw the Commonwealth Government shift to using self-contained units for resettlement services for accepted refugees.[34] The Migrant Transitory Flat Scheme that became the focus of the Department of Immigration (and its successor, the Department of Immigration and Ethnic Affairs) for refugee resettlement is discussed towards the end of this chapter.[35]

In August 1963, the Cabinet approved in principle that the migrant hostels known respectively as Bunnerong and Bradfield Park in Sydney and Brooklyn and Holmesglen in Melbourne should be replaced with three new hostels.[36] Locating suitable replacement sites for these hostels included considering other sites in country New South Wales, namely outside the town of Orange.[37] The new hostel in Randwick, in its initial operational requirements, aimed to provide lodging and related services for approximately 250 migrant families at any one time.[38] Slated to cost £1.9 million initially and increasing to £4.25 million at the time of the Endeavour's construction, Randwick was in a heavy industrialized area of Sydney's southeast.[39] Commonwealth sponsored migrant accommodation in Sydney was strategically located next to developing hubs of industry. Tabled in the *Report Relating to the Proposed Erection of a Migrant Hostel at Randwick*, the Endeavour was proposed on the grounds as a replacement for both the Bunnerong Hostel and Bradfield Park Hostel in West Lindfield, Sydney, both with easy access to surrounding industries:

> The proposed Randwick hostel is planned to make good the unavoidable loss of Bunnerong in June 1967 and its location will ensure that the surrounding industrial areas will be continued to be serviced.[40]

The design, construction and costs were consistently communicated, debated and adjusted by the major actors in the design process. These included the Department of Immigration, the Department of Labour and National Service, the Commonwealth Department of Works and to a lesser degree Commonwealth Hostels Limited (CHL). Intermingled with the departmental records, including letters and minutes, is media coverage of the proposed erection of the hostel in Randwick and descriptions of local council meetings, which demonstrate a concern about the broader reception of the new hostels. Among these transcripts of departmental communication are alternative sketch designs for the new hostel at Randwick. In these alternative propositions, for which little contextual information is available, the accommodation blocks are not planned in the radial arrangement.[41] However, ideas about retrofitting the facilities foreshadowed the gradual winding down of the migrant recruitment programme and associated CHL accommodation in the 1970s, and it is possible that institutional design of these two new hostels could readily be repurposed for accommodation in connection with educational, social services, or similar purposes (see Figure 7.4).[42]

The Endeavour and its Melbourne counterpart, the Enterprise, both feature in the Commonwealth Department of Works annual publication *Works Review*, which reported on the department's major projects both underway and complete. Set up after Federation, the department went through successive name changes and, in 1945, it became the Department of Works and Housing, partly in response to the need to address the housing shortage. Then, in 1952, it took on the title of the Department of Works and by the early 1970s, it had been spilt into four departments.[43] *Works Review* had a publication life from approximately 1956 to 1973, reflecting the emphasis on nation building through infrastructure development.[44] The periodical showcased through photographic documentation the building achievements in industry, education and large-scale municipal buildings in Australia and through its governmental mandate in Papua New Guinea prior to independence.[45] The inclusion of hostels in this documentation of nation building reinforces that the accommodation and resettlement of

Figure 7.4 New industrial-style kitchens at the Endeavour Hostel, circa 1970–78. Courtesy of the National Archives of Australia, NAA: B941, Food Processing/Kitchens/1.

migrants had become another division of public infrastructure in Australia, rather than only provisional barracks for a workforce.

These two new hostels are always referred to with the prefix 'modern' and stood alongside airports, major post offices and judicial buildings in a building catalogue of Australia's new infrastructure as part of nation-building programmes. Presented as representative of a new era in hostel accommodation, the Endeavour aimed to provide improved forms of domesticity:

> The new hostel at Randwick, opened in March 1970, represents a completely new concept for Australia's new settlers. It is the first large-scale centre entirely designed for migrants and replaces the system of draughty huts with modern brick buildings offering self-contained units and a 'home' atmosphere to migrant families.[46]

During the 1960s and 1970s, Sydney was projecting itself as a modern, global-orientated city, one that was artistically and culturally informed and, in part through its architecture, a coveted destination.[47] In *Works Review*, there was an emphasis on the new international airport in Sydney constructed over marine mud and billeted to bring 'world-class air travel facilities' to the region.[48] Sydney's emergence as a global destination coincided with changing policies to welfare services offered to incoming migrants and refugees, along with bipartisan political criticism for assimilation-based immigration policies. Framing Australia, via Sydney, as a progressive nation striding towards a cosmopolitan future gained momentum in the 1970s after the construction of the Endeavour. As built, it provides a useful example for considering how the new hostels were presented in Commonwealth Government publications such as *Works Review* and whether they had a perceived role in advancing new conceptions of national identity. In examining these and similar publications that bracketed and contextualized hostel design, it is possible to consider how hostel architecture was used to promote Australia as a destination built anew.

FROM HOUSING SHORTAGES TO MODERN ACCOMMODATION AND FACILITIES

Paralleling the overhaul of existing Commonwealth hostel sites, the construction of the Endeavour was also fuelled by concerns emerging within the government about Australia's ability to recruit European migrants. The drafting process and publication of reports produced by the Parliamentary Standing Committee on Public Works in relation to the construction of the two new hostels in Randwick, Sydney and in Springvale, Melbourne, outline the reasons for the need for an improved accommodation standard.[49] On the evidence of experiences in the recruitment of migrants from the competitive conditions in Europe, the reports assert that the quality of accommodation available to migrants on arrival in Australia was, increasingly, vital to the success of its migrant intake and long-term population growth.[50]

The Springvale report stated that: 'Growing prosperity, rising social standards and a high level of employment existed in most of the main European countries that migrants were being recruited from.'[51] This scenario contrasted with the political and economic conditions that stimulated migration immediately after the Second World War. It is suggested repeatedly in the drafting surrounding these committee reports that if Australia was to continue to attract and retain migrants in light of these global economic developments, the standard of transitory accommodation must be progressively improved.[52] And this was notwithstanding the fact that the already completed redevelopment of select hostels nationwide, including Villawood, had strategies in place to progressively improve the appearance and grounds of many hostels by 'programmes of landscaping, garden planning and provision of outdoor amenities' (such as playing equipment for children and sports areas).[53] In addition, in the late 1960s, wherever there was enough demand, childminding centres were provided at select hostels. However, many hostels still resembled military camps and were notorious for terrible accommodation. Brooklyn, which the hostel at Springvale would replace, was one of these described in parliamentary reports as 'retain[ing] the character of accommodation provided to meet the emergency of the immediate post war period and must create a poor impression on migrants.'[54]

The repeated publicity around poor facilities was also raised as an issue and equally counteracted with the need to reassure government benevolence:

> The proposed new hostel in Springvale to replace Brooklyn and eventually Holmesglen will remove a continual source of criticism which, in stressing the physical appearance of the establishment, more than neutralises the strong attempts that are made to care for the welfare of the migrant resident. And the more urgently this can be achieved the greater the potential benefits.[55]

On the need to improve hostels, it was outlined in these reports that it was difficult to foresee the rate of house construction in the future that would provide adequate dwellings for migrants and refugees on arrival.

During the mid-1960s, the conclusion was reached that even though housing construction affected the volume of transitory accommodation required, if the migrant intake was to increase beyond the present level without a marked increase in the rate of home construction, the long-term requirement for hostel accommodation would have exceeded the current capacity of existing hostels.[56] The need to construct new hostels in order to improve the reputation of CHL accommodation, along with the wider context of Australia's housing market, were justifications offered to help bolster public support. Communications between the Department of Immigration and the Department of Labour and National Service outlined concerns raised about the erection of a new hostel from both the Springvale Council and residents of southeast Melbourne. The Council initially placed formal reservations and then withdrew these concerns, which ranged from landscaping and building design to the number of occupants. In relation to the proposal for a hostel at Randwick, some residents felt that the 'hostel was not in keeping with a heavily developed residential areas and claimed its development would be a burden on rate-payers'.[57]

There was an emphasis that the new dwellings at both Randwick and Springvale be convenient and comfortable to help project Australia as modern, open and flush with possibility. However, equally stressed was the essentially temporary nature of the accommodation. The *Report Relating to the Proposed Erection of a Migrant Hostel at Springvale* states that: 'The prime objective is to provide reasonably comfortable surroundings which, however, must not be seen as a substitute for long-term accommodation.'[58] Under item 9 (a)–(f), the aims of transitory accommodation in migrant hostels are outlined and accentuate temporariness in the following:

> (c) not to discourage families from moving into the general community as soon as circumstances and resources permit;
>
> (d) permit the most intensive use of capital invested by encouraging families to move out into the community. Flexibility is needed in the transitory accommodation so that it is adaptable to families of varying sizes and varying period;
>
> (e) to provide opportunities for persons of a wide range of financial sources to develop the ability to make a move; and
>
> (f) allow for the vagaries of the economic climate.[59]

The report for Randwick expresses similar sentiments, albeit worded slightly differently. Both reports also offered an overview of the architectural brief that suggests a negotiation between ideas of modern domesticity that related a sense of comfort and modernity against ensuring the hostel was not considered a long-term dwelling option. The report's recommendations suggest a confusion about what physically and spatially constitutes home and unsettlement. This messy duality can be seen in the architecture that exhibits design strategies that draw from domestic models defined by temporary tenures such as hotel and motel, house and prison histories.

HOUSES, HOSTELS AND PRISONS

On 22 January 1965, *The Australian* published an article entitled 'A New Home, Motel Style', which reported on the two new hostels – the Endeavour and the Enterprise – to be built in Melbourne and Sydney. The article outlines the announcement by Mr Bruce Brown, General Manager of CHL, that the preliminary design in discussion was of blocks of two, three and four-bedroom family units with shared, modern bathroom and laundry facilities in each block. The article hints at the architectural templates bracketing the new designs, at interplay between motels, hotels and the house as inscribed in the apartment type along with more restrictive forms of institutional dwellings.[60] This spatial exchange was consistently renegotiated through changes in administrative directives and facility management. The Australian government aimed to package Commonwealth migrant hostels as a short stay in a migrant's journey towards home ownership. In the discussions for the brief for the Endeavour, there are debates about the inclusion or exclusion of certain domestic features, namely bathrooms.[61] In these departmental deliberations, there are suggestions that bathrooms and increased residential convenience and comfort within the family units would help attract 'desirable' migrants. In the early years of the migrant recruitment drive, explicit racialized hierarchies informed the Australian government's attitude on the selection of migrants. However, equally, there was an emphasis on not providing bathrooms in order to deter long-term stayers, demonstrating the established perceptions of what specific spatial arrangements might signal a place of permanent residency. The absence of the postwar suburban house's core planning features, such as private bathrooms and kitchen and dining spaces, reveal how domesticity was spatially defined in relation to hostel accommodation. By extension, it shows how the suburban house was the ideal model for domesticity during this period in Australia and arguably still is in the national consciousness (see Figure 7.5).

One aim behind the design of both the Endeavour and the Enterprise was to increase privacy for families. Initial planning for the Endeavour stipulated that the design cater only for family units of four or more, indicating a demographic shift in the type of migrants the department wanted to recruit, away from an emphasis on individual workers to families. In evidence to the Parliamentary Standing Committee on Public Works, the supporting documentation asserts that: 'The living accommodation

Figure 7.5 Laundry facilities at the Endeavour Migrant Hostel, 1971. Courtesy of the National Archives of Australia, NAA: A12111, 1/1971/22/20

is so planned as to provide the greatest flexibility in the use of the available space, and simultaneously to enable families to live in as normal a family setting as is practicable within a hostel system.'[62] This quote encapsulates the two pivotal design agendas: one, to maximize space for increased capacity and, two, to provide standards of accommodation akin to self-sufficient apartments to foster an environment conducive to 'home' making practices. In 1966, according to a newspaper article of the time, Mr Buchanan, the Chairman of the Parliamentary Public Works Committee told the House that the units should be more self-contained (see Figure 7.6). He felt that migrants should be able to expect reasonable accommodation in Australia and that although it was not possible to provide permanent units, the hostels should have their own toilets and showers.[63] In the following years, as the brief was amended and debated, these questions of what is deemed adequate on-arrival accommodation for migrants consistently resurface and are often centred on the provision of bathrooms and kitchens.[64]

The three accommodation blocks of the Endeavour's final design were replicas of each other, with minor adjustments, and were striking in scale and form for a hostel-housing development, mainly due to their radial planning of six accommodation wings.[65] In the core, connecting the six wings, were the shared gendered bathrooms along with a shared telephone booth and laundry drying rooms. The arrangement

Figure 7.6 Example of a room at the Enterprise Migrant Hostel, 1984. Courtesy of the National Archives of Australia, NAA: A12111, 2/1984/22A/159.

of units in each extruding wing from the core was planned with flexibility by using intercommunicating doors to cater for shifts in the number and the ages of children in each family. In the initial planning stages, each unit consisted of at least two bedrooms, and the main bedroom could be occupied by the parents, but also used as a family living room (see Figures 7.7 and 7.8).[66] It was equipped with a divan bed, which could be converted into a compact settee for seating when the programme of the room shifted to a living room and the secondary bedrooms were joined to the main bedroom. Select family units also contained toilets and hand basins. However, bathrooms were predominantly communal. On each floor of the accommodation blocks, internal corridors linked all bedrooms with services such as toilets, ablution facilities, cubicles for public telephones, main stairways and secondary stairways, and drying rooms. The entrance to each family's unit came off the internal corridors. Indeed, the corridor seen in hotels and motels remained, and needed to be navigated to get to the shower or to use the phone.

A key aim of the new hostel design, which was consistently reiterated in the departmental records and reports, was that the design was to be less institutional in appearance in order to move away from the perpetual criticisms of the military-style barracks of the earlier migrant camps in statements such as: 'Design was required to preserve privacy and recognize the emphasis on family living. There was also the requirement that the buildings should avoid having an institutional appearance.'[67] However, the use of the radial plan evokes the architectural heritage of the eighteenth and nineteenth-century prisons and asylums built as reformative institutions.[68] From the aerial photography of the hostel, the clusters of radial wings around an open core make an imposing impression. Sitting in stark contrast to the surrounding suburban houses, architecturally, it is hard not to make links to incarceration and confinement.[69]

The Enterprise in Springvale, Melbourne, which adopted a similar arrangement of this radial planning, was used for detention in 1988, when three women and their children were transferred from the Maribyrnong Immigration Detention Centre. These new detainees shared facilities with other residents, but were restricted from leaving the grounds.[70] The use of the accommodation for detention was due to the lack of facilities for women and children at the Maribyrnong Immigration Detention Centre and a provisional understanding of the role of the new and later notorious immigration detention centres emerging in Australia in the late 1980s. The deployment of onshore and offshore facilities for the discretionary and later mandatory detention of unauthorized arrivals that provoked increasingly negative perceptions of Australian migrant facilities globally are seemingly prefigured in these earlier and comparatively innocuous hostel plans. Indeed, the radial plans' historical institutional lineage points to planning strategies that enable greater punitive supervision and spatial control. Although migrants and refugees who were not detained were free to leave and return to the hostel as they pleased, and there were no explicit formal restrictions or security embedded in the design, the radial plan of Jeremy Bentham's panopticon prison already formalized at Darlinghurst Gaol in Sydney (constructed between 1822

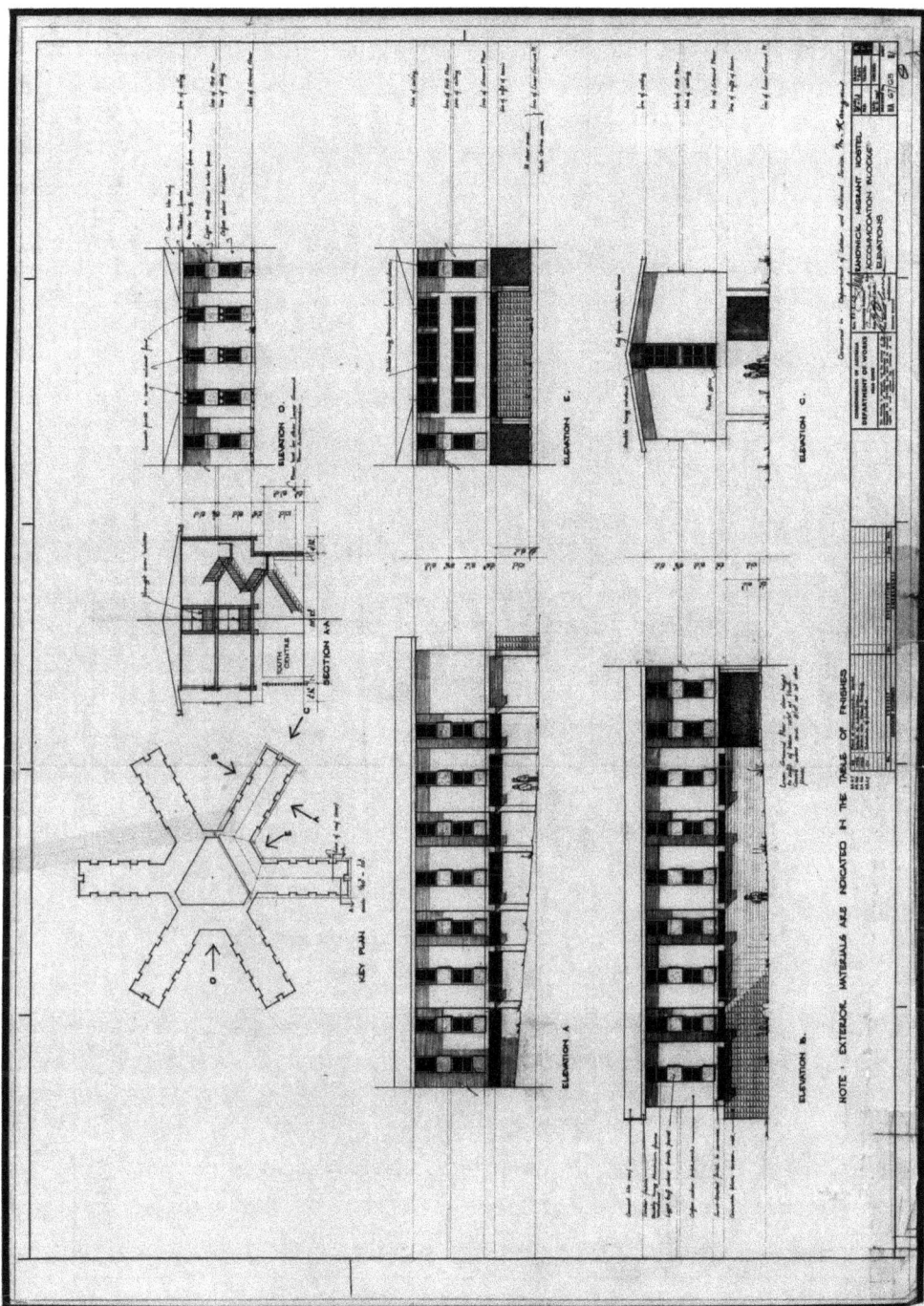

Figure 7.7 Accommodation blocks elevation, Endeavour Migrant Hostel, 1967. Courtesy of the National Archives of Australia, NAA: C4177, HA67/0065/B

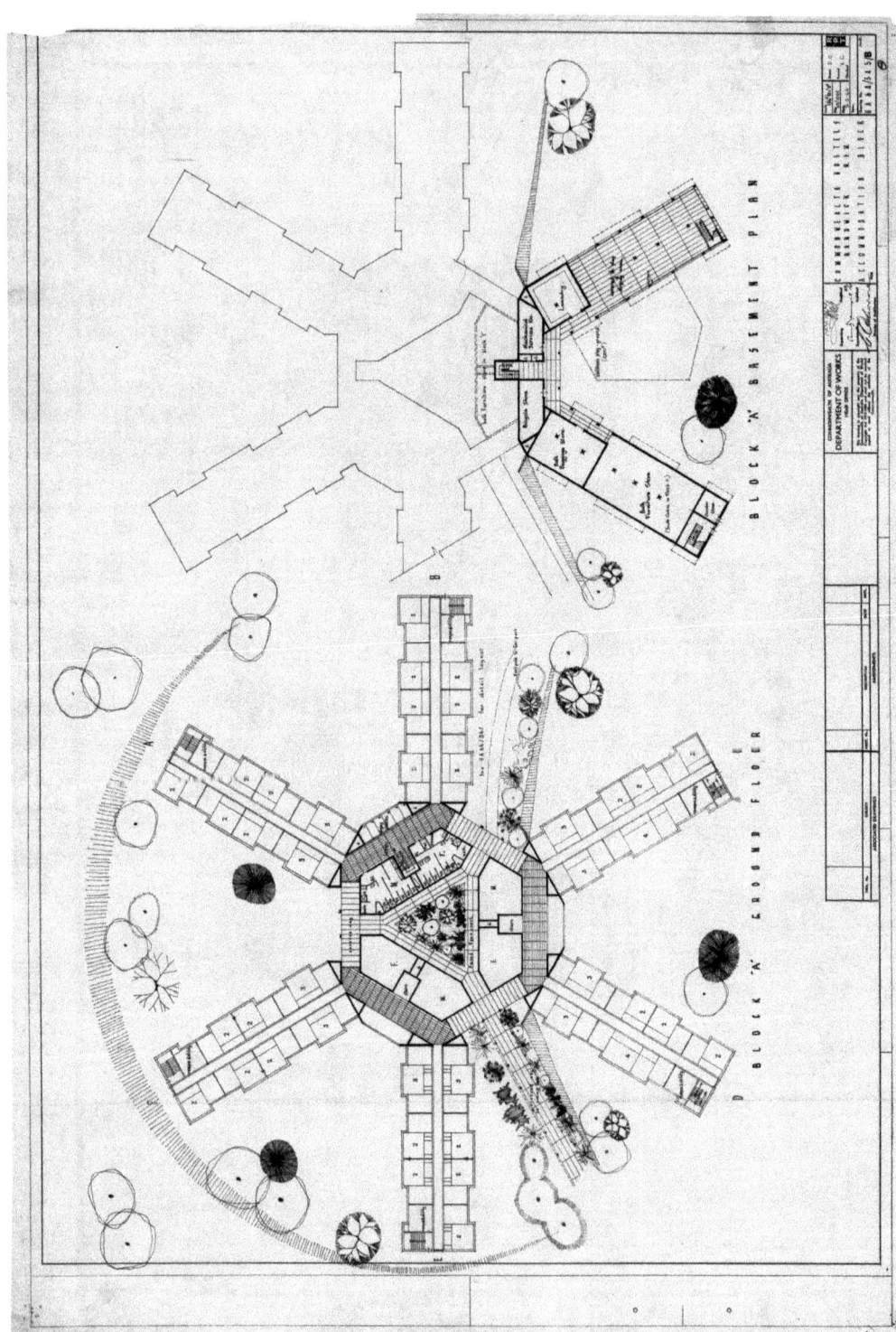

Figure 7.8 Accommodation block plan, Endeavour Migrant Hostel, 1964. Courtesy of the National Archives of Australia, NAA: C4177, HA64/0345/B

and 1885), with the implied centralised eye of surveillance by those in control, suggests a complicated layering of spatial ideals at migrant hostels. Considering this was the planning arrangement of choice for purpose-built designs for the resettlement of new migrants, after clearly testing the viability of other planning variants of housing blocks, it suggests conflicts around the type of accommodation and its inscribed agendas that should be offered to migrants and refugees. Read in combination with hostility in the wider community to erecting both the Endeavour and the Enterprise, these imposing wings, architecturally ripe for monitoring behaviour, foreshadow the often-racialized political tensions that emerge in the governmental discourse on how to treat and detain refugees seeking asylum in Australia in the following decades and the public perception of these spaces and buildings. In contrast, the new and improved Commonwealth migrant hostels were featured in government publications and promotional material, highlighting how hostel refurbishment was orchestrated to bolster migrant recruitment. The promotional drive also included reports on CHL's improved hostels televised on the national news on broadcaster, the Australian Broadcasting Commission, which featured a report on the new accommodation at Nunawading in Melbourne.[71] The novel collective living arrangements, surrounded by the expansive grounds seen at both the Endeavour and the Enterprise, provided increased privacy for individual families and included amenity updates such as telephones and improved bathroom facilities. However, equally, the innovative designs of the new Commonwealth migrant hostels were pitched to prospective migrants as a springboard for modern life in Australia. The two hostels discussed in this chapter were described textually and were displayed in images in pamphlets dispersed to prospective migrants both in Europe and on arrival in Australia. The new types of on-arrival accommodation showcase the better, more hospitable living arrangements that the Australian government now provided to incoming populations. The use of the modern buildings to promote Australia is seen in the Australia *Information for You* booklet series for incoming assisted migrants and refugees published by the Department of Immigration from 1967 to the late 1970s.[72]

BEYOND THE MIGRANT HOSTEL: TRANSITORY FLATS AND THE COMMONWEALTH GOVERNMENT'S RESETTLEMENT OF REFUGEES IN THE 1970S

By 1978, CHL had only eight migrant hostels in operation across the nation and accommodated about 7,625 persons with two hostels remaining in Sydney, the Endeavour and the Villawood/Westbridge Migrant Hostel.[73] The number of migrant families living in the new accommodation blocks was dwindling and a newspaper article on Villawood in 1974 for the *Sydney Morning Herald* suggests that a large number of the modern units at the Westbridge Hostel had been vacant for more than a year.[74] The article raises a point of contention that emerges in the political discourse accompanying the end period of Commonwealth migrant hostel accommodation. Due to the widespread vacancies, it was argued that hostel accommodation should be made available to the wider Australian populations, including low-income residents and the homeless. A version of this type of occupancy did occur at the Bradfield Migrant Hostel in Sydney that was adapted from a former RAAF training depot in 1947.[75] A section of the site, run by the HCNSW, provided self-sufficient, emergency housing for Australian-born citizens when the HCNSW had housing shortages. Additionally, it accommodated internally displaced people from the 1950s Redfern housing clearance programme in Sydney.[76] According to the 'Submission to the Review Group Examining Post-Arrival Programmes and Services to Migrants', 1976–78 accommodation surpluses in hostels nationwide were made available on a short-term basis to the wider Australian population, including apprentices, members of the defence forces and cultural, religious and sporting organizations.[77]

During the latter half of the 1970s, select Commonwealth hostels, including the Endeavour (Randwick) and the Enterprise (Springvale), were used to house many people arriving from mainland Southeast Asia. Refugees from Cambodia, Laos and Vietnam, who were displaced due to the Vietnam War and the Khmer Rouge regime, began arriving in Australia from approximately 1975–76 onwards. During the 1970s, the Commonwealth through the Department of Immigration and, subsequently, the Department of Immigration and Ethnic Affairs implemented myriad changes that shifted immigration policy around recruitment and resettlement. Underlying these changes are several influential contributing factors, including changes in the national economy, new understandings of national identities relating to multiculturalism, and global responsibilities regarding perceptions of humanitarianism towards displaced people.

The global recession in the early 1970s, which had a significant impact on the Australian economy by contributing to 'stagflation' and high unemployment, signalled the end of relatively unhindered economic prosperity and growth in the previous decades after the Second World War.[78] As these political economic histories impacted on the populations at migrant hostels, the economic instability contributed to the cessation of the mass recruitment of migrants seen in the earlier Australia Assisted Programmes and the emergence of new criteria and methods of selecting migrants. By the late 1980s and early 1990s, rather than the previous large-scale programmes, migrant recruitment targeted desired skill areas and labour shortages.[79] In conjunction with the economic instability of the 1970s, multiculturalism surfaced as a new mode of articulating national identity both through policy and wider nationally informed cultural practices, resulting in part from the successive removal of polices that came under the umbrella term of the White Australia Policy.[80] The pathway of multiculturalism's introduction as an approach to national identity and the inherent complications that informed on-arrival accommodation is beyond the scope of this chapter. However, its introduction contributed to a cultural framework that is interlinked to changes around the acceptance of refugees from outside Europe and the establishment of a targeted humanitarian programme.

Although resettling displaced people after the Second World War was part of a range of assisted passage schemes, these schemes sat within a wider policy of population expansion through the recruitment of migrants. It was not until 1977 that a specific refugee policy and a planned humanitarian programme that examined the protection claims of people seeking refuge were introduced.[81] However, this official programme emerged from policy shifts in response to international situations and allegiances during the early 1970s, including the arrival of people fleeing the Vietnam War by boat, combined with Australia's involvement in the Vietnam War as an ally of the United States and the South Vietnamese government.[82] Also influencing this trajectory were local and international perceptions about Australia's commitment to human rights from the Commonwealth governments led by Gough Whitlam (1972–75) and Malcom Fraser (1975–83).[83] A distinction between how arriving populations were classified begins to emerge in this period, defined by two distinct programmes, the skilled and family migrants' programme and the humanitarian program. The narratives that surround these two programmes would become distorted and manipulated by actors on all sides of the political spectrum in relation to border securitization in the late twentieth century and had a direct impact on the expansion and continuation of immigration detention facilities. Acceptance of refugees entering on humanitarian visas saw people arriving during the 1970s and early 1980s from Chile, the Czech Republic, West Papua, Vietnam, Cambodia and Laos as well as Lebanon, East Timor and later from the former Yugoslavia, with a large portion of people identifying as Serbian.[84]

Commonwealth migrant hostels gradually closed during the 1970s and 1980s due to the winding down of the large-scale population recruitment programmes and changes in the acceptance and selection of migrants and refugees. By the 1980s, the remaining hostels only accommodated refugees and humanitarian programme entrants. The Migrant Transitory Flat Scheme, first introduced in 1967, was the preferred form of on-arrival accommodation and the future trajectory of housing refugees arriving as part of the humanitarian programme and in need of housing provision (see Figure 7.9).[85] Part of the justification behind this shift in the type of on-arrival accommodation was that completely self-contained apartments allowed for a wider geographical distribution of migrants, and the future existence of migrant hostels, particularly in country areas, was increasingly economically untenable.[86] Migrant Transitory Flats, separate to the CHL-managed migrant hostels, provided self-contained flats with kitchen and bathroom facilities for families. The Commonwealth Government piloted these alternatives to migrant hostels as part of the wider programme to improve the general standard of on-arrival accommodation for migrants and refugees in the late 1960s and 1970s.[87] Initially, the Department of Environment, Housing and Community was responsible for the provision, management, and maintenance of the Migrant Transitory Flats. However, regarding policy matters and changes, the department would consult with the Department of Immigration of Ethnic Affairs.

The flats, which were intended to provide an alternative to the institutional style of living in the hostels, were provided exclusively for families, and in 1976, their opera-

Figure 7.9 Example of Commonwealth Migrant Flats in Adelaide, South Australia, 1973. Courtesy of the National Archives of Australia, NAA: A12111, 2/1973/21A/2

tion was transferred to CHL. On implementation, they were regarded as an experimental scheme that offered a potential financial advantage over the significant costs of running hostels, in particular the costs associated with providing meals. By 1974, there were 396 fully furnished flats located in mainland capital cities and it is notable that, unlike early migrant camps and hostels, flat locations were restricted to cities.[88] Families were selected to reside in flats rather than hostels if they were considered most likely to establish themselves in private accommodation, with initial priority going to English-speaking families in employment categories that showed labour shortages. Families would sign a six-month lease on induction and a bond was required, but occupants could end the lease on short notice without penalty. The average length of stay in the 1970s was approximately 23–24 weeks and rents were collected weekly by departmental officers.[89] In the mid-1970s, the flats were a better economic proposition for the Commonwealth Government than hostels, but were not considered a viable replacement option at that time.[90]

Broadly comparable terms of in size and standard to flats provided by the various state housing authorities, two-thirds of the migrant transitory flats were built under the supervision of state housing authorities, with the remaining being purchased from the private real estate market.⁹¹ From the few photographs available, the transitory flats were medium-density, two- to three-storey apartment blocks, which were often brick-faced. In NSW in 1976, there were 116 residences spread across Sydney and the Department of Immigration stipulated that the units be fully furnished, with the standard to be comfortable but modest.⁹² The flats' locations were selected to provide convenient access to shops, schools and transport services, and reasonable proximity to centres of employment. According to a report, there was a deliberate policy to avoid a concentration of migrants as the department saw that this would assist in migrant integration into the community.⁹³ Generally, they were not located close to existing migrant hostels and instead were scattered in metropolitan areas; in 1980, the average stay was for five months.⁹⁴ Although it is beyond the scope of this research, a preoccupation with the groupings of various migrant communities, particularly recently arrived and linguistically and culturally diverse groups and perceived anxieties around high concentrations of migrants living in specific areas, would become a recurrent thread in the national discourse in the late twentieth century. Narratives around 'ghettoization' and 'enclaves' would encircle the Vietnamese Australian communities and other communities from mainland Southeast Asia, including but not limited to Cambodian, Laotian, Hmong and Chinese, particularly in western Sydney during the 1990s.⁹⁵

CONCLUSION

The Australian Government's recruitment and accommodation of migrants and refugees after the Second World War from across Europe, including the British Isles, bolstered its population growth, but it is the other aim of providing labour for growth industries, such as agriculture and construction, that was intrinsically linked to hostel location and development. This is evident in the strategic mapping of hostel locations and the departmental debates about the location of new hostels such as the Endeavour in Randwick. The federal government's population orchestration and management were directly linked to the national economy, and its understandings of the economic utility of people arriving underscore the categorization and acceptance of migrants and refugees entering Australia – an understanding that continues in contemporary border management and refugee detainment and interdiction.⁹⁶

Hostels such as the Endeavour were defined by experimentation with housing forms: testing out new models for collective living. The Endeavour's completion contributed to a network of hostels across Sydney that began to decrease in terms of its operative scale during the 1970s. However, select hostels like the Endeavour remained open and were used to house refugees displaced by the Vietnam War. The Endeavour's completion additionally emphasized a significant intersection of political attitudes to migrants and refugees, materializing the necessity for better, more livable accommodation for economically disenfranchised populations. When compared with previous hostel designs, its formal and spatial alignment with housing reflected efforts at potentially humanizing arriving populations as more than industrial workers and recipients of government hospitality. On the other hand, tensions around ethnicity and integration that emerged in both Australian government discussions and in the broader community about the hostel's locale foreshadowed the central and divisive position that the resettlement of refugees arriving from outside Europe would hold in the national discourse in the following decades with the emergence of immigration detention practices.

ACKNOWLEDGEMENTS

This chapter expands on initial research presented in a conference paper at *Historiographies of Technology and Architecture: The 35th Annual Conference of the Society of Architectural Historians, Australia and New Zealand* in 2018 (Miller-Yeaman, Renee, 'From Emergency Reception Centres to Housing Experiments: Migrant Accommodation and the Commonwealth Department of Public Works', *Proceedings of Historiographies of Technology and Architecture: The 35th Annual Conference of the Society of Architectural Historians, Australia and New Zealand*, Wellington, New Zealand, 4–7 July, Wellington: SAHANZ, 2018). Research for this chapter was in part funded by the Australia Research Council project FT140100190, 'Temporal Cities, Provisional Citizens: Architectures of Internment', led by Professor Anoma Pieris.

Renee Miller-Yeaman is a Research Fellow in Urban Studies at the Melbourne Centre for Cities, Faculty of Architecture, Building and Planning, University of Melbourne. Her research looks at design histories of housing and institutions, examining the intersections between government policy, social histories and architecture.

NOTES

1. Jordens, *On Accommodating Migrants*, 2.
2. Ibid., 3–4.
3. NAA: C3076, WOB 714 (hereinafter NAA C3076, WOB 714), Commonwealth Hostels Limited (CHL), 'Correspondence Files', 1960–71; NAA: A446, 1972/78712 (hereinafter NAA: A446, 1972/78712), Department of Immigration, 'Commonwealth Migrant Hostels Administrative Responsibilities between Departments', 1968–76.
4. NAA: C3076, 1/1/46 PART 1, CHL, 'New Hostel for Migrants Randwick', 1964–66.
5. See Dellios 'Displaced Persons, Family Separation, and the Work Contract in Post-War Australia', 418–32; Sluga, *Bonegilla, 'A Place of No Hope'*.
6. NAA: C3076, 1/1/46 PART 1, (hereinafter NAA: C3076, 1/1/46 PART 1), Migrant Workers' Accommodation Division, Department of Labour and National Service, 'New Hostel for Migrants Randwick – Construction and Design', 1964–66.

7. Jordens, *On Accommodating Migrants*.
8. Standing Committee on Public Works, *Report Relating to the Proposed Erection of a Migrant Hostel at Randwick*, 4–8.
9. Examples of protests at the Villawood Migrant Hostel also in Sydney: '500 Protest to Menzies Migration', *Sydney Morning Herald*, 9 June 1958, 5; 'Heating of Villawood Hostel', *The Biz (Fairfield)*, 6 May 1959, 15; 'Angry Migrants Tied to Camp', *Sunday Mirror*, 29 October 1961; 'M.P., Seeks Probe on Migrant Camp', *Sunday Mirror*, 5 November 1961; 'Hostel Similar to Concentration Camps', *The Biz (Fairfield)*, October 1962, 1.
10. NAA: MP1760/1, 67/72502 (hereinafter NAA: MP1760/1, 67/72502), Department of Immigration, 'Enterprise Migrant Hostel, Springvale Victoria', 1956–66.
11. Commonwealth Experimental Building Station (CEBS), *Office Record/Dept. of Works and Housing, Commonwealth Experimental Housing Station*.
12. Standing Committee on Public Works, *Report Relating to the Proposed Erection of a Migrant Hostel at Randwick*, 4–8.
13. See Neumann, *Across the Seas*, 189–245, Higgins, *Asylum by Boat*.
14. Neumann, *Across the Seas*, 189–245; Examples of histories of refugees displaced from the Vietnam War and Commonwealth Policy from the period are found in: Standing Committee of Foreign Affairs and Defence, *Indochinese Refugee Resettlement*; Manne, 'Indochinese Refugees and Australia Political Culture', 10–14; Hawthorne, *Refugee*.
15. NAA: A446, 1975/80775, Department of Immigration (from 12 June 1974, Immigration Group, Department of Labor and Immigration), 'Working Party on Migrant Hostels – Part 1'.
16. See Wills, 'Between the Hostel and the Detention Centre', 263–80; Dellios, 'Migration Parks and Monuments to Multiculturalism', 7–32; Dellios, *Histories of Controversy*; Fung, 'A Place 'Midway between the Old Life and the New''; Sluga, *Bonegilla*.
17. Lozanovska, *Migrant Housing*; Lozanovska, Levin and Gantala, 'Is the Migrant House in Australia an Australian Vernacular Architecture?', 65–78.
18. For histories of urban space as a laboratory for projects of social engineering, see Rabinow, *French Modern*; Foucault, *Discipline and Punish*.
19. Mills, 'Refabricating the Towers', 1–27.
20. Tibbits, 'The Enemy within Our Gates', 123–62.
21. Williamson, 'Building and Construction Research', 115–16.
22. Bock, *The End Was to Build Well*, 11.
23. CBES, *Office Record/Dept. of Works and Housing*, no. 95.
24. Ibid.
25. Ibid.
26. Friedman, *The Adaptable Home*; Friedman, *Innovative Houses*.
27. NAA: A4905, 11 (hereinafter NAA: A4905, 11). Fifth Menzies Ministry, Cabinet Submissions, 'Building Standards for Migrant Workers' Hostels – Decision 14', 1951.
28. NAA: A4905, 11.
29. Dufty-Jones, 'A Historical Geography of Housing Crisis in Australia'. For postwar reconstruction, see Macintyre, *Australia's Boldest Experiment*.
30. Ministry of Post-War Reconstruction, *Commonwealth Housing Commission, Final Report*, 23–25; Appleyard, *Low-Cost Housing and the Migrant Population*, 7–10.
31. Jordens, *On Accommodating Migrants*, 1–3.
32. Appleyard, *Low-Cost Housing*, 7–10.
33. NAA: C424, PRO1976/523, (hereinafter NAA: C424, PRO1976/523), Australian Property Group, New South Wales, 'South Coogee- Review of Use', 1976–88; 'Migrants to Lose Coogee Hostel', *Daily Telegraph*, 3 October 1985.

34. NAA: C3076, 1/1/508 PART 1 (hereinafter NAA: C3076, 1/1/508 PART 1). CHL, 'Commonwealth Hostels Limited – Central – Organisation and Administration Policy – Migrant Transitory Flats', 1976–78.
35. Note: the Department of Immigration was renamed the Department of Labour and Immigration, which was in effect from December 1972 to December 1975, and then the Department of Immigration and Ethnic Affairs from December 1975 to March 1987.
36. NAA: A5827, Volume 12/Agendum 387.
37. NAA: MP1760/1, M1966/46354, 'New Migrant Hostel Planned for Randwick', *Sydney Morning Herald*, 21 June 1968; NAA: MP1760/1, M1967/72252, 'Formal Design for Migrant Centre', *Sydney Morning Herald*, 26 March 1970.
38. NAA: MP1760/1, M1966/46354; NAA: MP1760/1, M1967/72252.
39. NAA: A5827, VOLUME 12/AGENDUM 387, '£1.9 M. Migrant Hostel Planned for Randwick', *Daily Telegraph*, 28 October 1965.
40. NAA: MP1760/1, M1967/72252.
41. NAA: C3076, 1/1/46 PART 1.
42. Jordens, *On Accommodating Migrants*, 25–29.
43. Willis, 'Commonwealth Department of Works', 164–65.
44. NLA: Department of Works, *Works Review*.
45. Ibid., 35–39.
46. Ibid., 18.
47. Symonds, 'Outside the Spaces of Modernity', 67; Hogben and O'Callaghan, *Leisure Space*; Roe, *Twentieth Century Sydney*.
48. Department of Works, *Works Review*, 3.
49. The Enterprise Hostel built at Springvale had minor variations, but was almost identical in its design to the Endeavour. NAA: MP1760/1, 67/72502, Public Works, *Report Relating to the Proposed Erection of a Migrant Hostel at Springvale*; Public Works, *Report Relating to the Proposed Erection of a Migrant Hostel at Randwick*.
50. Public Works, *Report Relating to Migrant Hostel at Springvale*, 5–7; Jordens, *On Accommodating Migrants*, 20.
51. Public Works, *Report Relating to Migrant Hostel at Springvale*, 6.
52. NAA: MP1760/1, M1967/72252, 1962–66; NAA: MP1760/1, 67/72502.
53. Public Works, *Minutes of Evidence in Relation to the Proposed Erection of a Migrant Hostel at Springvale Victoria*, 3.
54. Public Works, *Minutes of Evidence Relation to the Proposed Erection of a Migrant Hostel at Springvale*, 3–4.
55. Minutes of evidence relating to the proposed erection of a migrant hostel at Springvale edited, draft copies in NAA: MP1760/1, 67/72502. Both new hostels where publicized by the government and reported on: 'New Hostel for Migrants', *Canberra Times*, 21 June 1968, 10; 'Migrant Accommodation Standards Improved', *Canberra Times*, 8 September 1969; 'New Migrant Hostel for Randwick', *Sydney Morning Herald*, 21 June 1968; '$8m on Hostels', *The Australian*, 1 September 1969; 'New Hostel to House 1,000', *The Messenger*, 16 March 1970.
56. Standing Committee on Public Works, *Report Relating to the Proposed Erection of a Migrant Hostel at Randwick*, 6.
57. Journalism on the presentation of Parliament Public Works Committees: 'Hostel Protests Pushed Down', *Sydney Morning Herald*, 23 March 1966.
58. Public Works, *Report Relating to Migrant Hostel at Springvale*, 4.
59. Ibid.
60. 'A New Home, Motel Style', *The Australian*, 22 January 1965.

61. NAA: C3076, 1/1/46 PART 1, Public Works, *Report Relating to Migrant Hostel at Randwick*, 9–10.
62. Public Works, *Report Relating to the Proposed Erection of a Migrant Hostel at Randwick*, 7.
63. 'Migrant Hostels Too Like Intuitions in Design', *Canberra Times*, 21 September 1966.
64. NAA: MP1760/1, M1967/72252; NAA: C3076, 1/1/46 PART 1, 1964–66.
65. NAA: C4177, HA64/0344/B; NAA: C4177, HA64/0348/B; NAA: C4177, HA64/0390; NAA: C4177, HA64/0415/C, Architectural drawings and documentation in Director of Construction, New South Wales, 'Randwick Migrant Hostel Accommodation', 1861–81.
66. NAA: C4177, HA66/1093/C1; NAA: C4177, HA66/1096/C1; NAA: C4177, HA66/1148/C; NAA: C4177, HA67/0064B; NAA: C4177, HA67/0065/B; NAA: C4177, HA67/0068/B, Architectural drawings and documentation in Director Construction, New South Wales, 'Randwick Migrant Hostel Accommodation Blocks', 1861–81.
67. Public Works, *Report Relating to Migrant Hostel at Randwick*, 7; 'Migrant Hostels Too Like Intuitions in Design', *Canberra Times*, 21 September 1966.
68. See Foucault, *Discipline and Punish*; Goffman, *Asylums*.
69. In the Australian context, this design precedents can be seen in the design of Parramatta Goal, Sydney. See Kerr, 'Designing a Colonial Gaol', 40–51; Kerr, *Out of Sight, Out of Mind*.
70. ; Immigration Museum (Victoria), *A Worthwhile Enterprise*, 18.
71. NAA: B6154, 1546246, 'New Migrant Hostel', Australian Broadcasting Corporation (ABC), 23 January 1967.
72. NAA: B146, 1966/1000, Department of Labour and National Service, 'Department of Immigration', 1966–70.
73. NAA: A4340, MR 1/164, Appendix A in Review of Post Arrival Programs.
74. 'Modern Govt Flats Left Unused', *Sydney Morning Herald*, 18 February 1974, 1, 9; 'Govts Plan Study into Hostel Use', *Sydney Morning Herald*, 19 February 1974 (front page); 'Vacant Flats', *Canberra Times*, 19 February 1974, 3; 'Modern Govt Flats Left Unused', *Sydney Morning Herald*, 18 February 1974, 1, 9.
75. NAA: A446, 1967/71794, Department of Immigration, 'Migrant Workers' Hostel – Bradfield Park', 1949–71.
76. Maddox, Gary, 'Bradfield Park, a Forgotten Part of Sydney's Urban History', *Sydney Morning Herald*, 28 April 2018.
77. NAA: A4340, MR 1/164, *Review of Post Arrival Programs*, 3.
78. For more on Australian economic history, see Wright, *Australian Economic History*; Millmow, 'Hardly the Age of Aquarius'.
79. Spinks, *Australia's Migration Program*, 1–3.
80. Koleth, *Multiculturalism*.
81. Phillips, *Australia's Humanitarian Program*.
82. See Neumann; *Across the Seas*; Higgins, *Asylum by Boat*.
83. Higgins, *Asylum by Boat*.
84. Neumann, *Across the Seas*, 135–291.
85. NAA: C3076, 1/1/508 PART 1, CHL, 'Commonwealth Hostels Limited – Central – Organisation and Administration Policy – Migrant Transitory Flats [Box 717]', 1976–78.
86. NAA: A4940, C3833 (hereinafter NAA: A4940, C3833), Secretary to Cabinet, 'Construction of New Migrant Hostels', 1963–67.
87. NAA: A4940, C3833.
88. NAA: A446, 1975/81349 (hereinafter NAA: A446, 1975/81349), Immigration Group, 'Commonwealth Hostels Limited and Migrant Flats – Briefs and Notes', 1975–76.
89. NAA: A446, 1975/81349.
90. Ibid.

91. Ibid.
92. NAA: C3076, 1/1/508 PART 2, Migrant Workers' Accommodation Division, 'Commonwealth Hostels Limited – Central – Organisation and Administration Policy – Migrant Transitory Flats', 1976–78.
93. NAA: A446, 1975/81349.
94. NAA: A446 1981/76637.
95. Hickey and Lim, *Once Upon a Time in Cabramatta*.
96. See Stratton, 'Uncertain Lives', 677–92; Klocker, 'Community Antagonism towards Asylum Seekers in Port Augusta, South Australia', 1–17.

BIBLIOGRAPHY

Archives

National Archives of Australia (NAA)
National Library of Australia (NLA)
Commonwealth Experimental Building Station (CEBS)

Publications

Appleyard, Reginald Thomas. *Low-Cost Housing and the Migrant Population*. Canberra: Committee for Economic Development of Australia, 1963.

Bock, Geoff. *The End Was to Build Well: A Half-Century of Australian Government Building Research*. North Ryde, NSW: CSIRO Australia, Division of Building, Construction and Engineering, 1995.

Dellios, Alexandra. 'Displaced Persons, Family Separation, and the Work Contract in Post-War Australia', *Journal of Australian Studies* 40(4) (2016), 418–32. https://doi.org/10.1080/14443058.2016.1224913

——. *Histories of Controversy: Bonegilla Migrant Centre*. Melbourne: Melbourne University Publishing, 2017.

——. 'Migration Parks and Monuments to Multiculturalism: Finding the Challenge to Australian Heritage Discourses through Community Public History Practice', *Public Historian* 42(2) (2020), 7–32.

Dufty-Jones, Rae. 'A Historical Geography of Housing Crisis in Australia', *Australian Geographer* 49(1) (2018), 5–23. https://doi.org/10.1080/00049182.2017.1336968.

Foucault, Michel. *Discipline and Punish: The Birth of the Prison*, Alan Sheridan (trans.). New York: Pantheon Books, 1995.

Friedman, Avi. *The Adaptable Home: Designing and Building for Choice and Change*. New York: McGraw-Hill, 2002.

——. *Innovative Houses: Concepts for Sustainable Living*. London: Laurence King Publishing, 2013.

Fung, Pamie. Ching. Tsz. 'A Place "Midway" between the Old Life and the New: A Case Study of the Migrant Hostel at Maribyrnong', Ph.D. Dissertation. Melbourne: University of Melbourne, 2013.

Goad, Philip, and Julie Willis. *The Encyclopaedia of Australian Architecture*. Port Melbourne, Vic: Cambridge University Press, 2012.

Goffman, Erving. *Asylums: Essays on the Social Situation of Mental Patients and Other Inmates*. Chicago: Aldine, 1961.

Gunew, Sneja, *Haunted Nations: The Colonial Dimensions of Multiculturalism*. New York: Routledge, 2003.

Hawthorne, Lesleyanne. *Refugee: The Vietnamese Experience*. Melbourne: Oxford University Press, 1982.

Hickey, Jacob, and Bernadine Lim. *Once upon a Time in Cabramatta*. Neutral Bay, NSW: SBS; Screen Australia; Madman Entertainment, 2012 (originally screened on SBS1, 8 January 2012).

Higgins, Clare. *Asylum by Boat*. Sydney: New South Publishing, 2017.

Hogben, Paul, and Judith O'Callaghan. *Leisure Space: The Transformation of Sydney, 1945–1970*. Sydney: New South Publishing, 2014.

Immigration Museum (Victoria). *A Worthwhile Enterprise: The Migrant Hostel in Springvale*. Melbourne: Immigration Museum, 2008.

Jordens, Ann-Mari. *On Accommodating Migrants*. Canberra: Administration, Compliance & Governability Program, Research School of Social Sciences, Australian National University, 1994.

Jupp, James. *From White Australia to Woomera: The Story of Australian Immigration*. Port Melbourne, Vic: Cambridge University Press, 2007.

Kerr, James Semple. *Out of Sight, Out of Mind: Australia's Places of Confinement, 1788–1988*. Sydney, NSW: S.H. Ervin Gallery, National Trust of Australia, 1988.

——. 'Designing a Colonial Goal', in Lenore Coltheart (ed.), *Significant Sites: History and Public Works in New South Wales* (Sydney: Hale & Iremonger, 1989), pp. 40–45.

Klocker, Natascha. 'Community Antagonism towards Asylum Seekers in Port Augusta, South Australia', *Australian Geographical Studies* 42(1) (2008), 1–17. https://doi.org/10.1111/j.1467-8470.2004.00239.x.

Koleth, Elsa. *Multiculturalism: A Review of Australia Policy Statements and Recent Debates in Australia and Overseas, Research Paper No. 6*. Canberra: Parliament of Australia Research Publications, 2010–2011.

Levin Azriel, Iris. 'Migrants' Houses: The Importance of Housing Form in Migrants' Settlement', Ph.D. Dissertation. Melbourne: University of Melbourne, 2010.

Lozanovska, Mirjana (ed.). *Ethno-architecture and the Politics of Migration*. New York: Routledge, 2016.

Lozanovska, Mirjana. *Migrant Housing: Architecture, Dwelling, Migration*. New York: Routledge, 2019.

Lozanovska, Mirjana, Iris Levin, and Maria Victoria Gantala. 'Is the Migrant House in Australia an Australian Vernacular Architecture?', *Traditional Dwellings and Settlements Review* 24(2) (2013), 65–78.

Macintyre, Stuart. *Australia's Boldest Experiment: War and Reconstruction in the 1940s*. Sydney: New South Publishing, 2015.

Manne, Robert. 'Indochinese Refugees and Australia Political Culture', *Migration Action* 3 (2–4, Spring 1976/Autumn 1978), 10–14.

Mills, Peter. 'Refabricating the Towers: The Genesis of the Victorian Housing Commission's High-Rise Estates to 1969', Ph.D. Dissertation. Caulfield: Monash University, 2010.

Millmow, Alex. 'Hardly the Age of Aquarius', in Alex Millmow, *A History of Australasian Economic Thought* (Abingdon: Routledge, 2017), pp. 175–203.

Ministry of Post-War Reconstruction. *Commonwealth Housing Commission, Final Report, 25th August 1944*. Sydney: Ministry of Post-War Reconstruction, 1944.

Neumann, Klaus. *Across the Seas: Australia's' Response to Refugees: A History*. Collingwood, Vic: Black Inc., 2015.

Phillips, Janet. *Australia's Humanitarian Program: A Quick Guide to the Statistics since 1947*. Canberra: Parliament of Australia Background Note, Social Policy Section, 2017. Retrieved 22 December 2023 from https://www.aph.gov.au/About_Parliament/Parliamentary_Departments/Parliamentary_Library/pubs/rp/rp1617/Quick_Guides/HumanitarianProg.

Rabinow, Paul. *French Modern*. Chicago: University of Chicago Press, 1995.

Roe, Jill (ed.). *Twentieth Century Sydney: Studies in Urban and Social History*. Sydney: Hale & Iremonger in association with the Sydney History Group, 1980.

Sluga, Glenda. *Bonegilla, 'A Place of No Hope'*. Parkville, Vic: University of Melbourne, 1988.

Spinks, Harriet. *Australia's Migration Program*. Canberra: Parliament of Australia Background Note, Social Policy Section, 2010. https://parlinfo.aph.gov.au/parlInfo/search/display/display.w3p;query=Id:%22library/prspub/272398%22.

Standing Committee of Foreign Affairs and Defence. *Indochinese Refugee Resettlement: Australia's Involvement*. Canberra: Australian Government Publishing Service, 1982.

Standing Committee on Public Works. *Report Relating to the Proposed Erection of a Migrant Hostel at Randwick, New South Wales*. Canberra: Parliament of Commonwealth of Australia, 1964–66.

——. *Report Relating to the Proposed Erection of a Migrant Hostel at Springvale, Victoria*. Canberra: Parliament of Commonwealth of Australia, 1964–66.

Stratton, Jon. 'Uncertain Lives: Migration, the Border and Neoliberalism in Australia', *Social Identities* 15(5) (2009), 677–92. https://doi.org/10.1080/13504630903205324.

Symonds, Michael. 'Outside the Spaces of Modernity: Western Sydney and the Logic of the European City', in Helen Grace, Ghassan Hage, Lesley Johnson, Julie Langsworth and Michael Symonds (eds), *Home/World: Space, Community and Marginality in Sydney's West* (Annandale, NSW: Pluto Press, 1997), pp. 66–98.

Tibbits, George. 'The Enemy within Our Gates', in Renate Howe (ed.), *New Houses for Old: Fifty Years of Public Housing in Victoria 1938–1988* (Melbourne: Ministry of Housing and Construction, 1988), pp. 123–62.

Williamson, Terence. 'Building and Construction Research', in Philip Goad and Julie Willis (eds), *The Encyclopedia of Australian Architecture* (Port Melbourne, Vic: Cambridge University Press, 2012), pp. 115–16.

——. 'Designing Houses for the Australian Climate: The Early Research', *Architectural Science Review* 56(3) (2013), 197–207. https://doi.org/10.1080/00038628.2013.807218.

Willis, Julie. 'Commonwealth Department of Works', in Philip Goad and Julie Willis (eds), *The Encyclopedia of Australian Architecture* (Port Melbourne, Vic: Cambridge University Press, 2012), pp. 164–65.

Wills, Sara. 'Between the Hostel and the Detention Centre: Possible Trajectories of Migrant Pain and Shame in Australia', in William Logan and Keir Reeves (eds), *Places of Pain and Shame: Dealing with Difficult Heritage* (New York: Routledge, 2009), pp. 263–80.

Wright, Claire. *Australian Economic History*. Canberra: ANU Press, 2022.

Chapter 8

From Enterprise to Enterprise
Refugees, Industry and Settlement in an Australian City

David Beynon

In this chapter I explore the impact of migrants from Southeast Asia on the development of Melbourne's metropolitan area, focusing on refugees who resided in Melbourne's migrant hostels from the late 1970s to their closure in the early 1990s. Part of this exploration is a response to the relative neglect of refugee and more broadly non-Western immigrant instigated settlement in Australian architecture and built environment discussions, despite its profound cultural and economic impact. This chapter takes up this question in relation to how notions of what is non-Western or Asian might be geographically reinterpreted through settlement of recent migrants to Australia from beyond Europe. Thinking of Australia as a 'Western' nation derives from its origins as a group of British (for this, read English) colonies, contrary to its geographical location southeast of the Asian continent. This conception of Australia has, as was outlined in previous chapters of this volume, led to non-English migrants being considered in relation to their cultural, ethnic or 'racial' distance from this colonially derived identity. Italian, Lithuanian, Macedonian and other Southern European immigrants found themselves prejudicially regarded. However, the first major influx of migrants from East and Southeast Asia provided a more existential challenge to Australia's self-identity. As Ien Ang puts it:

> the sense of danger associated with 'Asianisation' is more than a question of cultural xenophobia; it is intensified by the paradoxical geographical positioning of Australia, far from Europe and on the margins of Asia, an isolation that is manifest in persistent popular discourses on the 'distance' of Australia from the centres of US and European cultural and political power and influence, and on public debates on the 'place' of Australia, 'in' or 'out' of Asia, as quintessential to the nation's selfhood.[1]

While, as was discussed in earlier chapters of this volume, this was by no means the first influx of culturally differentiated immigrants or refugees into Australia, many of these new arrivals were of diverse and sometimes transcultural Asian backgrounds – Vietnamese, diasporic Chinese, Lao, Cambodian, Sri Lankan, Timorese and others – and represented a profound shift in Australia's demographic profile that is widely evident today. Moreover, Australia's location in the Asia Pacific region, with greater proximity to Southeast and East Asian homelands, has sustained continuous immigration from these regions since the late 1970s, including flows of refugees and interrupted only by changing immigration policies and border securitization. This chapter describes the first major influx of these immigrants and their diverse strategies for establishing communities and industries in Australia. What is emphasized here is that while many of their activities were small-scale in comparison with the heavy industrial industries and nation-building projects described in previous chapters, these immigrants from various parts of Asia have collectively had a profound impact on Australian society and its built environments. While heterogeneous in their identities and origins, their collective identification as 'Asian' has led to a broader sense of pan-Asian identity in the Australian context.

ARRIVING TO FRAGMENTED IMMIGRANT LABOUR OPPORTUNITIES

Unlike the roles and broad impact of migrants and refugees in Australia's post-Second World War nation-building projects previously discussed in Chapters 4 and 5, and heavy industries discussed in Chapter 3, by the 1970s, federally funded projects no longer supported or provided mass employment for refugees or immigrants. There was a relative lack of large new industrial infrastructure needing construction or mass labour. The manufacturing industries that provided ready employment for previous generations of refugees were starting to decline.[2] This necessarily shifted the industrial focus associated with new immigrant arrivals from large singular enterprises to more fragmented and dispersed subjects. Unlike the immigrants who had previously arrived to work on major government-financed or supported industries or infrastructure, new arrivals from the late 1970s onwards were only sometimes able to rely on state or local government for assistance with settlement and to find jobs in existing factories. Many had to draw on support from their own emerging immigrant communities to develop economic independence, leading to a proliferation of small enterprises, many starting in areas proximate to migrant hostels. Pursuing this change as its line of inquiry, this chapter introduces a number of individual or family stories, mostly drawn from community discussions and interviews, that link refugee arrival, settlement and developments in commerce, industry and community in these areas. The ways in which the outer-suburban and semi-industrial or fringe-rural built environments in the areas surrounding migrant hostels developed has illuminated several important issues. They include, first, how the adapted built environments of these areas embody a nexus of society and space in relation to Asian-identified environments. The most visibly 'Asian' parts of these suburbs are commercial/industrial districts rather than domestic/residential areas. Commercial/industrial districts involve clear demarcations of space, denoted as having particular sociocultural identities by signage advertising Asian products and/or in Asian languages. For example, the advertised display of particular goods such as noodles or tofu, suggests the identities of populations using, working in and engaging with the public realm in these built environments.

MINORITY IMMIGRANT COMMUNITIES AND SPATIAL OCCUPATION

The degree to which these environments are distinctive in themselves is one point of discussion, but more importantly this chapter explores the issue of spatial occupation in relation to Australia's prevailing conception of land ownership and identity that is still largely based on the nation's political origins as a collection of British colonies, despite the impact of developments detailed in previous chapters of this book. My empirical research correlates to a broader discussion about the production of spatial practices and representations and their relation to a still overarching 'governmental' sense of Australia's identity, notwithstanding recent progress in recognizing Indigenous Australians (Aboriginal and Torres Strait Islander First Nations/Peoples). Here, I use 'governmental' in both a literal and a positional sense, following Ghassan Hage's argument of how, despite apparent acceptance of multiculturalism, 'white' Australians retain a governmental sense of proprietorship of Australia's development.[3] And yet, this sense coexists with a population descended from a great diversity of immigrant backgrounds, and 'what is more part of Australia's multicultural heritage than the many towns and villages from which Australia's migrant population has originated?'[4] Despite this, ideas about Australian architectural heritage have generally avoided this 'transborder vision of migration',[5] reinforcing the sense that governmental proprietorship remains prevalent.

A couple of issues need to be borne in mind. First, while much of the built environment that I describe in this chapter involves the use of pre-existing architectural stock (largely utilitarian retail and light industrial buildings), interspersed occasionally with new typologies (Buddhist or Daoist temples and the premises of culturally specific organizations), the question of the nature of heritage in this environment needs to be asked. Second, and related to the first point, is that these communities of migrants from the 1970s to the 1990s represent neither the first nor the last wave of culturally identifiable settlers to these areas, raising the question of demographic dynamism and the fluidity of constructed and denoted identity in relation to the histories and legacies of individuals and communities, and their encounters with pre-existing diverse communities of immigrants and their descendants. What is being played out here could be described, using Kuan-hsing Chen's term, as the inter-referencing of diasporic and 'local' (for this, read settlers with a slightly longer history) expressions of belonging.[6] Acceptance of the idea of Australian identity being diversified is comparatively recent. Immigrants from non-British origins still have to contend with the persistent notion that Australian culture remains a received and adapted British (English) society.[7] To explore the question of geographical interpretation involves tracing histories of spatial occupations as well as obvious formal transformations. The areas studied as subjects of this chapter have undergone spatial and formal recontextualization of largely existing building stock. Since the late 1970s, this recontextualization has been, from inside refugee/immigrant communities, an often sudden transposition of identities due to conflict, into and onto Australian built environments. This chapter will thus argue that these transpositions across Australia's suburbs constitute a heritage of demographic diversification and evidence of what Jeffrey Hou has termed transcultural place making.[8] In approaching this, I am taking Bertacco and Vallorani's suggestion to 'imagine new schema of translation premised on the acknowledgement that we live in heavily translational cultures and most peoples, very likely, always have'.[9] If the past is not the unified and mutually agreed narrative of growing nationhood and the living present is a multiplicity of cultural identities that are themselves in a constant state of flux and mixing, then what about the built environment?

HOSTELS AND SUBURBS: FOOTSCRAY AND SPRINGVALE AS CENTRES FOR DIVERSE IMMIGRATION AND REFUGEE SETTLEMENT

The two areas of suburban Melbourne studied in exploring these questions have particular histories of diverse immigration and refugee settlement that have led to the distinctive development of commercial and industrial built environments and cultural identifications. Hostels scattered around Melbourne began to receive an influx of people fleeing from conflicts in Southeast Asia from the late 1970s. While some refugees passed through the Westona Hostel in Altona and the Eastbridge Hostel in Nunawading, the Midway Migrant Hostel in Maribyrnong and the Enterprise Migrant Hostel in Springvale became major recipients of Southeast Asians: Vietnamese, diasporic Chinese, Cambodians and Lao. Due to the locations of these hostels, the surrounding suburbs of Footscray and Springvale became major centres for their communities, along with some other areas of Melbourne such as Richmond, where social housing was available. Previously, Footscray had been developed as a working-class suburb in the late nineteenth century to the immediate west of the centre of Melbourne – a centre for heavy industry due to its proximity to the city's port. Springvale was largely established on the southeastern fringe of Melbourne's metropolitan area in the 1950s. By the 1970s, both suburbs were surrounded by industry and cheap housing. There were parallel developments in Sydney and other Australian cities in the 1970s, and together the arrival and settlement of this influx of migrants constituted a distinct change to Australia's demographic makeup.[10] As earlier chapters in this volume have discussed, these new settlers were certainly neither the first refugees to arrive in Australia nor the first to face the difficulties of negotiating cultural differences. However, their arrival constituted the first substantial number of migrants from anywhere in Asia since the repealing of the *Immigration Restriction Act* (the 'White Australia Policy'), which was discussed in Chapter 1.

The residents of the Midway and Enterprise Hostels initially sought employment and permanent housing in their surrounding areas, and some found work in nearby factories and other local businesses. However, as ethnically distinct ex-refugees, there were also substantial barriers to their finding employment, including difficulties with language, lack of recognition of qualifications and sometimes outright racial discrimination.[11] As a result, a larger proportion of them became self-employed than previous waves of migrants and by the 1990s had begun to establish themselves through small retail businesses and manufacturing.[12] This development also demonstrated the ability of many ex-refugees from Vietnamese, Cambodian, diasporic Chinese and other communities to identify, pursue and succeed in taking the entrepreneurial opportunities created by their communities' presence.[13]

Through hard work, enterprise, willingness to engage with existing commercial needs and an ability to provide products and services that were previously unavailable or unknown in Australia, these new communities have thrived. This variety of uses, indicative of rich histories and creative adaptations of found conditions, has elevated previously marginal parts of metropolitan Melbourne to become integral to the city's projections of multiculturalism, attractive to regional immigrants seeking an egalitarian reception of their different needs.

Working through and with the discriminatory processes initially encountered in these localities, enterprising refugees and immigrants have succeeded in transforming manufacturing, commercial and retail districts with new types of businesses and industries as well as new community, cultural and religious institutions. Sometimes these transformations have meant entirely new buildings and architectural types. However, in many cases, it is the uses of existing buildings rather than their physical forms that have been changed. Comparing the present-day streetscapes of Springvale, Footscray and many other suburbs with those of earlier decades, many of the buildings remain the same, but their usage, signage and identities have been profoundly transformed. The result has been that over forty years later, the suburbs of Footscray (the nearest substantial commercial district to the Midway Hostel), Springvale and Richmond (an inner eastern suburb where large numbers of these communities were settled in public housing) have become identified with these cultures. As Vietnamese are the most numerous community in these suburbs, Footscray, Springvale and Richmond have become identified with Vietnamese identity to the point of being referred to as 'Little Saigons'.[14]

NARRATIVES OF SETTLEMENT, ADAPTATION AND SPATIAL TRANSFORMATION

Interviews with individuals from these communities provide a rich repository of stories that bring these demographic changes to life. Their stories each tell of a weaving of chronology and geography, at first over considerable distances and involving great dangers, and then over smaller distances and with risks of a different kind. These stories collectively describe macropractices and micropractices of labour that occupied and spatially transformed many of Melbourne's existing spaces and buildings, and added new layers of spatial inscription to the land, leading to profound changes to the host city. They also tell of the disappearance of former lives and the slow and sometimes painful building of new ones, and with this building of lives, the concurrent development of business enterprises and places. Many of these people were refugees from Vietnam or Cambodia, arriving as children or young adults via arduous and dangerous journeys to first become residents of Melbourne's migrant hostels and then settlers in surrounding suburbs. Some have gone on to create successful businesses and others to (re)qualify themselves and become established in professional fields.

NEW NEEDS, PRODUCTS AND ADAPTED BUILT ENVIRONMENTS

The most obvious visual representations of industrial enterprise have been the transformation of commercial and retail streetscapes. One of my correspondents for this project is Cuc Lam, a councillor and former mayor for the City of Maribyrnong, who arrived as a refugee from Vietnam to Midway Hostel in 1978 after a lengthy and hazardous journey. Here Cúc Lam provides a sense of the need for new products and services in 1970s Melbourne:

> I think people started [making Vietnamese food business] because . . . Vietnamese people need their food culture. They want rice, noodles. During the time I was at the Midway hostel, we were not allowed to cook. We had to go to the canteen. I couldn't eat the food because food like lamb was not familiar to me . . . also as I was pregnant, I didn't like onion . . . they deducted about eighty-five percent of our money for accommodation and food . . . so we didn't have much left, about twenty or thirty dollars per fortnight for both my husband and I. I used the remaining money to go to the shops/groceries or Highpoint to buy noodles . . . we had hot water in the studio, so we could boil the noodles, pour it into the cup and have instant noodles. Being a refugee . . . it isn't easy where language gesture and culture are so different from your own country. But we managed to move forward with strong resilience and motivation to build a new better life in Australia with harmony and happiness.[15]

Enterprising ex-refugees developed a large number of new enterprises in Melbourne to meet this need, introducing new forms of retailing, manufacturing and other industries, as recounted by the following two people that I interviewed in 2020. As they wished to remain anonymous, I have designated them as Business Owners 1 and 2 (B1 and B2).

B1 is Chinese-Vietnamese and speaks fluent Cantonese. She arrived in Australia after a lengthy and traumatic journey, first in a small boat from Vietnam that sank in Thai waters (like many who initially fled the country), occasioning the rescue of B1 and her hundred-odd fellow passengers. From there she was put into a refugee camp in Thailand. Meanwhile, her husband successfully made it to Australia in a different boat and by 1979 was resident in the Enterprise Hostel and was able to have her flown to Melbourne under family reunion provisions. Following this, they shared residency at the hostel for a few months. While at the hostel, B1 looked for work, finding the forms of piecemeal employment packaging and sewing open to non-English speakers at the time. B1 left the hostel with her husband after a few months, renting in nearby suburbs of Westall and Clayton. By 1980, they had sufficient means to start a small business in Springvale. This was a milk bar (a convenience store in local parlance) previously run by Italian immigrants. The surrounding shops were greengrocers and butchers, as well as frozen meat shops, all owned, as B1 recollects, by previous generations of migrants of Italian, Greek and Jewish backgrounds:

> There was no chance I could loan money from [the] bank, I didn't have anything for a mortgage loan. So, it was our little saving, and our friend was operating a grocery store, so we borrowed stock from him ... it was not a big company, it was a small store like ours in Richmond. And our friend recommended us at the time and said 'I can supply you the stock, then you can operate your store'. So we got the stock from him every day, then we sold the stock by small amounts to start our store.[16]

However, gradually, the business grew. B1 and her husband expanded their range of products to cater for customers of other Asian backgrounds, as not only did imports of culturally specific products increase, but numerous small enterprises, manufacturing products such as tofu and noodles, also sprang up in Springvale and surrounding suburbs. With this growth, they moved to larger and more prominent premises on Springvale Road and established a pan-Asian supermarket that remains in business to the present day with B1 as the owner and proprietor. The building previously housed a furniture shop and despite the change of use and almost four decades as a supermarket has been little altered. The shopfront glazing and entry have been renewed, signage has been added to the awning and parapet, and some storage spaces have been created at the rear of the shop floor, but given the practicality of the space, the overall form of the single-storey building is the same as it was as a furniture shop in the early 1980s.

B2 also fled Vietnam in 1979 and is of mixed Chinese-Vietnamese background. She came from a wealthy background in Saigon and her family paid for their boat passage in gold bars. However, like B1, B2's boat ran into trouble and was intercepted by Thai pirates three times (stripping what remained of her family wealth) before they made it to Singaporean waters, where the boat was turned away and was eventually found drifting at sea by an oil tanker and brought to Darwin. B2 was in Darwin for three months before being transferred to Springvale in 1980. Here, she stayed at the Enterprise Hostel for one year and then rented a one-bedroom apartment in the nearby suburb of Oakleigh, while working in a restaurant. Like B1, B2 also started a small grocery shop in the early 1980s, though initially this was in Croydon, a few suburbs northeast of Springvale. Here the Asian proportion of the supplies was lower, and the customers were mostly Anglo-Australian (the only people of Asian background that B2 remembers were Filipinos married to Anglo-Australians). Then in 1992, with the developing demand for locally manufactured Asian food products, B2 took over a vacant warehouse in Westall, an industrial area near Springvale. At this premises she set up a business manufacturing Chinese/Vietnamese-style fishballs and fishcakes. As she initially had no kitchen facilities, B2 used a friend's restaurant kitchen until she had established the business sufficiently to get a bank loan and import her own equipment from Taiwan.

The retail centres of Footscray and Springvale are clearly marked by concentrations of such Asian-derived enterprises as these areas that have become major locations for retail shops, restaurants, food outlets and a diverse range of services oriented towards communities of Vietnamese and other Southeast Asian origins, more recently supplemented (and in some cases being supplanted) by the same kinds of businesses of African origin. However, while the presence of goods, services and signage in a proliferation of languages mark their physical environments as different from other suburbs in Melbourne, the architectural impact of these changes to built environments is more difficult to gauge. The character of Vietnamese or Cambodian-Australians' commercial architecture is not distinct in its physical form. In architectural terms, you could say there is nothing much that is really different here, if you look beyond the signs and unfamiliar products. As Sanaz and Wood argue in their discussion of Sydney's culturally diverse commerce, 'it would be difficult to sustain the argument that Bankstown's traders have adapted public/private interfaces in particularly novel ways. In countless main streets and town centres across Australia, buildings of similar vintage and (more or less) similar condition might be identified'.[17] The issue is perhaps that their territorializing practices do not really differ that much – details may change, social rituals or mores may change, but basic practices of trade and industry (exchange, market display methods, etc.) are hardly unique to particular cultures.

Yet, if they are not so typologically different, they *are* seen as ontologically different. The difference is in the literal embodiment of their highly differentiated practices of occupation. Buildings can be inhabited by a succession of people and reused (even without obvious formal or structural differences) for different purposes. The built environment of Springvale or Footscray is representative of the complex ways in which built environments are instrumentalized in the construction of identities. This is because buildings demarcate territorial occupation. The notion of settlement as the fundamental basis of cities is manifested in the apparent solidity of buildings and their constructed surroundings, placed and codified by the boundaries of zones, districts, suburbs, cities, states and nations. Because of this, the fact of a shop fitout being identified with a particular community or ethnicity and being in a district in close proximity with other shop fitouts (in equally generic physical surroundings) lends an underappreciated significance to an urban environment. While there is some historiography on the commercial aspects of culturally distinct migrancy,[18] there are many substantial urban districts that owe their identities to such migration. B1's supermarket (see Figure 8.1), for instance, is a well-known landmark in the local landscape, having remained for over forty years in the same location within a virtually unaltered physical envelope.

FROM FACTORIES TO GARAGES: IMMIGRANTS' COLLECTIVE NEEDS FOR BOTH FORMAL EMPLOYMENT AND THE DEVELOPMENT OF HOME-BASED INDUSTRY

Richard Lim, another Springvale resident and a pharmacist and current councillor, represents the Springvale Ward of the City of Greater Dandenong. Richard was born in Cambodia of Chinese-Cambodian parentage and was forced to flee due to its takeover by the Khmer Rouge regime in 1975. His account of establishing himself in Australia as a pharmacist is testimony to his resourcefulness, drive and sheer hard work:

Figure 8.1 Nan Yang Asian Supermarket, Springvale, Victoria, 2022. © David Beynon

I was working at night, night shift ... in a factory ... near Vermont, Heathmont was my first job. The factory, the first one, was Vulcan, they made ovens, hot water systems ... that was my first job there. Not long after, Vulcan decided to sell to another company therefore I got another job ... in a factory [Stokes] where they make elements for the stove ... My job was to print, to put the batch number on the element, and also to make the element for the stove ... I said to my boss, 'Can I work during afternoon shift? change my shift ... so I can go to school?' Very nice boss from England, he said OK. That's how I could go to school during the day, from 8:30 to 3:30. Then [at] 4 o'clock something I went to factory for afternoon shift until about 1 o'clock at night, then home, for two years. In 1983 I finished my high school certificate. By [19]84 I got into first year pharmacy school.[19]

Richard Lim's pharmacy was established in Springvale in 1990 and in its current site occupies a prominent street corner in the suburb's retail centre (see Figure 8.2).

Taken together, as well as being accounts of individuals' achievements, these are stories of the settlement and development of new communities in Australia. Finding themselves in a new and unfamiliar environment, these are people who reshaped their surroundings to better secure their sense of belonging and ownership. And their reshaping at an individual level was supported, whether explicitly (in allowing the use of a restaurant kitchen to start a fishball production business and starting a grocery by selling on stock in microquantities) or implicitly (by working in a factory to confirm professional qualifications already part-attained overseas), and replicated by others

Figure 8.2 Lim's Pharmacy, Springvale, Victoria, 2022. © David Beynon

in their broader migrant communities. There are of course many more stories that I could recount here. They reveal different aspects of these sociospatial processes of settlement and economic establishment, illustrating both their overt and unseen impacts on Australian suburbs' built environments.[20]

Studies of immigrant entrepreneurship have been carried out in Australia since the 1980s,[21] as has research into the social impacts of concentrations of businesses by people of shared ethnocultural backgrounds.[22] Refugee women, as represented by B1 and B2, were especially incentivized by this mixture of lack of existing employment opportunities and abilities to see business possibilities in the changing demography of which they were a part,[23] with larger proportions of self-employment amongst ex-refugees than for other types of migrants.[24] As was related by a number of my other correspondents, this often meant that families banded together in a mixture of employed and informal work arrangements, echoing the arrangements that residents in earlier migrant camps had to make, as discussed in Chapter 6. As Bon Nguyên, current President of the Vietnamese Community in Victoria, ex-refugee and now a leading scientist in the field of fluid dynamics, recalls:

> My mum was sitting in front of the sewing machine at home and she picked strawberries as well during the day . . . during the night she do that [sewing]. My dad worked for Cadbury, the chocolate factory in Ringwood. Dad was very proud of how he made chocolate.[25]

The reference to sewing is significant as it indicates the importance of recognizing industrial activities that have no public profile. Many men, like Richard Lim and Bon Nguyên, worked in the factories of Melbourne's western or southeastern suburbs. However, many women worked as machinists doing piecework or collectively filling contract orders of garment companies. And in the evenings, the men often joined entire families occupied in this way. As another correspondent, Kim Bùi-Quang, reflected about one of her contemporaries:

> She used to be owner of a machinist [business] giving people work to do, then they give back to her, and she said that the family, they have machine work twenty-four hours. Once two people sleep other ones wake up and do very hard work. Her husband during the day is an engineer. When he comes back, has a quick nap then after dinner he work[s] the overlocker until late.[26]

This machining work has been vitally important for livelihoods of these communities, but their spatial transformations of existing spaces and buildings has largely been invisible to the public. Nevertheless, the ingenuity of these workers is demonstrated by their invention of a number of tools to assist their work. A number of my contacts for this project are driving a proposal for a museum to celebrate Vietnamese-Australian culture and history, the forthcoming Vietnamese Museum Victoria (VMA), in which their emphasis on the many ways of making a living is celebrated:

> With [the] first influx of Vietnamese, a lot of people got involved in sewing, machinists to be exact, overlocking, more machinist than seamstress. So we had to make a few different

tools to help, to rationalize the work, to simplify, [make it] easier to work. So we have not only designed but created a few little tools like that. Say for example for the collar, how to turn it quickly inside-out, to thread elastic too . . . little tools that have now been developed into patents. People have actually patented [these tools] as well. So what we have is like a very, very early design of that kind of thing . . . prototype kind of thing . . . A lot of families actually turned their garage into a makeshift factory, and from there developed into a proper factory.[27]

A couple of important points are worth emphasizing here. First, considerable ingenuity was applied to the laborious and repetitive tasks of sewing large quantities of garments, as evidenced by the invention of apparently simple but extremely useful labour-saving tools. Second, this employment often involved multiple generations of extended family members working in domestic environments that were gradually modified into industrial workplaces. This meant a blurring of residential, industrial and commercial realms in ways that might sometimes have been imperceptible, but were actually profoundly transforming Melbourne's suburbs. And as the images of a current sewing business in Melbourne's northern suburb of Keilor Downs shows, this is still the case (see Figure 8.3).

What these examples indicate is that there is a distinct relationship of labour to spatial and formal developments in the built environment. The enterprise of refugees has introduced forms of manufacturing, retailing and other industries that were cul-

Figure 8.3 Sewing/machining workshop, Keilor Downs, Victoria, 2022. © David Beynon

turally new to Australia, while spatially extending existing industries beyond their previous bounds in the creation of sociospatial networks extending across suburbs, cities and the nation as a whole, creating important elements of the contemporary Australian built environment. At first glance, this importance might be hard to see in architectural terms. Beyond signage and shop or factory fitouts, few architectonic developments have obviously eventuated from B1 and B2's successful businesses. Both B1 and B2 have occupied a series of pre-existing buildings and made only minimal and pragmatic alterations. This is often the case with retail/light industrial architecture. Building for a shop can be very simple, needing nothing more than the provision of an envelope to house, protect and display goods and some signage to denote its existence. While some retail premises may be custom-designed to correlate with the products housed, in most cases this is not, or only minimally, the case. Identity in most shops is inscribed on the shopfront, not so much by its permanent aspects, its glazed façade or its entry, but by signage and by the visibility of the goods inside (and sometimes outside in front). While civic or residential buildings may clearly express the aspirations of those for whom they are built (as well as for those who design and build them) and represent the beliefs and priorities of their society through architectural expression, this is mostly not the case for the commercial and retail built environment. As well as being relatively simple, shop fitouts and signage can be applied and readily removed, so to a broad extent the set of business-specific elements necessary to sustain a shop is interchangeable as far as the physical building envelope is concerned.

However, there are a number of aspects of culturally defined buildings and uses that might be critically interrogated. The commercial zones in Footscray and Springvale have, as was noted earlier in this chapter, become major locations for retail shops, restaurants, food outlets and a diverse range of services oriented towards communities of refugee/immigrant origins. There are distinct identities being represented here within sociospatial contexts that call into question normative understandings of these everyday environments. One way of looking at both Footscray and Springvale is that two former racially 'white' working-class suburbs have been reterritorialized by these new arrivals, and this reterritorialization is an ongoing and dynamic process, as evidenced by the current gradual transformation of Footscray's retail businesses and food outlets from Vietnamese to African (largely Ethiopian, Sudanese and Somali)-owned or run businesses. Looking at the changes in this suburb in this manner raises questions as to their ontological and epistemological significance in terms of their meanings and representations for wider audiences.

These retail and commercial premises collectively occupy space and despite lacking distinctive architectural form, these spatial occupations denote and demarcate identities in territorial ways. Their existence makes visible the diversifying reality of these suburbs as the ground for myriad *tactical* activities,[28] making the most of the limited space and resources at their disposal to make identifiable places. These developments have made Footscray and Springvale into cultural centres, and from these centres, second and third-generation immigrant families are building on these communities' increasing influence on greater Melbourne through their business enterprises, cultural and religious organizations. Taking Lefebvre's idea of space as the repository of creative energy, 'stored in readiness for new creations',[29] and exposing meanings, whether political, philosophical or religious, suggests that these retail and commercial environments voice these meanings by providing both envelope and content to the everyday lives that happen within them. The implication is that buildings, like the other physical elements of a city, are not only filled by the meanings that their builders, architects and individual owners ascribe to them, but are also social and cultural constructions with collective impact. Here, the collective impact of a particular influx of refugees starting businesses is what is evident in the physical/cultural environments of Melbourne. This most immediately occurred in areas of Footscray, Springvale and Richmond, but has since been apparent in other suburbs of Melbourne (notably Noble Park, St Albans, Sunshine and Preston) and in a more diffused manner in nearly all of suburban Melbourne. Just one example of this correlation of culture, lived experience and space is the proliferation of outlets making and selling *banh mi* (Vietnamese filled bread rolls), to the extent that one Melbourne daily newspaper recently produced a map indicating where they are available in every one of the city's suburban districts.[30] Beyond that, as Bon Nguyên recalls:

> I'm fortunate to fly away for my job, away from [Melbourne's] Asian community for a week or two ... By the end of the journey you get to the [Melbourne] airport, you see some *banh mi*, 'Oh my god I really want that!' 'And what about a beer?' Imagine an Asian guy at the airport having a *banh mi* and a beer ... I can't complain.[31]

BROADER BUILT ENVIRONMENTS: BALANCING RELIGIOUS FUNCTIONS, WORKPLACES AND IMMIGRANT COMMUNITY NEEDS IN INDUSTRIAL ZONES

What this confluence of new cultures and purposes has also led to is an adjustment of urban neighbourhoods. While most of the buildings of light industrial zones are pragmatic and generic, despite whatever is being manufactured or sold within them, the industrial zones near Springvale and Footscray are interestingly also places where cultural and religious institutions can be found, and the presence of these buildings, with their more expressive architecture, is a result of the less visible changes to the environments around them. In the industrial district of Braybrook northwest of Footscray, for instance, the most dominant sight is the Quang Minh Vietnamese Buddhist Temple (see Figure 8.4). This is a large complex of buildings on a site overlooking the Maribyrnong River valley, incorporating a mixture of worship halls, event venues, shrines and accommodation for monks. As well as its religious function, the temple correspondingly hosts Vietnamese cultural and sporting events, and its Lunar New Year and other Vietnamese/Buddhist annual celebrations are attended by the wider

Figure 8.4 Quang Minh Vietnamese Buddhist Temple, Braybrook, Victoria, 2022. © David Beynon

population of the surrounding area and beyond. The abbott of the temple explained to me how the Quang Minh Temple came to be here:

> There's been a lot of change, I've been here since 1996... This whole area here used to be very heavily industrial... To find a large piece of land is very difficult, these were abandoned factories, cheap, so that's why we had to come here... we used to be at the edge of the community settlement, quite far away from Footscray... So now we become like a centre.[32]

He also discussed how the temple has come to be a cultural rather than purely a religious centre:

> Like any emerging community, we have to move from place to place, the reason is that you cannot move too far from your community members, but when you establish [a temple] a lot of people come... Two things happened, more refugee[s] arrived, but also more people come to the temple... for cultural identity rather than religion... That still exists nowadays, like when we organize a festival... around twenty percent are not Buddhist who come to the festival (also now people who are not Vietnamese, with their kids). In Vietnam a temple has to be a pure religious centre... But in Australia I think the cultural aspect is a lot more demand than the religious side. When we built the temple here, we got a $1

million grant from the government. Western governments like [to] separate community from religion, we presented a case that a lot of community activity happens in the temple . . . sporting club, youth association, Vietnamese language school . . . lion dancing group, dragon dancing group.[33]

Despite all these cultural developments centred on the temple, its immediate neighbours are automotive mechanics and panel shops run mostly by Vietnamese-Australians. Light industrial areas are among the cheapest real estate available in cities and are held in correspondingly low esteem. Consequently, such areas are often not subject to the kinds of heritage and planning controls that govern other areas (or, more pointedly, are less subject to the objections that are often raised to the construction of new religious and cultural institutions in other areas). As a result, the Quang Minh Temple is just one example of such developments across Melbourne's metropolitan area. The appearance of religious and cultural buildings in industrial zones has become a distinctive form of cultural transformation, their visibility only limited by the locations of such areas. In Springvale, the Guan Di Daoist Temple and Teochew (Chinese dialect group) Association is another example, at the edge of an industrial estate and next door to a cabinet-making workshop (see Figure 8.5), though nearby are the premises of the Vietnamese Women's Association and the Hakka (another Chinese dialect group) Cultural Association alongside Cambodian-Australian tyre fitters and other local businesses.

Figure 8.5 The Guan Di Daoist Temple and Teochew Association, next door to a cabinet-making workshop, Springvale, Victoria, 2022. © David Beynon

What is being provided in these once entirely industrial areas of Braybrook and Springvale are effective hubs for new communities, where they have been able to literally add to the diverse fabric of their physical surroundings. And, as is also noted in Footscray in relation to minority ethnic communities establishing themselves, the instigation of a culturally specific centre has led to a growth of a surrounding area's identity in relation to that cultural specificity.[34] These areas have grown in their ability to provide *affordances* for immigrant communities as they have increasingly become places for their embodied practices. This has been a mutually transformative process. As Kelum Palipane has put it, 'affordances are not already there, inscribed in space but are activated through peoples' sensory experiences by the moving through, touching, smelling, hearing seeing of objects and places'.[35]

But whether due to the economics of acquiring land, the difficulties of obtaining permits or the latent qualities of such places, the presence of a temple or cultural centre amongst workshops, warehouses and factories represents a clear shift in the identity of a built environment and the ability of immigrant communities to remake unpromising built environments into places of community belonging and identity. Their presence also raises various questions about the evolving urban landscape of a city that proclaims itself multicultural and cosmopolitan. In travelling through Melbourne's suburbs, what distinguishes one place from another? What punctuates the landscape? Denotations of particular identities in particular languages? By itself, it seems that little distinguishes a Cambodian-Australian tyre repair shop from an Anglo-Australian one (see Figure 8.6). Yet Angkor Tyres in its name evokes an identity built around an ancient Khmer monument so powerful in its resonance that even the Khmer Rouge protected it. Angkor is the symbol *sine qua non* for Cambodia, on the national beer and on the national flag. Being on a tyre repair shop in Springvale designates the importance of that identity, both symbolically and practically for those in need of a tyre mechanic who can speak Khmer.

There are various ways in which this confluence of specific identities, whether denoted as signage on generic industrial forms or formally expressed as religious architecture, can be seen. I have previously written about some of these aspects in relation to planning authorities, processes, and the latent and sometimes blatant undercurrents of discrimination that have also determined where such buildings are and are not located.[36] However, in this chapter, I wish to concentrate more on what is being created than on how the governments and majority cultures have influenced these activities. Yet, prioritizing certain forms of identity with formal qualities of urban space does reify those qualities as being the norm in the built environment and renders other formations as aberrant – in Hou and Chalana's terms, 'messy' – lacking the order that is associated with the normative.[37] In this sense, Hou and Chalana's book on *Messy Urbanism* is both a provocation of and resistance to the persistent, institutional, and cultural biases that persist in global thinking about urbanism. Their focus is on Asia's cities and their relations to legacies of postcolonial pasts and Western-centred views of urban environments – 'The interplay and overlays of order/disorder, formal/informal,

Figure 8.6 Angkor Tyres repair workshop, Springvale, Victoria, 2022. © David Beynon

legal/illegal, local/global constitute an experience that defines life and urbanism in many Asian cities'[38] – but I think it is also useful to think of the 'messy' as a productive/provocative way of thinking of Australia's changing urban environment as it becomes more culturally heterogeneous. Here, messiness denotes urban conditions and processes that do not follow institutionalized or culturally prescribed notions of order, which is not to say that they have no order at all. Instead, it suggests an alternative structure and hierarchy as well as agency and actions that, even if subjugated or ignored by the dominant hierarchy, create their own spatial and visual orders as well as adapting and developing social and political institutions and cultural norms in place. Each identifiable community has its own genealogies of practice – defined by specificities of product and process – that are not necessarily dissimilar to others (in the provision of shops, manufacturing enterprises, etc.), but are defined by particular intersections of histories, memories and translations, and then inscribed into a given locality. The process of adaptation to found conditions is a process of redefinition and reterritorialization, whether literally applied to pre-existing physical places or involving new constructions in pre-existing frameworks of spaces and zones.

From the point of view of the city as a whole, these developments are gradually turning once entirely industrial zones from peripheries into centres as they afford modes of usage and inhabitation. The increasing number of everyday cultural interactions may individually relate to specific and quite small communities, but together they contribute to the dynamism of Melbourne's demographic complexity. Returning to the idea of 'inter-referencing', these are places where multiple cultures exist and intersect.[39] The ordinary and everyday nature of this inter-referencing might also be rendered in architectural terms as variations on ethno-architecture (as Paul Memmott has used to describe Indigenous Australian buildings in the Australian context),[40] or even as 'commercial vernacular', evoking Venturi, Scott Brown and Izenour's analysis of US commercial developments in the mid-twentieth century to re-evaluate both the overtly symbolic and compositionally banal results of the 'Las Vegas Strip',[41] and the 'hidden' symbolic and compositionally accomplished works of feted modernist architects.[42] Bearing in mind later arguments over the use of 'vernacular' to describe increasingly corporatized commercial developments, emphasis was placed on the 'local street'[43] and its 'natural and instinctive' process of creation.[44] Applied in a culturally charged and inter-referenced way, such a position can then be related to the often prejudicial views of Western authorities toward non-Western districts of colonial and postcolonial cities, a point often made by postcolonial writers on the subject.[45] Accounts of the Chinese districts of nineteenth-century gold rush towns and cities provide evidence of this pejorative distinction in Australian urban history.[46] In the present, however, this kind of 'Messy urbanism implies plurality, multiplicity, and contradictions, a condition in which urban forms and processes don't fit into a singular hierarchy, structure, or meaning'.[47] However, for a multicultural and dynamic city this 'messiness' represents increasingly desirable attributes. In their roles as sites of implicit resistance against the top-down structures of governmental urban planning, these places of urban messiness might also serve as sites of innovation in the pursuit of new modes, understanding and collaboration among citizens, professionals and institutions. Architecturally speaking, it is worth thinking about how this range of buildings relates to conceptions of how architecture is constituted in relation to migrants. On an individual architectural level, these conceptions bring to mind Clifford's description of ways in which cultures *travel*,[48] a term he prefers to 'migration' as it conveys a process more complex than the simple displacement and settlement of immigrants.

THE OVERLAPPING AND CONTINGENT REALITIES OF IMMIGRANT SETTLEMENT: INDUSTRY, IDENTITY AND LENTICULARITY

Beyond individual tales of business success, a number of contingent realities can be derived from my correspondents' narratives. The first is that externally derived identities are more complex than they seem. Bon Nguyên, Kim Bùi-Quang and Venerable Phước Tấn Thich all arrived in Australia from Vietnam and identify as Vietnamese-Australians, whereas B1 and B2 also arrived in Australia as refugees from Vietnam, but identify as Chinese.[49] In the transit from Vietnam to Australia, identities such as Vietnamese and Chinese have become conflated – the Chineseness of 'Vietnamese' refugees such as B1 is noted but rarely discussed in detail, perhaps because it complicates broader stories of cultural influx and interaction or because the nuances of difference of refugees' cultural background were inconsequential in relation to the gravity of the cultural difference between any Asian culture and an Australia emerging from the White Australia Policy. Also, it might be considered that the greater difference between these refugees and their hosts necessarily brought individuals of different cultural backgrounds together in pragmatic solidarity. The results, as written on the signage of B1's supermarket, speak of this kind of solidarity, expanded to a pan-Southeast/East Asian range of goods indicated by the words 'Supermarket' being written on the shop's awning in Vietnamese, Lao, Tagalog (Filipino), Japanese, Malay/Indonesian and Khmer, as well as in Chinese characters and English on the parapet. Here cultural diversity is demarcated in a single place.

So, what does this mean for (Australian) urban history or planning history? The question that needs to be asked is how do traditional criteria for belonging, such as the primacy of occupation, length of tenure or identification with the historical majority, stand up under conditions of social and cultural change? And what of the buildings in this context? Do they speak of a kind of cultural dialogue that is illustrative of the area's cultural and societal changes? And what does it mean for relative newcomers (both people and buildings) to alter environments that pre-date their arrival? Environments identified as Asian in Australia are largely commercial/retail rather than domestic, involving clear demarcations of retail/commercial places with particular social/cultural identities. Their communities, by extension, are those who use particular services/goods and display these in particular ways. Whether these ways are distinctive in themselves or not, the issue of spatial occupation is important within the Australian/Western conception of property. The changed demography and identification of Footscray and Springvale, and their parallels elsewhere in Melbourne and across Australia, particularly in Sydney (Cabramatta, Bankstown) and Brisbane (Darra), are broadly based evidence that this influx of refugees comprises a significant event in Australia's history as a nation. Through their occupation of these buildings for particular purposes, they have changed the nature of utilitarian surrounds within a 'suburban utilitarian' built environment. Their apparently superficial alterations – signage, storage and display of goods, and manufacture of products – are reminders that buildings, like the other physical elements of a city, are not filled only by the meanings that their original builders, architects or owners ascribe to them, but are social and cultural as well as physical constructions, and this is not just symbolic. Because connections to family and friends were often severed or traumatically disrupted by the harrowing process of becoming refugees, subsequent decades have seen networks developing in increasingly multidirectional ways. My correspondents tell of their own travels since leaving Vietnam and of relatives in other states and territories of Australia:

> I came to Tasmania in 1980 we stayed in the convent of the Catholic Church and we stayed there for six months because I was nineteen at the time and I had two brothers, who were

eight and fourteen, and one sister who was eleven, one niece who was six and one nephew who was five. That's why I stayed there for so long. We were looked after by Father Philip Green ... We were very lucky that the Catholic Church tried hard to find a house for us, lent us money to buy the house in West Hobart. So we stayed there for seven years ... for the children to study. Very hard to get a job there. My brother went to Tasmania Uni [University of Tasmania], another brother went to Sydney to look for a job, and myself later on, two sisters and one brother came from Thailand, started looking but couldn't find jobs there. We moved to Melbourne. I had to go there first to look for a school for the children, and after that we slowly moved to Melbourne in 1987. And we start in business there ... sewing business. And later on with brother and sister we started another business until now, ductwork. We work in Sydney, Adelaide, New Zealand and around Melbourne.[50]

Several correspondents mentioned relatives and connections overseas, especially in places such as France, Canada and the United States that also received refugees from Vietnam in the 1970s and 1980s. Even if physical premises have already been erased from the former sites of business and residence, as in the case of B2's former fishball manufacturing plant, their narratives tell of intricate webs of interconnected geographies and chronologies. Borrowed restaurants, rented warehouses and shopfronts represent fragments of history in a changing economic as well as cultural environment. These stories started with accounts of necessary survival tactics,[51] circumscribed by initial tentative occupation of space and the contingent use of limited time, together, developing into communities that not only continue to exist in space but also have visible, tangible, usable markers of their presence, identifying as well as providing their community (as well as others) with services, goods and other means for useful and meaningful interactions.

The siting of a building in the present day is thus often seen in terms of its contextual relationship with the assumed identity of a given street, suburb or city, with cultural meaning and importance largely ascribed to origins. New buildings are judged on the degree of their departure from, or alteration to, elements that represent an area's putative cultural identity. Architecture is not just complicit in these definitions; it is the embodiment of them. Buildings and spaces, especially in diasporic/multicultural contexts such as Footscray and Springvale, express the plural identities, priorities and spatialities of those for whom they are built (as well as for those who design and build them). Hage's definition of 'lenticularity' is useful here in relation to the typological/ontological distinction.[52] Through the example of the Lebanese diaspora, both in places of emigration and in Lebanon itself, Hage takes up the idea of an ontological pluralism or multiplicity as a predominant way of being: 'the way the ontological multiplicity of the real can come to represent itself. It is an argument against all forms of epistemological and ontological monorealism and either/or-ism'.[53] Like lenticular images, the resultant buildings, spaces and urban environments of refugee/immigrant industry seem different depending on how you look at them because they *do* contain difference. In contrast to a single image that appears to change from different angles (akin to a governmental view of multiculturalism or different shoppers' perceptions of an Asian supermarket), a lenticular image has a number of different realities within it. Hage uses this idea to reflect on diasporic dwelling as a lenticular process, in which multiple realities exist for diasporic populations, between which individuals oscillate depending on context, purpose and positionality.[54] In terms of cultural heritage, I agree here with Byrne's statement that 'surely there is no other category of cultural heritage that in the very spread of its materiality – the sites, buildings and objects produced by or associated with transnational migration – so obviously exceeds and escapes the territorial frame of the nation-state'.[55]

Just as looking at a lenticular print from different angles reveals entirely different pictures in the same place, the idea of lenticularity provides an apt analogy for the multiplicity of identities of Vietnamese-Australian, Cambodian-Australian and Chinese-Australian settlers and their built environments. The viewpoint from which they are seen determines which of their identities comes into focus. The development of culturally distinctive commercial and industrial districts has made visible their diasporic identities to outsiders, with each shop or temple evoking distant locations, cultures and ways of life. However, for people within these communities, such environments have served to create new local identities for the streets of Footscray, Springvale and other suburbs. In such locations it is simultaneously real that a person can be an immigrant or refugee from a particular cultural, ethnic or geographical origin, a member of a diasporic community, a resident of a Melbourne suburb, an Australian citizen, a pharmacist and a local councillor. This does not mean that all these identities should be neatly collapsed into the singular reality: 'we are always relating to things in a multiplicity of ways that are also a multiplicity of realities'.[56] Multiple realities coexist and any apparently singular reality is just a specific time, place and relation seen through a particular lens.

The relationship of a discussion about culture to architecture and the built environment is grounded in the spatial nature of human interaction, as well as the symbolic power of physical surroundings to influence (and to be influenced by) the actions and intentions of those within it. In relation to the tales of my correspondents, the idea of lenticularity serves to remind us that their migration, settlement, development of industries and ongoing cultural adaptation and negotiation of identities have not been a simple series of movements, but an overlapping of networks, of transnational movement/interchange/exchange that has required oscillation between different ways of being. The role of the built environment in these oscillations has been both functional and expressive. In this chapter, I have traced a discrete sample of Vietnamese, Chinese-Vietnamese and Cambodian immigrant arrivals, struggles and successes in commerce and industry in suburban Melbourne. These stories relate to different forms of industry and their corresponding spatial, formal and representational needs, in the forms of workspaces, building envelopes and expressed/denoted uses. Whether formally expressive (as in the case of the Quang Minh Buddhist Temple), denoted (the Nan Yang Supermarket) or implicit (the house in Keilor Downs incorporating a sewing workshop in its garage), these examples illustrate the complexity of relationships between industry, immigrant subjects, identity, siting of buildings and space. The collective siting of such uses within a broader urban context – in Springvale the presence of a Daoist Temple next to a cabinet-maker's workshop, around the corner from both Vietnamese and Chinese community associations – indicates the multiplicity of such relationships within a shared landscape. As well as establishing new economies and cultures in an Australian city, these areas constitute territories of difference that enrich, complicate and contest Australia's self-identity.

ACKNOWLEDGEMENTS

Numerous people assisted in the providing material and background for this chapter, as part of the Australian Research Council Discovery Project. These include Andrew Dao, External Affairs Deputy for the Vietnamese Community in Victoria (VCA); Bon Nguyên, President of the VCA; members of the Vietnamese Museum Australia (VMA) who gave freely of their time in interviews, notably Hanh Do, Kim Bùi-Quang, Trung Nguyên and Khue Nguyên; Sophanara Sok; two business owners in Springvale who wished to remain anonymous; Cúc Lam, Councillor for the City of Maribyrnong; Richard Lim, Councillor for the City of Greater Dandenong; the Venerable Phước Tấn Thich, Abbot of the Quang Minh Buddhist Temple; Annie Wong of the Teo Chew Association/Guan Di Temple; Rhonda Diffey of the City of Greater Dandenong's Archive; Chris Keys of the Springvale Historical Society; Jan Trezise of the Enterprise Hostel Committee; Wai Kee Yeo; Wajie Chan; Jane McDougall; and especially my Research Assistants Freya Su and Van Krisadawat, who have been instrumental in providing fieldwork/documentary assistance with the overall project related to this chapter.

David Beynon is Associate Professor in Architecture at the University of Tasmania. His research involves investigating the social, cultural and compositional dimensions of architecture, and adaptations of architectural content and meaning in relation to migration and cultural change. His current work includes investigations into the multicultural and postcolonial manifestations of contemporary urban environments and the creative possibilities for post-industrial architecture in Australia and Asia.

NOTES

1. Ang, 'Introduction: Alter/Asian Interventions for 21st Century Australia', xviii.
2. Sharam and Stone, *Addressing Concentrations of Disadvantage*.
3. Hage, *White Nation*.
4. Hage, *Against Paranoid Nationalism*, 12.
5. Byrne, 'Heritage Corridors', 2373.

6. Chen, *Asia as Method*.
7. Hage, *White Nation*.
8. Hou, *Transcultural Cities*.
9. Bertacco and Vallorani, *The Relocation of Culture*.
10. Byrne et al., *Heritage-Making among Recent Migrants in Parramatta*.
11. Van Kooy, 'Refugee Women as Entrepreneurs in Australia'.
12. Stevens, 'Balancing Obligations and Self-Interest'; Collins, *Ignite*, 16.
13. Van Kooy, 'Refugee Women as Entrepreneurs in Australia', 72.
14. Hente, 'A Taste of the Spicy Warmth of Our Little Saigon', 1.
15. Cúc Lam, interview with the author, Footscray, Victoria, 14 April 2022.
16. Anonymous Business Owner 1, interview with the author, Springvale, Victoria, 9 March 2020.
17. Alian and Wood, 'Stranger Adaptations', 99.
18. Collins, *A Shop Full of Dreams*; Piperoglou, 'Migrant Labour and Their "Capitalist Compatriots"'.
19. Richard Lim, interview with the author, Springvale, Victoria, 29 August 2022.
20. Nguyen 'Vietnamese Australians' Community'.
21. Lee, 'Dimensions of Entrepreneurship'.
22. Sharam and Stone, *Addressing Concentrations of Disadvantage*, 4.
23. Van Kooy, 'Refugee Women as Entrepreneurs in Australia', 72
24. Collins, *Ignite*, 16.
25. Bon Nguyên, interview with the author, North Sunshine, Victoria, 18 April 2022.
26. Kim Bùi-Quang, interview with the author, Carlton, Victoria, 28 August 2022.
27. Ibid.
28. De Certeau, *The Practice of Everyday Life*, xix.
29. Lefebvre, *The Production of Space*.
30. Cowie, 'How Much Should a Banh Mi Cost?'.
31. Bon Nguyên, interview with the author, North Sunshine, Victoria, 18 April 2022.
32. Venerable Phước Tấn Thich, interview with the author, Braybrook, Victoria, 16 April 2022.
33. Ibid.
34. Oke, Sonn and McConville, 'Making a Place in Footscray', 326.
35. Palipane, 'Towards a Sensory Production of Urban Space', 13.
36. Beynon, 'Edge of Centre'; Beynon, 'Melbourne's Third World-Looking Architecture'.
37. Chalana and Hou, *Messy Urbanism*.
38. Ibid., 3.
39. Chen, *Asia as Method*; Lee et al., 'Trajectories, Institutions, and Re-locations', 345.
40. Memmott, *Gunyah, Goondie + Wurley*.
41. Venturi, Scott Brown and Izenour, *Learning from Las Vegas*.
42. Beegan and Atkinson, 'Professionalism, Amateurism and the Boundaries of Design', 311–312.
43. Yelavich, *The Edge of the Millennium*.
44. Beegan and Atkinson, 'Professionalism, Amateurism and the Boundaries of Design', 312.
45. Colombijn and Kusno, 'Kampungs, Buitenwijken and Kota Mandiri', 41.
46. Beynon, 'Beyond Big Gold Mountain', 185; Holthouse, *River of Gold*.
47. Chalana and Hou, *Messy Urbanism*, 243.
48. Clifford, James, 'Travelling Cultures'.
49. Lee, 'Dimensions of Entrepreneurship', 91; Coughlan, 'Changing Spatial Distribution and Concentration of Australia's Chinese and Vietnamese Communities'.
50. Trung Nguyên, interview with the author, North Sunshine, Victoria, 16 April 2022.
51. De Certeau, *The Practice of Everyday Life*, xix.
52. Hage, *The Diasporic Condition*, 202.

53. Ibid., 187.
54. Ibid., 188.
55. Byrne, 'Heritage Corridors', 2370.
56. Božić-Vrbančić, 'An Interview with Ghassan Hage', 242.

BIBLIOGRAPHY

Archival Records

City of Greater Dandenong Archive
Springvale Historical Society Archive

Publications

Alian, Sanaz, and Stephen Wood. 'Stranger Adaptations: Public/Private Interfaces, Adaptations, and Ethnic Diversity in Bankstown, Sydney', *Journal of Urbanism: International Research on Placemaking and Urban Sustainability* 12(1) (2019), 83–102.

Ang, Ien. 'Introduction: Alter/Asian Interventions for 21st Century Australia' in Ien Ang, Sharon Chalmers, Lisa Law, and Mandy Thomas (eds), *Alter/Asians: Asian-Australian Identities in Art, Media and Popular Culture* (Annandale: Pluto Press, 2021), xxiii–xxx.

Beegan, Gerry, and Paul Atkinson. 'Professionalism, Amateurism and the Boundaries of Design', *Journal of Design History* 21(4) (2008), 305–13.

Bertacco, Simona, and Nicoletta Vallorani. *The Relocation of Culture: Translations, Migrations, Borders.* New York: Bloomsbury, 2021.

Beynon, David. 'Melbourne's Third World-Looking Architecture', in Colin Long, Kate Shaw and Claire Merlo (eds), *Suburban Fantasies: Melbourne Unmasked* (Melbourne: Australian Scholarly Publishing, 2005), pp. 69–88.

———. 'Edge of Centre: Australian Cities and the Public Architecture of Recent Immigrant Communities', in Mirjana Lozanovska (ed.), *Ethno-architecture and the Politics of Migration* (London; New York: Routledge, 2016), pp. 29–42.

———. 'Beyond Big Gold Mountain: Chinese-Australian Settlement and Industry as Integral to Colonial Australia', *Fabrications* 29(2) (2019), 184–206.

Božić-Vrbančić, Senka, 'An Interview with Ghassan Hage', *Ethnološka tribina* 43(50) (2020), 238–244.

Byrne, Denis. 'Heritage Corridors: Transnational Flows and the Built Environment of Migration', *Journal of Ethnic and Migration Studies* 42(14) (2016), 2360–78.

Byrne, Denis, Emma Waterton, Sarah Barns, Sarah Jane Brazil and Kay Anderson. *Heritage-Making among Recent Migrants in Parramatta.* Sydney: Institute for Culture and Society Project, University of Western Sydney. Retrieved 2 January 2024 from https://www.westernsydney.edu.au/ics/projects/heritage-making_among_recent_migrants_in_parramatta.

Chalana, Manish, and Jeffrey Hou (eds). *Messy Urbanism: Understanding the 'Other' Cities of Asia.* Hong Kong: HKU Press, 2016.

Chen, Kuan-hsing. *Asia as Method: Toward Deimperialization.* Durham, NC: Duke University Press, 2010.

Clifford, James. 'Travelling Cultures', in Lawrence Grossberg, Cary Nelson and Paula Treichler (eds), *Cultural Studies* (London: Routledge, 1992), pp. 96–116.

Collins, Jock. *A Shop Full of Dreams: Ethnic Small Business in Australia.* Leichhardt, NSW: Pluto Press Australia, 1995.

———. *Ignite: From Refugee to Entrepreneur in Sydney in Less Than Three Years (Final Evaluation Report on the SSI Ignite Small Business Start-ups Program)*. Sydney: Cosmopolitan Civil Societies Research Centre, UTS, 2017.

Colombijn, Freek, and Abidin Kusno. 'Kampungs, Buitenwijken and Kota Mandiri: Naming the Urban Fringe on Java', in Richard Harris and Charlotte Vorms (eds), *What's in a Name? Talking about Urban Peripheries* (Toronto: University of Toronto Press, 2017), pp. 152–72.

Coughlan, James. 'Changing Spatial Distribution and Concentration of Australia's Chinese and Vietnamese Communities: An Analysis of 1986–2006 Australian Population Census Data', *Journal of Population Research* 25 (2008), 161–82.

Cowie, Tom. 'How Much Should a Banh Mi Cost? This Map Shows the Price of a Pork Roll in Melbourne', *The Age*, 19 February 2022. Retrieved 1 January 2024 from https://www.theage.com.au/national/victoria/how-much-should-a-banh-mi-cost-this-map-shows-the-price-of-a-pork-roll-in-melbourne-20220217-p59xa9.html. De Certeau, Michel. *The Practice of Everyday Life*. Berkeley: University of California Press, 1984.

Hage, Ghassan. *White Nation: Fantasies of White Supremacy in a Multicultural Society*. Sydney: Pluto Press, 1998.

———. *Against Paranoid Nationalism: Searching for Hope in a Shrinking Society*. Sydney: Pluto Press, 2003.

———. *The Diasporic Condition: Ethnographic Explorations of the Lebanese in the World*. Chicago: University of Chicago Press, 2021.

Hente, Corinna. 'A Taste of the Spicy Warmth of Our Little Saigon'. 2019, *Mojo Podcast: Spoonful of Melbourne*. Retrieved 2 January 2024 from https://www.mojonews.com.au/page/spoonful-of-melbourne-a-taste-of-the-spicy-warmth-of-our-little-saigon?amp=1.

Holthouse, Hector. *River of Gold: The Story of the Palmer River Gold Rush*. Sydney: Angus & Robertson, 1967.

Hou, Jeffrey. *Transcultural Cities: Border Crossing and Placemaking*. New York: Routledge, 2013.

Lefebvre, Henri. *The Production of Space*. Oxford: Blackwell, 1991.

Lee, Christopher, Kuan-Hsing Chen, Sneja Gunew, Michelle O'Brien, Audrey Yue and Alam Rusaba. 'Trajectories, Institutions, and Re-locations: A Conversation on Inter-Asia outside Asia', *Inter-Asia Cultural Studies* 20(2) (2019), 341–55.

Lee, Henri Kwok-Wai. 'Dimensions of Entrepreneurship: A Study of First and Second Generation Ethnic Chinese in Melbourne', Ph.D. dissertation. Melbourne: Swinburne University of Technology, 2009.

Leung, Helen Hok-Sze, and Christine Kim. 'Editorial Introduction: Inter-Asia beyond Asia', *Inter-Asia Cultural Studies* 20(2) (2019), 159–61.

Memmott, Paul. *Gunyah, Goondie + Wurley: The Aboriginal Architecture of Australia*, 2nd edn. London: Thames & Hudson, 2022.

Nguyen, Anh Tuan. 'Vietnamese Australians' Community: Realities and Prospect'. 2014, *Modern Diplomacy*. Retrieved 2 January 2024 from https://moderndiplomacy.eu/2014/11/18/vietnamese-australians-community-realities-and-prospects/.

Oke, Nicole, Christopher Sonn and Christopher McConville. 'Making a Place in Footscray: Everyday Multiculturalism, Ethnic Hubs and Segmented Geography', *Identities* 25(3) (2018), 320–38.

Palipane, Kelum. 'Towards a Sensory Production of Urban Space: Developing a Conceptual Framework of Inquiry Based on Socio-sensory Perception', *Dealing with Diversity in 21st Century Urban Settings, 7–9 July 2011*. Amsterdam; International Sociological Association (ISA).

Piperoglou, Andonis. 'Migrant Labour and Their "Capitalist Compatriots": Towards a History of Ethnic Capitalism', *Labour History* 121(2021), 175–94.

Sharam, Andrea, and Wendy Stone. *Addressing Concentrations of Disadvantage: Springvale Case Study Report*. Melbourne: Australian Housing and Urban Research Institute (AHURI_, 2017.

Stevens, Christine. 'Balancing Obligations and Self-Interest: Humanitarian Program Settlers in the Australian Labor Market', *Asian and Pacific Migration Journal* 6(2) (1997), 185–212.

Van Kooy, John. 'Refugee Women as Entrepreneurs in Australia', *Forced Migration Review* 53 (2016), 71–73.

Venturi, Robert, Denise Scott Brown and Steven Izenour. *Learning from Las Vegas*. Cambridge, MA: MIT Press, 1972.

Yelavich, Susan (ed.). *The Edge of the Millennium*. New York: Cooper-Hewitt, 1993.

Conclusion
Migration Heritage Landscapes in Australia Today

Alexandra Dellios, Anoma Pieris, Mirjana Lozanovska,
Andrew Saniga and David Beynon

Migration, the mobility of peoples into and within the continent, has been a constant across Australia's human history. And yet the mainstream and official recognition of settler-colonial Australia as a 'migrant nation' has been historically limited in scope and brevity. The authorized heritage of migration is celebratory and dialogically bound by the categories of early settler, postwar migrant and refugee Other, offering a simplified narrative of Australia's colonization.

This chapter is an exploration of the status and direction of 'migrant heritage' – especially as it pertains to authorized, national and industrial heritage – in Australia today. Presented according to each of our case studies, the chapter offers multiple and sometimes conflicting questions about the heritage and public history of post-Second World War immigration, industrialization and architecture. These are not prescriptive conclusions about migrant heritage, but rather points of discussion, which draw from all of our site-based research with migrant and implicated community groups across Australia. Drawing attention to the resources we have drawn upon to frame the arguments we broached in this book, we offer selective insights into the challenges entailed in writing on industry and migration, and the possibilities presented by our particular interdisciplinary orientations from architectural, urban, landscape and heritage studies.

Migrant and ethnic-minority communities themselves have long been invested in constructing, publicizing and conserving their histories. They are capable of locating their personal and familial pasts within a local, regional, national, and international history of migration, settlement and industrialization. However, their desires to publicly remember are frequently compromised by the effacement of the built and material environments that might give their experiences a sense of permanence and continuity, and due to the ways in which minority heritage remains marginal even in efforts at non-elite and vernacular heritage recognition. In Australia, as new attention towards Indigenous Australian (Aboriginal and Torres Strait Islander First Nations/Peoples) heritage enters both teaching and practice, it becomes important to integrate other minority experiences precluded from or absorbed into settler-colonial/anglophone framings of non-Indigenous identity. This concluding chapter will explore examples of (successful and unsuccessful) migrant community heritage making, the emotions and motivations that compel public remembering of migration and industrialization, and the interpretive power of storytelling for understanding the history of Australian labour markets, their ethnic segmentation and built structures in the postwar era.

OUTLINING KEY CONCEPTS: HERITAGE

First, it is necessary to provide a working definition of heritage as it is explored in the following discussion. Heritage (and its 'management') is a socially constructed process. In its broadest and simplest definition, heritage is about inheritance and legacy, implying that people make choices about what is worthy of being preserved or passed on to subsequent generations. This can transcend the tangible and intangible. Of course, heritage can include the tangible, but only as it is understood and interpreted through the intangible: the values and stories that people give it.[1] Heritage is best understood as a future-orientated process and a practice rather than as an object. Accordingly, heritage is contingent on power relations and on prevailing cultural norms.[2] In relation to migration histories and histories of the settlement of ethnic-minority peoples within an anglophone and settler-colonial nation-state, the expression of this heritage is contingent on political and affective power relations.

The heritage management context, particularly in the built heritage sector, reinforces the idea of 'heritage' as a noun or an object, something tied to a set of regulations and legislation administered by state bodies or so-called experts and ultimately authorized by politicians. In this context, the thing we call 'Heritage' in the West is not so much negotiated as it is regulated, codified and registered.[3] Heritage becomes a commodity and a device in governmentality, nationalism or a 'delocalised humanism'.[4] Laurajane Smith's concept of the 'authorized heritage discourse' (AHD) cuts through this and similar academic critiques of heritage.[5] The AHD is a way of thinking about the type of heritage that dominates the heritage sector at large – a discourse internalized by practitioners and perpetuated in policy and legislation, not just in Australia, but also across the Anglosphere and in new heritage practices in Asia. In summary, the AHD privileges Eurocentric cultural outlooks and symbols of the Western elite, is narrowly focused on materiality (on the monumental), lends itself to positivist and linear views of history and is dismissive of local, layered or diverse (and therefore difficult or contested) expressions of knowledge. It also limits the ability to identify and preserve heritage to those identified as 'experts', as Christobal Gnecco discusses.[6]

Within the Australian context, migrant heritage is minority heritage – it offers flavour, but remains marginal to the 'core' heritage of the nation, which is an anglophone settler-colonial and largely fabric-based heritage that denotes/symbolizes progress and expansion, and therefore possession and dispossession in a manner that erases Indigenous sovereignty and alternative modes of living on the land and valuing heritage.

That said, the AHD is inherently dissonant and can be actively challenged, not only by appointed experts themselves but also by subaltern groups who may be excluded by the AHD's (positivist, whitewashed and nationalistic) versions of history, or sidelined by the 'claims of professional objectivity' to which heritage managers cling when assessing places or objects as heritage-worthy.[7] While the critical heritage studies literature includes work on community engagements with heritage, informed recently by studies into audience reception and audience or visitor affect and emotion,[8] more attention is needed on how 'subaltern' publics themselves, including the migrants and racialized peoples who are the subject of many exhibitions and commemorations, actively create and publicize their own heritage. What exactly, in relation to migration and industrial and labour histories, can we learn from communities engaged in heritage and public history practices themselves? Why and how do we remember and commemorate places of migration reception, settlement and work, and what can alternative or community-minded approaches to this past do for our collective conception of postwar immigration and industrialization?

LABOUR HERITAGE AS MIGRANT HERITAGE AS INDUSTRIAL HERITAGE

Of relevance to a study of migration heritage is the status and visibility of industrial and labour heritage in Australia. As historical markers, migrant camps and former sites of industry that functioned as nodes in an industrial and highly regulated network are less able to avoid difficult histories of structural inequity and ethnic segmentation. Admittedly, the same cannot always be said about dynamic urban streetscapes; their layered histories of settler occupation are qualitatively different and David Beynon's section in this chapter speaks to this reality. The location of large industry and migrant camps in mostly regional areas of Australia, some of which are still suffering from the effects of deindustrialization, also makes their integration into a celebratory neoliberal heritage framework fraught with narrative dissonance and ambivalent memories.

In their investigation of the tangible and intangible heritage of the Australian labour movement, Reeves et al. describe the distinction drawn between industrial and labour heritage: 'If industrial history concerns itself with technologies, with sites of work and workforce development, labour history is above all concerned with the people who worked the machines, populated the factories, mines and mills or depended on them for their livelihood.'[9] The activities of the labour movement, of working lives, are often 'left out' of the process of heritage identification and interpretation.[10] More broadly, however, industrial heritage sites – let alone those that consider labouring people – are *under*represented in state, national and international heritage lists and registers in Australia. According to Smith, Shackel and Campbell, the industrial monoliths that garner heritage attention tend to centre on the might of industrial technology above or instead of working people or class struggle.[11] In effect, *migrant* labourers are absent from the historical narratives promoted by the heritage sector in Australia, except in the rare instances in which they appear as harbingers of a harmonious and industrially proficient multicultural nation state, as is the case in recent heritage discourses that surround the Snowy Mountains Hydro Electricity Scheme, whose labour force was predominately migrant men from Eastern and Southern Europe bound by two-year work contracts. One should aim to analyse the heritagization of such industrial sites alongside a desire to study the historical working experiences of the classed and ethnicized cohort behind their construction.

Analysing the muting of these political and social dynamics in heritage processes also lays bare the 'marketization of difference'.[12] As Meskell argues, heritage has been utilized as a tool in neoliberal government, in which the sanitized heritage of industrial ruins and capitalist success are implicated in processes of gentrification – they become real estate investments, impressive structures, but separated from the stories of past people and lives implicated (and sometimes destroyed by) that fabric.[13] Industrial heritage, in this context, is ephemeral infrastructure that can be repurposed as capital and redistributed in the market as a politically neutralized space – sometimes a space that can also have the added and marketable allure of ethnic diversity, but a 'phantasmatic' and depoliticized diversity that does not make demands on social hierarchies.[14]

Australia's heritage management regime limits the expression of migrant heritage and the heritage of migration. A system concerned with conserving and tracing a limited range of tangible structures, with categorizing discrete and isolated 'examples' of a place and with conforming to nation-building and progressive narratives, inevitably conceals the complex intersections between the personal and collective, between the structural and the emotional, between migration and migrants themselves (as workers, family members and members of civil society).

In the same way that the academic discipline of history and related histories of the built environment, rooted in a European past and the analysis of written sources, have ignored whole swathes of people and their experiences – notably, racialized and Indigenous peoples – heritage management too, in its inability to integrate effectively alternative methods of 'doing' heritage and history (stories and storytelling, which can also be contained in art, ritual, music and dance, communal gatherings, foodways and celebratory practices), has 'missed' the migrant presence in Australia. The AHD has not fully accounted for these histories *as part of* the history of nation building and modern capitalism. The migrant experience of working and living within these structures cannot always fit comfortably within progressive or celebratory historical narratives, but the non-British migrant was a pivotal part of past political and social economies.

ALEXANDRA DELLIOS: MIGRANT CAMPS, STORYTELLING AND IN/TANGIBLE MEMORIALS

The popular commemoration of the postwar immigration scheme began in earnest from the 1980s. Postwar migrant storytelling initially coalesced around the space of the migrant camp – the government or industry-run 'centres', 'hostels' or 'camps' that received, processed, accommodated and then 'dispersed' hundreds of thousands of migrants to industrial centres (both regional and urban) across Australia. The stories extend outward from these discrete places, linking the migrant camp to places of work, other sites of temporary accommodation and diverse suburbs and localities. In the late 1980s, and when the earliest group of displaced persons (DPs) were still with us, the impetus for camp reunions came from former residents themselves. They staged a series of camp reunions – Bathurst, Bonegilla, West Sale (Vic) and Greta (NSW) all hosted reunion events from the mid-1980s. While these reunions were initiated by migrants themselves, commemorations were eventually overtaken by state actors invested in capitalizing on the funding available to projects aligned with liberal multiculturalism.[15]

State-sanctioned public history pertaining to postwar migration holds up the migrant camp as a somewhat ambivalent example of both endurance and welcome. Some versions of this narrative admit that the camp was a tough space in which to live, but it welcomed hardworking migrants who 'demanded less', implying a contrast between the past deserving and present undeserving. In their endurance and through the oversight of a paternalistic state, the camp is cast as a place of harmony, a place in which we can locate the 'birthplace of multiculturalism'.[16] This narrative ignores the structural inequalities that weighed heavy on non-Anglo-Celtic migrants in the workforce and that the official introduction of multiculturalism as a policy by the Labor government in the early 1970s only partially allayed. It also ignores the long history of interethnic and sectarian conflict, and the race-based inequalities that shaped (and continue to shape) the settlement experiences of arrivals in Australia since colonization. The 'birthplace of multiculturalism' narrative is positivist and retrospective, refashioning Australia as a 'welcoming' place. Both state-sanctioned actors (councils backed by heritage funding, state-funded collecting institutions and government publications) and grassroots actors (including descendants of migrant groups who passed through these camps) can participate in this revisionist narrative, and for different emotional purposes. This memory work is not, to quote Michael Rothberg, a 'zero-sum game', in which one version loses out over the other or that has either a rigidly conservative or progressive bent.[17] The following discussion unpacks community-initiated examples of heritage-making, in the hopes of complicating the dichotomy and stressing the many uses to which 'camp heritage' can be (and is) put today.

Arguably, only Bonegilla, the largest and longest-running camp, has garnered national and authorized heritage attention, and this has come in the form of heritage listings, large grants for conservation and interpretation, and council-run commemorative structures erected over the last few decades (see Figure 9.1). Capturing the diverse heritage of migration and migrants has been limited by a management regime that is discursively and materially bound by a concern with conserving and tracing the tangible, with documenting and categorizing distinct places as part of a representative register of place, and with conforming to nation-building narratives that stress progress and transformation. While many narratives about postwar migration lend themselves to nationalist frameworks, these do not always serve the memorial interests of migrant and ethnic-minority community groups today. Narrow, parochial and fabric-based assessments of heritage places can 'miss' the intersections between migration and labour history, as well as the camps' connections with Australia's tangible and intangible industrial and labour heritage, providing only a partial view of Australia's immigration history – this is where storytelling and first-person testimony can have an effect.[18]

Less than fifteen years after its closure in 1971, Bonegilla re-emerged on the public stage under the initiative of an ex-residents' group in 1985, who had grand ambitions for an on-site museum. Later, alongside community-led efforts, state actors would adopt and re-appropriate the site as an apt symbol for the success of modern multiculturalism. In the twenty years since 2002, Bonegilla has received over AU$4 million in heritage grants from Federal and State bodies – for on-site conservation and interpretation, tourism and visitation improvements, and reunion events hosted by councils. It was listed on the Victorian Heritage Register in 2002 and on the National Heritage List in 2007. Bonegilla's integration into Australia's heritage management

Figure 9.1 Block 19, Bonegilla Migrant Experience, 2012. © Anoma Pieris

regime – primarily through its listings and success in various heritage funding grants – may in effect obscure a fuller narrative of postwar immigration and settlement, of the connected, co-dependent and networked nature of regional migrant centres and industry, as well as the individual lives shaped by these systems and places. As Sara Wills identified, Bonegilla is the most publicly 'remembered' of all Australia's postwar migrant camps.[19] It stands as a 'representative' example of migrant accommodation on heritage lists, sometimes to the detriment of other conservation efforts (most notably Benalla). Most migrants passed through multiple camps during the term of their two-year work contracts. But as a heritage place, Bonegilla stands alone. The grassroots storytelling efforts of ex-residents from other camps are undoing this exclusivity as they continue to do the work of telling a more layered history of postwar settlement.

Some ex-resident groups are more formally constituted, like the Benalla Migrant Camp Inc. Others require the support of local councils to organize, like the committees behind various reunions at Greta. In all cases, key individuals stand out as memory activists; they organize the events, apply for the grants, organize the temporary exhibitions and campaign for heritage listing. Community groups have encountered official resistance along the way – the most obvious case being the Heritage Council of Victoria's 2016 rejection to the bid from ex-residents to list Benalla on the heritage register and the cancellation of the 2017 Greta camp reunion in Maitland – all of which speaks to conflicting interpretations of the past and what accommodations can and cannot be made in the AHD for telling alternative accounts of migrant experiences in postwar Australia. Collectively, the migration and settlement stories of DPs and postwar assisted migrants' accommodation in camps – stories shared most freely in community forums, online message boards and at reunions themselves – reveal alternative truths about postwar society. Their stories speak to the complex negotiations of diverse family units living in intercultural spaces, the networked and discriminatory nature of labour relations and workplace conditions for non-English-speaking migrants, and social justice and gender politics that shaped their families' integration (and sometimes anti-assimilation) into postwar Australia.

Greta's first reunion in the late 1980s occurred alongside wider shifts in Australia's memorial culture, particularly in relation to sharing 'ordinary people's' history and migrant voices. The popular 1984 film *Silver City*, partially set at Greta's holding centre Silver City, was directed and written by Sophia Turkiewicz, who passed through the camp as a child with her single mother, a Polish DP. This film contributed to a communal desire to remember the migrant camps. Like the film, attendees at these memorials were not only interested in celebration, in lauding their success in contributing to a multicultural Australia, and nor were they only concerned with the moment of accommodation. Like *Silver City*, stories of settlement prominently featured stories of work and workplace exploitation of non-English-speaking migrants by both large and small Anglo-Australian employers, especially single women hired as 'domestics' in homes or institutions in Maitland or Newcastle or as factory workers in textile industries like Bradmill in Rutherford. The emotional fallout from dashed hopes and structural disadvantages is a consistent theme. Also featured in their public recollections were the political and interethnic tensions that arose between people living in close quarters at the camp, tensions based on grievances stemming from the Second World War (i.e., Eastern Europeans who were forced or volunteered to fight under Nazi command) and its aftermath (i.e., Soviet invasion). Rivalries emerged among the diverse DP cohort in Australia, thrown together and segregated by sex, in remote migrant camps.[20] Today, their children bring to light not just their contribution to the nation state through their labour in massive industrial projects like the Snowy, but, crucially, also the political baggage they brought with them from Europe.

The effects of traumatic wartime experiences and exile, combined with the restrictions of the employment contract and family separation they experienced in Australia, shaped the ability of DPs to adjust psychologically, which was the subject of early sociological study, contemporaneous psychological commentary (most notably Henry Murphy's 1950s work) and more recent historical work.[21] For DPs in particular, the migrant camp was one in a continuum of many camp stays, which for many began during the Second World War – as Chapter 6 explored with its focus on family recollections. In the communal and vernacular memorial context, the camp was both a symbol of sanctuary and of traumas. It could also morph into something more sinister: a sanctuary for Nazi war criminals.[22] For the first generation of DP arrivals, the camp could never be simply a national heritage site symbolizing their tangible economic and social contributions as migrants to Australia. The complex emotional reality of the migrant camp is less easily captured in an AHD that seeks to speak to national histories of progress and migrant contributions, of the offer of a 'national cuddle' to the displaced.[23]

For Greta, heritage management, listing and interpretation in the official sense is not an option, because of the lack of on-site remnants. None of the 672 buildings that once formed Greta is still standing onsite, unlike Bonegilla or Benalla (see Figure 9.2). What remains of Greta migrant camp are a few roads and some old footings from former buildings. In the late 1980s, the Commonwealth Defence Department sold the land (some 423 hectares) to Uri Windt, a Sydney-based developer with ambitious plans to develop 'Greta Estate', a tourist hub and golf course.[24] Since the 1980s, former residents demonstrated enthusiasm for collecting and exhibiting images of their time in Greta camp. Uri Windt's Anvil Creek collection amassed nearly 1,000 photographic contributions and a 2022 photographic display mounted at Branxton Community Hall (the structure was the former YMCA Hall from Greta camp), contained nearly 100 photos of life at Greta, sourced mainly from family photo albums. The 423 hectare site was sold in late 2020 to a Sydney-based property developer for an estimated AUD 40 million.[25] It has been flagged as a mixed-use residential space; heritage conservation is not on the cards.

Despite the lack of physical remnants, some former residents have opted to gather near or on-site during reunions held since the late 1980s. This spoke to the need for something 'tangible' – manifesting in the first instance in a to-scale model of Greta

Figure 9.2 What remains at the site of the former Greta Migrant Camp, 2019. © Alexandra Dellios

migrant camp by ex-resident and engineer Vitaly Lupish. Lupish's model was first displayed at the 1987 reunion and has been kept in storage and displayed at subsequent reunions. It sits across four trestle tables and depicts the 840 buildings of Greta. The model has been a drawcard for ex-residents attending reunions – seeing the landscapes of their past made tangible and using it as a way to share a sense of what life was like in that space.

Postwar migrant camps contained structures used by the Department of Defence, including Nissen huts and wooden barracks that were designed to be easily dismantled and relocated. It is the case with Greta and with other camps like Benalla and Balgownie (also known as Fairy Meadow) that structures have been relocated and re-appropriated. Some buildings are still in use today, even though they were designed and built as temporary structures, a cheap solution to the housing shortage. To the dismay of some ex-residents, these re-appropriated structures contain no marker to indicate that they were once 'birthplaces of multiculturalism', in the same way that Bonegilla was memorialized with a National Heritage Listing plaque in 2007. The army camp in Scheyville is said to contain some of the huts that were originally built for Greta camp in 1940 and that accommodated migrants throughout the 1950s. As mentioned earlier, the Branxton Community Hall was the former Greta YMCA Hall and it has been in constant use since it was erected in the late 1940s. In 2022, the local Cessnock City Council installed simple black silhouettes on the outside of the building – one a lone soldier, to mark Greta's military past, the other a migrant family of three. Helen Scott, who manages the active Facebook group 'Keep Greta Camp History ALIVE', described the silhouettes as: 'One job completed in preserving our History.'[26]

Other examples of the re-appropriation of Greta camp structures include St Anthony Catholic Church's Rutherford Guides Hall in Maitland, which was the migrant camp's hospital building. Like the migrants who once occupied these structures, they are dispersed across the country. Those who come together at annual reunions (and more recently in online forums and published anthologies) express an interest in visiting these remaining structures, but the main memorial impetus rests with intangible storytelling and collecting images. The stories told about this place in online forums, posted alongside photocopies of archival records and family photographs, depict Greta as part of a complex labour network that supported a mobile (and not always willingly so) workforce. An official heritage fixation on physical remnants and discrete places – the product of an 'antiquarian approach' to building conservation[27] – with identifiable (and somehow unchanging or inherent) values risks obscuring this reality. Reunion events and the offshoots of these gatherings in the form of published and collated storytelling (both digital and physical) offer that complexity. This is heritage work undertaken by implicated subjects, which is worthy of further study if we are to understand how migrants have occupied this country and the subjective justifications that underpin their claims to (un)belonging.

MIRJANA LOZANOVSKA: DIRTY INDUSTRIAL HERITAGE

Industrial structures and sites are threatened and demolished, largely because they do not quite fit into the paradigm of the heritage industries – they are dirty and do not fit well with the 'decarbonization' and neoliberal aspects of the environmental agenda; and can become easy targets for local government to illustrate their preparedness to erase colonizing inscriptions on the land.[28] Positive directives are selective, as shown by restoration of (at least small sections) of redbrick factories, warehouses and mills that were built in the late nineteenth and early twentieth centuries. And yet, these restorations are also avoiding and disavowing labour histories: racialized and ethnicized hierarchies, and immigrant labour.

In the early 1980s, BHP Steelworks in Port Kembla implemented a strategy of redundancies and closure of entire sections of the operations at the steelworks that were not deemed profitable in the new technological economies of artificial intelligence (AI) substitution for human workers. An official government document states that BHP's workforce was reduced by approximately 10,000 employees between May 1982 and May 1983.[29] The magnitude of the massive losses of jobs led to outmigration of immigrant workers and their communities, depleting residents in Port Kembla. Unemployment was higher among the non-English-speaking workers and not all could afford to live elsewhere.[30] Participant views reinforce the unfair processes of job cuts. One participant viewed the strategy as 'ethnic cleansing' in the steelworks. For him and many others, it was a terrifying prospect – in their thirties, forties and fifties, they worked a demanding shiftwork regime at the steelworks – while in the 1980s, many, who by that time were in their fifties, watched their work futures become non-existent. Following BHP Steelworks redundancies in the 1980s, shops, banks, service storefronts and even public bars that had lined Wentworth Street, the main street in Port Kembla, vacated the premises such that in 2019, except for the site of the Red Point Artists and café, it was an abandoned place. Participants who had worked at the steelworks tell of a vibrant, busy and crowded Wentworth Street in the 1960s, lined with immigrant businesses and enterprises. They also speak about the alcoholism and thriving sex worker business, in addition to a collective support of multiple ethnicities to offer protection against racial attacks, and whisper about the drug criminal activity that was rampant on the street.

Histories of multiple realities are not neat and entangle physical sites with operations that were tolerated if not considered necessary at the time, but that dominant heritage discourse and practices tend to avoid and disavow, and, more often, heritage experts tend to erase effectively due to lack of interest. I will briefly discuss the postwar immigrant labour at the BHP Steelworks by focusing on it as a site of difficult histories and traumatic heritage, with a question about 'dirty' industrial heritage (see Figure 9.3).

In 2021 our research team led two tours of past BHP workers organized by the Macedonian Welfare Association (MWA) and the Multicultural Communities Council of Illawarra (MCCI). This included a bus tour with twenty participants of the BHP Steelworks organized with the support of BlueScope Steel (which purchased the plant from BHP in 2002) and a professional film crew that documented the event.[31] Small sections of the film were shown as part of the *Immigrant Networks* exhibition in November 2022–March 2023. While the role of the tour as a methodology for heritage discourse requires further analysis, the film documentation of the BHP Steelworks tour develops a record of the immigrant workers' experience and contribution, before these first-generation labour immigrants become too frail or pass on. It also offered the participants an alternative position from which to view their relation to their industrial employer, one from which they could speak and tell their story of an otherwise silenced history contributing towards a collective accounting of immigrant labour history. Community engagement was the highlight of the research project as a totality. The tour superimposed the gravitas of the dark, dirty, exploitative history of the BHP Steelworks and the individual trajectories of twenty past migrant workers onto one another. But it was their stories and their voices that were the focus and that brought about an alternative agency in each of their personal trajectories of horrendous conditions and hardship. Huge sections of the steelworks are already closed to the public or demolished, and we were not able to exit from the bus to walk around the now defunct coke ovens, likened to the subterranean factories in the powerful 1927 film *Metropolis*. Walking through the still-operative tin mill and slab yards, the participants became more animated and were keen to explain how it all worked and what it was like when they worked there. Their voices immersed in the operations – the noise and heat – and diminished by the massive volumes and scale of the equipment were nonetheless captured and recorded on film.

Figure 9.3 Past immigrant workers climb the stair tower to the mill at the BHP Steelworks in Port Kembla, 2021. Photo by Pia Solberg, courtesy of the Multicultural Communities Council of Illawarra (MCCI)

Heritage discourse and practices are interwoven with the histories that we construct about Australia and Australians. In 'Histories of Migrants and Refugees in Australia', a 2018 state of the field review essay in the journal *Australian Historical Studies*, historians Ruth Balint and Zora Simic discuss the ambivalence of the place of migration within Australian historical scholarship: 'Migration is everywhere and nowhere, as evidenced in the two volume, *Cambridge History of Australia* (2013).'[32] They note the innovative work that has built knowledge on the 'Australian mosque' and 'Chinese Australian history', which offer a more diverse framing for Australian history. While scholarly research deploying oral and archival histories, as well as community activism, has generated new and profound histories on the early postwar period, Balint and Simic note how the immigrant history of the 1960s is lacking. Surprisingly, the immigrant heritage of the postwar period, including the 1960s, is introduced in local heritage studies such as Meredith Walker's invaluable report *First Accommodation for Migrants Arriving in Wollongong Post World War 2*, which was part of Wollongong's Migrant Heritage Places Study (2007).[33]

The bus tour was organized for the participants to tell their stories, to collect and record their voices about immigrant labour history alongside a visit to the actual site of the steelworks (see Figure 9.4). While the interviews that were conducted elsewhere are invaluable, questions arise as to whether there is something additional to being on site. And is it only valuable for the past immigrant steelworks workers or is there value to the proposition to preserve parts of the steelworks for all Australians, as inheritance and as a site of postwar immigrant labour?

Figure 9.4 Past immigrant workers point to the coke ovens at the BHP Steelworks in Port Kembla and speak about their experiences and the skill required for their work, 2021. Photo by Pia Solberg, courtesy of the MCCI

Tangible heritage is the major national heritage investment, but industrial heritage comprises about 5% of registered heritage sites. Migrant-built heritage confronts further challenges in the assessment procedures, as illustrated in Winkler's analysis of the St Eleftherios Greek Orthodox Church in Brunswick.[34] This was assessed as being socially significant for the changing demography of its context, but architecturally significant as an example of interwar brick (former Methodist) churches. The outcome is that the church is listed as having tangible heritage significance as though this is unrelated to its social and cultural value. In addition, if 'tangible expressions of Australian identity and experience . . . [that] reflect the diversity of our communities, [and] tell us about who we are and the past that has formed us', the narrowing of those artefacts preserved as tangible heritage tells a very skewed history.[35]

Heritage practitioners confront very challenging environmental metrics when charged with assessing industrial structures and sites. Along with BlueScope and BHP, for the local council, creative industries and the environmental agenda, it would be better for the old 'non-green' parts of the Port Kembla Steelworks, like the coke ovens and the sinter plant, precisely the sites where immigrants spent decades growing the nation, to disappear. This tendency to erase dark parts from history and, with the passing of the immigrants, from memory, is troubling.

ANOMA PIERIS: THE WORK OF THE DEAD

Among the concerns raised in relation to militarized past-heritage of migrant camps was competition between settler, military and migrant histories for ownership of the physical space and resultant compromises. Rushworth Migrant Camp failed to attract comparable interest following its closure in June 1953 and release for private grazing. The nearby Tatura Irrigation and Wartime Camps Museum is focused on the site's wartime history as an internment camp and has over the years collected substantial quantities of memorabilia from that period, both creating and featuring publications on that topic rather than on the Rushworth Migrant Camp. This is partly because the proximity of both the Tatura German Military Cemetery and the Italian Ossario at Murchison, interring the deceased prisoners of war (POWs) from the 1939–46 period attract diplomatic interest in annual remembrance ceremonies, bringing Melbourne-based consuls, officials and a few descendants of former POWs or internees to these rural towns. The wartime history of these individuals and the scattered archaeological debris still visible among the tangled barbed-wire spinifex and random cactus plants highlights this earlier relationship, marginalizing the much shorter and poorly represented DP camp period. In these admittedly rare examples, wartime histories of violence – of forced displacement, conscription and racialization – have effectively suppressed any similar types of violence we might find in subsequent migration histories of the same site. The presence of human remains lends the site added gravitas and the possibility of continuity, where other sites may be erased. A similar overshadowing of one history by another is evident at Cowra, a site that is equally poorly documented when compared to the nearby Cowra POW camp property made notorious by the attempted breakout and deaths of Japanese POWs on 6 August 1944. Europa Park with a memorial and plaque marks the site where the migrant camp once stood, in a spot some distance from the town along the highway, but it is a sad stepchild of the robust wartime narrative that has accumulated multiple sites and structures over the years, including a Japanese war cemetery, the Cowra Japanese Garden and a segment of the former POW camp site. Settler, immigrant and internee identities jostle for recognition in these small country towns. A similar accretion of disparate monuments can be found at Cooma, the Snowy Hydro company town, a reminder of the cumulative layers of the settler narrative, but also its fragmentation along axes of identity at the intersection of militarization and industry.[36] This is particularly evident if we look at the memorials to the workers who died on the Snowy Scheme.

In his remarkable study *The Work of the Dead*, Thomas Laqueur links necronominalism – the practice of naming dead persons – to Western modernity; when the public cemetery first replaced the churchyard and when ordinary individuals were commemorated on headstones, previously reserved for elite families or important figures.[37] He notes the revolution in such naming practices sanctified by the 1863 Gettysburg Address and following it with the making and marking of uniformly patterned graves in the cemeteries of the two world wars. The wording on three plaques ceremonially unveiled to a crowd of around 600 persons at the opening of Jindabyne pumping station on 8 February 1969 (outlined below)[38] and later set in granite at the Jindabyne surge tank illustrate this tension between Australian (settler) and New Australian (immigrant-settler) identities in memorializing the dead. The first plaque was dedicated (in capital letters):

> The men and women of the Snowy Scheme who carried out the pioneer work
> of investigation and early construction in the remote regions of the
> Snowy Mountains area. Their efforts have brought many of the dreams
> of the early pioneers of the Monaro and Murrumbidgee Valleys to a reality.[39]

This is followed by a poetic verse attributed to Merle Harvey, a clerk for the Snowy Mountains Authority (SMA),[40] saying:

> No man really dies who leaves behind
> Something of good that other men share;
> If aught he's done shall benefit mankind
> Some part of him shall live forever there.[41]
>   (Merle Harvey)

This heroic proclamation was followed by a sombre second plaque (also worded in capital letters) that dampened its impact:

> The members of the Snowy Workforce who lost their lives during construction of the Snowy Mountains Hydro-electric Scheme.[42]

The third plaque was dedicated to:

> The early pioneers of the Snowy Mountains Area – These great men and women have been immortalized in verse text and song for their horsemanship and the manner in which they suffered privation, cold and hunger to fulfil their dreams.[43]

This was embellished with the last lines of Banjo (A.B.) Paterson's poem:

> The man from Snowy River is a household word today,
> And the stockmen tell the story of his ride.[44]
> (A.B. Patterson)

The men and women of the Snowy Scheme were being made complicit in the greater settler-colonial project of Indigenous Australian dispossession and destitution, their foreignness subsumed into the Snowy's successes that was later to be excavated as evidence of the scheme's commitment to 'multiculturalism' long before it became government policy in the late 1970s.[45]

The Snowy workers, dissatisfied with the brevity of the memorial to their mates, lobbied tirelessly for a further decade for a proper memorial listing the names of those who lost their lives. Around 500 people gathered on 21 February 1981 at the opening of the Snowy Mountain Scheme Workers Memorial at Cooma, designed by local architect R.J. Rolfe and built by Italian builder E. Fachin.[46] This listed 119 men who had lost their lives during construction of the scheme. The figure was later raised to 121 men. Key among the speakers, Mr C.T. Oliver, President of the New South Wales State Union of Australian Workers stressed their cultural diversity and mateship, and described the risks taken as 'arduous' and 'dangerous', but, he said, they broke all world records. A bronze relief showing a tunnel entrance, a crane and construction vehicles with a snowy mountainous backdrop was embedded on the memorial's surface. The unionist attributed the success of the project in part to their preventing imposition of Federal awards on two separate occasions; if not, he believed, the project would still be under construction.

Irish author and documentary film maker Siobhan McHugh, who arrived in Australia in 1985, assiduously investigated these deaths in SMA records and coroners' reports attributing many deaths to the bonuses associated with record completions of international contractors. Her 400 or so interviews included piercing questions regarding risks taken and safety practices. Among the most serious accidents was a tunnel disaster on 21 December 1963, when an avalanche of concrete burst through the pipes to bury three men at Island Bend, also injuring four others.[47] Although the SMA maintained that numbers were less than the international fatality figures and enforced stricter safety procedures from the 1960s onwards when US contractors entered the Scheme, the trauma of losing members of what was described as 'the Snowy Family', and others with lifelong injuries, persisted as a niggling undercurrent beneath the evident pride that workers took in being associated with the nation-building scheme and their admiration for the Snowy Mountains Authority (see Figure 9.5).[48]

Figure 9.5 Injured worker and companion at Snowy Mountains Hydro Electric Scheme work camp, 1957–60. Photo by Jeff Carter, courtesy of Jeff Carter Archive (Powerhouse collection)

The SMA installed a number of new headstones at Cooma cemetery for the scheme's seventieth anniversary in October 2019. A central pedestal was erected: 'In memory of the Snowy workers who lost their lives during construction of the Snowy Mountains Scheme 1949–1974' (see Figure 9.6). Headstones indicated the workers' name, age, date of death and camp. In their minimalism, the inscriptions appeared similar to those on military headstones. Although neither family members nor country of origin linked them back to their homelands, multilingual names in an otherwise Anglo-Celtic cemetery opened up a transnational cartography linked directly to the geography of camps: Ernesto Vecchiato, aged 29, River Camp; Lajos Nemeth, aged 22, Tantangara; Jazeps Briska, aged 33, Jindabyne; Nikola Cacic, aged 31, Deep Creek; Salvatore Dramisino, aged 26, Cabramurra; Louis Peter Van Hoof, aged 32, Section

Figure 9.6 Memorial to the Snowy workers who lost their lives during construction of the Snowy Mountains Scheme 1949–74, Cooma Cemetery. Erected in October 2019 for the 70th anniversary of the Snowy Scheme, 2022. © Anoma Pieris

Creek; Luigi Savegnago, aged 26, Junction Shaft, etc. Earlier graves erected by workmates were identifiable by Joe Roncari's rebar crosses and his friend Angelo Rosetti's stonework (see Chapter 2). As the few workers who stayed on in Cooma passed on with old age, their headstones introduced more intimate details of family, children and epitaphs, suggestive of lives lived in their fullness through Australian citizenship. And yet, residual traces of that other collective clung to their identities. A granite boulder memorial erected for Rinaldo Fabbro, a stonemason employed by Legnami Pasotti, who has lived a full life, depicted him at a 1953 ball in Cooma with five dapperly dressed Italian workmates.

When the Snowy Scheme closed in the early 1970s, Cooma reverted to a settler town and these new pioneers, like Joe Roncari, dispersed to other cities in Australia. The industrial landscape likewise lost its gritty temporary scaffolding lending itself more readily to the romanticized spectacle of progress. The company town became an appendage to Cooma and the houses were bought or rented by townspeople and the few, former workers who remained. Only the dead in their cemetery plots resisted the Anglo-Australian dream.

The final word must go to The Settlers, a musical group formed by Irish concreter Ulick O'Boyle. Through songs evoking and celebrating both good and bad aspects of their labouring lives, the intangible heritage of immigrant industry entered and persisted in the popular imagination, as in 'The Dozer Driver Man':

> Well longer grew the tunnels and short grew Olaf's life span.
> From rock to dust was the savage must for the dozer driver man.
> *Hit that rock, don't ride, jump clear as the big cat starts to slide.*
> *As she tumbles down the mountain if you can,*
> *leap for your life, you dozer-driver man!*[49]

The song evocatively captured the risks posed by the steep alpine terrain for Norwegian Olaf Groden, a friend of O'Boyle's who died in an accident while working on the Snowy Scheme.

ANDREW SANIGA: INTERPRETING RUINS IN REMOTE LANDSCAPES.

Isolation, remoteness and ruin are key to understanding Woomera as a heritage place. Added to this is the nature of its managers – the Australian government's Department of Defence largely controls all the goings on in Woomera and still uses its vast weapons-testing range as a working laboratory for war. The Indigenous Kokatha people, who are the traditional custodians of the land upon which Woomera Village and the core of the range were built, are increasingly involved and have been successful in demarcating no-go zones (like the Woomera Golf Course) and in ensuring their voice is present in proposals for development. This has been a significant development, because after seventy-five years of operation, the extent of impact on sites of Indigenous Australian cultural significance has long been in need of redress. Regardless, Defence is in a commanding position, to the extent that the security protocols and prohibitions that were born partly due to the presence of European immigrants amid broader fears of espionage at the dawn of the Cold War years has cast a long shadow. A sense of isolation is exacerbated by highly restricted physical access in place today, a condition that is also reflected in a lack of available archival access that is considered normal in other realms of research.[50]

In acknowledging the impact that Woomera has had on the Indigenous landscape, it is also the case that Woomera's infrastructure represents the most expansive and dramatic evidence of Australia's involvement in the Cold War. The places often have physical evidence linked with historic, scientific, aesthetic and social significance. There is rocket-testing hardware and military industrial heritage out on the range – or the 'footprints' of where they once stood – but also sites found in standalone buildings or structures or apparatus or trees through to the entire modern planned village of Woomera, which was once inclusive of all the services and facilities required to house a population of more than 6,000 people upon a harsh and treeless gibber plain. Water had to be piped 173 km as a lifeline for the unlikely act of creating a suburban oasis, an innovative grey water sewerage treatment system giving life to a vegetative setting full of plants that were totally foreign to the environment.

Woomera as a village still exists today, but its infrastructure is not even the skeleton of its former self. Its population hovers precariously between 100 and 200 people. These are mostly caretakers of its remaining defence infrastructure and activities, which although a shadow of the peak years is still highly valued and heavily guarded (and increasingly in demand) for modern trials. Relics of industry and infrastructure, including the now defunct detention centre for 'unauthorized arrivals', are cast despondent in the Australian desert, or given over to adaptive reuse. Natural degeneration has produced ruinous places and settings, making tangible the forces of boom and bust in the context of the arid and remote landscape. Much of the fabric has been completely erased: roads and rail, most of the houses and service buildings, trees and gardens, sports fields and the like. This has occurred to such an extent that, indeed, the presence of 'something' seemingly out of context and isolated in the extreme – a relic, a trace – often stands out and becomes a potent reminder of what you are 'not' seeing (see Figure 9.7).

The contributions of European migrants who served here are embedded at all levels, some more obvious than others, if you know what to look for. When walking around what remains of the village and in stumbling upon a concrete culvert or sections of stone revetment, I 'see' the immigrants who surveyed, designed and drafted within the Department of Works and Housing's Drawing Office – and the labourers who mixed concrete and laid stone. When walking around the site of the Phillip Ponds construction workers' camp and finding a rusted nail, beer bottle tops, or tent peg, I walk between the long rows of canvas tents and makeshift washing lines. In discovering a rusted, corroded fragment of fencing bar lying adjacent to a rail bridge and only recently exposed in the Woomera floods of January 2022, I can grasp the backbreaking conditions of the twenty-five-strong gangs who were sometimes driven to the point of suicide by unrelenting gangers. All this is 'from the debris', unfettered and raw, hot

Figure 9.7 Wirrawirralu Waterhole (Phillip Ponds), 2021. © Andrew Saniga

and dusty, and far removed from the curated and air-conditioned museum where any appreciation of the immigrants' contribution is yet to be told.

When J.B. Jackson discussed 'the necessity for ruins' in the US context, he proposed that in order for a particular aspect of the past to become valued and preserved, society must first perceive that aspect in a state of ruin or neglect and discontinuity – renewal and reform follow death and rejection.[51] Forgotten or neglected spaces or landscapes can challenge us with a sense of abject failure, serving as powerful instigators for reflection. Others such as Gisli Pálsson argued that in semi-natural landscapes, far removed from urban or developed areas, ruins have enabling potential, as 'ruined sites . . . places of dereliction clearly illustrate the interconnected nature of the landscape's formation processes, between the supposedly natural and cultural'.[52] In Pálsson's analysis, remote ruins potentially allow mental space and energy for imaginative interpretation.[53] Ruins discovered in far-flung and inaccessible places have special gravity or weight. They take effort to get to, and to understand, and they are often augmented by new or unfamiliar sensorial environments and sequential experiences. In this way, discovering ruins in Woomera harks back to the first moments of arrival when immigrant workers finally 'landed', somewhere, when they otherwise had nowhere else to go.

DAVID BEYNON: COMMERCIAL/INDUSTRIAL STREETSCAPES AND LAYERS OF IMMIGRANT HERITAGE

There are a few issues associated with evaluating the heritage of Footscray and Springvale's commercial and industrial streetscapes. The first is the comparatively modest scale and form of most of the constituent buildings and spaces. Apart from the occasional temple or cultural association's premises, these buildings of retail, commercial and light industrial areas provide functional envelopes. They have an unself-conscious ordinariness and a banality of form and detail, the main benefit of which is to be adaptable to different users and uses. However, the overall effect of the streetscapes of these suburbs is not banal (see Figure 9.8). As Meaghan Morris once suggested, banality is a property associated with Western notions of modernity and its relation to taste, an idea of images and surfaces covering an underlying mundanity and lack of originality rather than being of intrinsic value.[54] Yet, here the signs and symbols on these ordinary buildings speak of enterprise, adaptation and creativity. And collectively, they constitute the reinscribing of an urban environment with new meanings and identities.

This leads to the second issue with considering these buildings and their urban environments as heritage. With the addition or subtraction of early applied signage and functions, the identities of these buildings tend to be denoted rather than compositionally or spatially expressed. A case in point is the Nan Yang pan-Asian Supermar-

Figure 9.8 Vietnamese-Chinese hairdresser (in a shop that once was a clothing factory outlet), next to an East African *injera* bakery and grocery in Footscray, 2020. © David Beynon

ket discussed in Chapter 8. Prior to its current use, the building housed a furniture store and prior to that, an outlet selling rubber goods and equipment. But while each of these changes of use necessitated a change of signage on the parapet and front walls/windows of the building, only minimal spatial or physical alterations have been required to the building's essential envelope. The changes have been in specific uses housed within these spaces and in the identities of each business' proprietors or their communities. The name 'Nan Yang' itself is demonstrative of this, being a Chinese term for the lands and waters south of China, the region now known as Southeast Asia. The identity expressed in the signage states the geographical region encompassed by the supermarket's range of produce, reinforced by the use of other Asian languages and scripts on the shop's awning. This aspect of difference being more in terms of identity than typology has already been argued in Chapter 8's discussion of the ontological difference embodied within proprietors, users and communities of particular ethnic origins. Concentrations of racially differentiated and 'non-white' cultural groups associated with Asian immigrants also act as signifiers of welcome liberal values to some, while being threatening to others. The refugee origins of many within these communities have added an extra layer of challenge to overcome. In contrast to more recently established populations of East Asian and South Asian origin who have settled in Melbourne's wealthier eastern suburbs, these communities have had to develop their enterprises in traditionally working-class areas.

To take this discussion into a broader context of change within a city such as Melbourne, what happens when one wave of immigrant settlers of particular origins starts to make way for the next? The settlement of refugees is by its nature contingent. Vietnamese, Cambodian and other immigrants who arrived in the late 1970s or 1980s did not settle in Springvale or Footscray because they had the choice of residing and working anywhere in Melbourne. The Midway and Enterprise Hostels provided catalysts for their concentration in the particular areas, and these, unsurprisingly, were areas that previous waves of migrants had settled. In Hopkins Street in the centre of Footscray's retail district, surrounded by Vietnamese and Chinese retailers and cafés, is T. Cavallaro & Sons' Pasticceria. This is a business founded by Sicilian immigrants in 1956 and still makes Sicilian sweets today.[55] It is also a reminder that prior to the 1970s, Footscray was already a centre for recent immigrants, being home to large communities from Italy,[56] as well as Greece, Malta and the then Republic of Yugoslavia. However, while communities of these origins are still present in the area, their business and presence are much less obvious than those of Southeast Asian immigrants. And Footscray is still changing. Over the course of researching this book, a cultural shift has been observable, in which the number and geographical extent of Vietnamese and other Asian-Australian business has reduced and the number of African-Australian businesses has grown, as more recent immigrants from Ethiopia, Somalia, Sudan and other parts of Africa have settled and established shops, restaurants and other businesses in Footscray and the surrounding suburbs. New trajectories of immigrant enterprise are emerging. As the Vietnamese *banh mi* has gone from being a specialized food item only found where Vietnamese immigrants have settled to being an Australian staple found at airports, the bakeries now opening in Footscray make Ethiopian *injera* bread for a gradually expanding market (Figure 9.8). However, this new wave of African immigrants is still overcoming ethnic and racial tensions as they establish themselves. The Vietnamese and other Southeast Asian arrivals in the late 1970s challenged notions of a British or European Australia, and now arrivals from Africa represent a further contestation to the ideas of 'whiteness' and 'blackness' in relation to Australian identity.

The cumulative effects of waves of immigrants making apparently superficial changes to ordinary buildings are not only urban adaptations of place but also elements of Australian heritage being layered in place. The temporal aspect of these migrants' layered heritage, the ephemerality of concentrations of identity in particular places at particular times, is something that architectural and urban historians need to be able to capture. Understanding Australia's recent settlement history requires an appraisal of the real effects of waves of immigrants in transforming the identities of commercial and industrial built environments.

CONCLUSION

Our collaborative task of piecing together material fragments and memories has been the greatest challenge and joy of writing this book. We have ventured far from both familiar sources and authorized discourses to dig deep into unorthodox archives. These include community archives and ephemera, social media platforms, exhibitions and physical traces on abandoned and deindustrialized sites, and, equally, life stories of individuals and families who never thought them sufficiently remarkable to be captured in print. We have acknowledged the extraordinary value of their precious ordinary objects. More importantly, this book has unearthed the messy, violent histories typically buried or overlooked in both built environment disciplines and heritage discourse: of militarized accommodation, workspaces and routines, and of the dirty, noisy and dehumanizing hard labour in heavy industries that leave permanent scars on both the workers and the landscape. It has raised questions of how these spaces of labour shape migrant subjectivity. Our interest in the physical and material worlds of migrant labourers has focused attention on camp and hostel environments, company towns, factories, work camps and small businesses as the host environments for our study, departing from the private homes, ethnic suburbs and commercial strips previously covered by many scholars in our disciplines.

Because of this focus, this book has ventured beyond the usual parameters of migration studies by addressing the environmental impact of infrastructure projects, including in terms of changing place associations and meanings – identifying work environments as development ecologies continuing settler practices of Indigenous dispossession and environmental damage – and has also examined how the military discipline required for building infrastructure in harsh and remote environments forged pathways into professions for some. Throughout this book, we have drawn attention to how families and single women with children navigated living and working environments designed for single men and survived family separation and uncertainty. And, finally, shifting to a period after government industries no longer 'absorbed' migrants, we have noted their dispersal and survival in and transformation of outlying industrial suburbs. Through these many studies ranging across infrastructure, heavy industry and manufacturing, crossing both European and Asian labour-migrant experiences, we have uncovered the vein of racialization that insinuates itself into 'Australian' interpretations of culture and class.

The period of our focus does not engage with the later more reactive nationalist politics that responded to government multicultural policies after 1978 or the mandatory detention of unauthorized arrivals, including offshore detention in the 1990s and 2000s. Unlike racialization within whiteness during the White Australia Policy era, these later developments have isolated and targeted certain migrants of colour from conflict zones in South Asia, Africa and the Middle East, alongside greater border securitization and more explicitly racialized expressions of what are perceived as acceptable pathways to citizenship. Australian humanitarian responses have also aligned with the so-called 'global war on terror' and the later 'refugee crisis'. The waves of migrants entering through these many pathways are visible and present in the already mentioned industrial suburbs and many inner-city public housing estates.

This final chapter has raised a number of questions on what this means for reconceptualizations of migrant heritage. Looking towards the future, we have posed questions about the function of heritage in erasing or sanitizing difficult and dangerous pasts, we have argued in favour of the need for community connection and its visibility, even in officially sanctioned heritage forums, and we have explored the limits of the AHD and community-initiated ways around this through digital storytelling that challenges elitist or exclusionary narratives of economic and national progress. Our exploration of the heritage landscape has spoken to the valuation as well as the *de*valuing of migrant heritage places in the Australian context – these are largely nonmonumental or aesthetically devalued spaces that have little hope of heritage conservation in the conventional (and tangible) sense. We hope that this anthology, alongside the wealth of community-initiated storytelling that propels and imbues it, constitutes an intangible and critical testament to these pasts. Like the vernacular, the pasts explored here are messy and unable to adhere to the fantasy of a containable heterogeneity as homogeneity, which is arguably the logic behind Australia's liberal multicultural agenda and its ahistorical celebration of a depoliticized diversity. Questions about the messy heritage of Australia's industrial and migrant labour past should continue to be explored in reference to a nation state that is still decolonizing.

Alexandra Dellios is Senior Lecturer in the Centre for Heritage and Museum Studies at the Australian National University. She is the author of *Heritage Making and Migrant Subjects in the Deindustrialising Region of the Latrobe Valley* (2022) and *Histories of Controversy: Bonegilla Migrant Centre* (2017), and co-editor (with Eureka Henrich) of *Migrant, Multicultural and Diasporic Heritage: Beyond and Between Borders* (2020). She is Chair of the Editorial Board for *Studies in Oral History*, a founding member of the Australian Migration History Network, and Executive Committee member of the Association of Critical Heritage Studies.

Anoma Pieris is Professor of Architecture at the Melbourne School of Design. Her most recent publications include the anthology *Architecture on the Borderline: Boundary Politics and Built Space* (2019) and *The Architecture of Confinement: Incarceration Camps of the Pacific War* (2022), co-authored with Lynne Horuchi. She was guest curator with Martino Stierli, Sean Anderson and Evangelos Kotsioris of the 2022 MoMA exhibition *The Project of Independence: Architectures of Decolonization in South Asia, 1947–1985*.

Mirjana Lozanovska is Professor in Architecture and Director of the Architecture Vacancy Lab at Deakin University. Her work investigates the creative ways that architecture mediates human dignity through multidisciplinary theories of space. Her books include *Migrant Housing: Architecture, Dwelling, Migration* (2019) and *Ethno-Architecture and the Politics of Migration* (2016). Her creative works include *Venetian Blinds* (European Cultural Centre, Venice 2021), and, with David Beynon, Cameron Bishop, Diego Fullaondo and Anne Scott-Wilson, the exhibition *Iconic Industry* (2017, National Wool Museum, Geelong). She was co-editor of Fabrications: *Journal of the Society of Architectural Historians Australia and New Zealand* from 2018 to 2021.

Andrew Saniga is Associate Professor of Landscape Architecture, Planning and Urbanism at the University of Melbourne. His research includes a history of landscape architecture in Australia and his writings have documented and explained key designers and projects with an emphasis on the mid-twentieth century. His book *Making Landscape Architecture in Australia* (2012) won the Victoria Medal from the Australian Institute of Landscape Architects. *Campus: Building Modern Australian Universities* (2023), a book he co-edited with Robert Freestone, is a collaborative history that sheds light on the origins and evolution of campus design in Australia from the Second World War to the current day. Andrew teaches design and history of landscape architecture, and is a registered landscape architect with the Australian Institute of Landscape Architects. He is also a member of DOCOMOMO International.

David Beynon is Associate Professor in Architecture at the University of Tasmania. His research involves investigating the social, cultural and compositional dimensions of architecture, and adaptations of architectural content and meaning in relation to migration and cultural change. His current work includes investigations into the multicultural and postcolonial manifestations of contemporary urban environments and the creative possibilities for post-industrial architecture in Australia and Asia.

NOTES

1. Munjeri, 'Tangible and Intangible Heritage', 13; Kirshenblatt-Gimblett, 'Intangible Heritage as Metacultural Production'.
2. Smith, *Uses of Heritage*; Harrison, 'Forgetting to Remember'; Smith and Campbell, 'Nostalgia for the Future'.
3. According to Cristobal Gnecco, who analysed the function of multicultural heritage in relation to governmentality, (global) humanism and the market: 'Its regulation becomes a purely technical matter: it defines who can find it (the archaeologist on the excavation, the historian in the archive), who can embellish it (the restorer), who can display it (the museum curator), who must watch over it (officials of state agencies)': Gnecco, 'Heritage in Multicultural Times', 266.
4. Gnecco, 'Heritage in Multicultural Times', 266.
5. As a discourse, the AHD accounts for how language figures practically in our constructions and understandings of heritage, along with how a discourse is being used and why. See Smith and Waterton, 'The Recognition and Misrecognition of Community Heritage'.

6. While this discourse and the Eurocentric elitism that underpins it have been the subject of much academic and practitioner criticism in the last few decades, the official global remedies proffered (in the form of the UNSECO Intangible Cultural Heritage Convention, for example) do little to challenge the underlying logic and power of the AHD, perpetuated and constituted by bodies like the World Heritage Council at an international level and the Australian Heritage Council (and its list) at a national level.
7. Smith and Waterton, 'Constrained by Commonsense', 160.
8. Smith, *Emotional Heritage*; Smith, '"We Are . . . We Are Everything"'; Witcomb, 'Understanding the Role of Affect'; Cooke and Frieze, 'Affect and the Politics of Testimony in Holocaust Museums'.
9. Reeves et al., 'Rethinking the International Significance', 313
10. Spearritt, 'Money, Taste and Industrial Heritage', 34–35.
11. Shackle, Smith and Campbell, 'Labour's Heritage'.
12. DesRoches, 'Working-Class Heritage and the Marketization of Difference', 1053.
13. Meskell, 'Heritage, Gentrification, Participation', 996–98.
14. Gnecco, 'Heritage in Multicultural Times', 266
15. Dellios, 'Commemorating Migrant Camps', 252–71.
16. Ashton, 'The Birthplace of Australian Multiculturalism', 381–98.
17. Rothberg, *Multidirectional Memory*, 21.
18. Such criticisms of official heritage practice – from academia and from practitioners – are familiar in the critical heritage studies literature. For decades, scholars have called for heritage management and conservation practice to engage more thoughtfully with implicated communities – for heritage work that is 'people-centred'. See Madgin and Lesh, *People-Centred Methodologies for Heritage Conservation*.
19. Wills, 'Between the Hostel and the Detention Centre', 269.
20. Smith, Persian and Fox, 'Introduction: Fascism and Anti-Fascism in Australian History' 1–19; Fitzpatrick, *White Russians, Red Peril*.
21. Murphy, 'The Assimilation of Refugee Immigrants in Australia', 179–206. Kevin and Agutter, 'From Forced to Coerced Labour', 1–13.
22. Aaron, *Sanctuary*.
23. Wills, 'Between the Hostel and the Detention Centre', 266.
24. Throughout the decades, Windt (who migrated from Israel with his parents) maintained an interest in the migrant heritage of the place and launched the online photo gallery (supported by Newcastle and Hunter Region Ethnic Communities Council). The thousands of images once accessible online today appear lost, although some speculate that they were donated to Newcastle University Library after the Anvil Creek website was scrapped almost ten years ago.
25. Donna Sharpe, 'Greta Migrant Camp Site Sold for Millions', *The Advertiser*, 6 March 2021. Retrieved 2 January 2024 from https://www.cessnockadvertiser.com.au/story/7153921/historic-greta-migrant-camp-site-sold-for-millions/?cs=4077.
26. Helen Scott, post on 'Facebook Group: Keep Greta Camp History ALIVE', 25 February 2022.
27. Mydland and Grahn, 'Identifying Heritage Values in Local Communities', 575.
28. An example is the 750 m concrete structure traversing the Barwon River in Geelong. After twenty years of seeking ways to restore this structure, the Council handed this particular site over only to the Wathaurong people, the Indigenous Australian custodians of the site on which Geelong was built.
29. Joint Committee of Public Accounts, *Australian Iron and Steel Industry*, 13.
30. Lever-Tracy and Quinlan, *A Divided Working Class*, 193.
31. Greg Ellis, 'Memories Flood Back on Steelworks Tour', *Illawarra Mercury*, 6 April 2021, 6.

32. Balint and Simic, 'Histories of Migrants and Refugees in Australia', 378.
33. Walker, 'First Accommodation for Migrants Arriving in Wollongong Post World War'. See also Walker and Peterson, *Every Story Counts*. Significant research is carried out by the Migration Heritage Project in Wollongong, which is run by volunteers and on a shoestring budget.
34. In 1969, the St Eleftherios Greek Orthodox Church, Lygon Street, Brunswick, adapted a former Methodist Church that was originally built in 1934. See Winkler, 'Post-War Migrant Built Heritage in Melbourne', 370.
35. Australia ICOMOS, *The Burra Charter for Places of Cultural Significance*, 1.
36. Lang, Skurjat-Kozek and Molski, 'Kosciuszko and Strzelecki'.
37. Laqueur, *The Work of the Dead*.
38. Siobhan McHugh, Oral History Transcripts, Mitchell Library, State Library of New South Wales (hereinafter MLOH 287, McHugh) 287, Siobhan McHugh, Snowy People – Box 4. 'The Opening of the Jindabyne Pumping Station'.
39. Ibid.
40. Merle Harvey and Akos Olah, both clerks at the SMA office, wrote the lyrics for *The Mountain Lark*, the first Australian opera dealing with migrants, sung to music composed by Bela Dolesko, who had studied in the academies at Budapest and Vienna including under the composer Ravel.
41. McHugh, Snowy People – Box 4. 'The Opening of the Jindabyne Pumping Station'.
42. Ibid.
43. Ibid.
44. Ibid. See NLA: Patterson, Banjo. 1890. 'The Man from Snowy River', *The Bulletin* 11(53), 26 April 1890, 13. Retrieved 2 January 2024 from http://nla.gov.au/nla.obj-443549096.
45. Harry Pearl, 'How the Snowy Hydro Scheme Helped Build Multicultural Australia', *SBS News*, 28 June 2017. Retrieved 2 January 2024 from https://www.sbs.com.au/news/article/how-the-snowy-hydro-scheme-helped-build-multicultural-australia/5zo1fuk9o.
46. '500 Attend Snowy Memorial Unveiling: 119 Persons Remembered', *Cooma Monaro Express*, 24 February 1981; MLOH287, McHugh, Snowy People – Box 4.
47. NLA: 'Three Die in Snowy Disaster', *Canberra Times*, 23 December 1963, 1. Retrieved 2 January 2024 from http://nla.gov.au/nla.news-article104283135.
48. 'History', Snowy Hydro.
49. 'The Dozer Driver Man', *Songs of the Snowy Mountains*, 67, reproduced with permission from Shannon O'Boyle.
50. Wohltmann, *Looking Back to See the Future*, 16–17.
51. Jackson, *The Necessity for Ruins*, 102.
52. Pálsson, 'Situating Nature', 174.
53. Ibid., 176.
54. Morris, 'Banality in Cultural Studies', 12.
55. T. Cavallaro & Sons' Pasticceria, 'Our Story'.
56. Cresciani, *The Italians in Australia*.

BIBLIOGRAPHY

Archival Records

McHugh, Siobhan. Oral History Transcripts, Mitchell Library, State Library of New South Wales (MLOH 287, McHugh).

National Archives Australia (NLA)

Publications

Aarons, Mark. *Sanctuary: Nazi Fugitives in Australia*. Melbourne: W. Heinemann Australia, 1989.

Agutter, Karen, and Catherine Kevin. 'From Forced to Coerced Labour: Displaced Mothers and Teen Girls in Post-World War Two Australia', *Labor History* (2022), 1–13.

Ashton, Paul. '"The Birthplace of Australian Multiculturalism?" Retrospective Commemoration, Participatory Memorialisation and Official Heritage', *International Journal of Heritage Studies* 15(5) (2009), 381–98.

Australia ICOMOS. *The Burra Charter for Places of Cultural Significance*. Melbourne: Australia ICOMOS, 2013.

Balint, Ruth, and Zora Simic. 'Histories of Migrants and Refugees in Australia', *Journal of Australian Historical Studies* 49(3) (2018), 378–409.

Cooke, Steven, and Donna-Lee Frieze. 'Imagination, Performance and Affect: A Critical Pedagogy of the Holocaust?', *Holocaust Studies* 21(3) (2015), 157–71.

Cresciani, Gianfranco. *The Italians in Australia*. Cambridge: Cambridge University Press, 2003.

Dellios, Alexandra. 'Commemorating Migrant Camps: Vernacular Memories in Official Spaces', *Journal of Australian Studies* 39(2) (2015), 252–71.

DesRoches, Davina M. 'Working-Class Heritage and the Marketization of Difference: The Limits of New Museology at Manhattan's Tenement Museum', *International Journal of Heritage Studies* 27(10) (2021), 1051–63.

Fitzpatrick, Sheila. *White Russians, Red Peril: A Cold War History of Migration to Australia*. Sydney: Black Inc. Books, 2021.

Gnecco, Cristóbal. 'Heritage in Multicultural Times', in Emma Waterton and Steve Watson (eds), *The Palgrave Handbook of Contemporary Heritage Research* (London: Palgrave Macmillan, 2015), pp. 263–80.

Harrison, Rodney. 'Forgetting to Remember, Remembering to Forget: Late Modern Heritage Practices, Sustainability and the "Crisis" of Accumulation of the Past', *International Journal of Heritage Studies* 19(6) (2013), 579–95.

Harvey, Meile. *The Mountain Lark* (Opera in One Act). Sydney, 1962. Retrieved 2 January 2024 from https://trove.nla.gov.au/work/209420750.

'History'. Snowy Hydro website. Retrieved 2 January 2024 from https://www.snowyhydro.com.au/about/history/.

Jackson, John B. *The Necessity for Ruins and Other Topics*. Amherst: University of Massachusetts Press, 1980.

Joint Committee of Public Accounts (Report Australia Parliament). *Australian Iron and Steel Industry*. Canberra: Govt. printer of Australia [for the] Joint Committee of Public Accounts, Report no. 253. PP no. 260 of 1987. Retrieved 28 July 2022 from https://nla.gov.au/nla.obj-2085012257.

Kirshenblatt-Gimblett, Barbara. 'Intangible Heritage as Metacultural Production', *Museum International* 56(1–2) (2004), 52–65.

Lang, Ursula, Ernestyn Skurjat-Kozek and Felix Molski. 'Kosciuszko and Strzelecki: The Men, the Mountain, the Monument'. Retrieved 2 January 2024 from https://monumentaustralia.org.au/themes/people/exploration/display/21672-sir-paul-edmund-de-strzelecki.

Laqueur, Thomas. *The Work of the Dead: A Cultural History of Mortal Remains*. Princeton: Princeton University Press, 2015.

Madgin, Rebecca, and James Lesh. *People-Centred Methodologies for Heritage Conservation*. Abingdon: Routledge, 2021.

Meskell, Lynn. 'Heritage, Gentrification, Participation: Remaking Urban Landscapes in the Name of Culture and Historic Preservation', *International Journal of Heritage Studies* 25(9) (2019), 996–98.

Morris, Meaghan. 'Banality in Cultural Studies', *Discourse* 10(2) (1988), 3–29.
Munjeri, Dawson. 'Tangible and Intangible Heritage: From Difference to Convergence', *Museum International* 56(1–2) (2004), 12–20.
Murphy, Henry, and Brian Megget. 'The Assimilation of Refugee Immigrants in Australia', *Population Studies* 5(3) (1952), 179–206.
Mydland, Leidulf, and Wera Grahn. 'Identifying Heritage Values in Local Communities', *International Journal of Heritage Studies* 18(6) (2012), 564–87.
O'Boyle, Shannon. *Songs of the Snowy Mountains: The Settlers*. Cooma: South East Printing, 2014.
Pálsson, Gísli. 'Situating Nature: Ruins of Modernity as *Natturuperlur*', *Tourist Studies* 13(2) (2013), 172–88. https://doi.org/10.1177/1468797613490374.
Reeves, Kier, Erik Eklund, Andrew Reeves, Vicki Peel and Bruce Scates. 'Rethinking the International Significance of the Material Culture and Intangible Heritage of the Australian Labour Movement', *International Journal of Heritage Studies* 17(4) (2011), 301–17.
Rothberg, Michael. *Multidirectional Memory: Remembering the Holocaust in the Age of Decolonization*. Stanford: Stanford University Press, 2009.
Smith, Evan, Jayne Persian, and Vashti Jane Fox. 'Introduction: Fascism and Anti-fascism in Australian History', in Evan Smith, Jayne Persian and Vashti Jane Fox (eds), *Histories of Fascism and Anti-fascism in Australia* (Abingdon: Routledge, 2022), pp. 1–19.
Smith, Laurajane. *Uses of Heritage*. London: Routledge, 2006.
——. '"We Are . . . We Are Everything": The Politics of Recognition and Misrecognition at Immigration Museums', *Museum and Society* 15(1) (2017), 69–86.
Smith, Laurajane, and Gary Campbell. '"Nostalgia for the Future": Memory, Nostalgia and the Politics of Class', *International Journal of Heritage Studies* 23(7) (2017), 612–27.
Smith, Laurajane, Paul A. Shackel and Gary Campbell (eds). *Heritage, Labour and the Working Classes*. Abingdon: Routledge, 2011.
Shackel, Paul, Laurajane Smith, and Gary Campbell, 'Labour's Heritage', *International Journal of Heritage Studies* 17(4) (2011), 291–300.
Smith, Laurajane. *Emotional Heritage: Visitor Engagement at Museums and Heritage Sites*. London: Routledge, 2020.
Smith, Laurajane, and Emma Waterton. 'Constrained by Commonsense: The Authorized Heritage Discourse in Contemporary Debates', in R. Skeates, C. McDavid and J. Carman (eds), *The Oxford Handbook of Public Archaeology* (Oxford: Oxford University Press, 2012), pp. 153–171.
Spearritt, Peter. 'Money, Taste and Industrial Heritage', *Australian Historical Studies* 24(96) (1991), 33–45.
T. Cavallaro & Sons' Pasticceria. 'Our Story', 2024. Retrieved 18 January 2024 from https://www.tcavallaroandsons.com.au/about.
Walker, Meredith. 'First Accommodation for Migrants Arriving in Wollongong Post World War 2', *Migration Heritage Project, Wollongong's Migration Heritage Thematic Study, 'Places Project'*, 2007. Retrieved 2 January 2024 from https://www.mhpillawarra.com.au/pdf/places_accommodation_essay.pdf.
Walker, Meredith, and John Peterson (eds). *Every Story Counts: Recording Migration Heritage: A Wollongong Case Study*. Wollongong, NSW: Illawarra Migration Heritage Migration Heritage Project Inc., 2015.
Waterton, Emma, and Laurajane Smith. 'The Recognition and Misrecognition of Community Heritage', *International Journal of Heritage Studies* 16(1–2) (2010), 4–15.
Wills, Sara. 'Between the Hostel and the Detention Centre: Possible Trajectories of Migrant Pain and Shame in Australia', in William Stewart Logan and Keir Reeves (eds), *Places of Pain and Shame: Dealing with Difficult Heritage* (London: Routledge, 2008), pp. 277–94.

Winkler, Sally. 'Post-war Migrant Built Heritage in Melbourne: From Assimilation to Multiculturalism', in *Association of Architecture Schools Australasia (AASA) Proceedings* (Geelong: Deakin University, 2011), pp. 366–74.

Witcomb, Andrea. 'Understanding the Role of Affect in Producing a Critical Pedagogy for History Museums', *Museum Management and Curatorship* 28(3) (2013), 255–71.

Wohltmann, Michael. *Looking Back to See the Future: A Revisionist History of Woomera 1947–1980*. Adelaide: Digital Print Australia, 2022.

Index

Page numbers in *italics* refer to illustrations.

Abbots Smith, Johnny, 108, 114–15
Aboriginal Australians. *See* Indigenous Australians
Aboriginal Welfare Board (previously Aborigines Protection Board), 88
Aborigines Protection Board (APB, later Aboriginal Welfare Board), 86–87, 90, 104
Acclimatisation Society, 103
accommodation and housing, 3; in barracks and hostels, 39–46; for men, 28, 197; prefabricated, 27, 119; private, 27–28; at regional camps, 25–27; shortages of, 26, 27, 190, 196, 198; on Snowy Scheme, 112–13; technical advances in, 195–98; temporary, 203; wartime, 39–46. *See also under* names of individual camps and hostels
acculturation, 116, 125
Acosta, Joe, 77
Adaminaby (NSW), 99, 104, 106, 107, 118
Adelaide (SA): CDWH in, 147, 153, 158; 'German villages' near, 18; Latvian community in, 153; Lithuanian community in, 149; migrant accommodation in, *212*
Adelaide United Trades and Labour Council (AUTLC), 145
advertising, 223, 233, 240
affordances, 237
Afghan immigrants, 17, 18
Africa, immigrants from, 7, 228, 233, *269*, 270, 271

agency, bounded, 166
agriculture, 62, 181; industrial-scale, 59
alcohol: abuse of, 29, 81, 83, 140, 144, 175, 258
Alice Springs, 18
Aliens Act, 30
Allan, David, 90
Allied Works Council (AWC), 50
Altona (Melb.), 224
Andrean, Nevina, 169, 175
Angkor Tyres repair workshop, *238*
anglophone/nonanglophone distinctions, 2–3, 212; in cemeteries, 264; and class, 2, 62, 77–78; in employment, 23, 34, 43, 77–78, 85; in historiography, 2, 18, 31, 91; in housing, 27, 31; in immigration, 18–20, 74; at Port Kembla, 74, 85; on Snowy Scheme, 101–2, 113–16, 123
Anthropocene epoch, 103
architecture: adaptations of, 62, 225–28; commercial and retail, 228, 233, 237–39; domestic, 41, 59, 195, 203–13; histories of, 1–12, 221–23; of hostels, 203–9; industrial, 71, 76, 91, 237–39; landscape, 142; military, 8, 40, 45; modernist, 239; punitive, 192, 203–9; as social and cultural construct, 233–34, 240–41; vernacular, 239
Architon Construction Co., 112, 118, 122
Arendt, Sophia, 182
Armstrong, John, 140
army camps. *See* military camps
artificial intelligence, 70, 257

279

Asia: Australia's relationship with, 221; diaspora of, 3, 19; immigrants from, 11, 62, 124–25, 221–43. *See also* names of specific countries

Asia Pacific region: Australia's relationship with, 1, 222; decolonization of, 5; during Second World War, 39

assimilation, 3, 5, 75–76, 117, 178; by changing names, 56; of children, 48, 174, 179; criticism of and resistance to, 201, 254; economic, 21; and home ownership, 59, 123, 195–96; and hostels, 190; and Indigenous Australians, 102; linguistic, 40, 140, 142, 178–79; and Northern Europeans, 116; two-way, 62, 123; of women, 32, 174; at Woomera, 156

assisted immigrants, 17, 22; accommodation of, 27, 41, 48, 190; and labour shortage, 21, 50; from Malta, 135; for population expansion, 211; and Snowy Scheme, 117; and trauma, 39

Auschwitz, 114

Australian Architon Construction Co., 118

Australian Council of Trade Unions (ACTU), 24

Australian Iron and Steel Ltd (AI&S), 67–68, 90

Australian Paper Mills, 23

Australian Security Intelligence Organisation (ASIO), 146

Austria: immigrants from, 21, 47; refugee camps in, 21, 41

authorized heritage discourse (AHD), 249–50, 254–55, 272

Avstralija, Avstralija (film), 84

Backaitis, Juozas, 150

Bain, Robert, 44

Balcombe camp, 43

Balgownie camp (Fairy Meadow), 31, 256

Ball, Heather, 88

Baltic states, immigrants from ('Balts'), 24, 43, 109; and communism, 179; at Woomera, 142, 145, 147, 153. *See also* Estonia, immigrants from; Latvia, immigrants from; Lithuania, immigrants from

Bandiana camp, 43, 50

Bankstown (Sydney), 228, 240

Barwick, Linda, 104

Bashford, Bruce, 117

Baska, Jonathan, 116

Bathurst camp, 44, 175, 252

Beadell, Len, 139

Bega, 103

Belgiorno-Nettis, Franco, 77

Belgium and Belgians, 22, 30, 41, 110, 119

Benalla: industries at, 177–78

Benalla camp, 10, 26, 43; buildings relocated from, 48, 256; children's services at, 48–49, 172; closure of, 182; informal economy at, 181–82; layout of, *173*; number of people at, 172

Benalla Migrant Camp Inc., 167, 177, 254

Bennett's Camp (Woomera), 139

Berents, Ina, 116

Berger, Sándor, 114

Bergtals, Sergejs and Nicolajs, 143–44

Berkeley, 31

Berridale, 116

Berri (SA), 136

Bhaka Nangal Dam, 99

BHP (Broken Hill Proprietary), 8, 23; and Arthur Calwell, 24; at Newcastle (NSW), 29, 170; and trade unions, 75; Vietnamese employees of, 28. *See also* Port Kembla

BHP Steelhaven, 77

BHP Steelworks, 72–75, *73*; closure and heritage of, 257–61. *See also* Port Kembla

Bidawal people, 103

Birdsville track, 17

Blazejowski, Bronislaw, 139–40, *141*, 149

BlueScope Steel, 258, 261

Blūmentāls, Arvids and Millija Erna, 142, 151–53

boarding houses, 7, 27–29, 74

Bombala, 104, 110

Bonegilla Immigrant Reception and Holding Centre (Vic.), 25; British immigrants at, 49; children's services at, 48–49; closure of, 253; distribution of workers from, 29–20; exhibition about, 40–41; heritage of, 252–54; huts at, 44; Italian POWs at, 50; layout of, *45*; number of people at, 26, 42; protests at, 43; reunion at, 252; services provided at, 43, 44

Bonegilla Migrant Experience, 49, *253*
Borejko, Jerzy, 139–40, *141*
Bouch, A.D., 142–43, 147–48, 150–51, 153
Bouwbedrijf, 119
Bowning (NSW), 182
Boyd, Robin, 119
Bradfield Park hostel, 199, 210
Bradford Cotton Mills (Aust) Pty Ltd / Bradmill Industries, 177. *See also* Burlington Mills
Braidwood, 103
Branxton Community Hall, 256
Braybrook (Melb.), 234
Bredero, 119
'bride flights,' 33
Bridge, Rod, 117
Briska, Jazeps, 264
Britain. *See* United Kingdom of Great Britain and Northern Ireland (UK)
Broken Hill Proprietary (BHP). *See* BHP
Brooklyn hostel, 199, 202
Brown and Root Sundamericana Ltd, 112
Brown, Bruce, 203
Browne, W.R., 106
Brown, G.W., 42
Buchanan, Mr, 205
Buchenwald, 114
Buddhism, 223, 234–39
Building Trades' Federation (BTF), 145
Building Workers' Industrial Union, 24
Bùi-Quang, Kim, 231, 239
Bundian Way, 104
Bunnerong Hostel, 199
Burlington Mills, *176*–177, 183–84
'bush carpenters,' *141*

Cabramatta (Sydney), 28, 104, 240
Cabramurra (NSW), 110, 116, 119, 264
Cacic, Nikola, 264
Cairns camp: children's services at, 48
Cairns (Qld), 48
Calwell, Arthur, 20, 26; and BHP, 75; and 'New Australians,' 24; and trade unions, 24; and the White Australia Policy, 21
Cambodia: symbols of, 237–38
Cambodia, immigrants from, 5, 11, 19, 25, 210–13, 222–29, 236–37
Cameron, Bill, 114

camps: locations of, *9*. *See under* names of individual camps
Canada, 22, 102, 151
capitalism, 85; and class, 183; excessive, 90; and heritage, 251; industrial, 134; in USA, 41
Captain Bennett's Camp (near Woomera), 139
Carson, Fripp & Williams, 119
Catholic Church, 54, 56, 156, 240–41
cemeteries, 59, 82, 261–65
Cessnock (NSW), 59, 181, 256
chain migration, 22, 26–28
Cheesman, Jack, 197
Chifley, Ben, 20, 108
childcare, 32, 33, 48, 172, 174, 202
children: abuse of, 175; as immigrants, 32; raising of, 10; services for, 48–49. *See also* childcare
Chile, refugees from, 195, 211
China, immigrants from, 4, 5, 11, 18, 25, 225, 239–40
Chocolate City. *See under* Greta camp
Ciotti, G., 122
Citizenship Act 1948, 99
Civil and Civic (later Lendlease Corporation), 119, 122
Civil Constructional Corps, 50
Clayton, E.S., 106
Clayton (Melb.), 227
Clews, Hugh, 109
climate change, 4, 103
clothing industry. *See* textiles and clothing industry
coal mining. *See under* mining
Colarusso, Nadia, 82, 90
Cold War, 144, 255; and Baltic immigrants, 43; and Egypt, 99; and espionage, 266; infrastructure of, *9*; and nationalism, 179; and Woomera, 9–10. *See also* communism; Woomera
Colombo Plan, 19
colonization: and architecture, 239; of Australia, 17–18, 86–90, 198, 221; heritage of, 257; and memorialization, 263. *See also* Indigenous Australians
Commonwealth Employment Office, 168
Commonwealth Employment Service (CES), 25, 26, 181

Commonwealth Experimental Building Station (CEBS), 195, 196–98
Commonwealth Government departments. *See under* various listings: Department of . . .
Commonwealth Hostels Limited (CHL), 10, 27, 190–214
Commonwealth Housing Commission (CHC), 198
Commonwealth Immigration Advisory Council, 42
Commonwealth Immigration Planning Council (CIPC), 23, 75
Commonwealth Investigation Service, 146, 147
Commonwealth Reconstruction Training Scheme, 136
Commonwealth Scientific and Industrial Research Organisation (CSIRO), 196
communism, 10, 75, 144–45; refugees from, 21, 135, 145; and Woomera, 145–46. *See also* Cold War
Communist Party of Australia, 24, 145
company towns, 116–23; locations of, *9. See also* Cooma; Woomera
concentration camps, 41, 42, 44, 114, 137
convict era, 6, 17, 39
Coolawye, 108
Cooma, 51, *58*, 99, 104, 116–23; architecture and layout of, 118–19, *120–21*; cemetery in, *265*; class divisions in, 117; East, 117, 119; entertainment in, 117–18, 124; heritage of, 262; housing in, 117–23, *120–21*; North, 9, 56, 110, *112*, 119, 124; North–South division of, 117; racial distinctions in, 118; South, 57; women in, 117–18
Coomaditchie, 70, 86, 88–91
Corio, 27, 28. *See also* Geelong
Cornale, Johnny, 56
Country Party, 46
Cowra camp, 26, 54, 262; heritage and preservation of, 261; huts at, *45*
Cowra Japanese Garden, 262
Cringila, 68, 74; ethnic makeup of, 31; housing in, 28, 29
critical race theory, 7
Cúc Lam, 226
Cunderdin camp, 32, 44
Czechoslovakia

Czechoslovakia, immigrants from, 21, 211; at Benalla, 180; men, 33; on Snowy Scheme, 114; at Woomera, 136

'dago,' 24
Dalgety, 105
Dančauskis, Aleksandrs, 143, 151, 153
Dandenong (Melb.), 11, 28, 59, *60–61*, 229–30
Daoism, 223, 236, 243
Dapto housing estate, 27
Darlinghurst Gaol, 206
Darra (Brisbane), 240
Darwin, 31, 227
'decarbonization,' 257
Decentralization Board, 22
decentralization / regionalization, 22, 168; demise of, 25, 178; and labour, 27, 31, 40; and Port Kembla, 72; and women, 32
decolonization, 5, 7, 91, 99, 272
defence, 43; industries, 7, 146; and population growth, 20; research, 144, 146. *See also* Cold War; Department of Defence; Woomera
deindustrialization, 250, 271
Delegate Aboriginal reserve, 104
delicatessens, 28
demographics of Australia, 19–20
Denisenko, Wasli and Leokadija, 43
Department of Defence, 9, 256, 266; and Indigenous land rights, 87–88; training facilities of, 169. *See also* Cold War; Woomera
Department of Environment, Housing and Community, 211
Department of Immigration (DOI, later Department of Immigration and Ethnic Affairs), 167, 192, 199, 211; Department of Information of, 21; establishment of, 20
Department of Labour and National Service (DLNS), 25, 27, 167, 192
Department of Post War Reconstruction, 196
Department of Public Works, 10, 192
Department of Social Services, 20
Department of War Organization of Industry, 50
Department of Works and Housing (CDWH, aka Department of Works), 9, 47, 50, 132, 135, 195–96, 199–200, 267. *See also*

Commonwealth Experimental Building Station (CEBS)
deportation, 168
detention: history of, 6; of refugees and asylum seekers, 206, 209–14, 266
Dhawaral people, 86–91
Dhgillawarah (aka Red Point), 70, 72, 86–91
Dhurringile camp, 49
displaced persons (DP) camps, 4, 6; in Europe, 169, 170, 176, 255. *See also* names of individual camps
displaced persons (DPs), 20; definition of, 168; and government work contracts, 24, 168, 169; and post-traumatic stress disorder, 175, 255; on Snowy Scheme, 113–16
Djilamatang people, 103
Doherty, Eddy, 107
domestication, generalized, 76–77
domestic design and innovation, 10, 119, 192, 196
domestic environments, 2, 4, 40, 42, 201–4, 232; and violence, 47, 175
domestic heritage, 123
domestic labour, 21–23, 32–33, 104, 172, 176, 182, 254
Dramisino, Salvatore, 264
Draper, Earl, 118, 119
Drobot, Peter and Nina, 170
drugs, abuse of, 83
Dubinskas, Česlovas and Stefanija, 139, 144, 146–47, 154–57, 158
Duke of Edinburgh, 106
Dumez France-Australia, 112
Dunedoo (near Dubbo), 54
Dusseldorp, Gerardus Jozef (Dick), 119

Eastbridge Hostel (Nunawading, Melbourne), 224
Eastern Europe: immigrants from, 18, 74, 113, 115, 135, 158, 180 (*See also* displaced persons); male immigrants from, 29; and Second World War, 21, 255; and unskilled labour, 23
East Timor, immigrants and refugees from, 11, 195, 211
economies, informal, 10, 168, 174, 181–85
Econo Steel, 112
Eden (NSW), 103–4

education: of children, 32, 48, 49; in Germany, 114; at hostels, 200; unrecognised (*See* qualifications); in Yugoslavia, 74
Eggeling, H.F, 109
Egypt, 99
Elder Park Hostel, 26
Electric Power Transmission (EPT), 23, 31, 77
Elizabeth II, Queen, 106
Endeavour hostel (Randwick, Sydney), 10; capacity of, 199; closing of, 198–99; construction of, *194*; cost of, 199; design and layout of, *191*, 193–94, 199–200, 205–9; facilities and services at, 193–94, 204–9, *205*; laundry facilities at, *204*; location of, 198; meals and catering at, *193, 200*; name of, 198; objections to, 203–4; opening of, 191, 201; and Vietnamese refugees, 213
Enterprise hostel (Springvale, Melbourne), 10, 11, 200, 224–25, 270; as detention centre, 206; opening of, 193
entrepreneurialism, 1, 67, 183, 225–28; research on, 231. *See also* small business owners
essential industries, 29, 50
Estonia, immigrants from, 21, 24; and cultural activities, 179; on Snowy Scheme, 109; at Woomera, 136, 140, 150. *See also* Baltic states, immigrants from ('Balts')
Ethiopia, immigrants from, 233, 270
ethno-architecture, 239
Études and Enterprises, 112
Eucumbene (NSW), 107, 110; Observation Building & Tea House, 107; reservoir, 106
Europa Park (Cowra), 262

Fabbro, Rinaldo, 265
Fachin, E., 263
Fairy Meadow (Balgownie) hostel, 31, 256
families: breakdown of, 83; reunions of, 29; separation of, 28–29, 48, 49, 169–77
Farken, Horst and Rena, 185
Farm Security Administration (USA), 41
Federated Ironworkers Association of Australia, 75, 91
Federation of Australia, 18
Fergin, Teodor, 181–82
Festival of the Snows, 118, *124*

First Nations Australians. *See* Indigenous Australians
Five Islands (in Illawarra), 87–*88*, 90
food and diet, 183–85; complaints about, 192; at Cowra, 54; at Endeavour hostel, *193*; Ethiopian, 270; at Greta, 183; of Indigenous Australians, 86, 103, 104; on Snowy Scheme, 77; Vietnamese, 226–28, 234, 270; at Woomera, 144–45, 156. *See also* gardens and gardening
Footscray (Melb.), 224–25, 228, 233; heritage of, 268–70; T. Cavallaro & Sons' Pasticceria, 270
Ford motor factory (Geelong), 27
forest industries, 17, 18, 87, 112, 183
Fowell, Mansfield and Maclurcan, 107, 118
France, 22, 30, 41, 110, 112, 241
Fraser, Malcolm, 211
Fremantle, 77
Frezza, Pino, 117
Frino, Francesco, 77
Fripp and Williams, 112

gambling, 81, 83, 117, 140
gardens and gardening, 4, 45, 119, 184; at Bonegilla, 48; at Cooma, 57, 59; at Cowra, 54; historiography of, 4; at Woomera, 142, 156–58, *157*. *See also* food and diet
Gebhardt, Franek and John, 181
Geehi (NSW), 109, 110
Geelong Gas Company, 27
Geelong Small Goods, 27
Geelong (Vic.), 6, 40; housing in, 28; major industries in, 27, 31, 48; social housing in, 27
gender: and accommodation, 170, 205; and employment, 23, 32–33, 169; imbalances of, 28, 33; and immigration, 28–29; and labour recruitment, 29; and migrant camps, 166, 169, 197; politics of, 254; and Snowy Scheme, 101. *See also* women
gentrification, 251
Gepps Cross hostel, 26
Germany: refugee camps in, 21, 41, 169, 176, 182; Templer religion, 47; temporary guest workers in, 22, 30; wartime internees from, 46, 47, 49, 122, 154. *See also* Nazi regime
Germany, immigrants from, 22, 46, 147; at Benalla, 174, 175, 180, 185; at Bonegilla, 48; cemetery for, 261; at Port Kembla, 31, 74, 82; skilled, 43, 78, 158; on Snowy Scheme, 109, 113–15, 117, 122; in South Australia, 18; suspicions against, 117; via assisted passage, 21
Geromin, Heinz, 114
ghettoization, 213
Gippsland (Vic.), 30, 103, 105
globalization, 3, 5, 84, 210, 238
global warming, 4, 103
Gold Rush era, 6, 11; architecture of, 239; immigration during, 18
Golonski, Bruon, 182
governmental assemblage, 90
Graf, Adam, 170
Gray, J.J.W., 140, *141*
Great Britain. *See* United Kingdom of Great Britain and Northern Ireland (UK)
Greece: and Northern European immigration, 30; women from, 32, 33
Greece, immigrants from, 21–24, 30–33, 91, 179, 261; in Footscray, 270; in Springvale (Melb.), 227
Greta camp (NSW), 10, 25, 44; children's services at, 48–49, 169–70; Chocolate City at, 45, 169, 175; destruction and dispersal of, 255–57, *256*; facilities and services at, 169–72; family separations at, 169–72; heritage of, 255–57; huts at, 44–45, 169, 256; Italian POWs at, 50; layout of, *171*; location of, 169; number of people at, 26, 45, 169; reunions at, 252, 254, 255–56; Silver City at, 45, 169, 254; transport to, 29, 170, 175, 183; women at, 172
Greytown (Vic.), 43
groceries and grocery stores, 18, 226, 227, 230, *269*
Groden, Olaf, 266
Grozdanovski, Dragan, 77, 82, *83*
Grunnsund, Eva, 116
Guan Di Daoist Temple, 236, *236*
Guthega (NSW), 51, 59, 108–9, 114; dam, 107, 110

Hakka Cultural Association, 236
Harris, R. Keith, 118
Harvey, Merle, 262
Havyatt, Valerie, 116

healthcare and hospitals, 23, 33, 43–45, 48–49, 170, 177, 185, 257
Heinrich, Heinz, 82
heritage: authorized, 249–51; commercial and industrial, 268–70; controls over, 236, 249, 251; definitions of, 249–51; histories of, 248; industrial, 6, 250–51, 257–61; intangible/tangible, 4, 249–50, 257, 261; of labour, 250–51; layers of, 270; military, 261–62, 264
Heritage Council of Victoria, 254
Heyes, T.H.E., 48
Hilde's Hairdressing (Benalla), 182
Holden camp (WA), 25, 44
holding centres, 4, 25–27, 41, 113, 169, 172, 174; closure of, 26. *See also* names of individual camps and centres
Holmesglen hostel, 199, 202
homesickness, 82
Hosking, Aubrey, 115
Hoskins Company, 67
hostels, 27; closure of, 210, 211; company, 27; development and employment near, 222–23; inner-suburban, 25; locations of, *9*; numbers of, 209; purpose-designed, 41; purposes and origins of, 190–92; for UK immigrants only, 26. *See also* names of individual hostels
housing: public, 10, 191, 194, 196, 225, 272; relocation of, 107, 256; social, 31, 224, 227. *See also* accommodation and housing
Housing Commission of New South Wales (HCNSW), 196, 210
Housing Commission of Victoria (HCV), 196
Hudson, William, 105, 106, 117
human bodies: as a commodity, 68, 78, 80, 85
Hume camp (NSW), 50
Hungary, immigrants from, 21, 33, 109, 176
Hunter Region (NSW), 50, 169
Hutchison Bros, 112
huts, 30, 48; at Bonegilla, 44; discomfort of, 48; at Greta, 44, 169, 175–76, 183–84; military, 8, 44; P- and C-series, 44–45, *45*; at Randwick hostel, 201; relocations of, 48; at Rushworth, 47–49; on Snowy Scheme, 112, 113; at Wooomera, 140. *See also* Nissen huts

identity, Australian, 61, 224; definitions of, 18, 270; expressions of, 261; new, 116; transformation of, 7

Ilic, Voy, 174–75, 179
Illawarra Aboriginal Land Council, 86
Illawarra district (of NSW), 22, 67–68, *69*; Indigenous history and European colonization of, 70; women in, 32. *See also* Port Kembla; Wollongong
Immigrant Networks (exhibition, 2022–23), 258
immigrants: dispersal of, 31; gender disparity among, 33, 172; hierarchies of, 2; nonanglophone, 2, 7, 18, 22–23; recruitment of, 5, 17–19, 28–30, 74–78, 113, 190–98, 201–2, 204, 210. *See also* individual countries
immigration: administration of, 19–20; family, 75; policy, 5, 19–20, 75, 78, 113, 190, 201, 210, 222; and reciprocity, 75–76; waves of, 19, 22. *See also* chain migration; Department of Immigration
Immigration Advisory Council (IAC), 24
Immigration Planning Council, 197
Immigration Restriction Act 1901, 2, 18, 19, 225. *See also* White Australia Policy
India, 99; immigrants from, 17, 18, 19; POW camps in, 49, 50, 54, *55*
Indigenous Australians, 84; architecture of, 239; custodianship and management of land by, 17, 103–4, 250; dispossession of, 4, 11, 18, 102–9, 263; exclusion of, 2; genocide of, 18; heritage of, 249; and inequality, 77; labour of, 18, 39, 67; and land rights, 87, 102; of the Monaro, *111*; population of, 20; racial attitudes towards, 104; and the Snowy Scheme, 102–9; violence against, 18; in Wollongong, 86–90; at Woomera, 136. *See also* Bidawal people; Dhawaral people; Djilamatang people; Kokatha people; Krauatungalung people; Ngarigo people; Ngunawal people; Wadi Wadi people; Walgalu people; Wandidian people
industry: economic benefits of, 4; environmental impacts of, 4, 86–87; heavy, 1, 19, 29, 177, 224 (*See also* mining; Port Kembla); heritage of, 257–61; light, 223, 233–36, 268; locations of, *9*, 236; social impacts of, 4; types of, 17; zoning for, 236
informal employment, 181–85
interculturalism, 19
International Harvester, 48
internationalization, 124

International Refugee Organization (IRO), 20–21, 135, 168
Ireland, immigrants from, 20, 31, 113, 263, 265–66; at Port Kembla, 74; on Snowy Scheme, 101, 114, 115; at Woomera, 156. *See also* United Kingdom of Great Britain and Northern Ireland (UK)
Iron Curtain, 21, 39, 132. *See also* Cold War
Iron Knob (SA), 136
Island Bend (NSW), 59, 110, 114, 263
Italian Ossario (Murchison, Victoria), 261
Italy: and Northern European immigration, 30; ornamental features from, 57, 59; prisoners of war from, 49–51, 122, 169 (*See also* Roncari, Giuseppe (Joe) and family); return emigration to, 26; wartime internees from, 46, 47, 49–51, 57, 62; women from, 33
Italy, immigrants from, 21–24, 30–31, 46, 91; at Bonegilla, 48; at Cringila, 29, 31; in Footscray, 270; at Port Kembla, 74; prejudice against, 221; and return immigration, 26; skilled, 158; on Snowy Scheme, 57, 59, 77, 115, 122, 265; in Springvale, 227; unskilled, 43; and women, 33

Japan: internees from, 46, 54, 62, 262
Japanese war cemetery (Cowra), 262
Jenkins, Robert, 90
Jewish immigrants and refugees, 21, 24, 46
Jindabyne (NSW), 59, 99, *100*, *108*, 110; destruction of, 106–8; planning of, 118

Kaiser Engineering Company, 119
Kaiser-Walsh-Perini-Raymond, 112, 118
Kalgoorlie (WA), 31
Kantaroski, Jovanče, *83*
Kapooka camp, 44
Keilor Downs (Melb.), *232*, 242
Kenny's Knob (NSW), 109
Khancoban (NSW), 110, 118
Khancoban Visitor Centre, 100
Khoury, Abdullah, 118
Kiandra (NSW), 104
Kidman, Alice, 107
Kilma, Jan, 114
kindergartens, 48
Kmak, Zenon, 183–84
Kobal, Ivan, 101

Kokatha people, 134, 138, 266
Kornienko, Irene (née Chlebnikowski), 182
Kosciusko, Mount, 103, 106
Kościuszko, Tadeusz, 103
Kozaczynski family, 184
Krauatungalung people, 103
Kružas, Algis, 145
Kunama Namadji (aka Mount Kosciuszko), 103, 106
Kwinana (WA), 31, 77

labour: coerced, 87; conscription of, 8, 39, 50, 77–78; dispersal of, 26; ethnic divisions in, 22–23, 77–78; forced, 169; indented, 39, 87; itinerant, 31; and nation building, 33–34; and postwar immigration, 20; shortages of, 135, 149–50; skilled, unskilled and semi-skilled, 20, 31, 43, 75–78, 149, 168, 210
Laikve, Guido and Erich, 136, 140, 144–45, 150–51, *152*, 158–59
Lake Koolymilka (Woomera), 136, *138*, 139, *141*
Lake Richardson (Woomera), 139
Lake Tyers (Vic.), 104
land grants, 18, 44, 70, 86–87, 90, 91. *See also* colonization
land rights, 87, 102
Landsburg camp, 114
language, 178–79; classes in, 185; and employment conditions, 24–25, 77–78; and interpreters, 184; racist, 24–25; on signage, 269; and solidarity, 240; and trade unions, 180
Laos, immigrants from, 11, 210, 211, 213
Latoof and Calill, 177–*78*, 180, 185
Latrobe Valley (Vic.), 3, 27, 31
Latvia, immigrants from, 179; and anti-communism, 21; racism against, 24, 147; on Snowy Scheme, 109; at Woomera, 136, 140, 142–44, 147, 150–51, 153–55. *See also* Baltic states, immigrants from ('Balts')
Lazic, Rosa and Slavo, 158
Lebanon, immigrants and refugees from, 23, 118, 211, 241
Le Corbusier (Charles-Édouard Jeanneret), 41
Legnami Pasotti Società per Azioni, 57, 115, 119, 122, 265

Lelli, Nando, 91
Lemega, Anna, 180
'lenticularity,' 241–42
Lim, Richard, 229–30, 231
Lim's Pharmacy (Springvale), *230*
Lithuania, immigrants from, 21, 24; in Adelaide, 149; men only, 33; at Woomera, 134–36, 139–42, 153–54. *See also* Baltic states, immigrants from ('Balts')
'Little Saigons,' 225
Liverpool (NSW), 54
Lobs Hole (NSW), 109
Long Range Weapons Establishment (LRWE). *See* Woomera
Lupish, Vitaly, 256
Lutheran Church, 18, 47, 147

Macaulay, Robert, 134
MacDougall, W.B., 134
Macedonia, immigrants from, 24, 31, *83*, 84; at Port Kembla, 74–75, 91, 258; prejudice against, 221; women, 32. *See also* Yugoslavia, immigrants and refugees from
Macedonian Welfare Association (MWA), 71, 74, 80, 258
Maclurcan, D.G., 118
Macquarie, Lachlan, 87
Mader, William, 176–77
Maitland (NSW), 175, 177, 257. *See also* Greta camp (NSW)
Malaya, 47
Malta, 21, 32, 135, 270
Man from Snowy River, 105
manufacturing industry, 17, 240; at Benalla, 178; cars, 22; and centralization, 25; and decentralization, 31, 72; decline of, 32, 222; farm equipment, 51, 59; in the 1990s, 225–27, 232, 241; in Springvale, 227, 234. *See also* BHP; Port Kembla; textiles and clothing industry
Maralinga (SA), 146, 159
Maribyrnong hostel, 27
Maribyrnong Immigration Detention Centre, 206
Maribyrnong (Melb.), 11, 226
market gardens. *See* gardens and gardening
marriage, 28, 83, 116, 172; by proxy, 33
'Marta Plan,' 33

Matt, Elizabeth, 183
Matulevičius, M., 149
Mazins, P., 158
McEwen, John, 46
McHugh, Siobhan, 263
McMahon, William, 21
McQuade, Georgina, 116
memory studies, 4
men: as a commodity, 78–81; preference for, 27, 28–29, 75
mental illness, 5, 29, 82. *See also* alcohol, abuse of
Menzies, Robert, 20, 145–46
Meškauskas, Jonas, 144, 150, 154–57, 158
'messy urbanism,' 237–39
Mexico, 6
Middle East, immigrants from, 3, 19, 23, 271. *See also* Lebanon, immigrants and refugees from; Turkey, immigrants from
Midway hostel (Maribyrnong, Melbourne), 11, 224–25, 226, 270; food at, 226
migrant camps, 7; conditions in, 41–42; and heritage, 252–57; women in, 167. *See also* names of individual camps
Migrant Transitory Flat Scheme, 195, 199, 211–13
migration theory and historiography, 2–7
Mildura camp, 26
military camps, 8, 25–26, 48, 50, 256; repurposing of, 39–46, 191, 202
milk bars, 227
Miloradovic, Dusca (Duke Milford), 114
mining, 4; coal, 29, 67, 74, 87; and colonization, 67; gold, 6, 11, 18, 104, 239. *See also* BHP
Mockunas, Jonas, 139, 140
Monaro region, 99; environmental harm to, 106; and Indigenous people, 102–9. *See also* Snowy Mountains Hydro Electricity Scheme
Moon, C.L., 59, *60*
mosques, 3, 260
Mount Kosciuszko, 103, 106
Multicultural Communities Council of Illawarra (MCCI), 71, 80, 258
multiculturalism, 2–3, 210, 223; 'birthplace' of, 9, 49, 124, 252, 256; in Melbourne, 225; origins of, 20; in Whitlam era, 77, 252
Munyang powerhouse, 110

Murchison POW Camp 13, *44*
Murchison (Vic.), 44, 47, 261
Murray River, 103, 105, 134
Mussolini, Benito, 51
Mūsų Pastogė (Our Shelter), 142
Myrtleford POW camp (Vic.), 50

Nan Yang Asian Supermarket (Springvale, Melbourne), *229*, 242, 268–69
National Heritage List, 253
Native Patrol Officers, 134
Nazi regime, 21, 46, 114, 145, 147, 255
Nehru, Jawahar Lal, 99
Nemeth, Lajos, 264
neoliberalism, 250, 251, 257
Netherlands: migrant camps in, 41; return emigration to, 26; and Southern European emigrants, 30
Netherlands, immigrants from, 21, 30; in Geelong, 28; at Port Kembla, 31, 74; skilled, 22, 78, 115; on Snowy Scheme, 110, 119, 170; at Woomera, 158
'New Australians,' 24, 42, 113–14, 116, 142
Newcastle (NSW), 29, 31, 72–74, 170
New Deal, 100, 124
Neylan, E.M., 142–43
Ngarigo people, 103–4
Ngunawal people, 103
Nguyễn, Bon, 231, 234, 239
Nikolsky, George, 185
Nissen huts, 26, 45, 169, 197, 256. *See also* huts
Noble Park (Melb.), 234
Northam camp (WA), 25, 44, 50
Northern Europe: emigration from, 5, 22–23, 116; immigration to, 30
Norway, 107, 108, 110, 116, 266
NSW Railways, 26
nuclear weapons, 9, 133, 159. *See also* Woomera
Nunawading (Melb.), 209, 224

O'Boyle, Ulick, 265–66
Ohrdruf (Germany), 114, 119
Ohridsko, Cvetko, 82
Ohridsko, Lazec and Ivan, 82
Oliver, C.T., 263
Orbost (Vic.), 105
orphanages, 49

Pacific Islands, 18, 62, 181
Paez, Margot, 184
Palestine, 47
Panich, Catherine, *172*
Papagallo, Jorge, 82
Papua New Guinea, 47, 153, 200
Parkes, Rodney, *58*
parks, 4, 99, 106, 142
Parks, E.J., 43–44, 48
Pasqualin, Carlo, 82
pastoral industry, 4, 17, 67, 86, 102–5, 136, *138*
Paterson, A.B. ('Banjo'), 105, 263
Patterson, R.H., 142
Pauls, Eric, 117
Petruskevičiene, Viltis-Lodze, 151–52
Petruskevičius, Jonas, 152
pets and animals, 183–84
Phillip Ponds (Woomera), 137, *152*, *155*, *267*
Phillips, G., 147
Pimba (Woomera), 147, *148*, *159*
Pinkerton, Ivor, 118
Poland, immigrants from, 21, 28, 135, 170; at Benalla, 43, 174, 179; at Bonegilla, 43, 48, 170; at Greta, 170, 181–84, 254; men, 33; at Port Kembla, 74; on Snowy Scheme, 109, 114; at Woomera, 135–36, 139, 150, 155
Polo Flat (Cooma), 59, 110, 117
Poposki, Sisoja, 84
Popov, Stale, 84
'populate or perish,' 20
population of Australia, 39
Port Kembla Harbour Act 1898, 90
Port Kembla Ironworker (magazine), 91
Port Kembla (NSW), 8, 43, *69*; and colonization, 67–68; decline of, 257–58; ethnic makeup of, 31, 73–75; housing in, 28; itinerant workers at, 31; population of, 68, 72–74, 85, 257; racial and ethnic structures at, 68; Vietnamese workers at, 28. *See also* BHP
Portland Cement, 27
post-traumatic stress disorder (PTSD), 175, 255
Potter, Noel, 107
prefabrication: at Cooma, 119, *121*, 123; done overseas, 119, 122, 197; in high-rise housing, 196; and Snowy Scheme, 103, 110, 119; at Woomera, *141*

preschools, 48
Preston (Melb.), 234
prime ministers of Australia. *See* Chifley, Ben; Fraser, Malcolm; McMahon, William; Menzies, Robert; Whitlam, Gough
prison design, 192, 194, 203–9
prisoners of war (POWs), 41, 46; as agricultural labourers, 50; cemeteries and commemoration of, 261
protests: about accommodation, 42, 192; at Bonegilla, 43; at Woomera, 145
public housing, 10, 191, 194, 196, 225, 272
Puckapunyal camp, 43, 182

qualifications, (non-)recognition of, 23, 117–18, 149–51, 153, 168, 176, 225
Quang Minh Vietnamese Buddhist Temple, 234–36, *235*, 242
Queensland Housing Commission, 119

race: hierarchies of, 11; and multiculturalism, 3
racial slurs, 24–25, 76, 113, 122
racism, 5, 18–19; and displaced persons, 21; and housing, 27; and language, 24–25; and population growth, 20; at Port Kembla, 75–78; scientific, 21; and Southeast Asian immigrants, 225; structural, 24–25
railways, 26, 68, 110, 150, 170, 175, 183
Randwick (Sydney). *See* Endeavour hostel
reciprocity, 84, 85
Redfern (Sydney), 210
Red Point (aka Dhgillawarah), 72, 258
'reffos,' 24
refugees and asylum seekers, 209–13; as a 'burden,' 5; camps for, 6, 21; detention of, 206. *See also* names of individual countries
religion, 54, *55*, 57, 147, 156, 234–39. *See also* Buddhism; Catholic Church; Daoism; Lutheran Church
Renmark (SA), 136
Renold Chains (Aust) Pty Ltd, 177–78, 185
reterritorialization, 233
return emigration, 33, 42, 168, 176–77
Richmond (Melb.), 224–25
Rieck, Karl, 114
Robinson, Roy, 114
Rodwell, Frank, 113

Rolfe, R.J., 263
Roncari, Giuseppe (Joe) and family, 8, 40, 51–62, 123, 265
rooming houses. *See* boarding houses
Rosetti, Angelo, 57, 59, 265
Rowville camp (Melb), 50
Royal Australian Air Force (RAAF), 109, 139, 142–43, 210
Royal Australian Institute of Architects (RAIA), 197
Royal Dutch Harbour Co., 119
ruins, 268
Rushworth camp (Vic.), 26, 43–44, 46–50; closure and heritage of, 261; layout of, *47*
Russia, immigrants from, 43, 146, 170
Rutherford (Maitland, NSW), 176

Saliba, Michel, 78
Salteri, Carlo, 77
Savegnago, Luigi, 265
Šavkulevski family, 74
Scammels Spur (NSW), 109
Scandinavia, immigrants from, 22, 158
Schaller, Christine, 175
Scharkejewic, Anton (later Ivan Lipin), 146
Scheyville camp (NSW), 48–49, 179, 256
Schmertz, Ferdinand, 48
schools, 118; at Cringila, 28; at Cunderdin, 32; at Endeavour hostel, 194; at Greta, 45, 170, 175; at Rushworth, 47, 49; for Snowy Scheme, 123–24; at Woomera, 142
Schulha, Alek, 167, 175, 181
Scone (NSW), 170
Scott, Helen, 256–57
Seamen's Union, 24
Second World War: accommodation during, 41–46; commemoration of, 261; internees during, 41; and Italy, 51–52. *See also* military camps; Nazi regime
Seidler, Harry, 119
Selenitsch, Alex, 40–41
self-employment, 23
Selma Engineering Pty Ltd, 107, 110, 116
The Settlers (musical group), 265–66
sewerage systems, 27, 28; at Woomera, 142, 148, 150, 151, 153, 156, 266
sex work, 83, 117–18, 258
Seymour camp (Vic.), 43, 48

Shepparton (Vic.), 43, 48
Sidorko, Lucy, 170, 184
Silver City. *See under* Greta camp
Silver City (film), 254
Simpson, Dee, 116
Singapore, 47, 227
single-parent families, 172–74, 182
Singleton, 183
sinter plant, 68, 72, 78, 80, 82, 261
skiing, 116
slavery, 85
'slum' reclamation, 196
Slusarczyk, Irena and Tosia, 182
small business owners, 23, 28, 181–85, 222–23, 225–28
Snowy 2.0, 101
Snowy Hydro Discovery Centre, 100
Snowy Mountains Engineering Company (SMEC), 100–101
Snowy Mountains Hydro Electric Authority (SMHEA or SMA), 56, 100, 105–25; headquarters of, 99, 110, 116, *122*
Snowy Mountains Hydro Electricity Scheme, 8–9, 29, 56, *101*; beginnings of, 105–7; completion of, 59, 265; construction of, *110*–13; cost of, 100, 101; deaths of workers on, 115, 262–66; environmental consequences of, 102, 106–7; and family separation, 170; heritage of, 251, 262–66; and Indigenous Australians, 102–9; international contractors involved in, 110–12, 114; opposition to, 106; publicity for, 106–7; surveying and planning of, 109; wages paid by, 118; and women, 101, 116; workers camps of, 109–13; workforce of, 101, 109, 113–16, 123–25, 251
Snowy Mountains Scheme Workers Memorial (Cooma), 263
Snowy River, 99, *108*; course of, 103, 105; and Indigenous owners, 104
social workers, 23, 167, 172, 174, 178–79
Società Anonima Elettrificazione Spa (SAE), 77
Somalia, immigrants from, 233, 270
Somers camp (Vic.), 26, 43
South America, immigrants from, 195
South Asia, immigrants from, 7, 271
South Australian Housing Trust (SAHT), 151

Southeast Asia, immigrants from, 195, 210, 213, 221–43; in Footscray, 270
Southern Europe, immigrants from, 3, 31, 43, 75, 78, 116
Soviet Union (USSR), 21, 39, 99, 114, 132, *133*, 144–47, 255. *See also* Cold War
Spain: immigrants from, 115; and the 'Marta Plan,' 33; and Northern European emigration, 30; women from, 33
spatial analysis, 223–24
Spence, W.G., 67
Spodar, Stanley, 48
Springvale (Melb.), 193, 202, 224–25, 228, 233; heritage of, 268–70. *See also* Villawood hostel
Sri Lanka, immigrants from, 11, 222
St Albans (Melb.), 234
St Anthony's Catholic Church (Rutherford, Maitland), 257
State Electricity Commission of Victoria (SECV), 3, 23, 26, 30
stateless people, 21
Station Pier (Melb.), 31
steel: production process of, *79*, 80–82, *81*. *See also* Port Kembla
St Eleftherios Greek Orthodox Church (Brunswick, Melb.), 261
Stephansdach Holzbau, 112
Stevens, Jock, 183
Stevenson, A.J., 147, 149
St Ives (NSW), 54
Stoneham, C.P., 178
stone masons, 115
Strzelecki, Paul, 103
Sudan, immigrants from, 233, 270
Sue City (NSW), 114, 119
sugar industry, 17, 18, 30, 48
Sunshine (Melb.), 234
superannuation, 84
Sweden, 30
Switzerland, 30, 41, 110, 158
Sydney: airport at, 201; migrant communities in, 30; modern image of, 201
Sylvestro, Charlie, 57
Szymming, Jerzy Gabriel, 150, *155*, 158

Tadic, Velimir (aka 'Tarzan'), 158
Taiwan, 228
Talbingo (NSW), 106, 107, 110

Talgarno Prohibited Area (Vic.), 134
Tatura (Vic.): camp, *47 (See also* Dhurringile camp; Rushworth camp); German Military Cemetery, 261; Irrigation and Wartime Camps Museum, 261
Taube, Vilis, 150, 151
T. Cavallaro & Sons' Pasticceria (Footscray, Melb.), 270
Temelkovska, Borjanka, 82
temples, 223–37, 268. *See also* Guan Di Daoist Temple; Quang Minh Vietnamese Buddhist Temple
temporary immigrants, 19
Tennessee Valley Authority, 6, 41, 100, 105, 107, 118, 124
tents and tent cities, 26–27, 140, *141, 155*
Teochew Association, 236
terra nullius, 17, 18
textiles and clothing industry, 23, 32, 176–77, 180, 242; decline of, 33; and outwork, 33; and piecework, 231–32
Thailand, immigrants from, 241
Theiss Bros, 112
Thich, Venerable Phước Tấn, 239
Thredbo (NSW), 104, 107
Three Mile (NSW), 109
Timbery, Joseph, 87
tin mill, 68, 258
Tocumwal camp, 48
Topor, Helen, 174, 175
Townsville (Qld)
trade unions, 23–24, 180–81; and BHP, 75; racism in, 25; and Snowy Mountains Scheme, 263; and women, 32–33, 180; at Woomera, 145
Traeger, F.H., 147
transcultural place making, 224
Transfield, 77
translational cultures, 224
Troy, Jakeline, 104
Tuckalong (aka Tom Thumb Lagoon), 68, 70, 86, *89–91*
Tumut (NSW), 103–4, 109, *110*
Turkey, immigrants from, 23, 31, 32, 78, 91, 195
Turkiewicz, Sophia, 254
Tymukas, Kathleen and Kostas, 134–35, 146, 150–51, 153–*55*, 159

Ukraine, immigrants from, 21, 28, 33, 43, 114, 136, 179, 182
Ukraine, invasion of, 159
unions. *See* trade unions
United Kingdom of Great Britain and Northern Ireland (UK): Australia's relationship with, 1, 17, 99–100, 133, 134, 221–24; immigrants from, 2, 19, 74, 78, 135; preferential treatment of immigrants from, 7, 18–20, 26–27, 31, 33, 42, 49, 102, 169
United States Bureau of Reclamation (USBR), 100, 105, 115
United States of America (USA): Australia's relationship with, 1, 99–100, 105, 146, 211; displaced persons in, 41; immigration quotas of, 18; industrial towns in, 6; and postwar immigration, 22; racial divisions in, 118; wartime projects for, 50; worker camps in, 41
Upper Tumut Project, 110
Uranquinty camp, 26, 44, 182
urbanism, 237–38; histories of, 240
USSR. *See* Soviet Union
Utah Australia Ltd, 112

Vandyke Bros, 112, 119
Van Hoof, Louis Peter, 264
Vecchiato, Ernesto, 264
Veigurs, Albert, 140
Venerable Phước Tấn Thich, 239
Victor Emmanuel III, King, 51
Victorian Heritage Register, 253
Victorian Housing Commission, 27
Vietnamese Community in Victoria, 231
Vietnamese Museum Victoria (VMA), 231
Vietnamese Women's Association, 236
Vietnam, immigrants and refugees from, 5, 11, 19, 23, 25, 28, 68, 210–11, 221–43
Vietnam War, 5, 11, 195, 211
Villawood hostel (Springvale, Melb.), 27, 193–94, 199, 202
violence, 8, 271; domestic, 175; and repurposed camps, 49; of Second World War, 39, 261

Wacol camp, 44; children's services at, 48
Wadi Wadi people, 70, 71–72, 86–91
Walgalla Lake, 104
Walgalu people, 103

Wallace, James and Co., 112, 119
Wandidian people, 86
Waranga (Vic.), 48
Wasserman, Wally, 109
Waterside Workers' Federation, 24
water supply, 27, 44, 154
WeBuild, 101
Wee Warrah sheep station, 56
Westall (Springvale, Melb.), 227, 228
Westbridge hostel (Sydney), 199, 209
Westona hostel (Altona, Melb.), 224
West Papua, 211
West Sale camp (Vic.), 26, 30; reunion at, 252
Whiskey Swamp (Woomera), 139
Whitburn Colliery, 50
White Australia Policy, 62; and Asian cultures, 240; and biological racism, 18; demise of, 5, 20–21, 210, 225; and Snowy Mountains Scheme, 103, 125; and trade unions, 23–24
Whitlam, Gough, 77, 211
Whyalla (SA), 31, 147
'wife starvers,' 115
Williams and Co., 112, 119
Willow Tree sheep station (NSW), 56
Windt, Uri, 255
Winston, Denis, 118
Wirrawirralu Waterhole (Phillip Ponds, Woomera), *267*
Wisniewski, Charlie, 183–84
'wogs,' 24, 76, 113, 122
Wolff and Zimmer, 119
Wollongong (NSW), 31; boarding houses in, 28; population of, 68; social housing in, 27; transport to, 29; women in, 32. *See also* Port Kembla
women: accommodation of, 32; agency of, 169; employment of, 23, 32–33, 172, *178*, 254; and entrepreneurialism, 231; exploitation of, 154, 169; and immigration, 31; in migrant camps, 167; and Snowy Scheme, 101, 116; and trade unions, 33; and two-year work contracts, 172; and violence, 175. *See also* gender

Woodside camp (SA), 48–49
Woomera (SA), 9–10, 48; accommodation and housing at, 140–42; and Cold War, 266; conditions at, 136–42, *148*, 266; dismantling of, 158; and displaced persons, 135; entertainment and leisure at, 139, 140, 150, 155–56; Golf Course, 266; heritage and preservation of, 266–68; History Museum, 132; Immigration Reception and Processing Centre, 158; Indigenous custodians of, 266; landscaping and layout of, 142, *143*, 156, *157*; politics at, 145–46, 266; population of, 134, 135–37, 266; Prohibited Area (WPA), 9, 43, 133; racism at, 147, 156; security measures at, 146–49, 266; services provided at, 142; social hierarchy at, 156; surveying at, 139, 150, *152*; wages earned at, 136, 150; West, 137; women at, 148; workforce of, 135–40. *See also* Kokatha people
work contracts (two-year), 24, 168, 169; exemptions from, 172
workers' compensation, 81, 82
working conditions, 19, 123; and racism, 11, 24–25; in steelworks, 78–82, 258; at Woomera, 145
workplace injury, illness, death and danger, 80–85, 115, 261–66
World War II. *See* Second World War
worship, places of, 3, 234. *See also* religion; temples

Yugoslavia, immigrants and refugees from, 22, 23, 30–31, *83*, 211; at Bonegilla, 43; in Footscray, 270; at Greta, 174–75; to Northern Europe, 30; at Port Kembla, 31, 74, 84, 91; racism against, 24; and Snowy Scheme, 109, 115; at Woomera, 136, 158. *See also* Macedonia, immigrants from

Žabjani, Andrew, 82
Žilinskas, Algimantas, 154, *155*
Zintschenko, Maria, 170, 179

www.ingramcontent.com/pod-product-compliance
Lightning Source LLC
Chambersburg PA
CBHW080214040426
42333CB00044B/2653